BLENDER 3D SIMPLE & CLEAR 2024 GUIDE FOR NEW DESIGNERS

FARUSA REICHAR

Copyright © 2024 Farusa Reichar
All rights reserved.

INTRODUCTION

Creating a book introduction that encompasses the broad and multifaceted domain of Blender 3D without delving into specific chapters or outlining the book's structure is both a challenge and an opportunity to lay a solid foundation for the reader's journey. "Blender 3D Simple & Clear 2024 Guide for New Designers" is designed not just as a manual but as a companion in your voyage into the world of 3D modeling, animation, and rendering. This introduction aims to set the stage for a transformative learning experience, guiding you through the conceptual and practical landscapes you will navigate as you unlock the power of Blender 3D.

Blender, as a software, stands at the intersection of art, technology, and storytelling. It's a tool that has democratized 3D creation, offering capabilities that rival those of industry-standard software without the barrier of cost. The 2024 edition of Blender is a testament to the evolution of this open-source project, reflecting both the advancements in computing and the community's relentless pursuit of an accessible, powerful tool for creators everywhere. Our book is tailored for those at the beginning of their Blender journey, providing a pathway from the rudimentary understanding of 3D concepts to the mastery of creating complex animations and simulations.

At its core, Blender is about bringing ideas to life. Whether it's the inception of a character that's been brewing in your imagination, the architectural model of a dream home, or a scene from a story you wish to tell visually, Blender offers the canvas and the tools necessary for realization. The journey through Blender is as much about understanding the software as it is about understanding the principles that govern the digital art world. Concepts like modeling, texturing, and lighting are universal, with Blender offering a unique blend of tools and features to explore them.

Embarking on this journey, the beginner might find the expanse of Blender's capabilities daunting. This book is designed to alleviate that overwhelming feeling by breaking down the software into digestible segments, each building upon the last. The progression is deliberate, ensuring that foundational knowledge is cemented before moving on to more complex subjects. The aim is not just to teach you how to use Blender but to cultivate an understanding and appreciation for the art of 3D modeling and animation.

Learning Blender is also about joining a global community. The open-source nature of Blender has fostered a culture of sharing and collaboration, with countless tutorials, forums, and resources available. This book is a gateway into that community, encouraging you to leverage the wealth of knowledge and experience that exists beyond its pages. As Blender continues to evolve, so too will the ways in which we use it and learn from it. This book is but a snapshot of Blender in 2024, offering guidance and insight that will remain relevant as both the software and its users grow.

Technology in the realm of 3D art is perpetually advancing, and with it, the capabilities of Blender are expanded. The 2024 edition introduces features and improvements that enhance efficiency, realism, and creativity. These advancements are not just technical milestones; they represent new opportunities for expression, experimentation, and storytelling. Our book explores these features in the context of practical applications, ensuring that you not only understand what's new but also how to integrate these tools into your workflow.

The transformative potential of Blender is not limited to the digital space. Skills honed in Blender have real-world applications in industries ranging from film and animation to game development, virtual reality, and architectural visualization. Learning Blender is thus not merely an exercise in software proficiency but an investment in a versatile skill set that opens doors to numerous career paths and creative endeavors.

"Blender 3D Simple & Clear 2024 Guide for New Designers" is, at its heart, about unlocking potential—both the software's and your own. As you turn these pages and embark on projects, experiments, and creations, remember that the journey through Blender is one of constant learning and discovery. There will be challenges and frustrations, certainly, but also moments of triumph and beauty. This book is designed to be your guide through all of it, providing the knowledge, techniques, and inspiration needed to navigate the world of Blender and beyond.

In the end, mastery of Blender is not just about achieving technical proficiency; it's about how you harness this tool to bring your visions to life. The journey is long and the landscape ever-changing, but the possibilities are limitless. Welcome to "Blender 3D Simple & Clear 2024 Guide for New Designers"—your first step into a world where imagination meets creation.

Embarking on the journey to master Blender is akin to learning a new language. This language, however, is visual, expressive, and boundless in its potential to create worlds that extend beyond the limits of our physical reality. As you dive deeper into the Blender 3D 2024 guide, you will start with the alphabets and grammar—the basic tools and interfaces—and gradually progress to forming sentences and narratives through complex models, textures, and animations. The beauty of this journey lies in its iterative learning process, where each step builds upon the last, transforming novice users into proficient creators who can articulate their visions with precision and creativity.

The foundational chapters of this guide are meticulously crafted to ease you into the Blender interface, a space where creativity meets technology. This interface is your canvas, toolset, and studio all in one. You will learn to navigate it with the same fluidity with which an artist selects their brush and palette. Keyboard shortcuts, often overlooked by beginners, are the secret language of efficiency in Blender. Mastering these shortcuts is like learning to play an instrument, where initially complex sequences become second nature, allowing you to focus on the art and not just the technique.

As you become comfortable with the essentials, the guide leads you into the heart of 3D modeling and sculpting. Here, the true potential of Blender unfolds. You will learn to see objects not just for what they are but for what they could be, understanding the importance of meshes, vertices, edges, and faces in bringing your imagination to life. This is where the tactile feeling of sculpting in the digital world becomes real, allowing you to mold and shape your creations as if they were clay in your hands.

Moving beyond the creation of static models, the guide introduces you to the vibrant world of materials and texturing, a realm where your models gain character, realism, and mood. The art of texturing is like painting, but with a complexity that mirrors the real world. You will learn to appreciate the nuances of light and shadow, reflection, and texture, and how these elements interact to create the illusion of reality. This knowledge is not just technical; it's sensory, enhancing your ability to observe and replicate the world around you.

The illumination of your scene with lighting techniques marks the transition from the static to the dynamic, from models to environments. Lighting in Blender is your sunrise, your spotlight, your mood setter. It's here that you learn the subtleties of setting a scene, drawing the viewer's eye, and creating atmosphere. This is cinematic storytelling in the digital age, where you are the director, cinematographer, and editor.

The penultimate phase of your journey with Blender is animation and rigging—the breath of life into your creations. Animation in Blender is more than just movement; it's the embodiment of character and story. Through rigging, your models gain the ability to move and express, transforming from sculptures to actors in your digital narrative. This process, complex as it may seem, is demystified in the guide, ensuring that you understand not just the how but the why of animation.

The culmination of your journey through Blender is the realization that you are no longer just a user of software; you are a creator of worlds, a storyteller whose medium is the boundless landscape of 3D digital art.

This book aims not just to teach you the functionalities of Blender but to inspire you to explore, experiment, and express. As the chapters unfold, you are encouraged to not just follow along but to diverge, make mistakes, and learn from them.

In the spirit of the Blender community, this guide is a starting point, a spark for your creative journey. The landscapes you create, the characters you bring to life, and the stories you tell are yours alone. The path to mastering Blender is continuous, marked by constant learning, sharing, and growth. As you turn each page, remember that the essence of creativity lies in exploration and the courage to transcend boundaries. Welcome to a world where imagination takes form, where art and technology converge to create the extraordinary. Welcome to "Blender 3D Simple & Clear 2024 Guide for New Designers."

CONTENTS

INTRODUCTION iii
CONTENTS ix

Part 1: Mastering the Basics of Blender 1
Chapter 1: About Blender 3D 2024 2
Chapter 2: Keyboard shortcuts in Blender 20
Chapter 3: Exploring the Essentials of Blender 37
Chapter 4: How Blender Operates 42
Chapter 5: First Steps in Blender Modeling 64
Chapter 6: Editing and Object Mode Techniques 72

Part 2: Sculpting Your Vision in 3D 84
Chapter 7: Crafting with Meshes: From Simple to Complex 85
Chapter 8: The Art of 3D Sculpting 100
Chapter 9: Beyond Meshes: Exploring Blender's Primitives 106
Chapter 10: Customizing Materials for Realism 117
Chapter 11: Texturing Techniques for Detailed Models 123
Chapter 12: Illuminating Your Scene 133

Part 3: Bringing Your Creations to Life 143
Chapter 13: Basics of Animation in Blender 144
Chapter 14: Rigging Essentials - Breathing Life into Models 154
Chapter 15: Advanced Animation - Deforming Objects 167
Chapter 16: Automation in Blender: Simulations and Effects 174

Chapter 17: Exporting And Rendering Scenes 185

Chapter 18: Editing and Enhancing Video Animations 188

CONCLUSION 203

PART 1: MASTERING THE BASICS OF BLENDER

CHAPTER 1: ABOUT BLENDER 3D 2024

1.1. WELCOME TO BLENDER 3D

In the ever-evolving world of digital art and animation, a powerful tool has emerged as a beacon for creators ranging from hobbyists to professional studios. This tool is Blender 3D, a comprehensive, open-source software suite that facilitates the entire 3D creation pipeline. From sculpting and modeling to rendering and animation, Blender 3D stands as a testament to what open-source communities can achieve.

1.1.1. What is Blender 3D?

Blender 3D is a free, open-source 3D creation suite that supports the entirety of the 3D pipeline, including modeling, rigging, animation, simulation, rendering, compositing, and motion tracking, even video editing and game creation. Its comprehensive feature set, high-end capabilities, and commitment to fostering creativity and collaboration make it a unique tool in the digital art world.

Originally conceived in the early '90s, Blender started as an in-house tool for a small animation studio. However, it rapidly evolved beyond its initial scope, driven by a growing community of users and developers. In 2002, Blender was released as open-source software, a move that exponentially accelerated its development and adoption worldwide.

Blender's philosophy is rooted in its open-source nature, which ensures that it is not only free to use but also constantly improved upon by contributions from users and developers from all corners of the globe. This community-driven approach has led to Blender being at the forefront of innovation in the 3D world, continually introducing cutting-edge features and capabilities that rival, and often surpass, those of its commercial counterparts.

1.1.2. The Scope of Blender 3D in the World of Digital Art and Animation

Blender 3D's impact on the digital art and animation landscape cannot be overstated. It democratizes access to high-quality 3D creation tools, removing the barrier of cost that often restricts the ability of individual artists and small studios to compete in the industry. By offering a full suite of tools that cater to a wide range of 3D art and animation disciplines, Blender enables users to explore their creativity without limitations.

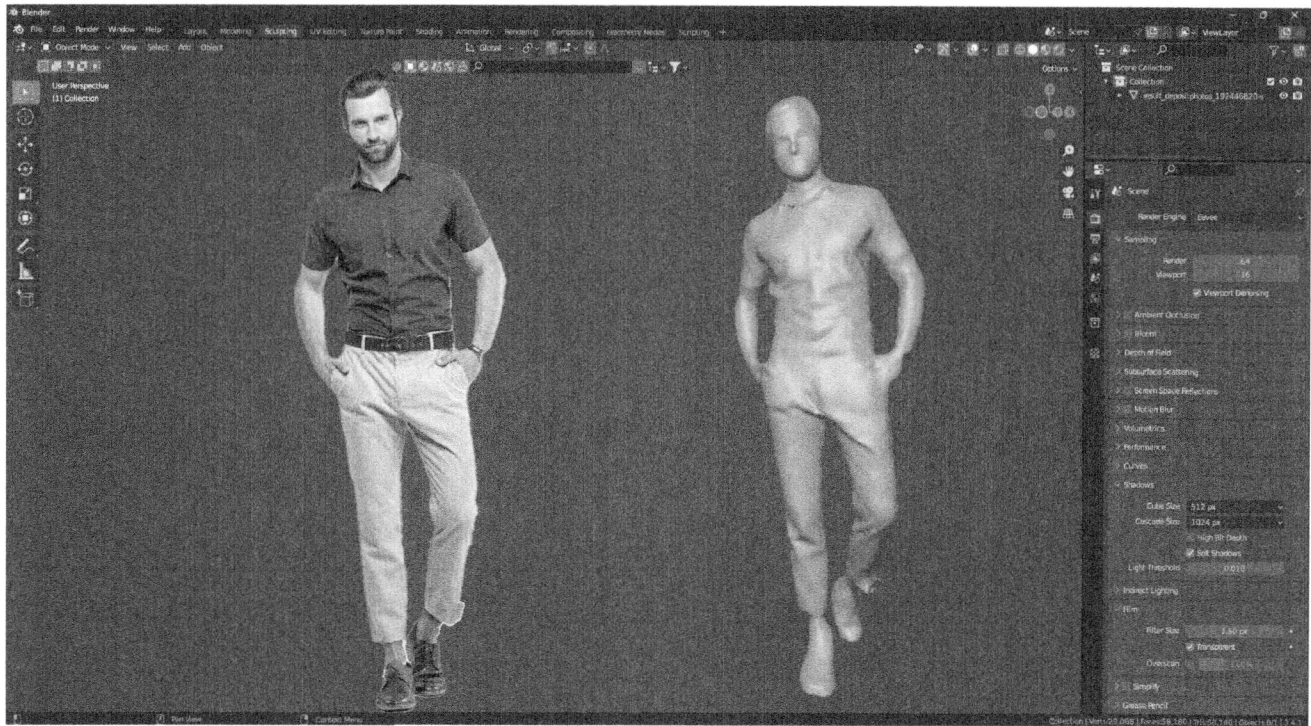

Artists use Blender for creating animated films, visual effects, art, 3D printed models, interactive 3D applications, and video games. Its ability to handle complex simulations, including fluid, smoke, hair, and particle effects, makes it a go-to solution for artists working on ambitious projects that require a high level of detail and realism.

In the realm of animation, Blender provides a robust set of tools for character rigging and animation. The software includes features for inverse kinematics, allowing for natural movement and poses for characters, and a non-linear animation mixer, enabling complex animations that can be edited and refined with ease.

For game developers, Blender offers an integrated game engine, enabling the creation of interactive 3D content. While the focus in recent years has shifted towards better integration with external game engines like Unreal Engine and Unity, Blender remains a valuable asset for game asset creation, including modeling, texturing, and animation.

The software's architecture is designed for extensibility, allowing users to customize and extend its capabilities through scripting with Python. This openness has led to a vibrant ecosystem of plugins and add-ons, further enhancing Blender's functionality to meet specific needs, such as architectural visualization, scientific visualization, and more.

Blender 3D's commitment to providing a comprehensive, open-source 3D creation suite has established it as a beloved tool in the global community of digital artists and animators. Its continual development, driven by feedback and contributions from its user base, ensures that Blender remains at the cutting edge of 3D technology, making it an invaluable resource for anyone looking to explore the vast potential of digital creation.

1.2 A BRIEF HISTORY OF BLENDER 3D

1.2.1 The Origins and Evolution

Blender 3D's journey began in the early 1990s in the Netherlands. It was initially developed by Ton Roosendaal, the co-founder of the animation studio NeoGeo, which was one of the largest animation studios in the Netherlands at the time. The initial goal was to create an in-house tool that would streamline and enhance their 3D content creation process. This need led to the birth of Blender as an integrated application that facilitated modeling, animation, and rendering processes within a single program.

The decision to release Blender as an open-source project in 2002 marked a pivotal moment in its history. This transition was facilitated through a unique crowd-funding campaign, "Free Blender," which raised over 100,000 euros from the community. This effort allowed Blender's source code to be released publicly under the GNU General Public License, ensuring that it would remain free and open to users and developers worldwide.

1.2.2 Milestones in Blender Development

Since becoming open-source, Blender has seen an explosive growth in features, capabilities, and user base. Significant milestones in Blender's development include:

- **The Introduction of Cycles Rendering Engine (2011):** Blender's own rendering engine, Cycles, brought photorealistic rendering capabilities to the software, allowing for more complex and visually stunning outputs.

- **Blender 2.8 and the User Interface Overhaul (2019):** This update introduced a more intuitive and user-friendly interface, making Blender more accessible to new users and streamlining the workflow for all users. It also introduced the Eevee real-time render engine, providing a powerful tool for real-time visualization and game development.

- **Blender 2.83 LTS (2020):** The first long-term support release, offering stability and support for two years, making it a preferred version for studios and individuals working on longer-term projects.

- **Everything Nodes Project:** An ongoing initiative aiming to make all aspects of Blender driven by a node-based system, enhancing the flexibility and power of procedural generation and effects within the software.

1.2.3 Blender's Impact on the Industry

Blender 3D's impact on the digital art and animation industry is multifaceted. Its role in democratizing 3D content creation has been perhaps its most significant contribution, allowing individuals and small studios to access high-quality tools without the burden of expensive licenses. This has led to a surge in creativity and innovation in digital arts, with Blender being used in everything from independent films to major studio productions.

Academically, Blender has become a valuable tool in education, offering students a comprehensive platform to learn 3D modeling, animation, and game design without financial barriers. This has enabled a wider range of individuals to enter the digital arts field, fostering diversity and innovation.

Professionally, Blender's open-source nature has encouraged a culture of collaboration and continuous improvement, with developers and users contributing to its development. This collaborative ecosystem has accelerated Blender's growth and capabilities, making it competitive with, and sometimes superior to, commercial alternatives.

Blender's influence extends into the realms of scientific visualization, architecture, and virtual reality, demonstrating its versatility beyond traditional entertainment industries. Its ability to adapt and integrate with various workflows and industries underlines the power and potential of open-source software in driving innovation and accessibility in digital content creation.

In conclusion, the history of Blender 3D is a testament to the power of community, open-source principles, and the vision of its founders and contributors. From its humble beginnings to becoming a cornerstone in the digital art and animation industry, Blender has continually evolved, reflecting the needs and aspirations of its users. Its impact on the industry, education, and individual creators around the world is a compelling narrative of how technology can empower creativity and change the landscape of digital content creation.

1.3 ACQUIRING BLENDER 3D

1.3.1 Understanding Blender's Subscription Model

Blender 3D, at its core, remains free and open-source, accessible to anyone with a computer and an internet connection. This approach ensures that the software remains inclusive, fostering a diverse community of users and developers. Beyond the software, Blender offers additional resources and services that can enhance the user experience, including advanced tutorials, asset libraries, and professional support. These services operate on a subscription model, designed to provide valuable extras for users who seek to deepen their engagement with Blender's ecosystem.

The subscription model for these services is not a paywall for the software itself but an avenue for users to access enriched content and support. It serves a dual purpose: offering users professional-grade resources and supporting the ongoing development of Blender through financial contributions. This model is a testament to Blender's commitment to remaining free while also offering avenues for growth and sustainability.

1.3.2 Subscription Options and Pricing

Blender offers several subscription options tailored to different user needs. These can range from access to the Blender Cloud, offering assets, courses, and project collaboration tools, to professional support subscriptions for studios and enterprises requiring direct assistance from Blender developers.

1. **Blender Cloud Subscription:** This subscription grants access to an extensive library of training materials, textures, and models. It's designed for individual artists and educators seeking to expand their skills or incorporate Blender into their curriculum. The pricing is structured to be affordable, offering monthly and annual payment options to accommodate different budgets.

2. **Professional Support Subscription:** Aimed at businesses and studios, this subscription provides direct support from Blender developers, prioritizing issue resolution and offering guidance on complex projects. Pricing varies based on the level of support required, with options for small teams to large enterprises.

3. **Blender Development Fund Membership:** While not a subscription for additional services, joining the Blender Development Fund is a way for users to support the software's development financially. Members can contribute monthly, with different tiers offering varying levels of recognition and perks, such as insights into upcoming features and Blender merchandise.

1.3.3 How to Purchase a Subscription

Purchasing a subscription to Blender's additional services is a straightforward process, designed to be as accessible as the software itself. The following steps outline the general process:

1. **Visit the Official Blender Website:** All subscriptions can be initiated from Blender's official site, ensuring security and ease of access.

2. **Choose Your Subscription:** Navigate to the services section and select the subscription that best fits your needs, whether it's Blender Cloud access, professional support, or membership in the Blender Development Fund.

3. **Create an Account:** If you don't already have one, you'll need to create an account on Blender's website. This account will manage your subscriptions and provide access to the services you've subscribed to.

4. **Payment Information:** Enter your payment information. Blender typically accepts various payment methods, including credit cards and PayPal, to accommodate users worldwide.

5. **Confirmation and Access:** Once your payment is processed, you'll receive confirmation, and your subscription will be active immediately. You can then access the resources or support channels as per your subscription plan.

In conclusion, while Blender 3D remains a free and open-source tool, offering unparalleled access to 3D creation software, it also provides additional paid services for those looking to enhance their Blender experience. These subscription options support both the users in their creative pursuits and the ongoing development of Blender, ensuring its sustainability and growth for years to come.

1.4. INSTALLING BLENDER 3D

Before embarking on your journey with Blender 3D, it's essential to ensure your computer system meets the necessary requirements and understand the installation process. This guide will walk you through the system requirements, a step-by-step installation guide, and how to troubleshoot common installation issues.

1.4.1 System Requirements

To ensure Blender 3D runs smoothly on your computer, it's crucial to check if your system meets the software's minimum and recommended requirements. Blender 3D is designed to be compatible with various operating systems, including Windows, macOS, and Linux. However, the software's performance significantly depends on your system's hardware.

Windows

	Minimum	Recommended
OS	Windows 8.1 (64-bit)	Windows 10 or Windows 11
CPU	4 cores with SSE4.2 support	8 cores
RAM	8 GB	32 GB
GPU	2 GB VRAM with OpenGL 4.3 (see below)	8 GB VRAM

macOS

	Minimum	Recommended
OS	macOS 11.2 (Big Sur)	macOS 14 (Sonoma)
CPU	Apple Silicon or Intel	Apple Silicon
RAM	8 GB	32 GB
GPU	GPU with Metal 2.2 (see below)	

AMD, **Apple Silicon**, or **Intel** (Skylake and newer).

Linux

	Minimum	Recommended
OS	Distribution with glibc 2.28 or newer (64-bit)	
CPU	4 cores with SSE4.2 support	8 cores
RAM	8 GB	32 GB
GPU	2 GB VRAM with OpenGL 4.3 (see below)	8 GB VRAM

Minimum System Requirements:

- **Operating System:** Windows 8.1, macOS 10.13, or Linux
- **Processor:** 64-bit dual-core 2Ghz CPU with SSE4.2 support
- **Memory:** 8 GB RAM
- **Graphics:** 2 GB RAM, OpenGL 4.3
- **Storage:** 700 MB available space

Recommended System Requirements:

- **Operating System:** Windows 10, macOS 10.15, or a recent Linux distribution
- **Processor:** 64-bit quad-core CPU
- **Memory:** 32 GB RAM
- **Graphics:** 8 GB RAM, NVIDIA GeForce GTX 1050 Ti or better (with CUDA support for optimal rendering)
- **Storage:** 2 GB available space (SSD preferred)

For users interested in more complex projects, including high-polygon modeling, advanced simulations, or 4K video rendering, investing in hardware that exceeds the recommended specifications is advisable. A powerful GPU will significantly reduce rendering times and improve the overall workflow.

1.4.2 Step-by-Step Installation Guide

Windows:

1. Visit the official Blender website and navigate to the download section.

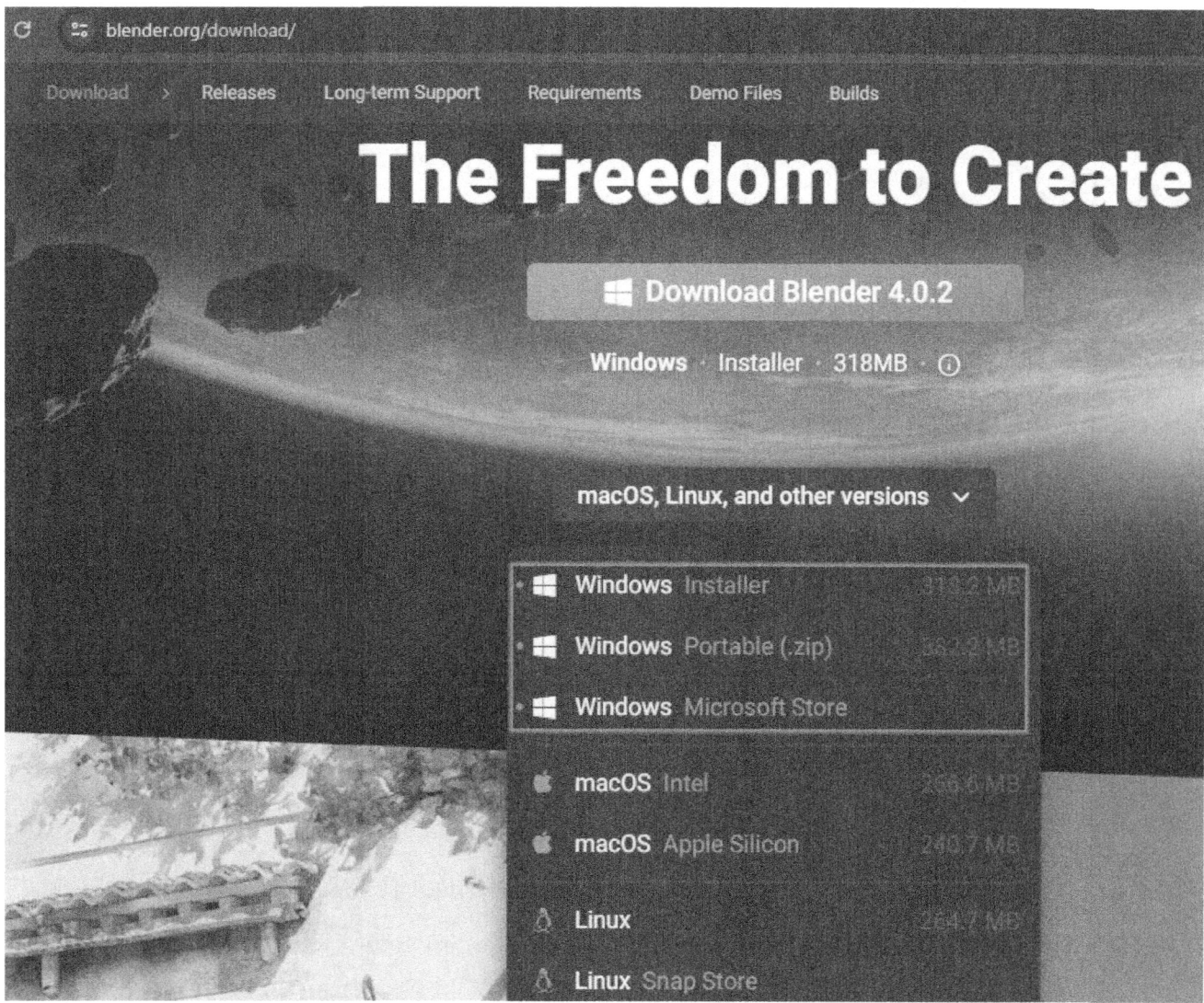

2. Choose the version compatible with your operating system and download the installer.

3. Once the download is complete, run the installer. If you encounter a security prompt from Windows Defender or your antivirus, confirm that you trust the source.

4. Follow the on-screen instructions. You can choose the installation path during this process; the default location is usually sufficient for most users.

5. After completing the installation, you can launch Blender from the Start menu or the desktop shortcut, if created.

macOS:

1. Download the macOS version of Blender from the official website.

2. Open the downloaded file. Drag and drop the Blender icon into the Applications folder.

3. You might need to authorize the application the first time you open it due to macOS security preferences. Go to System Preferences > Security & Privacy and allow Blender to run.

4. Double-click Blender in your Applications folder to start using it.

Linux:

1. For most Linux distributions, Blender can be installed directly from the official package manager. For example, in Ubuntu, you can use the command **sudo apt-get install blender** in the terminal.

2. Alternatively, download the Linux tarball from the Blender website, extract it, and run the Blender executable from the extracted folder.

3. You might need to install additional dependencies depending on your Linux distribution. Refer to the Blender documentation for detailed instructions.

1.4.3 Troubleshooting Common Installation Issues

Even with a straightforward installation process, users might encounter some issues. Here are common problems and their solutions:

Installation Fails or Freezes:

- Ensure your system meets the minimum requirements.

- Run the installer as an administrator (right-click the installer and select "Run as administrator").

- Check your antivirus software, as it might be blocking the installation. Temporarily disable it or add an exception for Blender.

Blender Crashes on Startup:

- Update your graphics card drivers. Outdated or corrupted drivers are often the cause of crashes.

- If you're using a dual graphics card setup (integrated and dedicated), ensure Blender is set to use the dedicated card. This setting can be adjusted in your graphics card's control panel.

- Disable any incompatible add-ons. Start Blender in Safe Mode to see if the issue persists.

Performance Issues:

- Make sure your graphics drivers are up to date.

- Adjust Blender's performance settings, such as reducing the viewport samples or lowering the subdivision surface modifier's viewport levels.

- Consider upgrading your hardware if you consistently encounter performance issues with complex scenes.

By following these steps and troubleshooting tips, you'll be well on your way to starting your 3D modeling journey with Blender. Remember, the Blender community is vast and supportive. If you encounter any issues not covered here, chances are someone has faced and solved the same problem. Forums, official documentation, and tutorials are great resources to help you overcome any obstacles.

1.5 BLENDER 3D'S DESIGN PHILOSOPHY

1.5.1 The Core Design Concepts Behind Blender

- **Open Source and Free Access:** At the heart of Blender's design philosophy is its status as open-source software. This foundational principle guarantees that Blender remains free to use for anyone, anywhere. This open access is more than just about cost; it's about lowering barriers to entry into the digital creation world, fostering a diverse and vibrant community of users and contributors. It ensures that Blender evolves in response to the needs and feedback of its community, rather than the profit motives of a corporation.
- **Comprehensive Toolset:** Blender is designed to be a 'one-stop-shop' for all things 3D. This means providing a suite of tools that support the entire 3D pipeline—modeling, rigging, animation, simulation, rendering, compositing, and editing. This integration ensures that artists can work within a single software environment without the need for costly plugins or external software, streamlining the creative process and fostering a more intuitive workflow.
- **Customizability and Extensibility:** Recognizing the diverse needs of its user base, Blender is built to be highly customizable. Users can tailor the interface to their workflow, create their own shortcuts, and even develop scripts and add-ons to extend Blender's capabilities. This flexibility ensures that Blender can adapt to the specific needs of individual artists and projects, promoting efficiency and creativity.
- **Community and Collaboration:** Blender's design philosophy places a strong emphasis on community and collaboration. The software is not just developed by its core team but also by contributions from users around the world. This collaborative approach extends to how users interact with Blender, with the community sharing tutorials, resources, and support through forums, social media, and events. Blender's open-source nature fosters a culture of sharing and mutual assistance, which accelerates learning and innovation within the community.

1.5.2 How Blender's Design Philosophy Benefits Users

- **Accessibility and Inclusivity:** By being free and open-source, Blender makes high-quality 3D creation tools accessible to everyone, regardless of financial resources. This inclusivity has opened the doors of digital creation to a global audience, enabling people from diverse backgrounds to express their creativity, learn new skills, and contribute to various fields, including film, animation, video games, and virtual reality.
- **Empowerment Through Education:** Blender's comprehensive toolset, combined with its vast library of community-generated tutorials and documentation, makes it an excellent platform for education. Students and educators have access to a professional-grade software package at no cost, facilitating the teaching and learning of 3D modeling, animation, and more. This accessibility has made Blender a popular choice in schools, universities, and online learning platforms.
- **Innovation and Flexibility:** The customizable and extensible nature of Blender allows users to adapt the software to their specific needs, promoting efficiency and creativity. This flexibility ensures that Blender can be used for a wide range of projects, from small-scale hobbyist creations to large commercial productions. Furthermore, the ability to

extend Blender through scripting and add-ons means that it can keep pace with the latest developments in the 3D field, driving innovation within the community.
- **A Stronger Community:** Blender's emphasis on community and collaboration has cultivated a supportive ecosystem where users share knowledge, resources, and feedback. This collaborative environment accelerates learning and innovation, enabling users to improve their skills and contribute to Blender's development. The community-driven approach also ensures that Blender evolves in a direction that reflects the needs and desires of its users, making it a tool that is continually refined and improved by those who use it the most.

In conclusion, Blender 3D's design philosophy is a reflection of its commitment to openness, inclusivity, and community. By providing a comprehensive, customizable, and free toolset for 3D creation, Blender empowers users around the world to explore their creativity, learn new skills, and contribute to a wide range of projects and industries. The benefits of this philosophy are evident in the vibrant community that has grown around Blender, characterized by a spirit of collaboration, innovation, and shared progress. As Blender continues to evolve, it remains a powerful testament to the impact of open-source principles on the world of digital creation.

1.6 DEVELOPING THE RIGHT MINDSET FOR 3D MODELING

Mastering 3D modeling, especially in a versatile environment like Blender 3D, is as much about cultivating the right mindset as it is about learning the software's ins and outs. This chapter delves into the foundational attitudes and perspectives that can significantly enhance your journey through the 3D modeling landscape.

1.6.1 The Importance of Patience and Persistence

The path to proficiency in 3D modeling is often long and fraught with challenges. Initial excitement can quickly give way to frustration as newcomers confront the complexity of creating their first models or animations. It's here that patience becomes indispensable. Understanding that each obstacle is a stepping stone towards mastery is key. Like learning a musical instrument or a new language, 3D modeling skills are honed over time, through consistent practice and perseverance.

Persistence plays a pivotal role, particularly when progress seems to stagnate or when faced with seemingly insurmountable challenges. The ability to push through, to find solutions to complex problems, and to continue learning and experimenting, even in the face of failure, is what separates those who succeed from those who give up. Remember, every expert in Blender started as a beginner, and their expertise is largely a result of their persistence.

1.6.2 Embracing Creativity and Continuous Learning

Blender 3D offers an expansive set of tools and features, enabling artists to bring even their most ambitious visions to life. However, the true potential of these tools is unlocked only by those who approach their work with creativity and an open mind. Creativity is not just about originality but also about problem-solving. It's about seeing the myriad ways a tool can be used, often in manners not initially intended by its creators.

Continuous learning is equally critical. The field of 3D modeling and Blender's capabilities are continually evolving. New tools, techniques, and best practices emerge regularly. Staying informed about these developments and incorporating them into your work ensures your skills remain relevant and your creations continue to innovate. Fortunately, Blender's vibrant community and wealth of online resources make it easier than ever to keep learning. From official tutorials and forums to user-generated content on social media and video platforms, there's a wealth of knowledge available at your fingertips.

1.6.3 Community and Collaboration in the Blender Ecosystem

One of Blender's greatest strengths is its community. From novices to seasoned professionals, the Blender ecosystem is home to a diverse group of individuals united by their passion for 3D creation. This community is an invaluable resource for learning, inspiration, and support. Engaging with the community can dramatically enhance your learning experience. Sharing your work for feedback, participating in challenges, and contributing to collaborative projects are just a few ways to engage with other Blender users.

Collaboration is another cornerstone of the Blender experience. Whether it's working together on a project, contributing to the open-source code, or sharing assets and resources, collaboration enriches the Blender ecosystem. It fosters a culture of sharing and mutual growth, where more experienced users mentor newcomers, and innovation is driven by collective effort rather than competition.

The community is also a testament to the power of open-source philosophy. Blender's development is significantly shaped by its users, with feedback and contributions directly influencing its evolution. This reciprocal relationship between the developers and the community ensures that Blender continues to meet the needs and exceed the expectations of its user base.

1.7 PREPARING FOR THE FUTURE WITH BLENDER 3D

Blender 3D's evolution is a testament to its adaptability and the forward-thinking approach of its community and developers. As we look to the future, Blender continues to position itself at the forefront of 3D modeling, animation, and rendering technologies, embracing new trends and integrating cutting-edge features. This chapter explores the anticipated directions for Blender in 2024, how users can keep abreast of these developments, and Blender's expanding role in future technologies and industries.

1.7.1 Upcoming Features and Updates in 2024

The roadmap for Blender in 2024 highlights a commitment to innovation, with several key features and updates poised to enhance its functionality, user experience, and application in professional workflows. While specific updates depend on the ongoing development and community feedback, several areas of focus reflect the broader trends in 3D technology and digital content creation:

- **Enhanced Realism in Rendering:** Continuing improvements to both Cycles and Eevee rendering engines aim to achieve greater realism with less computational overhead. This includes better handling of light, shadow, and materials, making photorealistic outputs more accessible to users.

- **AI-Assisted Modeling and Animation:** Leveraging artificial intelligence to streamline the creation process is a significant trend. Blender is expected to incorporate AI-based tools for tasks such as auto-rigging, facial expression generation, and perhaps even AI-driven animation, reducing the time and expertise required to bring characters and scenes to life.

- **Improved Simulation Capabilities:** Simulations for fluids, cloth, and particles are set to become more accurate and less resource-intensive, enabling more complex and dynamic scenes, especially useful in visual effects and scientific visualization.

- **Augmented and Virtual Reality Integration:** With the growing interest in AR and VR, Blender aims to enhance its support for creating content directly usable in these environments, including better real-time previews and integration with popular AR and VR platforms.

- **Interoperability and Industry Standards:** Emphasizing compatibility with other tools and adherence to industry standards remains a priority. This includes improvements in file format support, making Blender more seamless to integrate into mixed-software pipelines.

1.7.2 How to Stay Updated with Blender Developments

Staying informed about the latest Blender developments ensures users can take full advantage of new features and improvements. Several resources and strategies can help:

- **Official Blender Channels:** The Blender website, along with official social media accounts, provides announcements, detailed release notes, and insights into ongoing development projects.

- **Blender Developer Blogs and Forums:** Developers and contributors often share updates, tutorials, and discussions on upcoming features in blogs and forums, offering a deeper understanding of the changes and the rationale behind them.

- **Blender Conferences and Meetups:** Events like the Blender Conference and local Blender meetups are fantastic opportunities to learn from developers and experienced users directly, gaining insights into future directions and networking with the community.

- **Online Tutorials and Courses:** Many educators and content creators regularly update their offerings to include tutorials on new Blender features, providing practical guidance on how to leverage these in your projects.

1.7.3 The Role of Blender in Future Technologies and Industries

Blender's flexibility and comprehensive feature set position it as a key player in the future of various technologies and industries:

- **Film and Animation:** Blender's continued advancements in rendering and animation tools make it increasingly viable for large-scale film and animation projects, challenging the dominance of high-cost proprietary software.

- **Game Development:** With enhancements in real-time rendering and AR/VR support, Blender is set to become an even more integral tool in game development pipelines, facilitating the creation of immersive and complex game worlds.

- **Virtual Production:** The intersection of live-action filming and CGI benefits from Blender's capabilities in real-time rendering and visualization, making virtual production techniques more accessible to filmmakers.

- **Education and Training:** As a free tool, Blender is an invaluable resource for educational institutions, allowing students to develop marketable skills in 3D modeling, animation, and design without financial barriers.

- **Scientific Visualization:** Blender's advancements in simulation and rendering technologies enhance its application in scientific research, enabling more accurate and visually compelling representations of complex data.

In conclusion, preparing for the future with Blender 3D involves not only familiarizing oneself with upcoming features and developments but also understanding Blender's evolving role in broader technological and industrial contexts. As Blender continues to push the boundaries of what is possible in 3D creation, its users stand at the forefront of these changes, equipped to leverage the software's capabilities to explore new horizons in digital art, design, and beyond.

1.8 CHAPTER SUMMARY

1.8.1 Key Takeaways from This Chapter

- **Introduction to Blender 3D:** Blender is a comprehensive, open-source 3D creation suite that supports the entire 3D pipeline. It's accessible to beginners yet powerful enough for professionals, fostering a diverse community of users.

- **The Origins and Evolution of Blender:** Blender's journey from an in-house tool to a global open-source project underscores the power of community and the impact of open-source philosophy on software development.

- **Acquiring Blender 3D:** Despite being free and open-source, Blender offers additional resources through subscription-based services like Blender Cloud and professional support, providing users with enhanced learning tools and support options.

- **Installing Blender 3D:** The installation process is straightforward across different operating systems. System requirements are clearly defined to ensure optimal performance, and the community offers solutions to common installation issues.

- **Blender 3D's Design Philosophy:** Blender's development is guided by principles of openness, innovation, and community collaboration, which manifest in its versatile toolset and adaptive workflow.

- **Developing the Right Mindset for 3D Modeling:** Success in 3D modeling with Blender requires patience, persistence, creativity, and a commitment to continuous learning and community engagement.

- **Preparing for the Future with Blender 3D:** Blender's roadmap is marked by continuous improvement and adaptation, with future updates focusing on realism, AI integration, and support for emerging technologies like AR and VR.

These takeaways underscore Blender's role not just as a software tool but as a platform for learning, creativity, and community. Blender empowers users to explore the vast potential of 3D creation, regardless of their skill level or professional background.

1.8.2 What to Expect in the Next Chapter

As we move forward, the next chapter transitions from Blender's foundational aspects to practical guidance on beginning your 3D modeling journey. It will cover:

- **Navigating Blender's Interface:** An in-depth look at Blender's user interface (UI), including customization options to streamline your workflow and improve efficiency.

- **Basic Modeling Techniques:** Step-by-step tutorials to guide you through the process of creating your first 3D model in Blender, from simple objects to more complex shapes.

- **Material and Texturing Fundamentals:** Understanding how to apply and manipulate materials and textures to bring your models to life with realistic details.

- **Lighting and Rendering:** Techniques for effectively lighting your scene and rendering your creations to produce stunning visuals.

- **Animation Basics:** An introduction to animating objects in Blender, covering keyframes, timelines, and simple animations to bring motion to your models.

- **Project Management and Workflow Tips:** Strategies for managing projects within Blender, including file organization, version control, and efficient use of resources.

- **Community Resources and Further Learning:** A guide to leveraging the Blender community for support, inspiration, and ongoing education.

The upcoming chapter is designed to equip beginners with the necessary skills and confidence to start creating in Blender. Through hands-on tutorials, practical advice, and insights into the software's capabilities, readers will be prepared to embark on their own 3D modeling projects, laying the foundation for more advanced exploration in subsequent chapters.

CHAPTER 2: KEYBOARD SHORTCUTS IN BLENDER

WINDOW HOTKEYS

Certain window managers also use the following hotkeys. So **ALT-CTRL** can be substituted for **CTRL** to perform the functions described below if a conflict arises.

CTRL-LEFTARROW. Go to the previous Screen.

CTRL-RIGHTARROW. Go to the next Screen.

CTRL-UPARROW or **CTRL-DOWNARROW**. Maximize the window or return to the previous window display size.

SHIFT-F4. Change the window to a Data View **SHIFT-F5**. Change the window to a 3D Window **SHIFT-F6**. Change the window to an IPO Window **SHIFT-F7**. Change the window to a Buttons Window

SHIFT-F8. Change the window to a Sequence Window **SHIFT-F9**. Change the window to an Outliner Window **SHIFT-F10**. Change the window to an Image Window **SHIFT-F11**. Change the window to a Text Window **SHIFT-F12**. Change the window to an Action Window

UNIVERSAL HOTKEYS

The following Hotkeys work uniformly in all Blender Windows, if the Context allows:

CTRL-LMB. Lasso select: drag the mouse to form a freehand selection area.

ESC.

- This key always cancels Blender functions without changes.

- or: File Window, Data View and Image Select: back to the previous window type.
- or: the Render Window is pushed to the background (or closed, that depends on the operating system).

SPACE. Open the Toolbox.

TAB. Start or quit Edit Mode.

F1. Loads a Blender file. Changes the window to a File Window.

SHIFT-F1. Appends parts from other files, or loads as Library- data. Changes the window to a File Window, making Blender files accessible as a directory.

F2. Writes a Blender file. Change the window to a File Window.

SHIFT-F2. Exports the scene as a **DXF** file

CTRL-F2. Exports the scene as a **VRML1** file

F3. Writes a picture (if a picture has been rendered). The file format is as indicated in the Display Buttons. The window becomes a File Select Window.

CTRL-F3 (**ALT-CTRL-F3** on Mac OSX). Saves a screen dump of the active window. The file format is as indicated in the Display Buttons. The window becomes a File Window.

SHIFT-CTRL-F3. Saves a screen dump of the whole Blender screen. The file format is as indicated in the Display Buttons. The window becomes a File Window.

F4. Displays the Logic Context (if a Buttons Window is available).

F5. Displays the Shading Context (if a Buttons Window is available), Light, Material or World Sub-contexts depends on active object.

F6. Displays the Shading Context and Texture Sub-context (if a Buttons Window is available).

F7. Displays the Object Context (if a Buttons Window is available).

F8. Displays the Shading Context and World Sub-context (if a Buttons Window is available).

F9. Displays the Editing Context (if a Buttons Window is available).

F10. Displays the Scene Context (if a Buttons Window is available).

F11. Hides or shows the render window.

F12. Starts the rendering from the active camera.

LEFTARROW. Go to the previous frame. **SHIFT-LEFTARROW**. Go to the first frame.
RIGHTARROW. Go to the next frame.

SHIFT-LEFTARROW. Go to the last frame.

UPARROW. Go forward 10 frames.

DOWNARROW. Go back 10 frames.

ALT-A. Change the current Blender window to Animation Playback mode. The cursor changes to a counter.

ALT-SHIFT-A. The current window, plus all 3DWindows go into Animation Playback mode.

I KEY. Insert Key menu. This menu differs from window to window.

J KEY. Toggle the render buffers. Blender allows you to retain two different rendered pictures in memory.

CTRL-O. Opens the last saved file.

Q KEY. OK? Quit Blender. This key closes Blender.

OBJECT MODE HOTKEYS

These hotkeys are mainly bound to the 3D Viewport Window, but many work on Objects in most other windows, like IPOs and so on, hence they are summarized here.

HOME. All Objects in the visible layer are displayed completely, centered in the window.

PAGEUP. Select the next Object Key. If more than one Object Key is selected, the selection is shifted up cyclically. Only works if the Anim Buttons->Draw Key is ON for the Object.

SHIFT-PAGEUP. Adds to selection the next Object Key.

PAGEDOWN. Select the previous Object Key. If more than one Object Key is selected, the selection is shifted up cyclically. Only works if the Anim Buttons->Draw Key is ON for the Object.

SHIFT-PAGEDOWN. Adds to selection the previous Object Key.

ACCENT. (To the left of the 1KEY in US keyboard) Select all layers.

SHIFT-ACCENT. Revert to the previous layer setting. TAB. Start/stop Edit Mode. Alternative hotkey: **ALT-E. A KEY**. Selects/deselects all.

CTRL-A. Apply size and rotation. The rotation and dimensions of the Object are assigned to the Ob Data (Mesh, Curve, etc.).

At first glance, it appears as if nothing has changed, but this can have considerable consequences for animations or texture mapping. This is best illustrated by also having the axis of a Mesh Object be drawn (**Edit Buttons->Axis**). Rotate the Object and activate Apply. The rotation and dimensions of the Object are 'erased'.

SHIFT-CTRL-A. If the active Object is automatically duplicated (see AnimButtons -> DupliFrames or AnimButtons -> Dupliverts), a menu asks Make dupli's real?. This option actually creates the Objects. If the active Mesh Object is deformed by a Lattice, a menu asks Apply Lattice deform?. Now the deformation of the Lattice is assigned to the vertices of the Mesh.

SHIFT-A. This is the Add Menu. In fact, it is the Toolbox that starts with the 'ADD' option. When Objects are added, Blender starts Edit Mode immediately if possible.

B KEY. Border Select. Draw a rectangle with the Left Mouse; all Objects within this area are selected, but not made active. Draw a rectangle with the Right Mouse to deselect Objects. In orthonormal View Mode, the dimensions of the rectangle are displayed, expressed as global coordinates, as an extra feature in the lower left corner. In Camera View Mode, the dimensions that are to be rendered according to the Display Buttons are displayed in pixel units.

SHIFT-B. Render Border. This only works in Camera View Mode. Draw a rectangle to render a smaller cut-out of the standard window frame. If the option Display Buttons->Border is ON, a box is drawn with red and black lines.

C KEY. Centre View. The position of the 3DCursor becomes the new centre of the 3DWindow.

ALT-C. Convert Menu. Depending on the active Object, a popup Menu is displayed. This enables you to convert certain types of Ob Data. It only converts in one direction, everything ultimately degrades to a Mesh! The options are:

- Font -> Curve
- MetaBall -> Mesh The original MetaBall remains unchanged.
- Curve -> Mesh
- Surface -> Mesh

CTRL-C. Copy Menu. This menu copies information from the active Object to (other) selected Objects.

Fixed components are:

- Copy Loc: the X,Y,Z location of the Object. If a Child is involved, this location is the relative position in relation to the Parent.
- Copy Rot: the X,Y,Z rotation of the Object.
- Copy Size: the X,Y,Z dimension of the Object.
- DrawType: copies Object Drawtype.
- TimeOffs: copies Object time offset.
- Dupli: all Duplicator data (Dupliframes, Dupliverts and so on)
- Mass: Real time stuff.
- Damping: Real time stuff.
- Properties: Real time stuff.
- Logic Bricks: Real time stuff.
- Constraints: copies Object constraints.

OBJECT MODE HOTKEYS

If applicable:

- Copy TexSpace: The texture space.
- Copy Particle Settings: the complete particle system from the AnimButtons.

For Curve Objects:

- a second **X KEY, Y KEY, Z KEY** constrains movement to **X, Y or Z** axis of the local reference.
- a third **X KEY, Y KEY, Z KEY** removes constraints.
- **N KEY** enters numerical input, as well as any numeric key directly. **TAB** will switch between values, **ENTER** finalizes, **ESC** exits.
- **ARROWS**: These keys can be used to move the mouse

- cursor exactly 1 pixel.

Grabber can be terminated with:

- Copy Bevel Settings: all bevelling data from the EditButtons.

Font Objects:

- Copy Font Settings: font type, dimensions, spacing.
- Copy Bevel Settings: all bevelling data from the EditButtons.

Camera Objects:

- Copy Lens: the lens value.

SHIFT-C. Centre Zero View. The 3DCursor is set to zero (0,0,0) and the view is changed so that all Objects, including the 3Dcursor, can be displayed. This is an alternative for HOME.

D KEY. Draw mode menu. Allows to select draw modes exactly as the corresponding menu in the 3D viewport header does.

SHIFT-D. Add Duplicate. The selected Objects are duplicated. Grab mode starts immediately thereafter.

ALT-D. Add Linked Duplicate. Of the selected Objects linked duplicates are created. Grab mode starts immediately thereafter.

CTRL-D. Draw the (texture) Image as wire. This option has a limited function. It can only be used for 2D compositing.

ALT-E. Start/stop EditMode. Alternative hotkey: TAB.

F KEY. If selected Object is a mesh Toggles Face selectMode on and off.

CTRL-F. Sort Faces. The faces of the active Mesh Object are sorted, based on the current view in the 3DWindow. The leftmost face first, the rightmost last. The sequence of faces is important for the Build Effect (AnimButtons).

G KEY. Grab Mode. Or: the translation mode. This works on selected Objects and vertices. Blender calculates the quantity and direction of the translation, so that they correspond exactly with the mouse movements, regardless of the ViewMode or view direction of the 3DWindow. Alternatives for starting this mode:

LMB to draw a straight line.

The following options are available in translation mode:

Limiters:

- **CTRL:** in increments of 1 grid unit.
- **SHIFT:** fine movements.
- **SHIFT-CTRL:** in increments of 0.1 grid unit.

MMB toggles: A short click restricts the current translation to the **X,Y or Z axis**. Blender calculates which axis to use, depending on the already initiated mouse movement. Click Middle Mouse again to return to unlimited translation.

X KEY, Y KEY, Z KEY constrains movement to **X, Y or Z** axis of the global reference.

- **LMB SPACE** or **ENTER**: move to a new position.
- **RMB or ESC**: everything goes back to the old position.

Switching mode:

- **G KEY**: starts Grab mode again.
- **S KEY**: switches to Size (Scale) mode.
- **R KEY**: switches to Rotate mode.

ALT-G. Clears translations, given in Grab mode. The **X, Y, Z** locations of selected Objects are set to zero.

SHIFT-G. Group Selection

- **Children:** Selects all selected Object's Children.
- **Immediate Children:** Selects all selected Object's first level Children.
- **Parent:** Selects selected Object's Parent.
- **Shared Layers:** Selects all Object on the same Layer of active Object

I KEY. Insert Object Key. A key position is inserted in the current frame of all selected Objects. A popup Menu asks what key position(s) must be added to the IpoCurves.

- **Loc:** The XYZ location of the Object.
- **Rot:** The XYZ rotation of the Object.
- **Size:** The XYZ dimensions of the Object
- **LocRot:** The XYZ location and XYZ rotation of the Object.
- **LocRotSize:** The XYZ location, XYZ rotation and XYZ dimensions of the Object.
- **Layer:** The layer of the Object.
- **Avail:** A position is only added to all the current IpoCurves, that is curves which already exists.
- **Mesh, Lattice, Curve or Surface:** depending on the type of Object, a VertexKey can be added

CTRL-J. Join Objects. All selected Objects of the same type are added to the active Object. What actually happens here is that the Ob Data blocks are combined and all the selected Objects (except for the active one) are deleted. This is a rather complex operation, which can lead to confusing results, particularly when working with a lot of linked data, animation curves and hierarchies.

K KEY. Show Keys. The Draw Key option is turned ON for all selected Objects. If all of them were already ON, they are all turned OFF.

SHIFT-K. A popup Menu asks: OK? Show and select all keys. The Draw Key option is turned ON for all selected Objects, and all Object-keys are selected. This function is used to enable transformation of the entire animation system.

LKEY. Makes selected Object local. Makes library linked objects local for the current scene.

OBJECT MODE HOTKEYS

Object will not be deformed. A popup permits to select the bone. This is the option if you are modeling a robot or machinery

CTRL-L. Link selected. Links some of the Active Object data to all selected Objects, the following menu entry appears only if applicable.

- **To Scene:** Creates a link of the Object to a scene.
- **Object IPOs:** Links Active Object IPOs to selected ones.
- **Mesh Data:** Links Active Object Mesh data selected ones.
- **Lamp Data:** Links Active Object Lamp data to selected ones.
- **Curve Data:** Links Active Object Curve data selected ones.
- **Surf Data:** Links Active Object Surf data selected ones.
- **Material:** Links Active Object Material to selected ones.

SHIFT-L. Select Linked. Selects all Objects somehow linked to active Object.

- **Object IPO:** Selects all Object(s) sharing active Object's IPOs.
- **Object Data:** Selects all Object(s) sharing active Object's ObData.
- **Current Material:** Selects all Object(s) sharing active Object's current Material.

Current Texture: Selects all Object(s) sharing active Object's current Texture.

MKEY. Moves selected Object(s) to another layer, a pop-up appers. Use LMB to move, use SHIFT-LMB to make the object belong to multiple layers. If the selected Objects have different layers, this is 'OR'ed in the menu display. Use ESC to exit the menu. Press the "OK" button or ENTER to change the layer seting. The hotkeys (ALT-)(1KEY, 2KEY, ... - 0KEY) work here as well (see 3DHeader).

CTRL-M. Mirror Menu. It is possible to mirror an Object along the X, Y or Z axis.

N KEY. Number Panel. The location, rotation and scaling of the active Object are displayed and can be modified.

ALT-O. Clear Origin. The 'Origin' is erased for all Child Objects, which causes the Child Objects to move to the exact location of the Parent Objects.

SHIFT-O. If the selected Object is a Mesh toggles SubSurf onn/ off. CTRL-1 to CTRL-4 switches to the relative SubSurf level for display purpouses. Rendering SUbSurf level has no Hotkey.

CTRL-P. Make selected Object(s) the child(ren) of the active Object. If the Parent is a Curve then a popup offers two coiches:

- **Normal Parent:** Make a normal parent, the curve can be made a path later on.
- **Follow Path:** Automatically creates a Follow Path constraint with the curve as target.

If the Parent is an Armature, a popup offers three options:

- **Use Bone:** One of the Bones becomes the parent. The
- **Use Armature:** The whole armature is used as parent for deformations. This is the choiche for organic beings.
- **Use Object:** Standard parenting.

In the second case further options asks if Vertex groups should not be created, should be created empty or created and populated.

ALT-P. Clears Parent relation, user is asked if he wishes to keep or clear parent-induced transforms.

- **Clear Parent:** the selected Child Objects are unlinked from the Parent. since the transformation of the Parent disappears, this can appear as if the former Children themselves are transformed.
- **... and keep transform:** the Child Objects are unlinked from the Parent, and an attempt is made to assign the current transformation, which was determined in part by the Parent, to the (former Child) Objects.
- **Clear Parent inverse:** The inverse matrix of the Parent of the selected Objects is erased. The Child Objects remain linked to the Objects. This gives the user complete control over the hierarchy.

RKEY. Rotate mode. Works on selected Object(s). In Blender, a rotation is by default a rotation perpendicular to the screen, regardless of the view direction or View Mode. The degree of rotation is exactly linked to the mouse movement. Try moving around the rotation midpoint with the mouse. The rotation pivot point is determined by the state of the 3DViewport Header buttons. Alternatives for starting this mode:

LMB to draw a C-shaped curve.

The following options are available in rotation mode:

Limiters:

- **CTRL:** in increments of 5 degrees.
- **SHIFT:** fine movements.
- **SHIFT-CTRL:** in increments of 1 degree.

MMB toggles: A short click restricts the current rotation to the horizontal or vertical view axis.

XKEY, YKEY, ZKEY constrains rotation to **X, Y or Z** axis of the global reference.

a second **XKEY, YKEY, ZKEY** constrains rotation to **X, Y or Z** axis of the local reference.

a third **XKEY, YKEY, ZKEY** removes constraints.

NKEY enters numerical input, as well as any numeric key directly. **ENTER** finalizes, **ESC** exits.

ARROWS: These keys can be used to move the mouse cursor exactly 1 pixel.

Rotation can be terminated with:

- **LMB SPACE or ENTER**: move to a new position.
- **RMB or ESC**: everything goes back to the old position.

Switching mode:

- **GKEY:** switches to Grab.
- **SKEY**: switches to Size (Scale) mode.
- **RKEY**: starts Rotate mode again.

OBJECT MODE HOTKEYS

ALT-R. Clears Rotation. The X,Y,Z rotations of selected Objects are set to zero.

SKEY. Size mode or scaling mode. Works on selected Object(s). The degree of scaling is exactly linked to the mouse movement. Try to move from the (rotation) midpoint with the mouse. The pivot point is determined by the settings of the 3D Viewport header pivot Menu. Alternatives for starting scaling mode:

LMB to draw a V-shaped line.

The following options are available in scaling mode:

Limiters:

- **CTRL:** in increments of 0.1.
- **SHIFT-CTRL:** in increments of 0.01.

MMB toggles: A short click restricts the scaling to X, Y or Z axis. Blender calculates the appropriate axis based on the already initiated mouse movement. Click MMB again to return to free scaling.

XKEY, YKEY, ZKEY constrains scaling to X, Y or Z axis of the local reference.

a second **XKEY, YKEY, ZKEY** removes constraints.

NKEY enters numerical input, as well as any numeric key directly. **ENTER** finalizes, **ESC** exits.

ARROWS: These keys can be used to move the mouse cursor exactly 1 pixel.

Scaling can be terminated with:

- **LMB SPACE or ENTER:** move to a new position.
- **RMB or ESC:** everything goes back to the old dimension.

Switching mode:

- **GKEY**: switches to Grab.
- **SKEY**: starts Size mode again.
- **RKEY**: switches to Rotation.

ALT-S. Clears Size. The X,Y,Z dimensions of selected Objects are set to 1.0.

SHIFT-S. Snap Menu:

- **Sel->Grid:** Moves Object to nearest grid point.
- **Sel->Curs:** Moves Object to cursor.
- **Curs->Grid:** Moves cursor to nearest grid point.
- **Curs->Sel:** Moves cursor to selected Object(s).
- **Sel->Center:** Moves Objects to their barycentrum.

TKEY. Texture space mode. The position and dimensions of the texture space for the selected Objects can be changed in the same manner as described above for Grab and Size mode. To make this visible, the drawing flag Edit Buttons->Tex Space is set ON. A Popup Menu asks you to select: "Grabber" or "Size".

CTRL-T. Makes selected Object(s) track the Active Object. Old track method was Blender default tracking before version 2.30. The new method is the Constrain Track, this creates a fully editable constraint on the selected object targeting the active Object.

ALT-T. Clears old style Track. Constraint track is removed as all constrains are.

UKEY. Makes Object Single User, the inverse operation of Link (**CTRL-L**) a pop-up appears with choices.

- **Object:** if other Scenes also have a link to this Object, the link is deleted and the Object is copied. The Object now only exists in the current Scene. The links from the Object remain unchanged.
- **Object & ObData:** Similar to the previous command, but now the ObData blocks with multiple links are copied as well. All selected Objects are now present in the current Scene only, and each has a unique ObData (Mesh, Curve, etc.).
- **Object & ObData & Materials+Tex:** Similar to the previous command, but now Materials and Textures with multiple links are also copied. All selected Objects are now unique. They have unique ObData and each has a unique Material and Texture block.
- **Materials+Tex:** Only the Materials and Textures with multiple links are copied.

VKEY. Switches in/out of Vertex Paint Mode.

ALT-V. Object-Image Aspect. This hotkey sets the X and Y dimensions of the selected Objects in relation to the dimensions of the Image Texture they have. Use this hotkey when making 2D Image compositions and multi-plane designs to quickly place the Objects in the appropriate relationship with one another.

WKEY. Opens Object Booleans Menu.

XKEY. Erase Selected? Deletes selected objects.

ZKEY. Toggles Solid Mode on/off. **SHIFT-Z**. Toggles Shaded Mode on/off. **ALT-Z**. Toggles Textured Mode on/off.

EDIT MODE - GENERAL

Again, Most of these hotkeys are useful in the 3D Viewport when in Edit Mode, but many works on other Blender Object, so they are summarized here.

Many Object Mode keys works in Edit mode too, but on the selected vertices or control points; among these Grab, Rotate, Scale and so on. These hotkeys are not repeated here.

TAB or **ALT-E**. This button starts and stops Edit Mode.

CTRL-TAB. Switches between Vertex Select, Edge Select, and Face Select modes. Holding **SHIFT** while clicking on a mode will allow you to combine modes.

AKEY. Select/Unselect all.

BKEY. Circle Select. If you press **BKEY** a second time after starting Border Select, Circle Select is invoked. It works as described above. Use **NUM+** or **NUM-** or **MW** to adjust the circle size. Leave Circle Select with **RMB** or **ESC**.

CTRL-H. With vertices selected, this creates a "**Hook**" object. Once a hook is selected, **CTRL-H** brings up an options menu for it.

NKEY. Number Panel. Simpler than the Object Mode one, in Edit Mode works for Mesh, Curve, Surface: The location of the active vertex is displayed.

OKEY. Switch in/out of Proportional Editing.

SHIFT-O. Toggles between Smooth and Sharp Proportional Editing.

PKEY. Separate. You can choose to make a new object with all selected vertices, edges, faces and curves or create a new object from each separate group of interconnected vertices from a popup. Note that for curves you cannot separate connected control vertices. This operation is the opposite of Join (**CTRL- J**).

CTRL-P. Make Vertex Parent. If one object (or more than one) is/are selected and the active Object is in Edit Mode with 1 or 3 vertices selected then the Object in Edit Mode becomes the Vertex Parent of the selected Object(s). If only 1 vertex is selected, only the location of this vertex determines the Parent transformation; the rotation and dimensions of the Parent do not play a role here. If three vertices are selected, it is a 'normal' Parent relationship in which the 3 vertices determine the rotation and location of the Child together. This method produces interesting effects with Vertex Keys. In Edit Mode, other Objects can be selected with **CTRL-RMB**.

CTRL-S. Shear. In Edit Mode this operation enables you to make selected forms 'slant'. This always works via the horizontal screen axis.

UKEY. Undo. When starting Edit Mode, the original Ob Data block is saved and can be returned to via **UKEY**. Mesh Objects have better Undo, see next section.

WKEY. Specials popup Menu. A number of tools are included in this Popup Menu as an alternative to the Edit Buttons. This makes the buttons accessible as shortcuts, e.g. Edit Buttons->Subdivide is also '**WKEY, 1KEY**'.

SHIFT-W. Warp. Selected vertices can be bent into curves with this option. It can be used to convert a plane into a tube or even a sphere. The centre of the circle is the 3DCursor. The mid-line of the circle is determined by the horizontal dimensions of the selected vertices. When you start, everything is already bent 90 degrees. Moving the mouse up or down increases or decreases the extent to which warping is done. By zooming in/out of the 3Dwindow, you can specify the maximum degree of warping. The CTRL limiter increments warping in steps of 5 degrees.

EDIT MODE - MESH

This section and the following highlight peculiar Edit Mode Hotkeys.

CTRL-NUM+. Adds to selection all vertices connected by an edge to an already selected vertex.

CTRL-NUM-. Removes from selection all vertices of the outer ring of selected vertices.

ALT-CTRL-RMB. Edge select.

CKEY. If using curve deformations, this toggles the curve Cyclic mode on/off.

EKEY. Extrude Selected. "Extrude" in Edit Mode transforms all the selected edges to faces. If possible, the selected faces are also duplicated. Grab mode is started directly after this command is executed.

SHIFT-EKEY. Crease Subsurf edge. With "Draw Creases" enabled, pressing this key will allow you to set the crease weight. Black edges have no weight, edge-select color have full weight.

CTRL-EKEY. Mark **LSCM** Seam. Marks a selected edge as a "seam" for unwrapping using the **LSCM** mode.

FKEY. Make Edge/Face. If 2 vertices are selected, an edge is created. If 3 or 4 vertices are selected, a face is created.

SHIFT-F. Fill selected. All selected vertices that are bound by edges and form a closed polygon are filled with triangular faces. Holes are automatically taken into account. This operation is 2D; various layers of polygons must be filled in succession.

ALT-F. Beauty Fill. The edges of all the selected triangular faces are switched in such a way that equally sized faces are formed. This operation is 2D; various layers of polygons must be filled in succession. The Beauty Fill can be performed immediately after a Fill.

CTRL-F. Flip faces, selected triangular faces are paired and common edge of each pair swapped.

HKEY. Hide Selected. All selected vertices and faces are temporarily hidden.

SHIFT-H. Hide Not Selected: All non-selected vertices and faces are temporarily hidden.

EDIT MODE - MESH

SHIFT-U. Redo. This let you re-apply any undone changes up to the moment in which Edit Mode was entered.

ALT-H. Reveal. All temporarily hidden vertices and faces are drawn again.

ALT-J. Join faces, selected triangular faces are joined in pairs and transformed to quads

KKEY. Knife tool Menu.

- **Face Loop Select: (SHIFT-R)** Face loops are highlighted starting from edge under mouse pointer. **LMB** finalizes, **ESC** exits.
- **Face Loop Cut: (CTRL-R)** Face loops are highlighted starting from edge under mouse pointer. **LMB** finalizes, **ESC** exits.
- **Knife (exact): (SHIFT-K)** Mouse starts draw mode. Selected Edges are cut at intersections with mouse line. **ENTER** or **RMB** finalizes, **ESC** exits.
- **Knife (midpoints): (SHIFT-K)** Mouse starts draw mode. Selected Edges intersecting with mouse line are cut in middle regardless of true intersection point. **ENTER** or **RMB** finalizes, **ESC** exits.

LKEY. Select Linked. If you start with an unselected vertex near the mouse cursor, this vertex is selected, together with all vertices that share an edge with it.

SHIFT-L. Deselect Linked. If you start with a selected vertex, this vertex is deselected, together with all vertices that share an edge with it.

CTRL-L. Select Linked Selected. Starting with all selected vertices, all vertices connected to them are selected too.

MKEY. Mirror. Opens a popup asking for the axis to mirror. 3 possible axis group are available, each of which contains three axes, for a total of nine choices. Axes can be Global (Blender Global Reference); Local (Current Object Local Reference) or View (Current View reference). Remember that mirroring, like scaling, happens with respect to the current pivot point.

ALT-M. Merges selected vertices at barycentrum or at cursor depending on selection made on pop-up.

CTRL-N. Calculate Normals Outside. All normals from selected faces are recalculated and consistently set in the same direction. An attempt is made to direct all normals 'outward'.

SHIFT-CTRL-N. Calculate Normals Inside. All normals from selected faces are recalculated and consistently set in the same direction. An attempt is made to direct all normals 'inward'.

ALT-S. Whereas **SHIFT-S** scales in Edit Mode as it does in Object Mode, for Edit Mode a further option exists, **ALT-S** moves each vertex in the direction of its local normal, hence effectively shrinking/fattening the mesh.

CTRL-T. Make Triangles. All selected faces are converted to triangles.

UKEY. Undo. When starting Edit Mode, the original Ob Data block is saved and all subsequent changes are saved on a stack. This option enables you to restore the previous situation, one after the other.

ALT-U. Undo Menu. This let you choose the exact point to which you want to undo changes.

WKEY. Special Menu. A Popup Menu offers the following options:

- **Subdivide:** all selected edges are split in two.
- **Subdivide Fractal:** all selected edges are split in two and middle vertex displaced randomly.
- **Subdivide Smooth:** all selected edges are split in two and middle vertex displaced along the normal.
- **Merge:** as ALT-M.
- **Remove Doubles:** All selected vertices closer to each other than a given threshold (See Edit Mode Button Window) are merged ALT-M.
- **Hide:** as HKEY.
- **Reveal:** as ALT-H.
- **Select Swap:** Selected vertices become unselected and vice versa.
- **Flip Normals:** Normals of selected faces are flipped.
- **Smooth:** Vertices are moved closer one to each other, getting a smoother object.
- **Bevel:** Faces are reduced in size and the space between edges is filled with a smoothly curving bevel of the desired order.

XKEY. Erase Selected. A popup Menu offers the following options:

- **Vertices:** all vertices are deleted. This includes the edges and faces they form.

- **Edges:** all edges with both vertices selected are deleted. If this 'releases' certain vertices, they are deleted as well. Faces that can no longer exist as a result of this action are also deleted.
- **Faces:** all faces with all their vertices selected are deleted. If any vertices are 'released' as a result of this action, they are deleted.
- **All:** everything is deleted.
- **Edges and Faces:** all selected edges and faces are deleted, but the vertices remain.
- **Only Faces:** all selected faces are deleted, but the edges and vertices remain.

YKEY. Split. This command 'splits' the selected part of a Mesh without deleting faces. The split parts are no longer bound by edges. Use this command to control smoothing. Since the split parts have vertices at the same position, selection with **LKEY** is recommended.

EDIT MODE - CURVE

CKEY. Set the selected curves to cyclic or turn cyclic off. An individual curve is selected if at least one of the vertices is selected.

EKEY. Extrude Curve. A vertex is added to the selected end of the curves. Grab mode is started immediately after this command is executed.

FKEY. Add segment. A segment is added between two selected vertices at the end of two curves. These two curves are combined into one curve.

HKEY. Toggle Handle align/free. Toggles the selected Bezier handles between free or aligned.

SHIFT-H. Set Handle auto. The selected Bezier handles are converted to auto type.

CTRL-H. Calculate Handles. The selected Bezier curves are calculated and all handles are assigned a type.

LKEY. Select Linked. If you start with an non-selected vertex near the mouse cursor, this vertex is selected together with all the vertices of the same curve.

SHIFT-L. Deselect Linked. If you start with a selected vertex, it is deselected together with all the vertices of the same curve.

MKEY. Mirror. Mirror selected control points exactly as for vertices in a Mesh.

TKEY. Tilt mode. Specify an extra axis rotation, i.e. the tilt, for each vertex in a 3D curve.

ALT-T. Clear Tilt. Set all axis rotations of the selected vertices to zero.

VKEY. Vector Handle. The selected Bezier handles are converted to vector type.

WKEY. The special menu for curves appears:

- **Subdivide.** Subdivide the selected vertices.
- **Switch direction.** The direction of the selected curves is reversed. This is mainly for Curves that are used as paths!

XKEY. Erase Selected. A popup Menu offers the following options:

- **Selected:** all selected vertices are deleted.

- **Segment:** a curve segment is deleted. This only works for single segments. Curves can be split in two using this option. Or use this option to specify the cyclic position within a cyclic curve.
- **All:** delete everything.

EDIT MODE - SURFACE

CKEY. Toggle Cyclic menu. A popup Menu asks if selected surfaces in the '**U**' or the '**V**' direction must be cyclic. If they were already cyclic, this mode is turned off.

EKEY. Extrude Selected. This makes surfaces of all the selected curves, if possible. Only the edges of surfaces or loose curves are candidates for this operation. Grab mode is started immediately after this command is completed.

FKEY. Add segment. A segment is added between two selected vertices at the ends of two curves. These two curves are combined into 1 curve.

LKEY. Select Linked. If you start with an non-selected vertex near the mouse cursor, this vertex is selected together with all the vertices of the same curve or surface.

SHIFT-L. Deselect Linked. If you start with a selected vertex, this vertex is deselected together with all vertices of the same curve or surface.

MKEY. Mirror. Mirror selected control points exactly as for vertices in a Mesh.

SHIFT-R. Select Row. Starting with the last selected vertex, a complete row of vertices is selected in the 'U' or 'V' direction. Selecting Select Row a second time with the same vertex switches the 'U' or 'V' selection.

WKEY. The special menu for surfaces appears:
- **Subdivide.** Subdivide the selected vertices
- **Switch direction.** This will switch the normals of the selected parts.
- **Mirror.** Mirrors the selected vertices

XKEY. Erase Selected. A popup Menu offers the following choices:
- **Selected:** all selected vertices are deleted.
- **All:** delete everything.

VERTEX PAINT HOTKEYS

SHIFT-K. All vertex colours are erased; they are changed to the current drawing colour.

UKEY. Undo. This undo is 'real'. Pressing Undo twice redoes the undone.

WKEY. Shared Vertexcol: The colours of all faces that share vertices are blended.

EDIT MODE - METABALL

MKEY. Mirror. Mirror selected control points exactly as for vertices in a Mesh.

EDIT MODE - FONT

In Text Edit Mode most hotkeys are disabled, to allow text entering.

RIGHTARROW. Move text cursor 1 position forward

SHIFT-RIGHTARROW. Move text cursor to the end of the line.

LEFTARROW. Move text cursor 1 position backwards. **SHIFT-LEFTARROW.** Move text cursor to the start of the line **DOWNARROW.** Move text cursor 1 line forward

SHIFT-DOWNARROW. Move text cursor to the end of the text.

UPARROW. Move text cursor 1 line back.

SHIFT-UPARROW. Move text cursor to the beginning of the text

ALT-U. Reload Original Data (undo). When Edit Mode is started, the original text is saved. You can restore this original text with this option.

ALT-V. Paste text. The text file /tmp/.cutbuffer is inserted at the cursor location.

UV EDITOR HOTKEYS

EKEY. LSCM Unwrapping. Launches LSCM unwrapping on the faces visible in the UV editor.

PKEY. Pin selected vertices. Pinned vertices will stay in place on the UV editor when executing an **LSCM** unwrap.

ALT-PKEY. Un-Pin selected vertices. Pinned vertices will stay in place on the UV editor when executing an **LSCM** unwrap.

EDGE SELECT HOTKEYS

ALT-CLICK. Selects an Edge Loop.

FACE SELECT HOTKEYS

ALT-CLICK. Selects a Face Loop.

TAB. Switches to Edit Mode, selections made here will show up when switching back to Face Select Mode with TAB.

FKEY. With multiple, co-planar faces selected, this key will merge them into one "FGon" so long as they remain co-planar (flat to each other).

LKEY. Select Linked UVs. To ease selection of face groups, Select Linked in UV Face Select Mode will now select all linked faces, if no seam divides them.

RKEY. Calls a menu allowing to rotate the UV coordinates or the VertexCol.

UKEY. Calls the UV Calculation menu. The following modes can the applied to the selected faces:

- **Cube:** Cubical mapping, a number button asks for the cubemap size
- **Cylinder:** Cylindrical mapping, calculated from the center of the selected faces

- **Sphere:** Spherical mapping, calculated from the center of the selected faces
- **Bounds to x:** UV coordinates are calculated from the actual view, then scaled to a boundbox of 64 or 128 pixels in square
- **Standard x:** Each face gets default square UV coordinates
- **From Window:** The UV coordinates are calculated using the projection as displayed in the 3DWindow

CHAPTER 3: EXPLORING THE ESSENTIALS OF BLENDER

GETTING TO KNOW THE INTERFACE

The unique and distinctive interface of Blender has been one of the most intimidating aspects for both newcomers and experienced 3D artists. It has undoubtedly been a contentious feature of Blender. There was a time when referring to the user interface as a feature might have caused anxiety for those who had attempted to use Blender in the past but gave up in frustration when it didn't function as intended. However, while it wasn't the main focus, the interface modifications introduced in the 3.5 series of upgrades have significantly reduced that frustration. For example, when you first start Blender, the splash graphic that appears is now more helpful, providing easy access to online instructions and a list of recently opened files. The splash screen displayed when launching Blender for the first time is shown in the accompanying image.

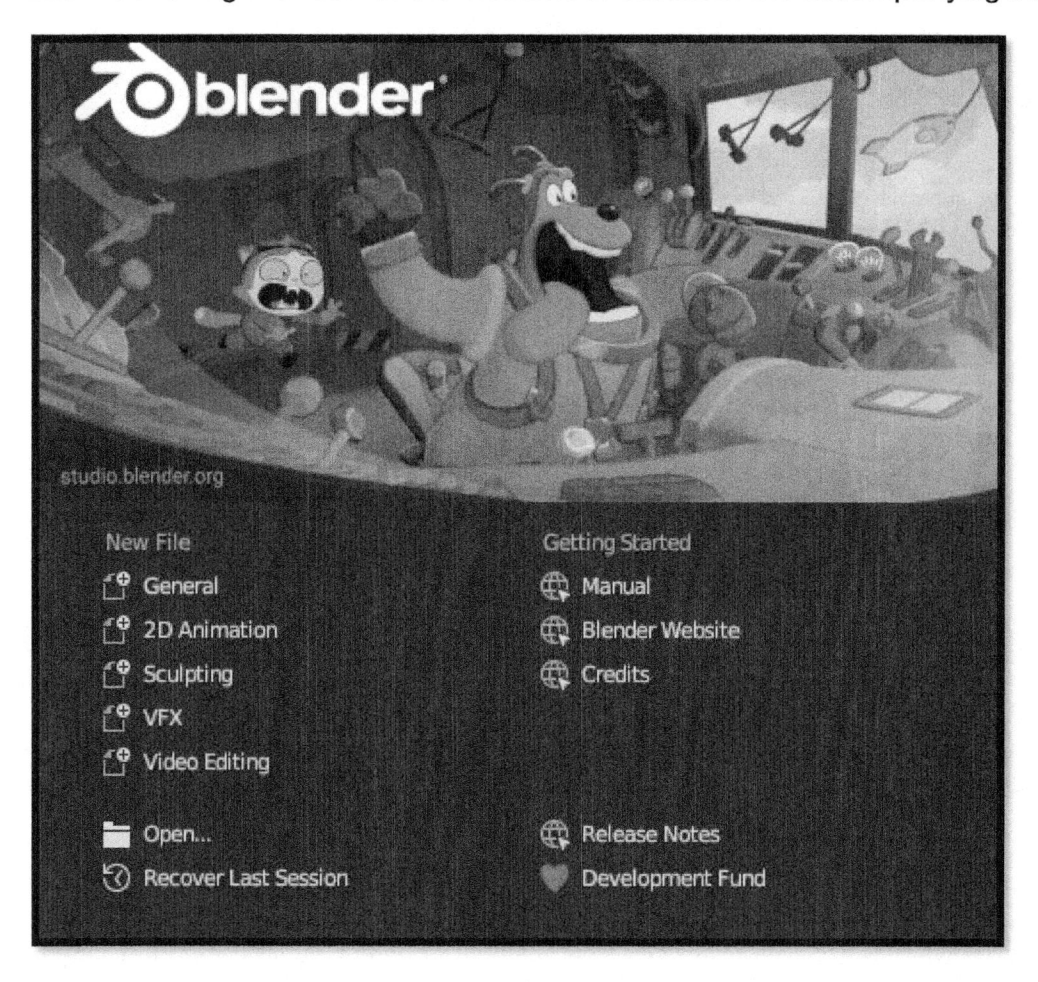

When you click anywhere outside the links provided on the splash screen, it disappears and is replaced by Blender's default interface, as depicted in the image below. Initially, the UI might seem a bit daunting, but the goal of this book is to make Blender more user-friendly by explaining some of the design choices behind the interface and ultimately enabling you to be productive. Who knows? You may even come to appreciate it and wonder why other apps don't offer similar flexibility and power.

WORKING WITH AN INTERFACE THAT STAYS OUT OF YOUR WAY

Understanding the basic structure of Blender's interface is the first step. The image presented here displays a single Blender window, but it's important to note that one or more regions can be separated, resized, and combined within each window according to your preferences. Typically, an area within the window represents a specific editor, such as the 3D View, where you make updates and adjustments to your 3D scene. Additionally, each editor may contain one or more regions that offer additional features or tools specific to that editor. An example of such a region is the header section at the top or bottom of the editor, which often contains menus and buttons granting access to functions within that editor. This concept of multiple regions within editors is consistent throughout Blender's interface.

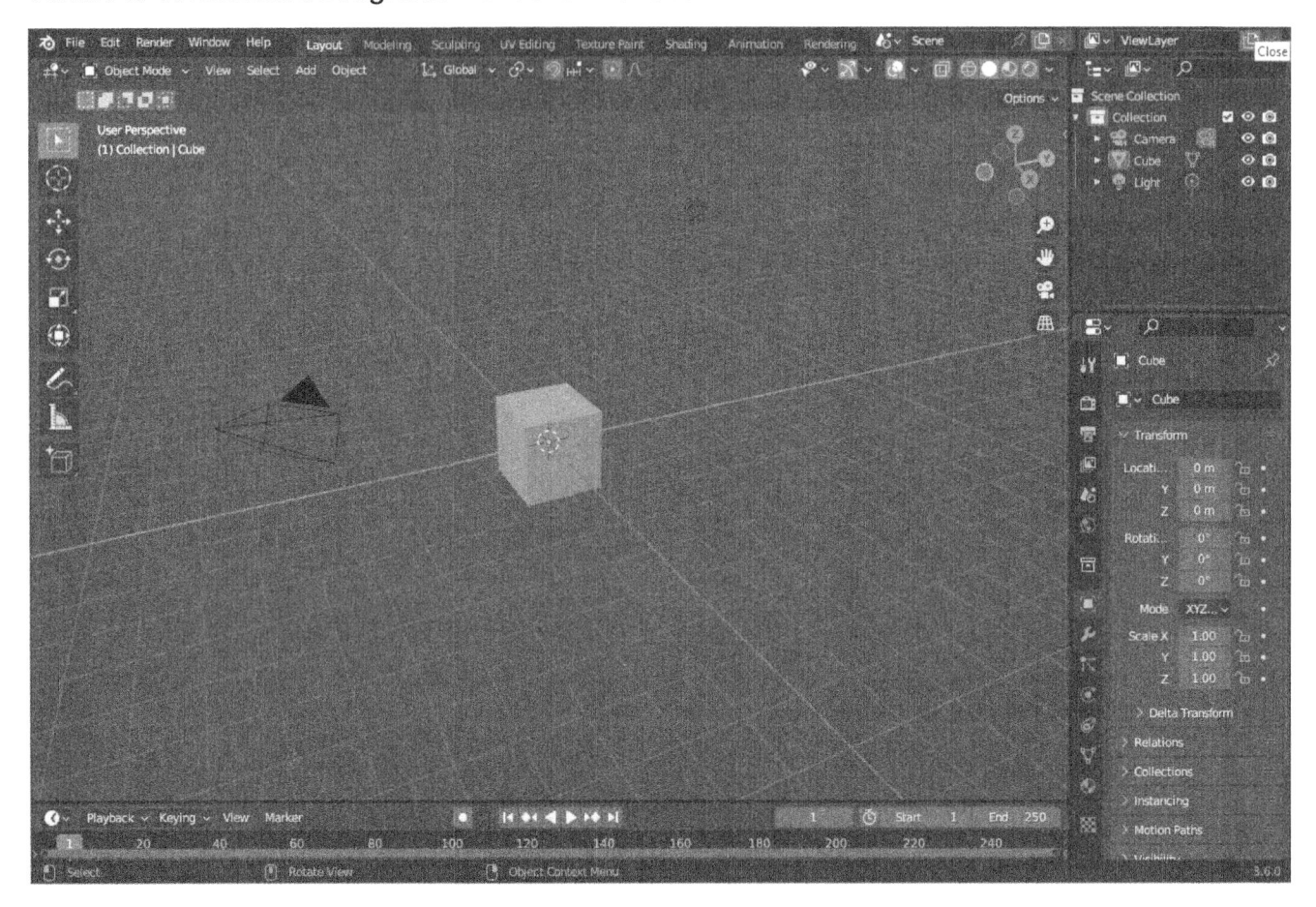

Blender's organizational structure is designed to provide a seamless user experience that is nonblocking and nonmodal. Unlike other software, Blender ensures that different features coexist without obstructing each other and that using one feature does not restrict access to others. In many software applications, when opening or saving a file, a file browser dialog appears as an overlapping window, blocking the view of underlying elements and often restricting modifications. However, Blender takes a different approach. The file browser in Blender is treated as an editor, allowing users to make adjustments to their scene while simultaneously accessing the file browser. This setup enables users to conveniently make tweaks before saving their work. The accompanying image illustrates a scenario where the file browser remains open while modifications are being made.

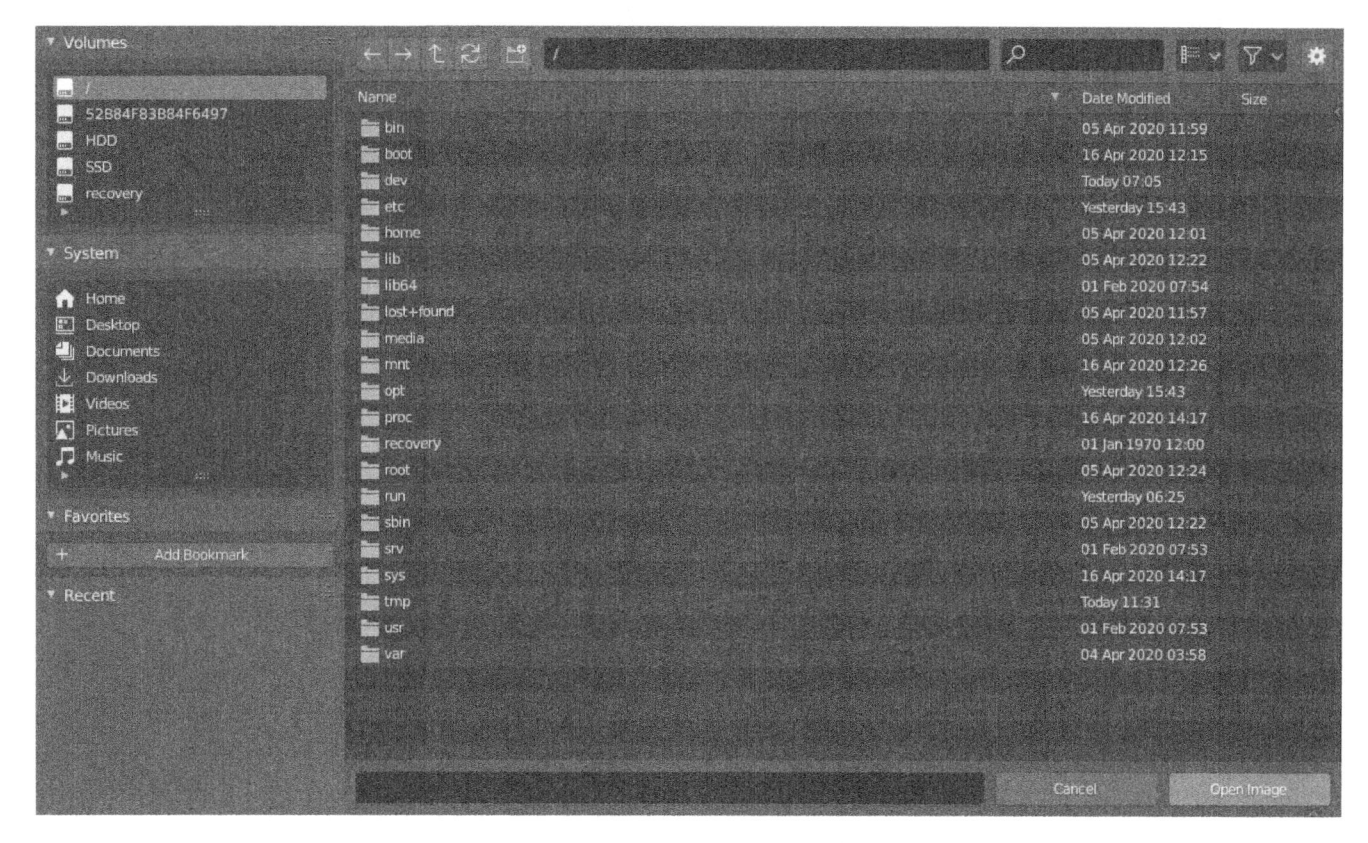

Working in a nonblocking, nonmodal interface may initially seem restrictive. You may question the various types of editors and whether you can have a simultaneous view of them or modify elements when everything seems fixed in place. Fortunately, all of these things are possible in Blender. The advantage of a clear workspace is the ability to quickly observe what's happening in your file. Additionally, starting with the Blender 2.5 development series, you have the option to have multiple windows that can overlap when needed.

RESIZING AREAS

You can adjust and resize each area within a Blender window in a similar manner. Simply left-click and drag the boundary between two regions to modify their sizes. When using this technique, one region expands while the surrounding regions shrink accordingly. If your Blender window consists of only one region, its size will be the same as the window itself. To increase the size of a single region, you will need to either adjust the size of its parent Blender window or create a new area within that space.

SPLITTING AND REMOVING AREAS

The default layout in Blender may not suit your preferences, but fortunately, you can customize it. Here are some actions you can take:

Splitting an area:

- Move your mouse pointer to the corner of an area until the cursor turns into a plus sign (+). In this case, you can activate splitting or joining by holding down the left mouse button (1MB).
- When you drag from a corner of an area inward, it will split the area.
- You can determine the direction of the split by dragging it horizontally or vertically.

Merging areas:

- If you want to eliminate a specific area, instead of dividing it into two, you can merge two areas. After left-clicking the corner widget, move your mouse cursor toward the edge of the region you want to combine with.
- The area your mouse is in will darken, and an arrow will indicate the region you want to delete.

Duplicating an area to a new window:

- Hold the Shift key and left-click on the corner widgets of an area, and then drag the mouse cursor away from it. This action will immediately duplicate the area and create a new Blender window to hold it.
- You can then close the additional Blender window by selecting the close button provided by the operating system on the window border.

Modifying the header:

- All editors in Blender have a header, which is a horizontal zone running along the top or bottom of each editor in a Blender area. The header often contains customized menus or buttons.
- **You have options for modifying the header:**
    - **Hiding the header:** If you drag the seam to the edge of the area, the header will be concealed and replaced with a small plus sign (+) in the corner of the area. The+ icon will appear in the bottom-right corner if the header is at the bottom of the editor, or in the top-left corner if the header is at the top. Left-clicking his icon will make the header reappear.
    - **Changing the header's location:** You can also change the header's location to either the top or bottom of the editor it belongs to. Right-click on the header and select "Flip to Top" or "Flip to Bottom," depending on the current position of the header.

MAXIMIZING AN AREA

There may be instances when you need to maximize an area in Blender to focus on a specific task or scene. This tool is particularly useful when you want to temporarily clear other areas and have more workspace.

To maximize an area:

Hover the mouse cursor over the area you want to work on. Pres s Shift + Spacebar.

This action will maximize the selected area, giving you more space to work.

To return to the tiled screen layout:

Select "View" from the menu.

Toggle to full screen from the editor's header.

Alternatively, right-click on the header and choose "Maximize Area" from the menu that appears. If the area is already maximized, it will show "Title Area" instead. This feature allows you to focus on a specific area and make the most of your workspace.

REVIEW QUESTIONS

What is Blender, and what sets it apart from other 3D modeling and animation programs?

How did Blender evolve from proprietary software to becoming open-source and freely accessible?

What are some of the unique features of Blender's interface, and how does it differ from other 3D software interfaces?

Can you explain the significance of the open movies and games produced by the Blender community and how they contribute to Blender's development and improvement?

Chapter 1 of the book introduces the reader to Blender, a free and open-source 3D modeling and animation program. The chapter emphasizes that learning Blender is an ongoing process, given its wide range of tools and functionalities. The Blender community's strength and dedication are highlighted, as they played a pivotal role in transforming Blender into powerful software.

The chapter covers the origins of Blender, its transition to open-source software, and the community's role in its development. The Blender Foundation was established to save Blender from financial difficulties, and the community raised funds to ensure its continuity. The chapter also delves into Blender's involvement in open movies and games, where artists collaborated using open-source tools, making their production files available for others to learn from and modify. The interface, initially intimidating, has been improved in the 3.5 series of upgrades, and the book aims to guide users in navigating it effectively, enabling them to harness Blen de r's full potential. It explains how to split, merge, duplicate areas, and maximize an area to make the most of the workspace.

In the next chapter, we are going to be taking you through how to think once you have opened the blender.

CHAPTER 4: HOW BLENDER OPERATES

Before diving into using Blender, it is crucial to familiarize yourself with the types of editors available and how to access them.

These editors provide the tools and functionality to create incredible graphics and images within Blender. Once you have gained this understanding, you can begin creating your graphics. However, it is also essential to grasp the fundamentals of working in the virtual three-dimensional space and how Blender interacts with 3D elements. In the following section, we will provide a detailed introduction to what you can expect from Blender and its interface, covering the ins and outs of working with Blend e r's powerful features.

LOOKING AT EDITOR TYPES

Blender areas typically consist of various types of editors. To view the available editor types, you can left-click on the button located on the far left of the editor's header. This button displays a dropdown menu that presents the different editor options accessible to you. By selecting an editor type from this menu, you can switch to that specific editor and access its unique set of tools and features.

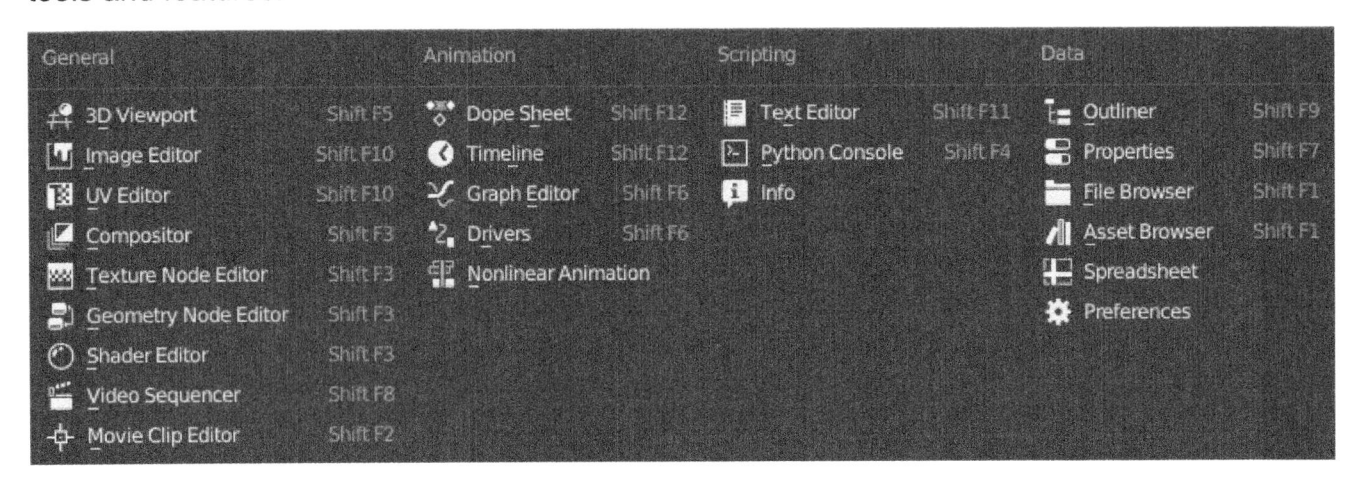

General		Animation		Scripting		Data	
3D Viewport	Shift F5	Dope Sheet	Shift F12	Text Editor	Shift F11	Outliner	Shift F9
Image Editor	Shift F10	Timeline	Shift F12	Python Console	Shift F4	Properties	Shift F7
UV Editor	Shift F10	Graph Editor	Shift F6	Info		File Browser	Shift F1
Compositor	Shift F3	Drivers	Shift F6			Asset Browser	Shift F1
Texture Node Editor	Shift F3	Nonlinear Animation				Spreadsheet	
Geometry Node Editor	Shift F3					Preferences	
Shader Editor	Shift F3						
Video Sequencer	Shift F8						
Movie Clip Editor	Shift F2						

In the subsequent section of this chapter, we are going to be breaking down all of the things that you see here.

GENERAL EDITORS

In the general editor of Blender, you will encounter the following editor types:

3D Viewport: This is the most frequently used editor in Blender. It provides a three-dimensional display of your model and allows you to manipulate and modify it.

Image Editor: This editor is used for basic image editing tasks.

UV Editor: The UV Editor is used for making basic edits to UV (texture) maps.

Compositor: The Compositor editor allows you to perform compositing tasks, where you can combine different image elements or apply effects.

Texture Nodes: This editor enables you to modify the structure of texture nodes, which control how textures are applied to objects.

Geometry Node Editor: With the Geometry Node Editor, you can edit geometry nodes, which control the procedural generation and manipulation of geometry.

Shader Editor: The Shader Editor is used to edit shaders, which determine the appearance of materials and how light interacts with them.

Video Sequencer: The Video Sequencer is a lightweight editor that allows you to assemble sequences of scenes and add basic effects, overlays, and transitions to create videos.

Movie Clip Editor: The Movie Clip Editor is used to work with movie clips and perform tasks such as tracking, stabilization, and masking to incorporate footage into your Blender projects.

These editors provide a wide range of functionalities for various aspects of your Blender workflow, from 3D modeling and texturing to compositing and video editing.

ANIMATION EDITORS

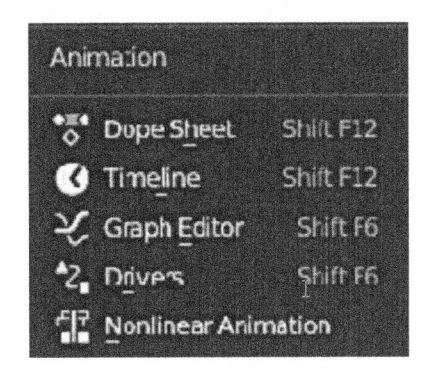

In addition to the general editors, Blender also provides several animation-specific editors:

1. **Dope Sheet:** The Dope Sheet editor gives you a bird's-eye view of keyframes in sheet format. It is inspired by the traditional hand-drawn animation process, where animators use charts to indicate the exact timing of each drawing, sound, and camera movement.
2. **Timeline:** The Timeline editor, represented by a clock icon, is used to manipulate keyframes and control the play back of the animation. It displays the current frame, keyframes of the active object, the star and end frames of the animation sequence, and user-set markers. The timeline provides a visual representation of the animation sequence.
3. **Graph Editor:** The Graph Editor allows you to adjust an improvement curve over time for any property you can mate. It provides precise control over how values change and interpolate during the animation.
4. **Drivers Editor:** The Drivers Edi wants to encourage you to create relationships between properties, allowing one property to drive or control another. It provides a powerful way to automate animation and create dynamic relationships between different elements.
5. **Nonlinear Animation (NLA) Editor:** The NLA Edi to r allows for the manipulation and repurposing of actions without manually handling keyframes. It is used for making extensive changes to a scene's animation, organizing and controlling motion sequences, and creating layered actions. The NLA Editor simplifies the organization and version control of your animation.

These animation editors in Blender provide specific tools and workflows tailored for animating objects, controlling keyframes, manipulating curves, creating relationships between properties, and managing complex animation sequences.

SCRIPTING EDITORS

When it comes to scripting in Blender, there are several editors available for you:

1. **Text Editor:** The Text Editor allows you to edit and write text-based scripts. You can write and save your scripts in this editor, making it a convenient tool for writing custom scripts and add-ons in various programming languages.
2. **Python Console:** The Python Console provides a quick way to execute Python commands directly within Blender. It grants access to the complete Python API, command history, and auto-complete functionality. It operates similarly to a command prompt, where the Python interpreter is loaded and ready to accept commands immediately at the prompt.
3. **Info Editor:** The Info Editor logs the operators that you execute in Blender and provides warnings and errors messages. It captures a history of your actions and can be a helpful reference for troubleshooting or understanding the sequence of operations performed. You can select a logged report by clicking on it, and if needed, you can choose multiple reports by holding the Shift key and left-clicking on the logs.

These editors provide essential tools for scripting in Blender, allowing you to write and edit scripts in the Text Editor, execute Python commands in the Python Console, and track the execution of operators in the Info Editor. They are valuable resources for customizing and automating tasks within Blender.

DATA EDITORS

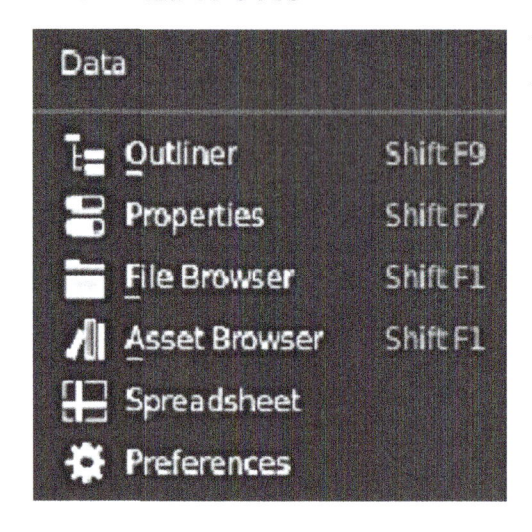

When working with data in Blender, you have access to various data editor tools:

- **Outliner:** The Outliner provides a comprehensive list for organizing and managing different types of data stored within a blend file. It allows you to view and manipulate scene data, video sequencer data, collections, objects, materials, and more.
- The Properties Editor allows you to view and edit properties in the **Properties Editor**: of active data, including objects, scenes, materials, and various settings. It provides access to a wide range of options and settings related to these collected data.
- **File Browser:** The File Browser is used for all file-related operations within Blender. It enables you to browse files, open, save, and import assets, and perform file management tasks.
- **Asset Browser:** The Asset Browser, introduced in Blender 3.0, serves as a central hub for managing assets and accessing external resources. It provides a convenient interface for browsing, organizing, and importing assets into your Blender projects.
- **Spreadsheet Editor:** The Spreadsheet Editor allows you to inspect and edit geometrical attributes of objects, such as vertex positions, UV coordinates, and other numerical data. It provides a tabular view for easy analysis and manipulation of data.

- **Preferences Editor:** The Preferences Editor allows you to modify various settings and preferences in Blender, including interface customizations, add-on management, input configurations, and many other options that affect the behavior of Blender.

These data editor tools provide a range of functionalities for organizing, managing, and editing different types of data with in Blender gives you control over your scenes, objects, materials, files, assets, and more.

UNDERSTANDING THE PROPERTIES EDITOR

Following the 3D View, the Properties editor is one of the most commonly used editor types in Blender. It allows you to modify the attributes of your scene and its elements using buttons and values. The Properties editor is organized into several sections, each responsible for specific aspects of the scene.

Here's a description of each section found in the Properties editor:

1. **Rende:** The Render Properties govern how the final output of your scene will look when rendered as an image or video.
2. **Scene:** The Scene Properties section affects the overall nature of your scene, including the active camera, measurement units, and physics settings like gravity.
3. **World:** The World Properties section controls the environment in which your scene is created, influencing the lighting, background, and overall ambiance of your scene.
4. **Object:** The Object Properties section allows you to modify the attributes of individual objects in your scene, such as their location, rotation, scale, and other object-specific settings.
5. **Object constraints:** Constraints are useful for defining relationships and interactions between objects. The Object Constraints Properties enable you to apply constraints that automate certain aspects of your scene and make it easier to control object behavior.
6. **Modifiers:** Modifiers provide a way to apply procedural operations to 3D models, allowing you to create complex effects and transformations. The Modifiers section lets you add, configure, and control modifiers that affect object geometry and appearance.
7. **Object data:** The Object Data Properties section allows you to interact with the core structural components of an object, such as its mesh data, materials, and vertex groups. The specific options available here depend on the type of object selected.
8. **Bone:** The Bone Properties section is accessible when an armature object is selected. It allows you to modify the properties of individual bones within an armature, which is used for character animation and skeletal systems.
9. **Bone constraints:** The Bone Constraints Properties section, available in pose mode with an armature selection, allows you to manage constraints specific to bones. Constraints restrict and control the movement and behavior of individual bones within an armature.
10. **Material.:** The Material Properties section lets you define and customize the appearance of objects by assigning materials to them. You can control properties like color, reflectivity, transparency, and more.
11. **Texture:** The Texture Properties section allows you to apply and modify textures to objects, which can dramatically alter their appearance. Textures can be used for surface details, creating realistic effects, or as brushes when painting and sculpting.

12. **Particles:** The Particles Properties section is used to manage particle systems, which are used for creating effects like hair, fur, smoke, and other dynamic elements. It offers extensive control over particle behavior and appearance.
13. **Physics:** The Physics Properties section allows you to simulate realistic physical behavior within your scene. It includes settings for rigid bodies, soft bodies, fluids, and other physics simulations.

These sections in the Properties editor provide a range of options and settings to customize and control various aspects of your scene, objects, materials, textures, particles, and physics. Understanding and utilizing these sections will enable you to achieve the desired look and behavior for your 3D projects in Blender.

NAVIGATING IN THREE DIMENSION

In Blender, the 3DView is undeniably one of the most frequently utilized window types. Furthermore, it presents users with a range of interface options that may appear unconventional compared to other 3D software. The purpose of this section is to assist you in mastering the use of this particular Blender feature effectively.

ORBITING, PANNING, AND ZOOMING THE 3D VIEWPORT

When navigating a 3D space in Blender, it's important to understand that the interaction differs. Imagine the 3D view as your window to a virtual world, where you move the entire world in front of you instead of physically moving through it. To navigate effectively in Blender, there are two basic techniques: orbiting and panning. Orbiting allows you to rotate the 3D world around a fixed point by holding the middle mouse button and dragging the cursor in the 3D view. On the other hand, panning enables you to move the world while maintaining the same viewing angle. To pan, hold Shift, then click and drag the middle mouse button in the 3D view.

To zoom in on objects in your scene, you can use the zoom function in Blender. There are two ways to zoom: using the scroll wheel on your mouse or holding Ctrl and middle-clicking in the 3D view. By default, scrolling forward zooms in, while scrolling backward zooms out. If your mouse doesn't have a scroll wheel or you prefer more control, you can hold Ctrl and middle-click, then drag the mouse up to zoom in or down to zoom out. You can adjust the zooming behavior in the Input section of User Preferences to match your preferred horizontal or vertical mouse movements.

In case your mouse doesn't have a middle button, you can enable the "Emulate 3 Button Mouse" option in User Preferences under Input. This allows you to emulate the middle mouse button by pressing Alt+left-click. With this setup, you can use Alt+left-click for orbiting, Shift+Alt+left-click for panning, and Ctrl+Alt+left-click for zooming.

CHANGING VIEWS

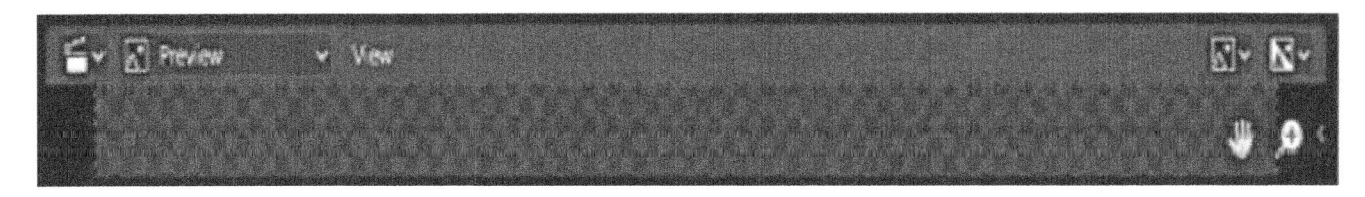

While navigating the 3D space using the mouse is common in Blender, the software also offers menu items and hotkey sequences that allow for faster and more accurate views. To quickly switch to specific views, Blender provides shortcuts for efficient navigation.

In the 3D View's header, you can find the **View menu**, which offers options for various angles and perspectives. You can choose to view the scene from the front, side, top, or camera angles using the shortcuts provided. These predefined views are helpful for quickly orienting yourself in 3D space.

ORTHOGRAPHIC VIEW

PERSPECTIVE VIEW

Additionally, the View menu allows you to switch between orthographic and perspective views. In the orthographic view, objects maintain their relative size regardless of distance, making it ideal for precise modeling based on blueprints or technical drawings. On the other hand, the perspective view mimics how we perceive objects in the real world, where objects appear smaller as they move away from the viewer. The perspective view is commonly used for creating realistic and immersive scenes. By utilizing the View menu and its shortcuts, you can easily access different views and choose the viewing mode that best suits your needs, whether it's for precise modeling or creating visually appealing scenes.

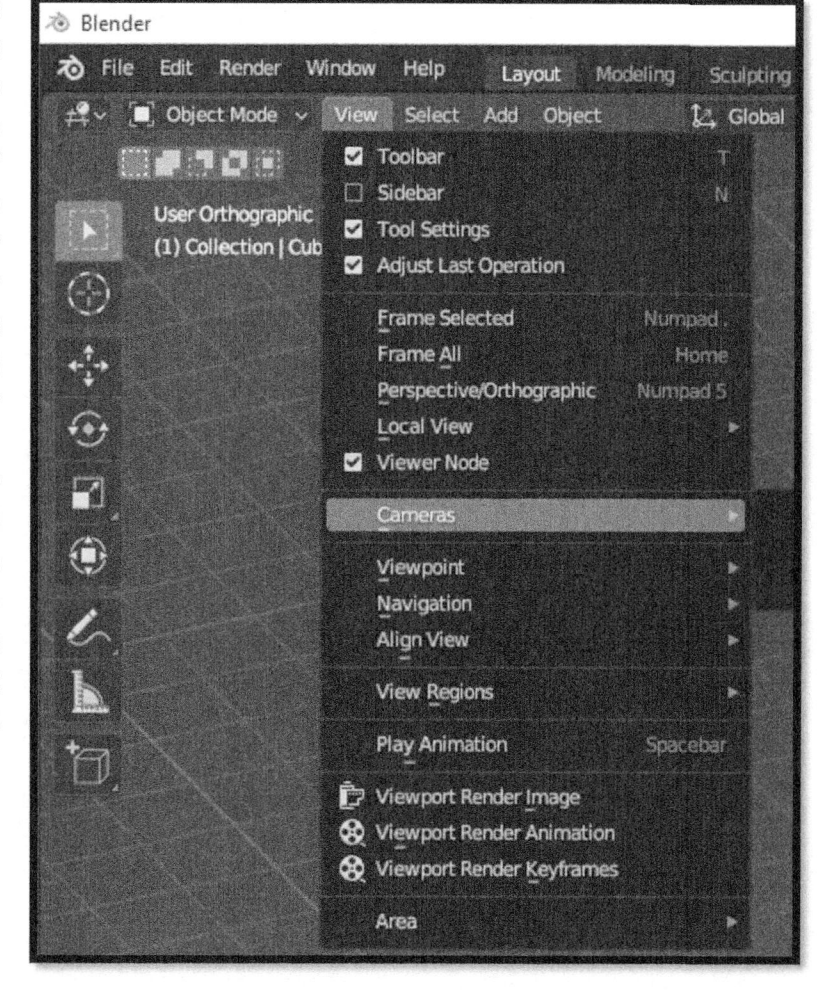

SELECTING OBJECTS

One of the most notable and debated design choices in Blender is how objects are selected. Unlike in most other software, where items are typically selected by left-clicking them, Blender diverges from this convention. In the 3D view of Blender, a left-click seems to have no effect other than moving a peculiar crosshair object known as the 3D cursor. This cursor holds significance in Blender, but at this point, you might be wondering how to select anything at all.

The solution is simple: In Blender, objects are chosen by right-clicking on them. To select multiple items simultaneously, you can use **Shift+right-click** to select or deselect multiple objects at once.

While using the right-click to select objects may seem unconventional, it serves a purpose and wasn't a random choice or merely a novelty. There are two underlying reasons for this design decision: one practical and one ergonomic. Firstly, it aligns with how the mouse is utilized in Blender. In Blender, the left mouse button is used to initiate or confirm actions. When moving, rotating, or scaling an item, the left-click is used to confirm that the operation has been completed. It is also used to position the 3D cursor.

Selecting an item itself doesn't fundamentally alter or affect it. Therefore, using the right-click to select objects allows for both picking items and halting an action in progress. While this may initially appear abstract, as you continue using Blender, this approach becomes more intuitive. Secondly, the choice of right-click selection helps prevent repetitive stress injury (RSI). People involved in computer graphics, such as 3D modelers and animators, often spend extensive periods in front of a screen. RSI is a significant concern in such professions. Reducing the repetitive strain on a single hand can help mitigate the risk. Blender contributes to this by not relying solely on the left mouse button forever. By adopting the right-click selection method, Blender offers a unique approach that balances practicality and ergonomics, providing a different workflow for its users.

TAKING ADVANTAGE OF THE 3D CURSOR

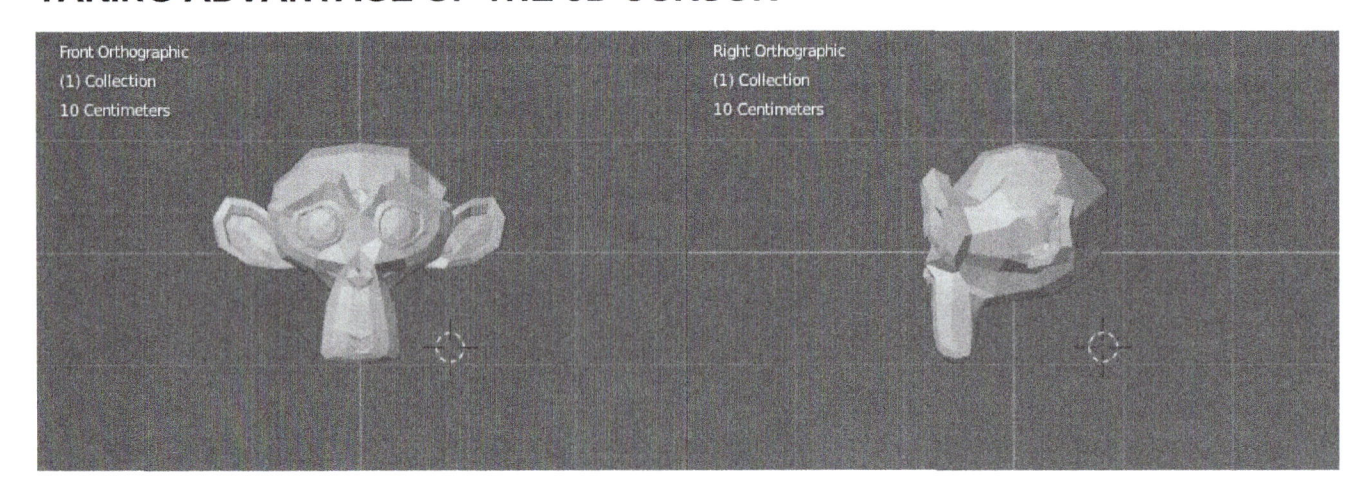

The moving crosshairs in Blender, known as the 3D cursor, may initially appear insignificant, but it serve a valuable purpose. It can be likened to a blinking cursor in a word processor or text editor that assists with adding or modifying text. Similarly, Blender's 3D cursor operates in three dimensions. It plays a role in determining the placement of new objects, serves as a reference point for rotation and scaling, and enables the snapping of objects to specific locations.

To center your view in the **3D view** using the 3D cursor, you can follow these steps: Left-click anywhere in the **3D View** to place the 3D cursor, and then press Ctrl +Numpad Dot(.) to readjust the view and center it on the cursor. This provides a quick way to center without selecting any objects. Another useful shortcut is Shift +C, which moves the 3D cursor to the origin coordinates of the 3D environment and brings all objects into view. It functions similarly to pressing the Home key, but it also resets the cursor to the origin.

SNAP MENU

The Snap menu in Blender allows you to snap your chosen item to different positions. You can snap it to the cursor's position, a specified point on the grid in the 3DView, or the center of the grid, which is referred to as the scene's origin. Additionally, the 3D cursor can be anchored to a specific spot on the grid, the active item in the scene, or the center of multiple selected objects. Thanks to the 3D cursor's flexibility, this technique provides an efficient way to move an item to a desired location in 3D space.

EXTRA FEATURES IN THE 3D VIEWPORT

Blender has undergone significant interface changes, particularly during the 2.5 series and subsequent versions. These updates have brought about notable transformations in various areas, including the Properties editor and the 3D View. In this section, we will explore some of these interface makeovers and discuss the key modifications that have taken place. One notable change is the reorganization of the Properties editor. In earlier versions of Blender, this editor consisted of several separate panels with different tabs, making it a bit overwhelming to navigate. However, with the interface updates, the properties editor has been redesigned to provide a more streamlined and user-friendly experience. The panels have been consolidated, and the tabs have been replaced with collapsible sections. This allows for easier access and management of the various properties related to objects, materials, physics, and more.

In addition to the Properties editor, the 3D View has also undergone significant improvements. One notable change is the introduction of viewport shading options. Previously, the 3D View only offered a solid shading mode, where objects were displayed with flat colors. However, the updated interface now includes options for wireframe, solid, material, and rendered shading modes. This provides users with more flexibility in visualizing and interacting with their 3Ds. Furthermore, the 3D View now features enhanced navigation tools and manipulators. The navigation gizmo, which includes controls for panning, rotating, and zooming, has been redesigned for better usability. Additionally, the manipulators for translating, rotating, and scaling objects have been proved, allowing for more intuitive and precise transformations.

These interface makeovers in Blender aim to enhance the user experience and improve workflow efficiency. By organizing and presenting the various properties and tools in a more accessible manner, users can navigate the software more easily and focus on their creative work. These changes reflect Blender's commitment to continually refining and optimizing its interface to meet the evolving needs of its users.

QUAD VIEW

If you're familiar with other 3D graphics programs, you may be accustomed to Quad View, where the 3D view is divided into four regions displaying different perspectives: top, front, right, and user perspective. In previous versions of Blender, recreating this layout was a tedious process of manually splitting areas and configuring each one as a specific 3D view. Finally, there was a risk of accidentally changing one of the orthographic views to the user's perspective without a way to lock them in place. However, Blender has made improvements in this area to provide a more convenient solution. To enable Quad View in Blender, you can click on "View" in the 3D View's header and select Toggle Quad View," or you can use the hotkey Ctrl+Alt+Q. This action will instantly switch your 3D view to the Quad View layout, where you can simultaneously view and work with the top, front, right, and user perspectives. When transitioning back to the full view from Quad View, Blender's behavior depends on how you make the switch. If you use the View menu option, you will always return to the top view. However, if you use the Ctrl+Alt+Q hotkey while your mouse cursor is positioned over one of the other views in the Quad View layout, Blender will set that view as the Full View upon exiting Quad View. By implementing the Quad View feature and offering a convenient hotkey, Blender allows users to switch between the regular view and Quad View more efficiently, resembling the functionality found in other 3D programs. This enhancement streamlines the workflow for users who prefer or require a quad-view layout for their 3D work.

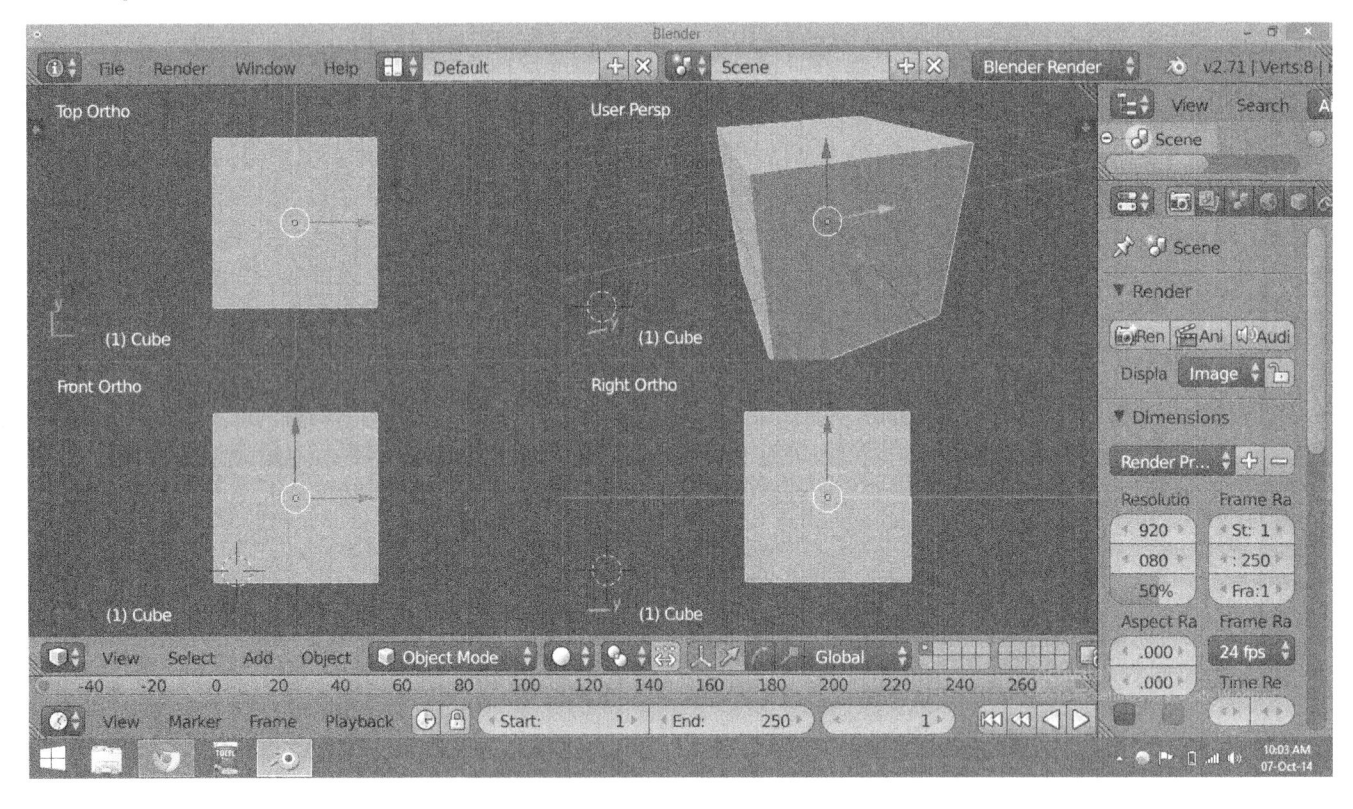

REGIONS

In the latest versions of Blender, regions have replaced the floating windows seen in older versions. These regions align with Blender's philosophy of avoiding overlapping interfaces and providing a more structured and organized layout. They consist of tabs and panels that contain buttons, widgets, and controls.

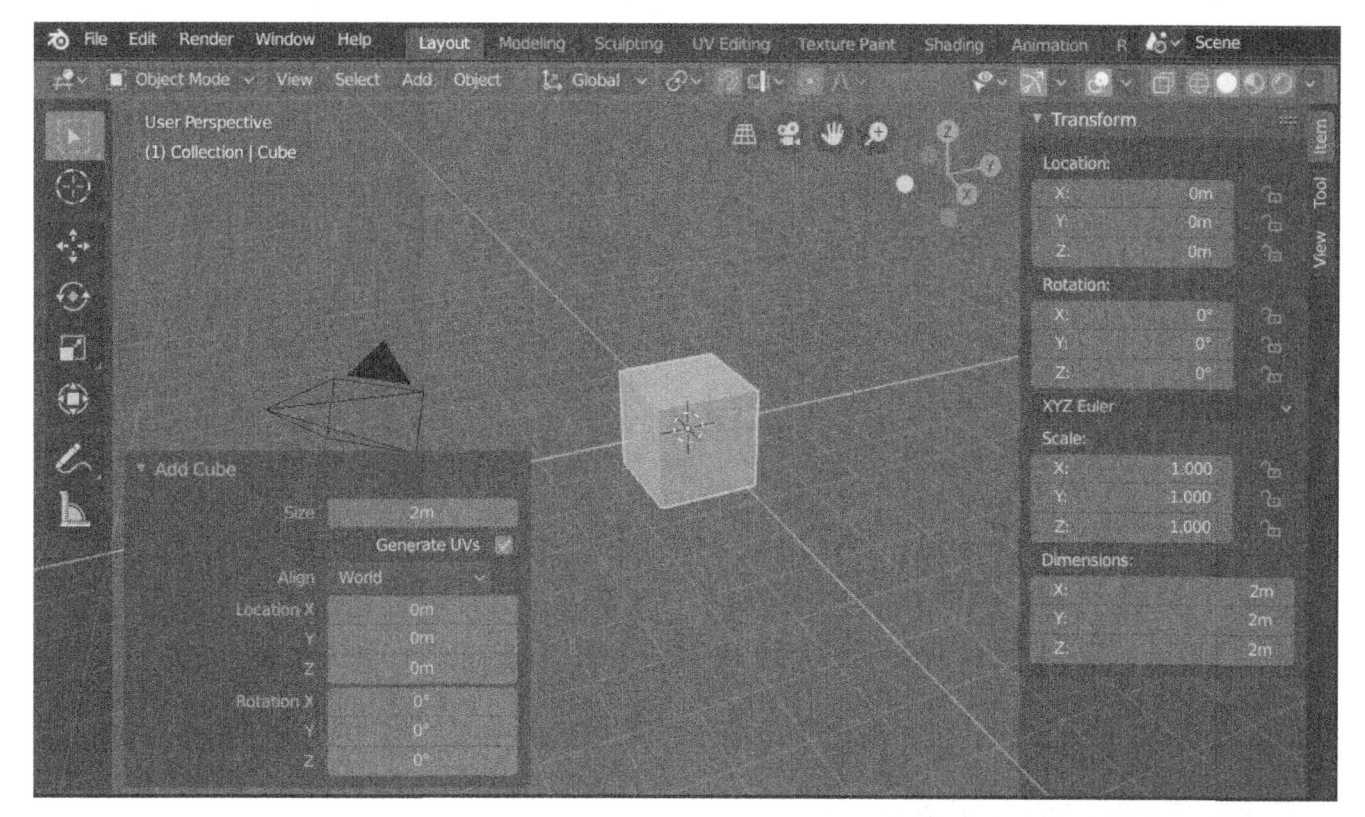

The image above illustrates the regions in the 3D viewport, including the sidebar and the Adjust Last Operation panel that appears when you add a cube.

THE PROPERTIES/INFORMATION REGION

To toggle the visibility of the Properties region in Blender, you can go to View->Properties in the header or press the N button on your keyboard while your cursor is in the 3D view.

The Properties region is available in various editors, except for Text Edit, and you can consistently open them using the Nkey. In the 3DView, the Properties region serves two main purposes. Firstly, it allows you to modify the selected object's location, rotation, and scale values in the Transform panel.

Secondly, it offers customization options for the 3D view, such as adjusting the 3D cursor position, displayed axis, grid floor appearance, and shading mode for textured viewport shading. Additionally, you can load a background image for modeling reference in the 3D view from this region.

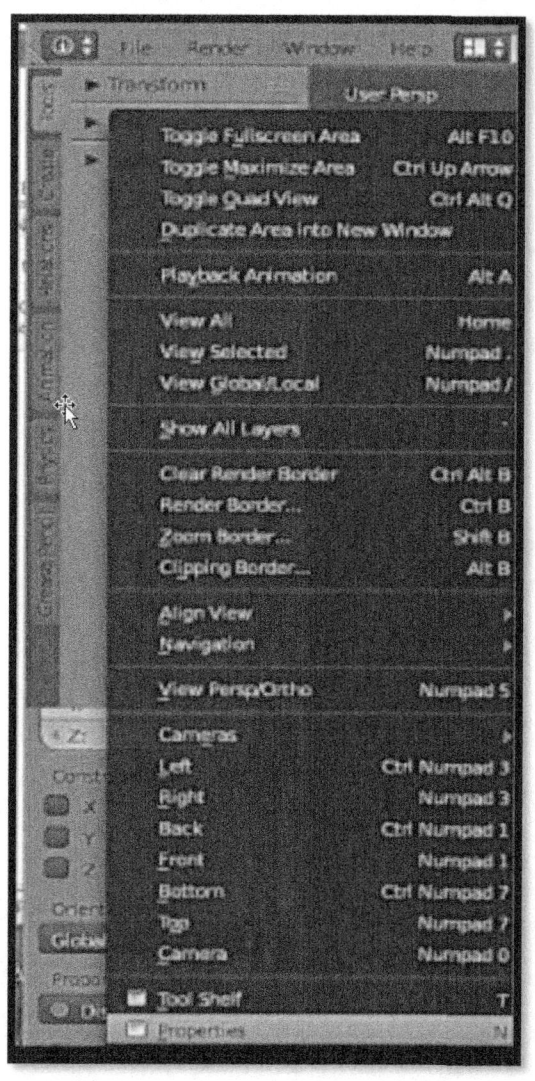

TOOL SHELF

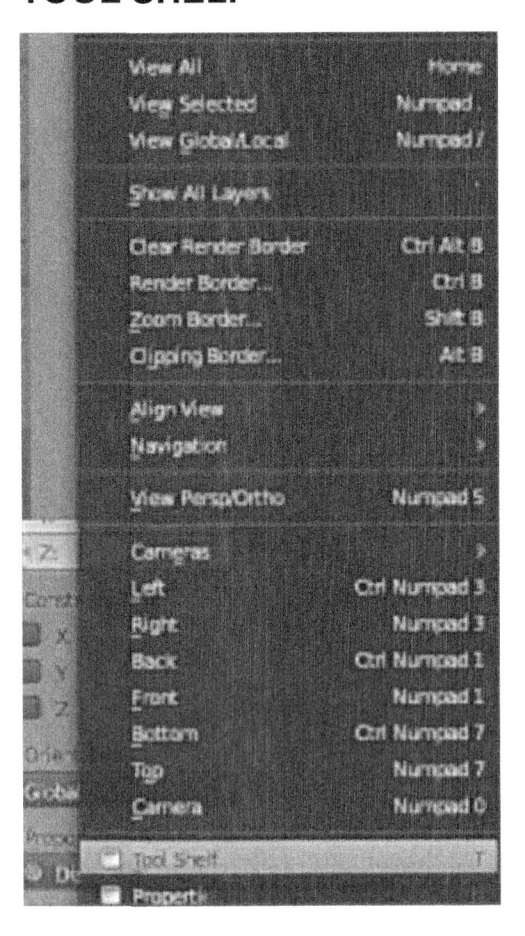

The tool shelf in Blender can be shown or hidden by going to View->Tool Shelf in the header or by using the T hotkey. The Tool Shelf provides a convenient location for frequently used tools and shortcuts, making your workflow faster, especially if you haven't memorized Blender's hotkeys. It offers easy access to commonly used tools with a single click, eliminating the need to navigate through menus. The tool shelf also includes the Last Operator panel at the bottom, which is highly useful. This panel dynamically updates to display relevant values for the most recent operation you performed, such as moving objects or adding new objects. It allows you to perform initial actions and then make precise adjustments using the displayed parameters. For example, if you add a UV sphere to your scene, the Last Operator panel lets you modify its location, number of segments, and rings. This panel provides a convenient way to fine-tune your actions and make adjustments to achieve the desired results.

Don't know how to do something? Hooray for a fully integrated search!

SEARCH

Blender's event system refactor has introduced a valuable feature for new users: an integrated search function within Blender's interface. This search feature enables users to quickly find and execute operations in Blender, even if they are unsure of where to locate them in the interface. By simply typing the name of the desired operation in the search field, Blender provides search results that match the query. Moreover, hotkeys associated with the operation are displayed next to the operator's name in the search results, allowing users to easily remember them for future use. For instance, pressing the spacebar brings up the search menu, and typing save would yield relevant operations related to saving.

The integrated search feature proves particularly beneficial for users who are new to Blender or transitioning from other software. It allows them to leverage their existing knowledge of the operations they wish to perform and effortlessly discover how Blender accomplishes them.

PATH-GUIDING IN CYCLES

Blender 3.4 introduces the major feature of path guiding in the Cycles Renderer. Path guiding enhances the rendering process by analyzing the light distribution and guiding the light paths that contribute the most to the final image. With path guiding enabled, cycles prioritize paths interacting with surfaces, resulting in faster noise reduction and improved sampling. This is especially beneficial for scenes with complex indirect lighting, such as multi-bounce diffuse illumination or multi-scattering in volumes like clouds. It's important to note that while path-guiding can help with caustics, it is not its primary focus. In terms of Geometry Nodes updates, Blender 3.4 brings several important changes. The introduction of the Viewer node allows users to preview the output.

of a node tree directly in the viewport, enhancing the debugging process and improving the overall user experience. Additionally, users can now retrieve attributes of instances created by geometry nodes, opening up new creative possibilities. New sets of nodes for retrieving topology information for meshes and curves have been added, and the Distribute Points in Volume node enables the creation of points inside volume grids. Although Blender 3.4 is not the major update for Geometry Nodes (reserved for Blender 3.5), it still introduces valuable features and enhancements that enhance the functionality and creative potential of Geometry Nodes.

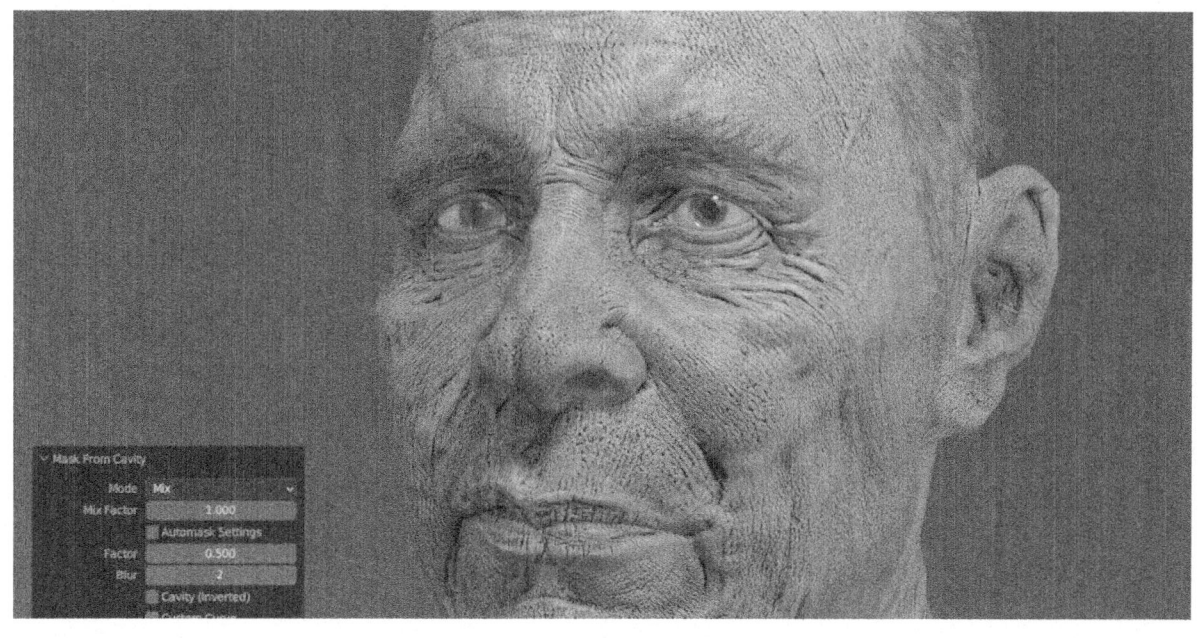

AUTO-MASKING OPTIONS

In Blender 3.4, the Auto-Masking options in Sculpt mode have been expanded to provide new methods for masking specific parts of a model's surface during sculpting or 3D painting. One notable addition is the automatic generation of a cavity mask. This feature allows users to paint details like dirt in the pores of a character's face without the need for manual application. The generated mask can be further adjusted by inverting or blurring it, as well as changing its blend mode, providing greater control and fine-tuning the results.

Another enhancement in Blender 3.4 is the ability to mask a sculpt based on the viewpoint. This feature enables users to paint or sculpt only the visible parts of the model's surface from a specific direction. This functionality enhances precision during the editing process, allowing for more accurate and targeted modifications.

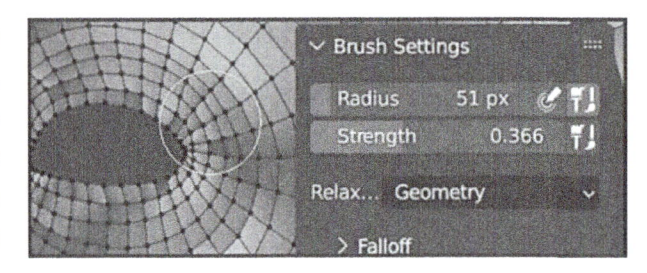

GEOMETRY-BASED UV RELAX BRUSH

Blender 3.4 introduces significant updates to its UV tools, including the new geometry-driven relax brush mode. Unlike the traditional Relax brush, which operates in 2D texture space, this new mode allows UVs to conform more closely to the model's geometry, resulting in improved UV mapping quality. The accompanying video demonstration demonstrates this enhancement, showcasing the benefits.

of the new brush mode. In addition to the relax brush mode, Blender 3.4 brings additional options for packing UVs, adding UV islands, and customizing the background grid in the UV Editor. These updates offer users more flexibility and control in their UV editing workflow, making it easier to achieve precise and desired results.

STORY PENCIL

Another notable addition to Blender 3.4 is the new Story pencil add-on. Developed by the team behind Blen de r's Grease Pencil 2D animation toolset, Story pencil is specifically designed for storyboarding. It integrates seamlessly with Blender's Video Sequence Editor, providing an efficient way to reorder shots and adjust their timing within the storyboard. Additionally, Story pencil allows for the export of both video and image sequences, giving users the flexibility to create animatics or static storyboards for presenting and sharing storyboard concepts.

CUSTOMIZING A BLENDER TO FIT YOU

Blender offers extensive customization options, allowing you to configure its screen layout according to your specific needs. However, its customization capabilities extend beyond rearranging window areas. With some time and effort, you can overhaul almost any part of Blender to create a comfortable and personalized work environment. This level of customization is particularly beneficial for users transitioning from other 3D graphics programs. While Blender may not replicate the exact behavior of other software, small adjustments like adopting familiar keyboard shortcuts can help smoothen the transition process.

USING PRESET WORKSPACES

In Blender, workspace layouts are screens that can be customized for different types of work. By default, Blender provides several preset screens, such as Animation, Compositing, Default, Game Logic, Scripting, UV Editing, and Video Editing. The default screen layout is the one you start with when launching Blender.

You can cycle through the screens using the Ctrl+ +- and Ctrl+ shortcuts or access them through the data block at the top of the window in the Info editor. A data block, in Blen der, is a block of data used to store various elements within Blender's interface and internal structure. Screens, scenes, objects, textures, and other critical components are stored as data blocks. Data blocks serve as more than just data storage; they enable Blender to treat the information as a database. By linking data blocks, you can share information between them, reducing redundancy and improving efficiency. For example, linking multiple objects to the same material data block allows them to have the same appearance. To create a new screen layout, it's recommended to start with a clean slate by restoring the default setup. This can be done by selecting File New or using the Ctrl+N shortcut. Blen der saves user settings in a special ".blend" file, which is loaded each time Blender starts. If you want to revert to the default setup, you can select File   Load Factory Settings. From there, you can recreate your custom layouts as desired. When adjusting screen layouts, you may feel the need to hide or show menus and buttons in the header to create more space. You can collapse the text menus by clicking the minus icon on the left side of the header. If that's not sufficient, you can middle-click and drag horizontally in the header or use the scroll wheel while hovering over the header to move its contents left or right. This feature is especially useful for users working on computers with limited screen space.

SETTING USER PREFERENCES

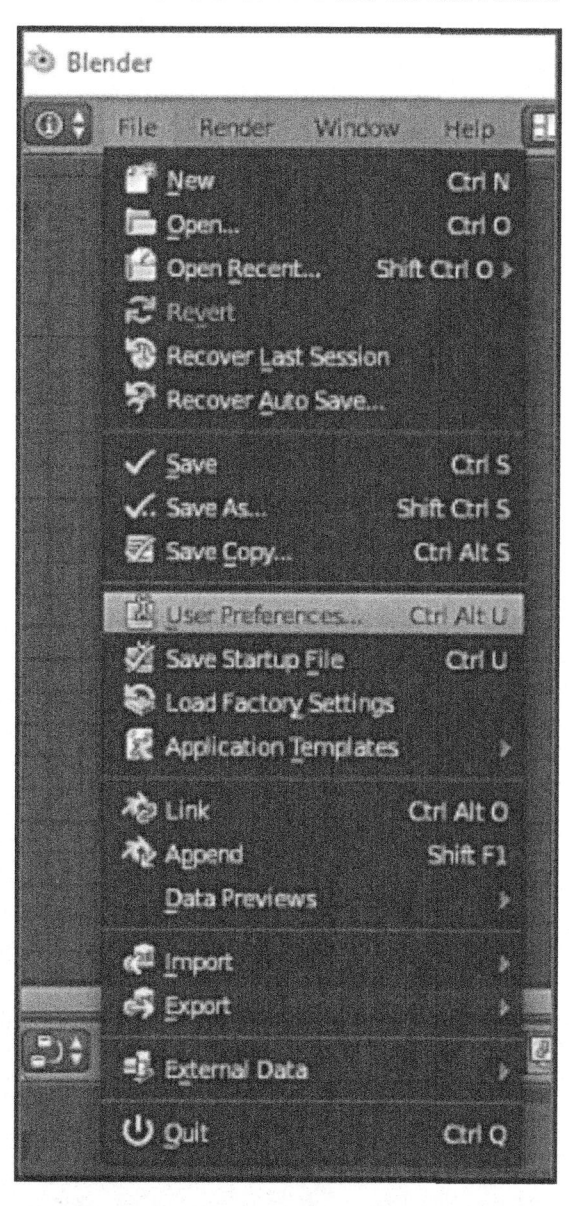

Please note that this section on user preferences provides only a basic overview. Blender's User Preferences editor offers an extensive range of options that can be overwhelming due to their sheer quantity. The goal here is to introduce you to the most useful and relevant options to enhance your productivity. For in-depth information on each button and setting, you can refer to the comprehensive online documentation available at www.blender.org. To access and modify your user preferences, navigate to File User Preferences (Ctrl+Alt+U). Blender will open a dedicated User Preferences editor window. While it's possible to convert any area into a User Preferences editor, using the File menu method is often more convenient as it eliminates the need to replace or split existing areas to accommodate the User Preferences editor.

If you select File User Preferences and the User Preferences editor doesn't open in a new window, it could be because your The current window is in full-screen mode, and your operating system's window manager prevents the User Preferences window from appearing on top. To resolve this, you can disable the full-screen view by clicking the icon on the far right of the Info editor's header or by pressing Alt + Fl 1. When you have customized your user preferences to your liking, you can save them as the default settings by selecting the "Save As Default" button at the bottom of the User Preferences editor or by using the Ctrl + U shortcut. In Blender's User Preferences, the first set of options pertains to interacting with your scene in the 3D view.

Here are some key options, from top to bottom:

- **Select with:** allows you to choose between left, right, or both mouse buttons for selection.
- **Zoom Axis:** Determines whether zooming is vertical or horizontal when using the scroll wheel.
- **Orbit Style:** Specifies the orbiting behavior when rotating the view in the 3D view.
- **Pan with:** Determines the mouse button used for panning the view in the 3D view.
- **Rotate Around Selection:** Enables or disables rotation around the selected object(s) in the 3DView.
- **Auto Perspective:** Automatically switches between orthographic and perspective views based on the zoom level.
- **Zoom to Mouse Position:** This controls whether zooming is centered around the mouse cursor position.
- **Auto Depth:** Determines whether selecting objects is based on their visible depth in the 3D view.

These are just a few examples of the many options available in Blender's User Preferences. Exploring and customizing these settings can greatly enhance your workflow and make Blender more tailored to your preferences.

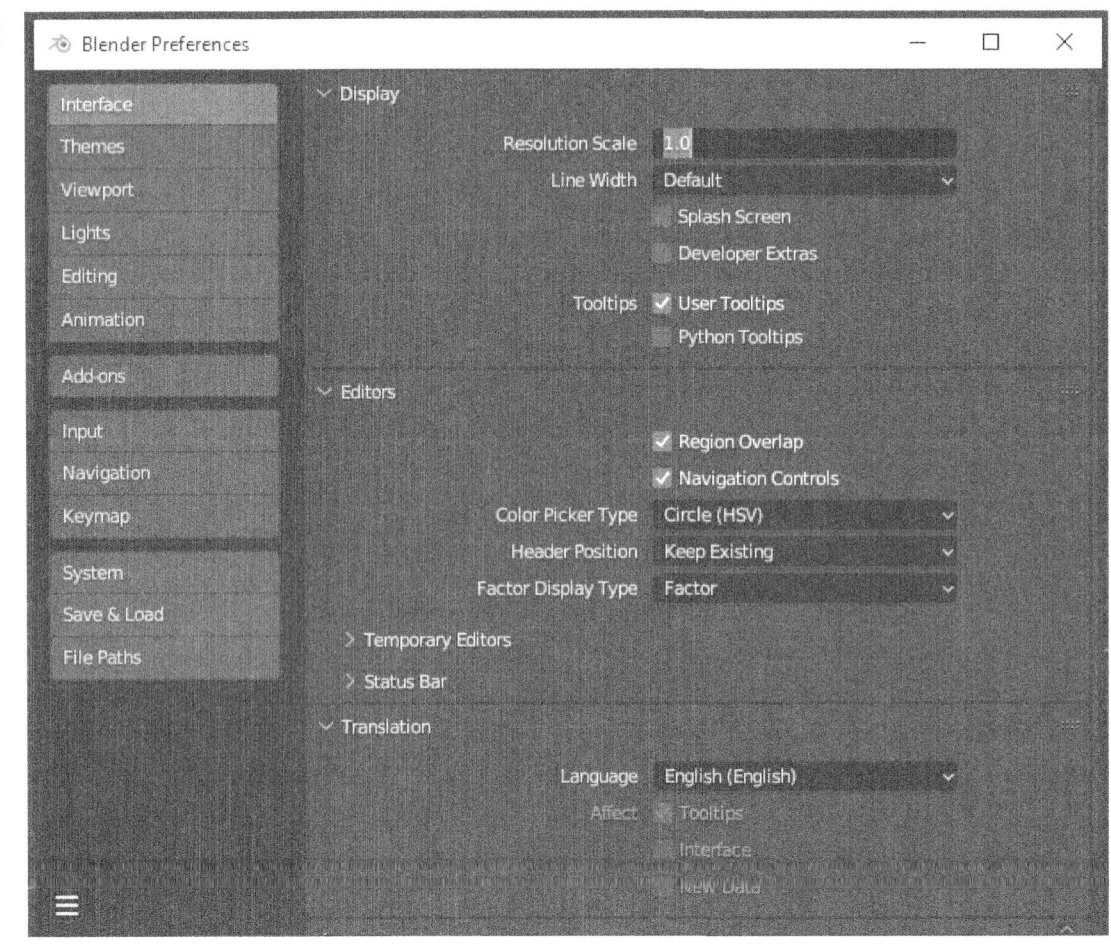

- **Display:** These options control the visibility of informational elements in the 3DView, such as tooltips, object information, and the mini axis in the corner.
- **Editors:** In this section, you can customize various aspects of the editor windows, including navigation controls and region overlap.
- behavior, color picker types, header position, and factor display type.
- **Temporary Editors:** When certain operations require opening a new window, you can modify this behavior in this section.
- **Translation:** Here, you can select the language used to translate the user interface.
- **Text Rendering:** This section allows you to adjust settings related to rendering text in Blender.
- **Menus:** Some users prefer menus to open automatically when the mouse cursor hovers over them. You can enable the "Open on Mouse Over" option and adjust the delay time for the menu to appear.
- **Pie Menus:** Pie menus are a type of context-sensitive menu that provides quick access to commonly used tools and functions. In this section, you can enable or disable pie menus and customize their appearance and behavior.

These are just a few examples of the options available in the Interface section of Blender's User Preferences. Exploring and adjusting these settings can help you tailor the Blen der Interface to your preferences and optimize your workflow.

THEMES

Blender offers a range of customization options for its appearance through themes. In this image, you can see the Themes settings.

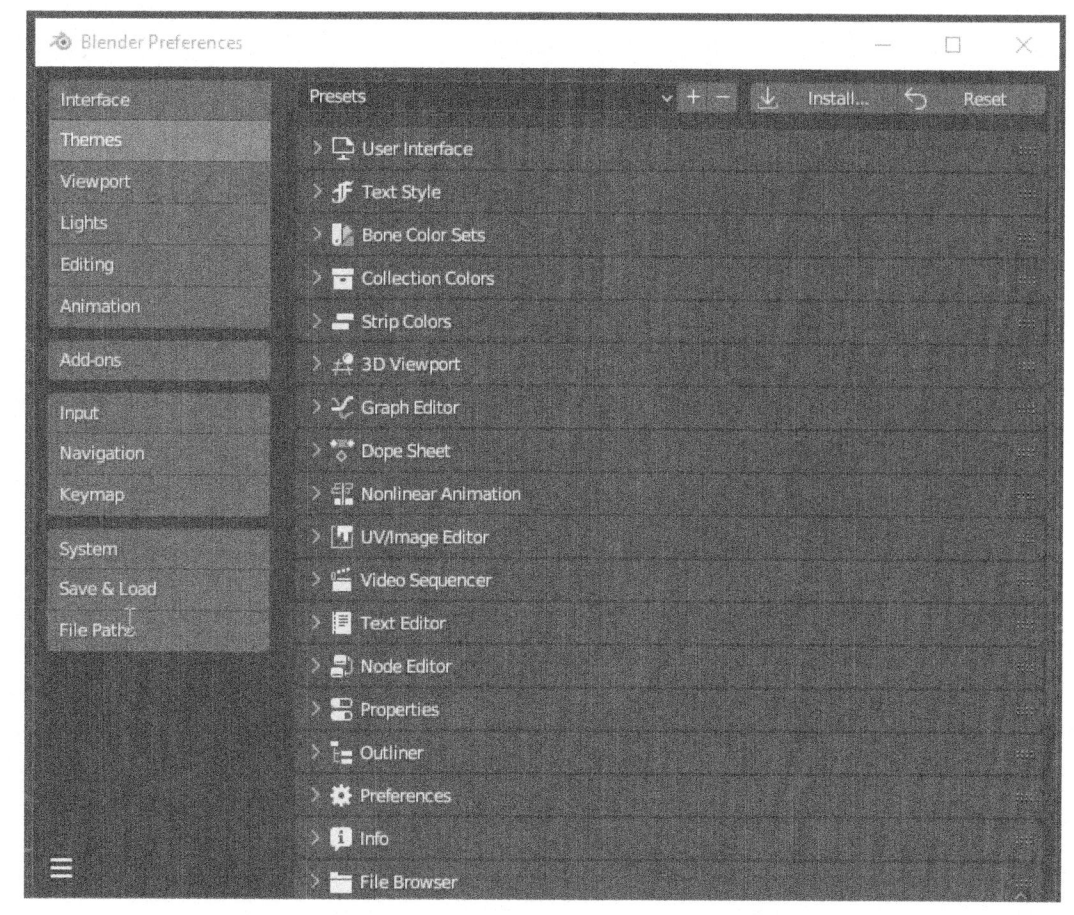

ADDONS

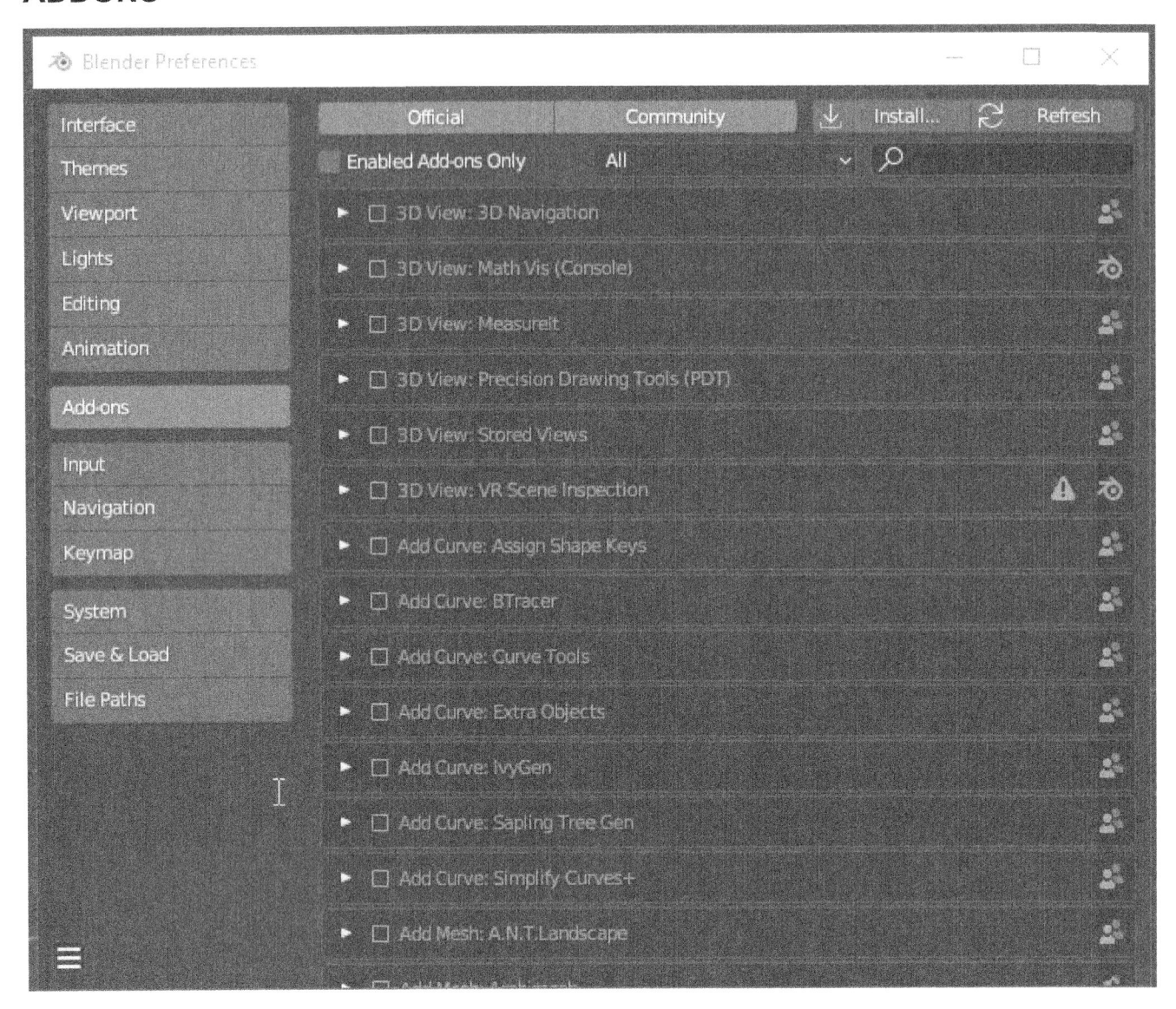

Blender includes add-ons, which are extensions that provide additional functionality within the software. These add-ons can enhance the user experience, modify the interface, introduce new objects, or offer tools to improve workflow efficiency. Managing add-ons can be done in the Add-Ons section of User Preferences. There are two main types of add-ons: officially supported and community-supported. You can filter and view these add-ons using the buttons on the left side of the Add-Ons section. By default, community-supported add-ons that come with Blender are disabled, while most officially supported add-ons are enabled. Enabling Disabling an add-on is as simple as clicking the checkbox next to it. Expanding a specific add-on box provides more details about its functionality.

Add-ons in Blender are categorized for easier navigation, and you can focus on a particular category using the buttons on the left side. Additionally, you can use the search field above the category buttons to quickly find specific add-ons. By exploring and utilizing the available add-ons, you can expand Blender's capabilities and customize the software to suit your specific needs and preferences.

FILE

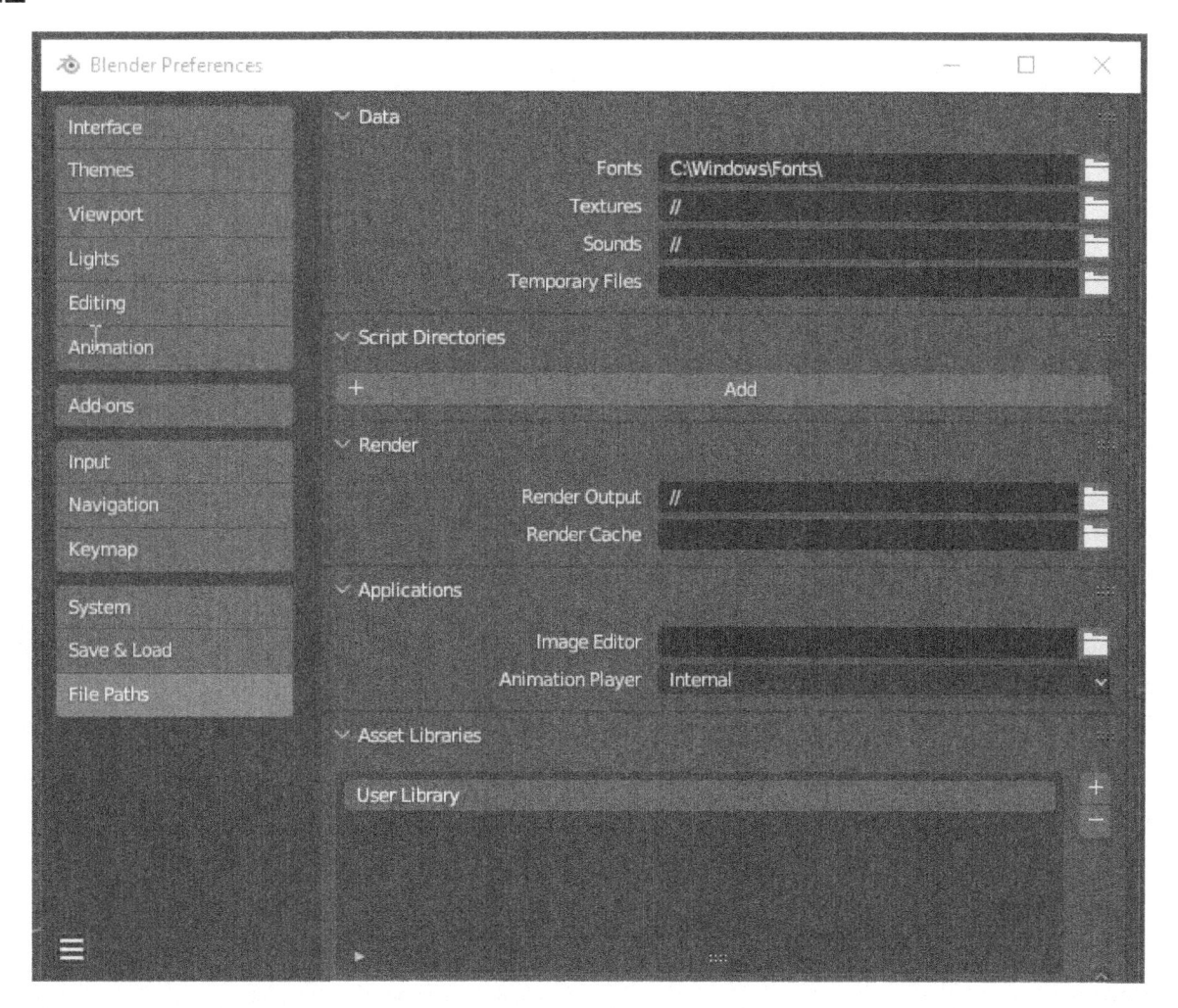

This section refers to the way Blender works with files, as shown in the screenshot above.

Let's break down the importance of each aspect:

- **File Paths:** In Blender, file management is crucial, and the File Paths options display the default locations where Blender stores or searches for various files. This includes fonts, render output, textures, sounds, and temporary files. The Temp path is particularly important as it stores auto-save files and the "quit.Blend" file, which allows you to recover your previous Blender session. By definition, temporary files are saved in the "/tmp/" directory.
  Tip: Windows users may face challenges with the default Temp location as it may not exist on their system. It is highly recommended for Windows users to either change the Temp location to "C:\Windows\Temp" or create a new folder namedtmp on their C:\ drive. Linux users may also need to consider changing the Temp location if their distribution clears the "/ tmp" directory during each boot. Failing to set the temperature path correctly can result in the loss of unsaved work when Blender is closed.
- **Save and Load Options:** These options determine how project files are handled in Blender. Two important options to note are "Compress File" and "Load UI." These options can be modified in the File Browser and define the default behavior. Enabling the "Compress File" option reduces the size of ".blend" project files when saving them. On the other hand, the "Load UI" option ensures that when you open a ".blendfile", Blender adjusts your screen layout to match the one used during the creation of that file. These

file management options in Blender allow you to customize the default behavior when saving and loading files, ensuring efficient storage and consistent user interface layouts.

SYSTEM

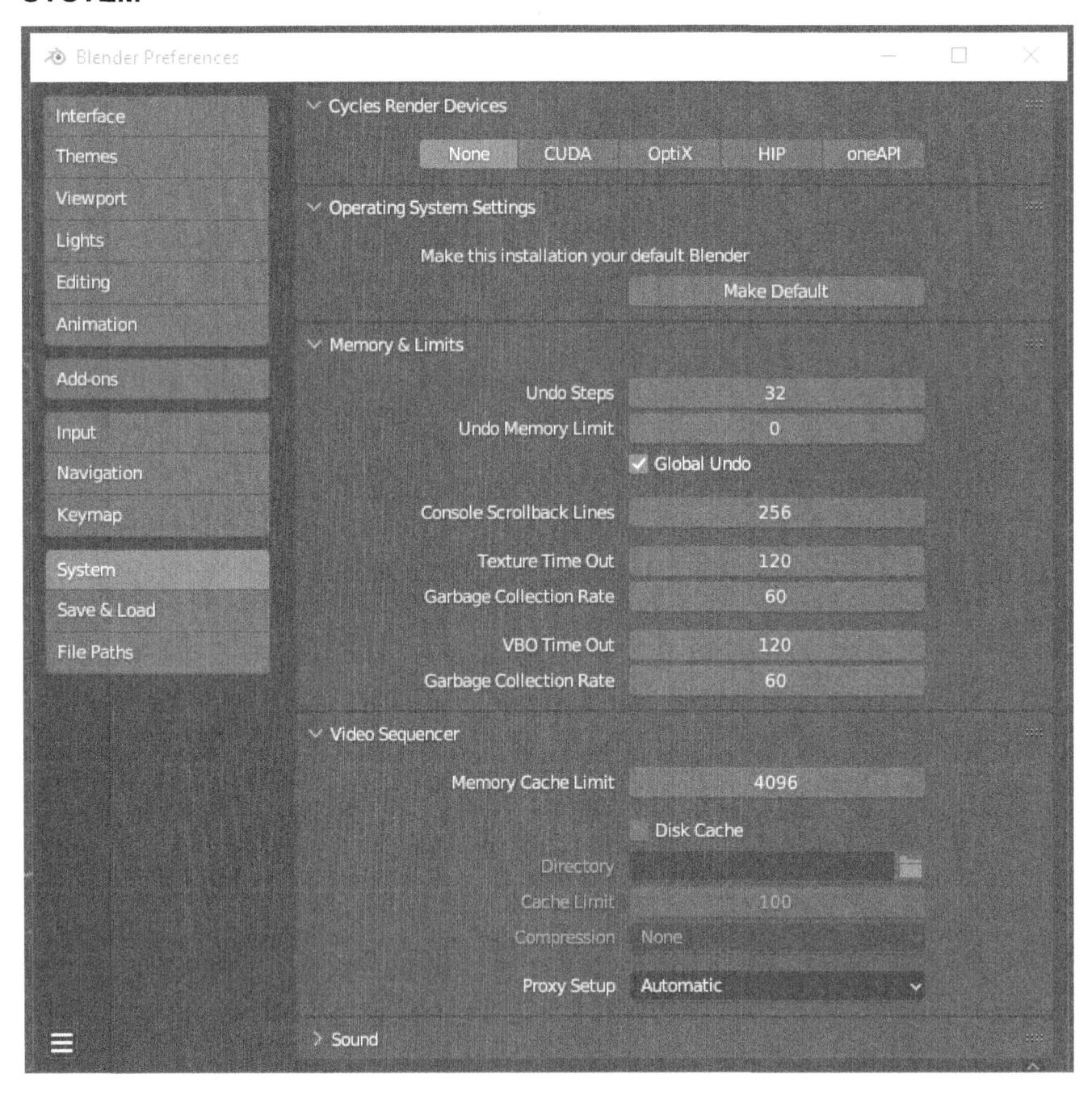

In the System section of Blender, you can configure graphics card options, memory limits, and sound settings. If your hardware doesn't support certain options mentioned in this section, they will either be hidden or automatically adjusted when Blender starts up.

INPUT

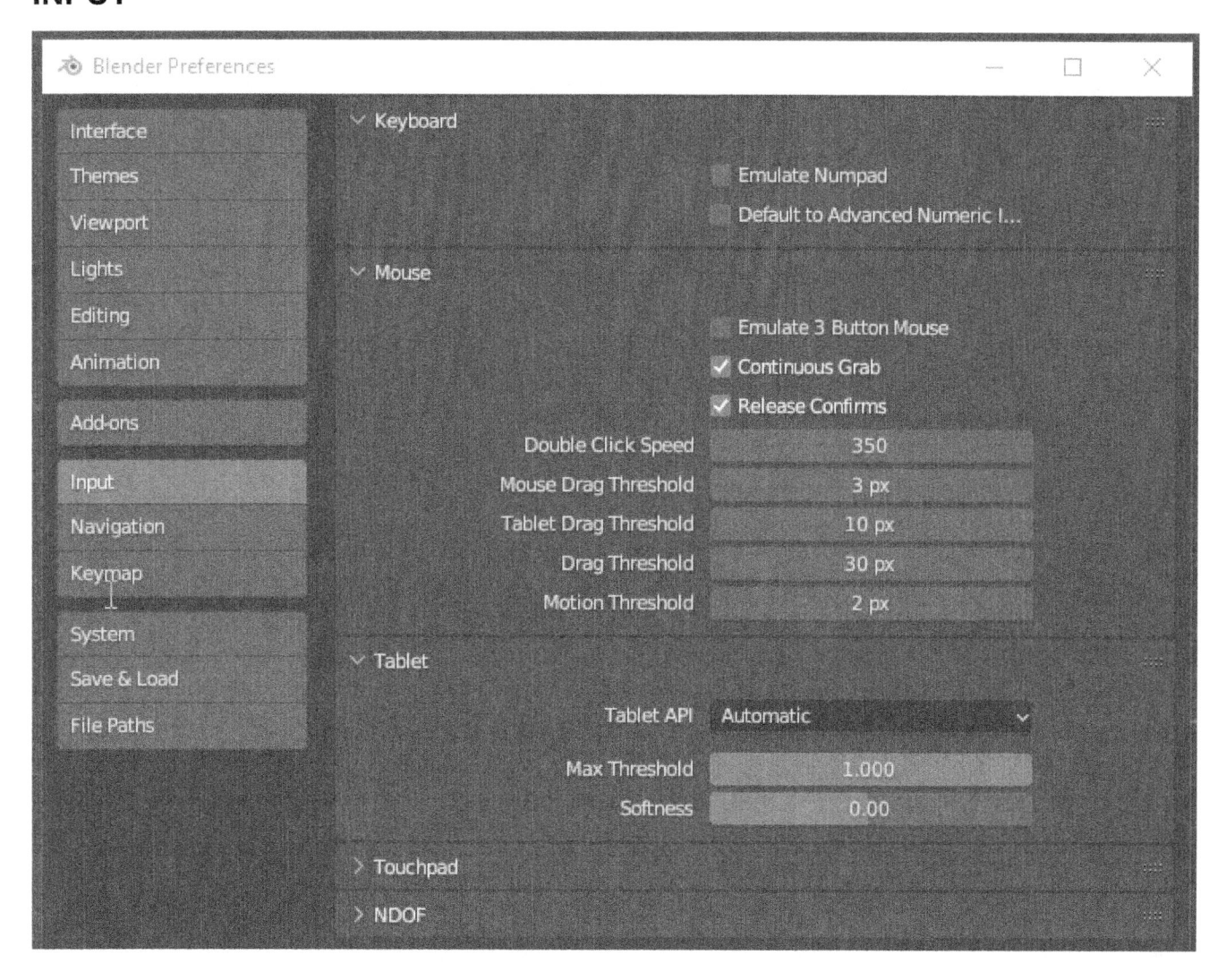

In the input preferences of Blender, you can customize the mouse and keyboard interactions as well as create your keymap.

Here are some important options in this section:

- **Emulate 3-Button Mouse:** This option is useful for users who don't have a three-button mouse, such as Macintosh or some tablet PC users. Enabling this option allows Alt+left-click to perform actions typically done with the mid-dle click. Continuous Grab: This feature allows you to keep moving an object even after reaching the edge of the editor. It's enabled by default, but tablet interface users may disable it if needed.
- **Emulate Numpad:** Laptop users can benefit from this option since laptops usually lack a dedicated numeric keypad. It allows using the number keys at the top of the keyboard to mimic the functionality of the corresponding Numpad numbers. However, it disables the normal layer-switching functionality of the number keys.
- **Release Confirmations:** By default, confirming a transformation in Blen der requires releasing the Left Mouse Button (LMB). Enabling this option allows releasing the LMB to act as confirmation for the "transform."
- **Mouse Drag Threshold:** This setting determines the number of pixels an interface element needs to be moved before Blender recognizes it as a drag event. Values below the threshold will be registered as click events.

- **Tablet Drag Threshold:** This threshold specifically applies to tablet events and determines the amount of drag required before Blender recognizes it as a tablet drag event.
- **Drag Threshold:** Similar to the previous setting, this threshold applies to non-mouse or tablet events such as keyboard or 3D mouse inputs. It determines the amount of damage needed for these events to be recognized. This setting also affects the Pie Menu on Drag keymap preference.
- **Motion Threshold:** This setting defines the number of pixels the cursor must be moved before the movement is registered. It is particularly useful for tablet pens, as slight pen movements can cause cursor stuttering. Adjusting this threshold can help reduce that issue. These options in the input preferences of Blender allow you to customize the behavior of your mouse and keyboard interactions to suit your preferences and hardware setup, providing a more comfortable and efficient workflow.

USING CUSTOM EVENT MAPS

In Blender's event system refactor, significant changes were made to improve the program's structure and responsiveness. The event system is crucial for user interaction in Blender, as every button press or mouse movement is registered as an event that triggers specific actions within the program. Previously, the event system in Blender was rigid and didn't provide immediate feedback. For example, editors wouldn't update until the mouse button was released, or resizing an area wouldn't update until the action was completed. However, with the refactor, Blender now offers more immediate feedback and customization options. To modify event handling and hotkeys in Blender, you don't necessarily need to access the User Preferences editor.

Instead, you can follow these steps:

1. Locate the desired operation in Blender's menu system, such as New," under the File menu.
2. Right-click on the menu item and select Change Shortcut.".
3. Input the new hotkey you want to assign, and it will be assigned to the operation.

For more advanced control over Blender's input settings, you can use the Input section in User Preferences. To navigate this section effectively, use the search feature to filter the options based on the operation you want to customize. From there, you can edit the events and modify their mappings and types.

In the Input section, you can activate or deactivate events, delete events, restore them to their original values, and expand their details for advanced controls. You can also export your customized event configurations to an external file, allowing you to share them with others or easily load them back into Blender when needed.

By customizing event handling and hotkeys in Blender, you can tailor the program to your workflow and preferences, improving your efficiency and overall experience.

Speeding up your workflow with Quick Favorites

The Quick Favorites menu in Blender is a convenient tool that allows you to gather and access your favorite or commonly used tools easily. It is accessible from the Toolbar, which is located on the left side of the 3DView by default.

To add a tool to your Quick Favorites menu, follow these steps:

- Activate the tool you want to add. This can be done by selecting it from the toolbar or using a hotkey associated with the tool.
- Right-click on the tool's icon or name in the toolbar.
- From the context menu that appears, select **"Add to Quick Favorites"**. The tool will now be added to your Quick Favorites menu. You can access the menu by clicking on the icon in the toolbar that looks like a star or by using the shortcut Q. The Quick Favorites menu provides a convenient way to access your frequently used tools without the need to search through menus or remember specific hotkeys. It allows you to customize your workflow and streamline your work process in Blender.

REVIEW QUESTIONS

1. What are the different types of editors available in Blender?
2. How can you switch between different editor types in Blender?
3. What is the purpose of the Quick Favorites menu in Blender's Toolbar?
4. How can you add a tool to the Quick Favorites menu in Blender?

SUMMARY

This section provides an overview of the importance of editor types, introduces various types of editors available in Blender, and highlights the significance of the primary editor in modifying attributes within the software.

CHAPTER 5: FIRST STEPS IN BLENDER MODELING

Blender is designed to optimize speed and efficiency, allowing users to work for extended periods without sacrificing productivity. In this chapter, we will explore the fundamental aspects of interacting with Blender's three-dimensional (3D) space, including object manipulation and polygon editing. If you have prior experience with other 3D software, you may encounter some unfamiliar concepts in Blender. However, recent updates have bridged the gap, minimizing the learning curve. Interestingly, if you're new to 3D work, you may have a slight advantage over professionals accustomed to different work. flows. Embrace the opportunity to start fresh!

In this section, we are going to be working around Blender.

GRABBING, SCALING, AND ROTATING

In a 3D scene, the three fundamental object operations are translation (grab), scaling (scale), and orientation (rotate). These operations allow you to position objects in 3D space, adjust their size, and change their orientation. Blender uses the terms grab, scale, and rotate to describe these operations, while other software may use move or size instead. With these operations, you have the flexibility to place objects in any position, size them as needed, and adjust their orientation to your preference. One of Blender's strengths is its consistent interface design. This means that you can use these transform operations not only in the 3D view but also in other areas of the software. For instance, you can utilize grab and scale operations when editing keyframes and motion curves in the Graph Editor. This level of convenience enhances your work flow and ensures a consistent experience throughout Blender. Blender is designed to prioritize efficiency and minimize repetitive stress while working. One way it achieves this is by reducing the need to hold down keys for extended periods. Instead, most operations in Blender are initiated by pressing and releasing a key, and they are confirmed by left-clicking with the mouse or pressing Enter. To cancel an operation, you can right-click or press Esc.

This approach applies to a wide range of operations in Blender, even those that typically require holding down a button. For instance, if you attempt to split an area by left-clicking and dragging a corner widget but change your mind, you can simply right-click while adjusting the boundary between areas to stop the operation. By streamlining the interaction process and providing intuitive ways to initiate, confirm, and cancel operations, Blender aims to enhance productivity and reduce strain on the user.

DIFFERENTIATING BETWEEN COORDINATE SYSTEMS

To effectively apply transformations in Blender, it's important to grasp the concept of coordinate systems in 3D space. Blender utilizes a grid composed of three axes: X, Y, and Z. Typically, the X-axis represents side-to-side movement, the Y-axis represents front-to-back movement, and the Z-axis represents vertical movement from top to bottom. This grid system, known as the Cart e-Siangrid, is fundamental in Blender.

The origin, or center, of the grid is located at the coordinates (O, 0, and 0). However, the variation in coordinate systems within Blender arises from how the grid is oriented relative to a selected 3D object. In the 3D View header, you can access the Coordinate System Orientation menu by left-clicking it. This menu allows you to visualize and manipulate the orientation of the grid, providing different reference points for transformations.

Understanding coordinate systems and their orientations is essential for precise object manipulation and positioning within Blender's 3D environment.

BELOW ARE THE FIVE POSSIBLE ORIENTATIONS.

- **Global:** The global orientation in Blender is represented by the base grid visible in the 3D view. It serves as the primary reference point for all other orientations. The X-axis (red) extends side-to-side, the Y-axis (green) moves front-to-back, and the Z-axis (blue) runs vertically. The origin, located at the center of the grid, is the starting point.
- **Local:** Each 3D object in Blender has its own local coordinate system, which is distinct from the global orientation. The local system is based on the object's origin, represented by an orange dot at its center. Initially, the local system aligns with the global axis, but as you move the object, its local orientation can differ significantly.
- **Gimbal:** The gimbal orientation addresses the issue of gimbal lock, which occurs when rotation axes coincide. Blender's Gimbal mode helps visualize the axes to avoid this problem. It uses Euler angles for rotation around the X, Y, and Z axes.
- **Normal:** The normal orientation is primarily used when editing meshes or working with Armatures for animation. It aligns with the "normal" of the surfaces and bones, providing a specialized local reference system.
- **View:** The view orientation adapts based on your perspective in the 3D view. The Z-axis always faces your view point, the Y-axis remains vertical, and the X-axis stays horizontal. It allows for consistent orientation regardless of camera movement or viewpoint changes.

TRANSFORMING AN OBJECT BY USING OBJECT GIZMOS

The 3D View incorporates the Transformation gizmo, which enables mouse-based manipulation of translation, rotation, and scaling. Each operation has its own distinct gizmo, which can be utilized individually or in conjunction with others.

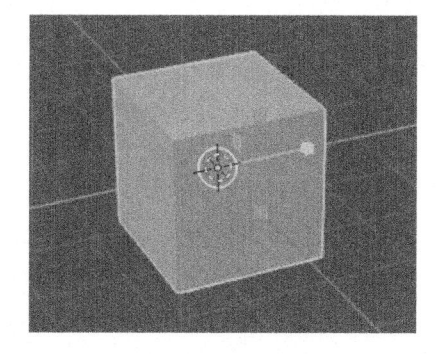

Figure 1: Move

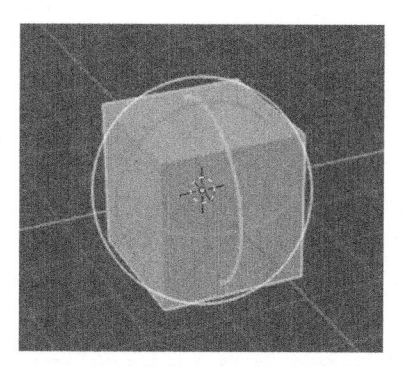

Figure 2: Rotate

The gizmo serves as a convenient tool for beginners seeking straightforward methods to transform objects. However, as you delve further into 3D modeling, the gizmos may become less advantageous. Their slower operation in comparison to shortcut keys makes them less efficient. Nevertheless, there are situations where the gizmo proves useful, such as when direct keyboard access is not available. For instance, when sculpting or drawing with a pen tablet, having a readily accessible tool for basic transformations can be beneficial.

ACTIVATING OBJECT GIZMOS

The Gizmo is initially hidden, but you can easily activate it from the Gizmo menu located in the top right corner of the 3D view port. Simply enable the checkboxes for move, rotate, and scale to make the gizmo visible again. Additionally, ensure that the gizmo icon is enabled, as the widget will not be displayed without it.

Using object gizmos

The transform gizmo consists of three distinct parts that can be activated independently or simultaneously. **This is what they look like:**

Move	Rotate Gizmo	Scale Gizmo

Here's a breakdown of their functionalities:

- To activate each part, access the Gizmo menu located in the top right corner. In the object gizmo section, check the move, rotate, and scale options.
- When all gizmos are active, you can click and drag the small white circle in the center to move the object based on the current view.
- The large white circle also utilizes the view but rotates the object instead.
- The circular lines represent the rotation axes: blue for Z, red for X, and green for Y. In case you forget the axis colors, you can refer to the navigation gizmo in the top right corner.
- The arrows allow you to move the object in the corresponding direction, while the square boxes enable scaling.
- When only the move widget is enabled, three small squares appear, each representing an axis. By clicking and dragging these squares, you can move the object within a plane.
- For instance, the red square moves the object along the Z and Y axes while excluding the X axis from the transformation.

If we enable only the scale widget, the larger white circle reappears. In this case, it serves as an indicator that we can position our mouse between the smaller and larger circles to scale the entire object. The sensitivity of the transformation depends on where we click and drag in relation to the outer circle. The closer we are to the outer circle, the less sensitive the transformation becomes.

Conversely, clicking and dragging further out, closer to the larger circle, allows for a more precise and refined transformation.

When the rotation widget is active on its own, it functions similarly to when all widgets are active, except that clicking and dragging in the middle creates a trackball-like rotation effect. One important detail to note is that when both the scale and move widgets are active but not the rotate widget, the small squares within the widget are dedicated to the move command rather than the scale command. These squares always disappear when rotation is enabled.

THE SETTINGS IN GIZMO AND HOW THEY WORK

When utilizing the selection tools or the 3D cursor from the left side tool panel, we have the option to enable or disable them individually via the gizmo menu located in the upper right corner of the 3D viewport. To toggle the visibility of gizmos, we can simply Click the show gizmo button next to each respective option. It's important to note that disabling gizmos in this menu also disables the control options found in the top right corner, which are specifically designed for navigation purposes.

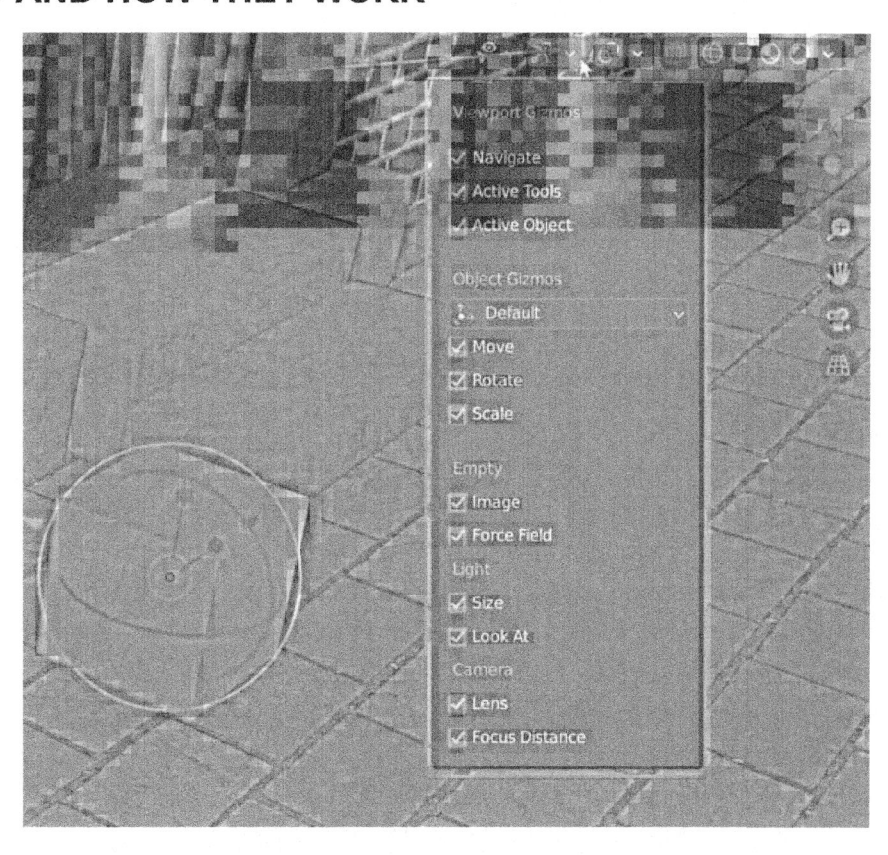

Within the viewport, you'll discover various options to customize your experience.

- The first checkbox, labeled "navigate," activates the navigation widgets mentioned earlier.
- The next checkbox, "active tool," determines whether the gizmo corresponding to the selected tool in the left-side tool panel is visible or hidden. Disabling this option ensures that the widget remains hidden when the move tool is subsequently enabled.
- The "active object" option acts as a toggle, enabling or disabling the use of the object groups as a group. These gizmos encompass the settings described previously and are displayed when no specific tool with its gizmo is enabled. It also includes all the subsequent settings in the menu.

- . The remaining gizmo options pertain to activating or deactivating empties, lights, and cameras. Empties require an attached force field or image to have gizmos available.
- For force fields, a yellow arrow appears, allowing adjustments to the strength.
- When working with images, clicking and dragging from the middle allows movement, while resizing can be done by manipulating the corners.
- Lights possess object-specific gizmos, enabling directional adjustments for sun, spot, and area lights, as well as size modifications for spotlights and area lights.
- Lastly, the camera gizmo allows modifications to the focal length by clicking and dragging the edges of the camera frame. To control the focus distance, access the object properties within the object data properties tab (identified by a green camera icon). In the viewport display settings, ensure that limits" is enabled.

Across hair will then appear on a line, allowing you to click and drag to adjust the plane on which your camera focuses.

MOVING THE GIZMO

The placement of the gizmo is determined by the transform pivot point, located in the center of the header within the 3D viewport, adjacent to the snapping menu. By default, the pivot point is set to the "median point." This means that when you select objects, the gizmo will automatically position itself in the center of the selected objects. Alternatively, if you set the pivot point to "3D cursor,"

The gizmo will follow the movement of the 3D cursor. However, there is one exception to this rule. If you choose "individual origins" as the pivot point, the gizmo will still be positioned at the median point.

To reset the position of the gizmo, simply select the "median point option as the transformation pivot point. The gizmo's appearance varies based on the object type and the tools being used. Different edit mode tools have their own specific gizmos, but the most commonly used one is the transform widget. For sculptors and painters, the transform widget provides a convenient method for basic object manipulation without relying on a keyboard. It serves as a helpful tool for beginners to learn object manipulation techniques. As we become more experienced in Blender, it is natural to transition towards utilizing shortcuts to enhance the speed of our modeling process.

SAVING TIME BY USING HOTKEYS

Many experienced Blender users often find that the manipulator can obstruct their view while working, leading them to disable it completely. To disable the manipulator, locate the manipulator mode buttons in the header of the 3DView and click the button featuring the color axis icon. Alternatively, you can press Ctrl+Spacebar. Now, you may wonder how to perform object transformations without the manipulator. Fear not, as Blender offers one of its most powerful features: hotkeys. The beauty of Blender's Hotkeys lie in their ability to reduce reliance on mouse movements and shorten the time required for mouse-based operations. By incorporating these time saving actions into your workflow, you can experience the true power of hotkeys.

TRANSFORMING WITH HOTKEYS

Hotkeys are a powerful way to access various functionalities in Blender, including object transformations. In Blender, the process of translating an object is referred to as "grabbing." This naming convention is specifically relevant to hotkeys.

Follow these steps to perform a Grab/Translate operation:

- Right-click the object you wish to move to select it.
- Press the "G" key.
- Congratulations! You are now able to translate your object.
- To confirm the translation, left-click or press Enter.
- To cancel the operation, right-click or press Esc.

HOTKEYS AND COORDINATE SYSTEMS

By default, when using hotkeys, all transformations in Blender occur within the view coordinate system, specifically the XY-plane of the 3D view, regardless of how you're viewing the scene. However, if you want to move your object along the global Z-axis, you can achieve this by following a specific key sequence.

Here's how:

1. Select your object and press the "G" key to enter Grab/Translate mode.
2. Without canceling the operation, press the "Z" key.

A blue line will appear, representing the global Z-axis. Your object will be locked to move only along this line. Similarly, pressing "Y" locks the movement to the global Y-axis, and pressing "X" locks it to the global X-axis. This technique works for rotation and scaling, too. For instance, "RZ" allows rotation around the global Z-axis, whileSX" scales along the global X-axis.

Now, let's explore the local orientation. It only requires an additional keypress in the sequence.

The following steps will help you grab an object and move it along its local Y-axis:

1. Imagine that you want to translate the object in the global Y-axis. Click "GY."
2. Press "Y" once more.

Now, you're translating along the local Y-axis. Pressing "Y" for the third time returns you to the default View coordinate system. This same sequence works for Norm-Al and Gimbal orientations too. Ensure that your coordinate system orientation is set to either normal or gimbal. Blender pays attention to this choice when you press the axis letter for the second time, even if the 3D manipulator is disabled. Remember, this sequence-based approach applies to scaling and rotation as well. For example, "RX" performs rotation around the local X-axis, while "SZ" scales along the local Z-axis. Furthermore, just like the 3D manipulator, you can work in a plane using hotkeys. Use Shift plus the letter of the axis perpendicular to the desired plane of movement. For instance, to scale an object in the global XY-plane, press "S" followed by "Shift+Z." Similarly, for the local XY-plan e, press "S" followed by "Shift +Z" twice.

This logic can also be applied to the grab operation, but note that it doesn't work for the rotate operation.

Grab	Scale	Rotate	Orientation
G	S	R	View
G⇔Z	S⇔Z	R⇔Z	Global Z-axis
G⇔Y	S⇔Y	R⇔Y	Global Y-axis
G⇔X	S⇔X	R⇔X	Global X-axis
G⇔Z⇔Z	S⇔Z⇔Z	R⇔Z⇔Z	Local Z-axis
G⇔Y⇔Y	S⇔Y⇔Y	R⇔Y⇔Y	Local Y-axis
G⇔X⇔X	S⇔X⇔X	R⇔X⇔X	Local X-axis
G⇔Shift+Z	S⇔Shift+Z	N/A	Global XY-plane
G⇔Shift+Y	S⇔Shift+Y	N/A	Global XZ-plane
G⇔Shift+X	S⇔Shift+X	N/A	Global YZ-plane
G⇔Shift+Z⇔Shift+Z	S⇔Shift+Z⇔Shift+Z	N/A	Local XY-plane
G⇔Shift+Y⇔Shift+Y	S⇔Shift+Y⇔Shift+Y	N/A	Local XZ-plane

NUMERICAL INPUT

In addition to using hotkeys for triggering different transform modes, you can also use the keyboard to specify the exact amount by which you want to modify an item. Once you activate the transform mode, you can simply enter the desired unit value to modify.

For example, let's consider rotating an item by 32 degrees around the global X-axis. To achieve this, you would use the hotkey sequence "R>X>32" followed by pressing Enter to confirm the rotation. Similarly, if you want to translate your object along its native Y-axis by 26.4 units, you can use the sequence "G -> i -> Y -> -26.4 -> Enter."

When it comes to mirroring an object, you can accomplish this by scaling the item by -1 along a specific axis. Following these steps with the 3D manipulator can be a quick and efficient way to flip or mirror an object.

REVIEW QUESTIONS.

1. How does the sensitivity of the transformation change based on the location of the click and drag about the outer circle in the gizmo?
2. What happens when both the scale and move widgets are active but not the rotate widget in the gizmo?
3. How can you toggle the visibility of gizmos in Blender, and what happens when you disable gizmos from the gizmo menu?
4. How can you reset the position of the gizmo in Blender's 3D viewport, and what options are available for determining the gizmo's placement?
5. What are hotkeys in Blender, and how can they be used for object transformations like grab/translate, rotation, and scaling? Also, how can numerical input be used to specify exact modifications during the transformation process?

Summary

The chapter discusses the functionality of the gizmo in Blender and how it can be used for object manipulation. When only the scale widget is enabled, a larger white circle appears, indicating the ability to scale the entire object by positioning the mouse between the smaller and larger circles. The sensitivity of the transformation depends on the distance between the click-and-drag point and the outer circle, with closer points resulting in less sensitive transformations. The rotation widget, when active alone, creates a trackball-like rotation effect when clicking and dragging in the middle. When both the scale and move widgets are active but not the rotate widget, the small squares within the widget are used for the move command. The text also covers the settings in the Gizmo menu, explaining how to enable or disable gizmos individually and customize the viewport gizmo's appearance for different object types.

Then we explore using hotkeys as a powerful alternative to the gizmo for object transformations in Blender. It explains how to perform the grab/translate operation using the "G" key and how to lock the movement along specific axes using key sequences (e.g., "GX" for the global X-axis and "GY" twice for the local Y-axis). The chapter emphasizes that hotkeys can be used for scaling and rotation as well, and numerical input can be utilized to specify the exact amount of modification. The chapter also briefly touches on using the 3D manipulator to mirror an object by scaling it along a specific axis. Overall, the text provides insights into both the gizmo and hotkey methods of object manipulation in Blender, catering to users with different preferences and skill levels.

CHAPTER 6: EDITING AND OBJECT MODE TECHNIQUES

In Blender, your primary focus is on selecting objects, modifying them, and connecting them as you work on a scene. This workflow involves transitioning between object mode, where you work with the overall model, and edit mode, where you make specific edits to the objects. It's important to note that this method is not limited to just modeling; it applies to many other tasks in Blender that require intensive work. The knowledge you gain in this chapter can be applied to various features in Blender, regardless of whether they are related to 3D modeling or not. Many of the concepts and operations discussed here are applicable in different areas of Blen der, similar to how transform operations are used in various editors beyond the 3D view.

In this section, we will be working on edit and object modes.

MAKING CHANGES BY USING EDIT MODE

While moving objects around can be enjoyable, true satisfaction comes from transforming them into your desired creations. If 3D modeling is your goal, you've come to the right place. In this section, you will delve into Edit mode, which is essential for making detailed modifications to objects in Blender. Blender places great importance on utilizing Edit mode for object alterations.

It's worth noting that many of the concepts and techniques discussed here apply not only to polygon modeling (or mesh editing) but also to editing curves, surfaces, armatures, and even text. So, even though the primary focus is on polygon modeling, the principles extend to various other aspects of Blender's editing capabilities.

SWITCHING BETWEEN OBJECT MODE AND EDIT MODE

In object mode, as the name implies, you work with complete objects. However, this mode is not suitable for making detailed internal modifications to your objects. Let's take the example of the cube in the default scene. You can select it by right-clicking. If you want to change the cube into a pyramid, simply scaling it along the axes won't be sufficient.

You need to modify the individual components of the cube. This is where edit mode comes into play.

There are two ways to access Edit mode: either through the mouse or by using a hotkey.

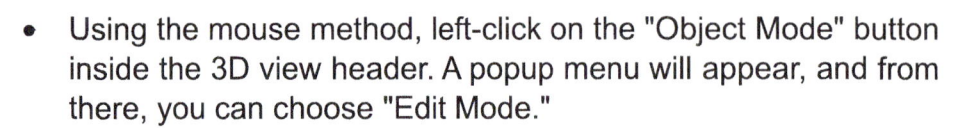

- Using the mouse method, left-click on the "Object Mode" button inside the 3D view header. A popup menu will appear, and from there, you can choose "Edit Mode."

- Blender provides a hotkey to quickly switch between object mode and edit mode. Pressing the Tab key toggles you back and forth between these modes. In fact, Tab is so commonly used for this purpose that Blender users often refer to it as "tabbing" into Edit mode or Object mode. This terminology is commonly used in Blender user forums and online documentation.

SELECTING VERTICES, EDGES, AND FACES

The cube changes color, and points appear at each of its corners as soon as you go into Edit mode. Every single point is a vertex, and an edge is a line that develops between two vertices. A polygon with three or four connected edges is called a face in Blender. Currently, faces in Blender are primarily limited to three-sided (tris) and four-sided (quads) polygons. While there are plans to introduce n-gons with virtually unlimited sides in the future, this functionality is only available in certain development versions of Blender at the moment. However, the current release still allows for extensive modeling using tris and quads. In fact, highly detailed character models are typically created using mostly quads with occasional triangles, and all 3D geometry is ultimately converted to triangles by computer hardware.

In Edit mode, there are different selection modes available for editing polygons: vertex select, edge select, and face select. By Definitely, Vertex Select mode is active when you enter Edit mode. Two visual indicators in the Blender interface show your current selection mode. Firstly, in Vert Ex Select mode, you can see each vertex of the model. Secondly, when you are in Edit mode, three additional buttons appear in the header of the 3DView, as shown here. The left button, with an icon of a cube and an orange dot on one corner, indicates that you are in Vertex Select mode when it is active.

To access different selection modes in Edit mode, there are buttons.

available in the 3D View's header. The button next to the Vertex Select button, depicted as a cube with a highlighted edge, activates Edge Select mode. In this mode, the individual vertices of your model are no longer visible. To enter Face Select mode, you need to select the last button in the group. It is represented by a cube with one side highlighted in orange. In Face Select mode, the vertices are hidden, and each polygon in your mesh is displayed with a square dot in the center. In the Browser interface, the Select Mode buttons for Vertex, Edge, and Face are grouped together. Similar to the 3D manipulator, you can actually activate multiple modes si-multaneously. To do this, simply hold down the Shift key and left-click on the desired Select mode buttons.

By enabling both Vertex Select and Edge Select modes at the same time, some Blender users find it more convenient to work efficiently. This allows for quicker selection and control at the vertex and edge levels. For example, you can use Blender's Lasso select tool (Ctrl+left-click+drag) to swiftly choose faces while benefiting from the combined selection capabilities of Vertex and Edge modes. When you enter Edit mode in Blender, all vertices, edges, and faces are initially selected by default.

The same selection principles that apply elsewhere in Blender also apply in Edit mode:

1. To select a single vertex, use the right mouse button.
2. By holding Shift and right-clicking, you can quickly select or deselect multiple vertices at once.
3. For selecting large groups of vertices, you have several tools available: Border Select (B), Circle Select (C), or Lasso Select (Ctrl+left-click+drag).
4. In Border and Circle Select, you can add items to your selection by left-clicking and dragging the mouse. This action creates a selection region, represented by a box in the case of Border Select. Circle Select is sometimes referred to as Brush Select because it

works similarly to painting. By holding down the left mouse button and moving the mouse pointer over a vertex, you can select that vertex.
5. Middle-click, then drag to remove from your selection, and right-click or hit the Esc key to leave the border or circle select.
6. If you want to use Lasso Select, hold Ctrl+left-click, then drag the cursor around the vertices you want to choose. Anything you choose within the region becomes part of your selection.

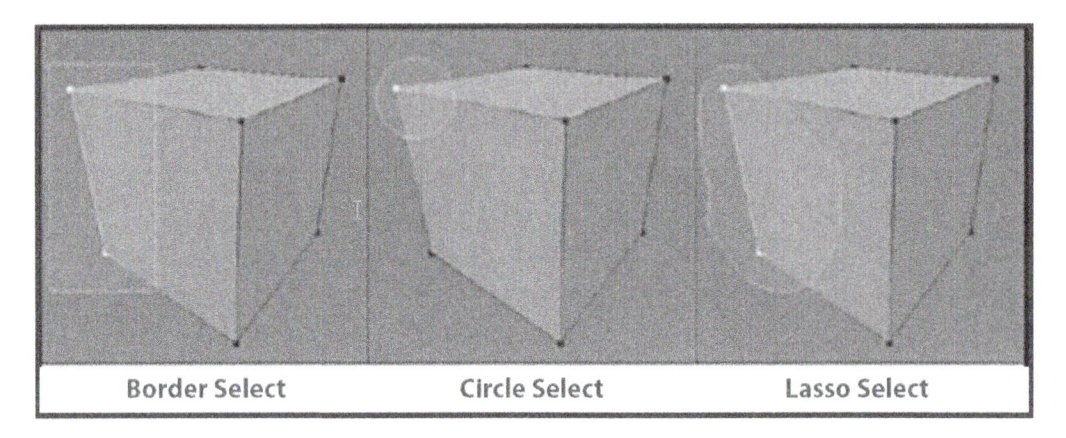

Border Select   Circle Select   Lasso Select

To select everything in Blender, you can press the Akey. This hotkey works as a toggle: if there was a previous selection, pressing A will select it, but if nothing was selected before, pressing A will select everything. You can use this hotkey repeatedly until you have either everything or nothing selected. By default, in Blender's default settings, you can't see or select the vertices, edges, and faces on the back side of your model unless you change the viewport shading or rotate the 3D view. However, there is a useful option to see and select those hidden vertices while in solid viewport shading. It's called the Limit Selection to Visible" button, also known as the "Occlude Background Geometry" button. It is located to the right of the Selection Modes block in the 3D View's header and has an icon of a cube with highlighted white vertices.

By default, his button is enabled, hiding the vertices on the back of your model, which is known as backface culling. It is a handy feature when working with complex models. We recommend keeping it enabled and temporarily switching to wireframe viewport shading (by pressing Z) if you need to quickly see or select those back face vertices.

WORKING WITH LINKED VERTICES

One way of selecting things in Edit Mode is by using linked vertices. They area of vertices is inside a mesh and connected by edges. Here's how it works:

1. Select (right-click) the default cube in Blender and enter Edit mode.
    - If all vertices are not selected, you can press A until they are.
2. With all the vertices selected, press Shift+D or choose "Add" -> "Duplicate" from the ToolShelf or 3D View's header to duplicate your selection.
    - Blender creates a copy of the selected vertices and switches to grab mode, allowing you to move the duplicate set of vertices, edges, and faces.
3. Use your mouse to move the new cube away from the original and confirm its placement by left-clicking a second time or pressing Enter.
    - The vertices of the original cube remain unselected, while the duplicated cube represents a set of linked vertices.

4. To select all the vertices in both cubes, position your mouse cursor near any vertex in the original cube and press L.
   - Now, all the vertices in both cubes will be selected simultaneously.

To deselect linked vertices, follow these steps:

1. Place your mouse cursor near any vertex on the duplicated cube and press Shift+L. All vertices connected to the one near your mouse cursor will be deselected. The hotkeys Land Shift+L are particularly useful when working on complex meshes. They allow for the quick selection and deselection of linked vertices. For example, when placing teeth in a modeled mouth, these hotkeys can be handy for efficient selection operations. In scenarios such as positioning teeth in a modeled mouth, we've found ourselves frequently using the Land Shift+L hotkeys. These hotkeys prove to be very useful for efficient vertex selection and deselection operations.

STILL, THE BLENDER'S NO. 1 MODELING TOOL IS: EXTRUDE

The Extrude function is one of Blender's most frequently used modeling tools after Transform. Extrusion is the process of creating new geometry by pulling existing elements outward in a specific direction. In Blender, extrusion allows you to extend selected vertices, edges, or faces in any direction, forming new geometry in the process. Blender has faced criticism for lacking certain advanced mesh-editing capabilities and tools. Some examples commonly mentioned include the absence of clear Boolean operations, the inability to perform per-edge beveling and the lack of support for n-gons (polygons with more than four sides). These limitations have sparked a demand for more sophisticated mesh-editing features in the software.

Historically, Blend's mesh structures relied on outdated code known as Edit Mesh, which contributed to these constraints. To address this, the Bmesh (Blender Mesh) project was initiated. It has been gradually evolving over the years with the efforts of just two developers, and it was integrated into Blender after the completion of the 2.5 series development and the release of Version 2.6. In Edit Mode, the extrude function provides multiple benefits. It grants quick access to various transform features, such as scaling and rotating, enabling efficient modeling without the need to switch between different modes. Axis-locking allows for precise movements or alignments during the extrusion process. Snapping can be enabled to align the extruded geometry with other elements in the scene. Furthermore, numerical input is supported for precise transformations when specific distances or dimensions are required.

However, the extrude function in grab mode also comes with a drawback. If you attempt an extrusion and then cancel it by right-clicking or pressing Esc, the newly extruded vertices, edges, or faces remain in the scene in their original positions. This can potentially lead to clutter and confusion if not handled properly. To address this, you can check for double vertices (duplicate vertices) and remove them using the "Remove Doubles" feature in Blender. In summary, the extrude function in Blender's grab mode transition offers numerous benefits, but it's essential to handle canceled extrusions properly to avoid any issues in the model. With a good understanding of the extrude function's features and limitations, Blender users can utilize this powerful tool for efficient and precise modeling.

ADDING TO A SCENE

If you're tired of seeing just the cube, there are other basic objects available that you can use as a starting point for your projects. When you add a new object to Blender, the origin of that object is placed where the 3D cursor is located. This allows for precise positioning and alignment of objects in the scene. One useful feature in Blender is how it remembers the last menu choice you selected and places it just under your mouse pointer for pop-up menus like the Dynamic Spacebar Menu. This workflow feature allows you to work more quickly and efficiently. The idea is that you often need to perform the same tasks repeatedly, so by reducing the distance your mouse needs to travel between each operation, Blender simplifies and speeds up these repetitive tasks.

In summary, Blender provides various basic objects to work with, and you can easily switch between them. Additionally, the Software's ability to remember your last menu choices and place them under your mouse pointer in pop-up menus enhances your productivity by minimizing mouse travel and making repetitive tasks more straightforward. This streamlined workflow makes Blender a powerful tool for 3D modeling and an imitator.

ADDING OBJECTS

In Blender, you can use the Shift+A hotkey to add new items to your scene. **Here are the different options available for adding primitives:**

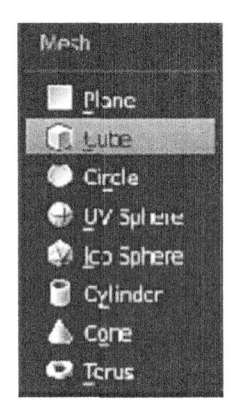

1. **Mesh:** Meshes are polygon-based objects composed of vertices, edges, and faces. They are the most common type of modeling object in Blender.
2. **Curve:** Curves are created using control points to form curved or straight lines. Blender offers two types of curves - NURBS curves and Bezier curves. Curves can also be used as paths to guide other objects.
3. **Surface:** Surfaces are similar to meshes but are defined by a collection of NURBS curves and their control points.
4. **Meta Ball:** Meta objects are unique primitives that can fuse together to create larger structures. They are useful for creating rapid, crude, clay-like models and various effects like blobby masses.
5. **Text:** You can add text to your 3D scene and modify it like other 3D objects using the text object.
6. **Armature:** Armature objects resemble skeletons and are made up of connected bones. They are used to deform other objects, allowing for animation and rigging setups.
7. **Lattice:** Lattices are used to deform other objects temporarily. They can be used to squash, stretch, and twist mod-els, providing precise control over their shape.
8. **Empty:** Empties are invisible in renderings and act as reference points for position, size, and orientation in 3D space. They are essential for animation and rigging setups as controllers and guides for other objects.
9. **Camera:** Camera objects determine the position and viewpoint from which your scene is rendered, defining the perspective and framing of your scene.
10. **Lamp:** Lamp items are used to illuminate your scene, just like real-world lighting is crucial for visibility and enhancing details.

11. **Force Field:** Force fields are empty objects that act as sources of physical forces like wind or magnetism. They affect the behavior of other objects in Blender's integrated physics simulation.
12. **Group Instance:** A group is a collection of related items in Blender. Group instances allow you to reference and place multiple instances of a group in your scene, facilitating the reusability and organization of objects.

These options provide a diverse range of primitives and functionalities to create and manipulate objects in Blender, enabling you to build complex 3D scenes with ease.

MEET SUZANNE, THE BLENDER MONKEY.

In 3D modeling and animation software, there is often a need for more complex objects to test renders, benchmarks, or demonstrations beyond simple shapes like cubes or spheres. To address this, many software packages provide generic, semi-complex functions. One famous example of such a primitive is the Utah teapot. The Utah teapot has become a standard test model used in various applications within the 3D industry. It serves as a versatile and widely recognized object for testing and showcasing the capabilities of 3D modeling and rendering software.

Blender, being known for its playful and creative community, offers something a little more intriguing and special: the monkey head, fondly referred to as "Suzanne." Suzanne is a humorous tribute to the ape characters from two of Kevin Smith's movies, "Jay and Silent Bob Strike Back" and "Mall Rats." To add Suzanne to your scene in Blender, you can simply press Shift+A, then select Mesh, and finally choose Monkey. The Blender community has embraced Suzanne, and references to her can be found all over Blender community forums and in a good portion of the release documentation.

The Suzanne Awards are named after her and represent the yearly awards ceremony at the Blender Conference in Amsterdam.

Suzanne's inclusion in Blender adds a fun and unique touch to the software, representing the creativity and humor that the Blender community values. It also serves as a versatile object for testing and demonstrating various 3D modeling and rendering features in Blender.

JOINING AND SEPARATING OBJECTS

In Blender, when you are building models for your scenes, there might be situations where you need to connect or separate items. For example, if you accidentally add a new primitive while in Edit mode, you might want to separate it from the current object without undoing it and go back to Object mode to add the primitive again. Fortunately, Blen der provides an alternative solution. When you add a new primitive in Edit mode, all of its components are selected, while none of the components from the previous object are selected. In this case, you can use the P key and then select "Selection from the menu to separate the newly added feature and turn it into a separate object.

After adding a new item in Blender, you can re-enter object mode and follow these steps to adjust its origin:

1. Select (right-click) the newly added item in object mode. The item's origin is initially set to the same location as the origin of the original object.
2. To move the origin of the new object to its true center based on its geometry, you have two options:
a) Press Shift+Ctrl+Alt+C and select Origin to Geometry" from the menu. This action will measure the size of the object and determine its precise center, repositioning the origin accordingly.
Or
b) Click Object" in the header of the 3DView, then go to "Transform and choose "Origin to Geometry." This achieves the same result as the previous method.

By using either of these methods, Blender recalculates the object's center based on its geometry, adjusting the origin accordingly. Furthermore, you can combine two items of the same kind into one. To do this, select multiple items in Object mode by Shift+right-clicking them or by using the Border Select or Lasso Select tools. The last object you select becomes the active object. Then, join the objects together by pressing Ctrl+J or choosing "Object" > "Join "from the 3DView's header while they are selected. This will combine the selected objects into one single object. By using these methods in Blender, you can easily connect or separate items, adjust their origins, and join objects together to create more complex models for your scenes.

CREATING DUPLICATES AND LINKS

In the previous section titled Working with linked vertices," we learned how to duplicate selected vertices using Shift+D (or Mesh).

> Add Duplicate). This duplication technique also works in object mode. However, in some cases, you might want the duplicated object in Edit mode to be an exact copy of the original. Moreover, it would be useful if any changes made in Edit mode were automatically applied to both the original and all of its duplicates. This is where linked duplicates come into play, allowing objects to share the same internal data blocks.

To create a linked duplicate in Blender, follow these simple steps:

1. Rig-click on the t he object you want to replicate to select it.
2. Press Alt+D or go to Object > Duplicate Linked from the 3D View's header while the object is selected.
3. After duplicating, the behavior is the same as standard duplication. Grab mode is automatically activated on the duplicated object.
4. Use the mouse to position the duplicated object in the desired spot, and then confirm its placement by left-clicking or pressing Enter.

Now, the duplicated object is a linked duplicate, meaning it shares the same internal data blocks as the original. Any changes you make to one of the linked duplicates in Edit mode will be applied to all the other linked duplicates and the original objects simultaneously.

To verify that an object is a linked duplicate, you can perform the following steps:

1. Enter Edit Mode on the original object or one of the linked duplicates.

2. When you do this, all objects linked to it will also go into edit mode.
3. Any changes you make to the vertices, edges, or faces in Edit mode will automatically update all the other linked duplicates and the original object instantly.

Using linked duplicates can be incredibly useful for creating variations of an object or maintaining consistency across multiple instances of the same model. It saves time and effort by allowing you to edit one object and see the changes propagate to all linked duplicates automatically.

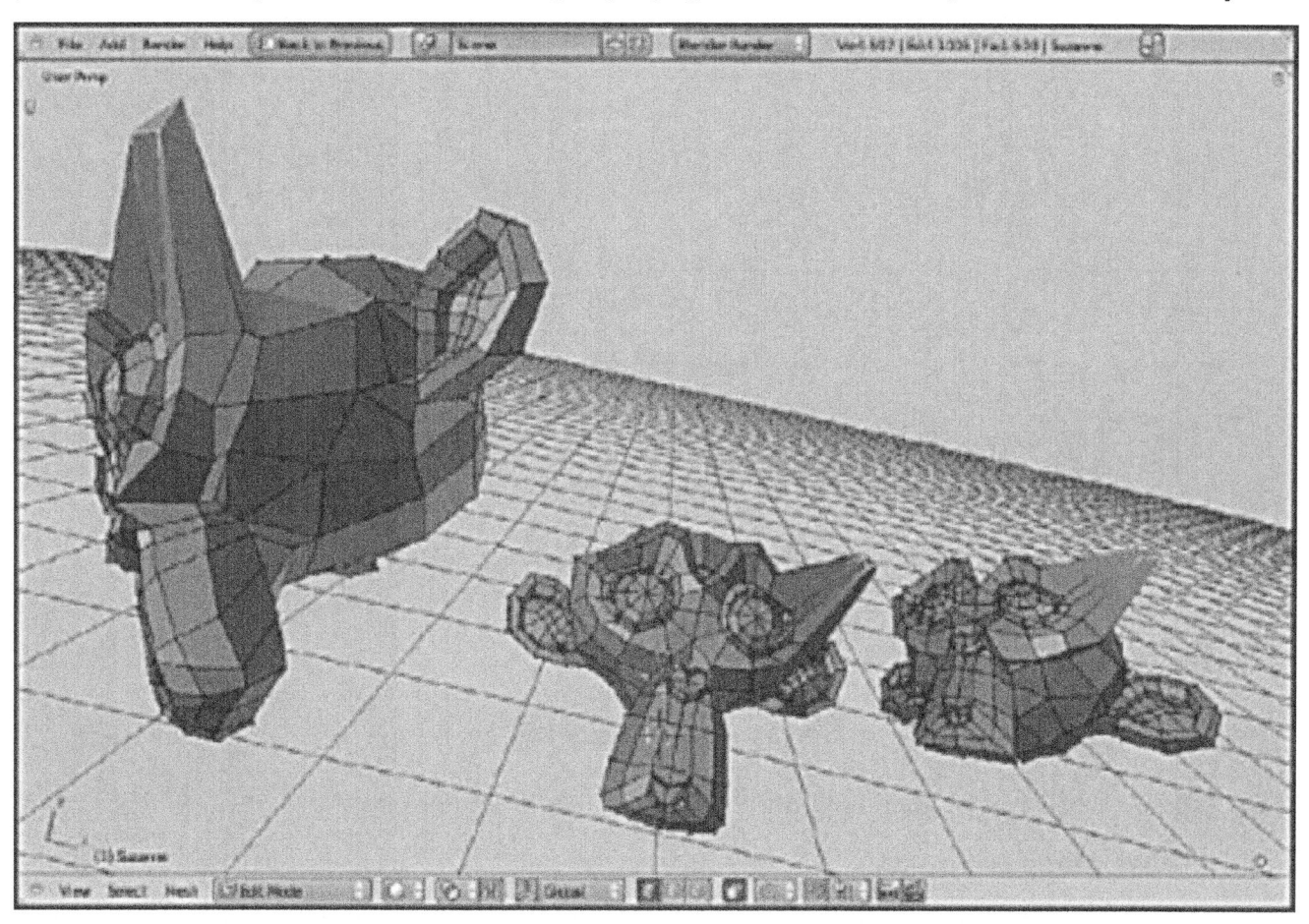

DISCOVERING PARENTS, CHILDREN, AND COLLECTIONS

Organizing objects into parent-child relationships in Blender is a powerful way to manage a collection of objects with a clear hierarchy. This technique allows you to group objects and control them collectively through the parent object.

Here's how you can establish a parent-child relationship between objects:

1. Select the objects you want to set as children. These objects can be of different types or have different properties.
2. Ensure that the last object you select (the active object) is the one you want to designate as the parent.
3. Press Ctrl+P and select "Object from the menu or go to Object > Parent > Set Parent in the header menu of the 3D view.

By parenting the selected objects to the active object, you create a hierarchical relationship. The active object becomes the parent, and the other selected objects become its children. Now, any transformation applied to the parent object will affect its children as well.

One practical example of using parenting is when you create a scene with a dinner table and chairs around it. Instead of individually scaling, grabbing, and moving each chair, you can parent all the chairs to the table. Then, when you transform the table, all the chairs will automatically move with it, maintaining their relative positions. Parenting is an essential tool for organizing complex scenes, animations, and rigs in Blender. It helps maintain structure and makes it easier to manage groups of related objects, saving time and effort during the 3D modeling and animation process too.

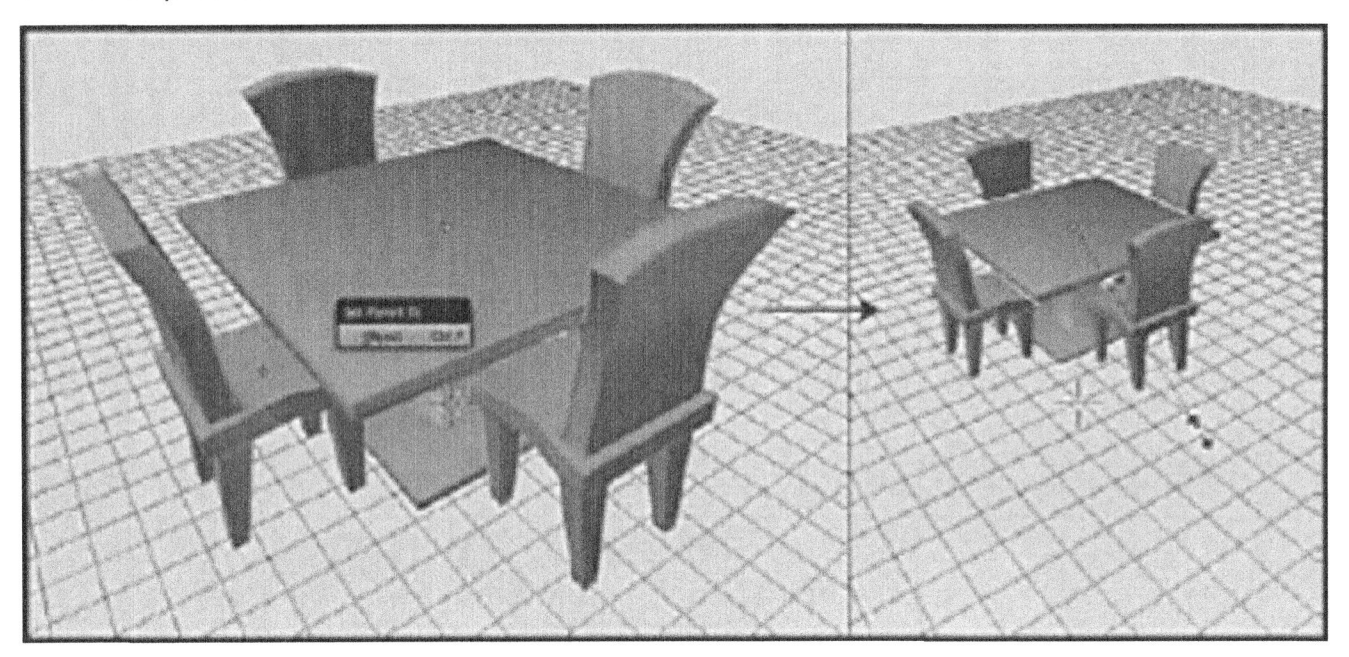

CLEARING A PARENT-CHILD RELATIONSHIP

Detaching a child's object from its parent in Blender is a straightforward process.

Follow these steps to do so:

1. Select the child object that you want to detach from its parent.
2. Press Alt+P or click Object > Parent > Clear in the header menu of the 3D View.

This will open a pop-up menu with three options:

a) Clear Parent: This option removes the parent-child relationship between the selected object and its parent. The child object will be completely independent and revert to its original position, scale, and rotation before it was parented.

b) Clear and Keep Transformation (Clear Track): This option also removes the parent-child relationship, but any transformations applied to the child object while it was a child will be preserved. It means the child object will maintain its position, scale, and rotation relative to the parent, even after the parent-child relationship is removed.

c) Clear Parent Inverse: This option clears the parent's transformation from the child object, but it doesn't sever the link between them. The child object will maintain its current position, scale, and rotation as if it had not been parented before any transformations were applied. This option can be useful in specific scenarios where you want the child to maintain its current transformation but no longer be affected by the parent's transformations.

Choose the appropriate option based on your needs. If you want the child's object to be completely independent of the parent, use "Clear Parent." If you want to keep the child's transformations but still remove the parent-child relationship, use "Clear and Keep Transformation (Clear Track)." If you need to maintain the child's transformations but eliminate the parent's influence, use "Clear Parent Inverse." By understanding these options, you can effectively manage parent-child relationships and detach objects as needed in your Blender projects.

SAVING, OPENING, AND APPENDING.

Saving and accessing files is indeed a crucial function in any software, and Blende provides efficient ways to manage project files. To save a file in Blender, you can use the Shift + Ctrl + S hotkey or choose File > Save As from the main header. In earlier versions of Blender, the F2 hotkey could be used for the same purpose. **Blender's approach to the Save dialog may seem different from traditional operating systems, and this is due to several reasons:**

1. Non-blocking interface principle: Blender follows a non-blocking interface principle, which means that it avoids using modal dialog boxes that block the user from interacting with the rest of the software. Instead of using a separate Save dialog box that pauses your workflow, Blender incorporates the file-saving functionality into its own interface, ensuring a smoother and uninterrupted user experience.
2. Consistent File Browser Interface: Blender uses its own File Browser interface for saving and opening files. This decision ensures that the file management functionality remains consistent across different platforms (Windows, Mac, and Linux). Regardless of the operating system, Blender's File Browser provides a unified and familiar experience for users.
3. Blender-specific features: The Blender File Browser offers additional features that are specific to Blender's workflow. It allows users to easily organize and manage their projects within Blender's file structure. Additionally, Blender's File Browser supports various Blender-specific file formats and features that may not be available in the default OS save dialogs.

By integrating the file-saving process into its interface and using its own file browser, Blender optimizes the user experience and ensures consistent functionality across different platforms. Blender's file management capabilities, combined with its rapid file reading and writing, contribute to a seamless workflow for users working on complex projects.

SAVINGS AFTER THE FIRST

Blender offers a convenient way to save evolving versions of your project without the need to manually rename the file each time.

To do this, follow these steps:

1. Press Shift + Ctrl + S or choose File > Save As from the main header to open the File Browser for saving your project.
2. In the File Browser, navigate to the folder where you want to save your project and enter a filename for the initial version (e.g., project_v1.blend).

3. Before clicking "Save," take note of the "Number" field located in the top-right corner of the File Browser. This field allows you to specify the version number that Blender will automatically increment for each subsequent save.
4. Click "Save" to save the initial version of your project with the chosen filename.
5. After making changes to your project and wanting to save a new version, simply use the Ctrl+S hotkey or choose File > Save from the main header.

Blender will automatically increase the version number and save the file with the new filename (e.g., project_v2.blend, project_t_v3.blend, and so on) without the need for manual renaming.

This method allows you to save evolving versions of your project quickly and easily, with each version being uniquely named based on the version number you specified in the "Number" field. It streamlines the process of keeping track of different iterations of your work, making it especially useful for larger and more complex projects.

OPENING A FILE

Indeed, opening a Blender file is a straightforward process. To open a Blend file, follow these simple steps:

1. Press Ctrl+O or choose File > Open from the main header to open the File Browser for loading a file.
2. In the File Browser, navigate to the folder where your ".blend files are located.
3. Left-click on the filename of the ".blend" file you wish to open.
4. If you want to load the selected file, click the "Open File" button in the top right corner of the File Browser.

Alternatively, if you are familiar with Blender's earlier versions, you can still use the Fl hotkey to open files. Additionally, if you have a wide display and want to quickly open a file without moving your mouse too far, you can simply double-click on the filename in the File Browser to load it. By following these steps, you can easily open ".blend" files and continue working on your projects in Blender.

APPENDING FROM AN EXTERNAL FILE

Correct! Blender's Append function is the perfect solution when you want to use a model or any other asset from one ".blend" file in another scenario or project. **Here's how you can use the append function:**

1. Press Shift+Fl or choose File > Append from the main header to open the File Browser for appending items from an external file.
2. In the File Browser, navigate to the ".blend" file that contains the character or asset you want to use.
3. Click on the ".blend" file to open it and explore its contents.
4. Inside the ".blend" file, you will see a list of various data blocks, including objects, materials, textures, animations, and more.
5. Select the data block you want to append from the external file. For example, if you want to import a character, model, select the object associated with that character.
0. Once you select the data block, click the "Append" button in the top right corner of the File Browser.

By using the Append function, you can bring in specific data blocks from one ".blend" file into your current project, effectively incorporating the character or asset into your scenario.

This way, you can reuse assets, save time, and avoid starting from scratch when working on complex projects. Blender's ability to precisely import selected data blocks along with their associated elements makes it a powerful and versatile tool for 3D modeling and animation.

REVIEW QUESTIONS

1. How do you establish a parent-child relationship between objects in Blender?
2. What are the three options available when detaching a child's object from its parent?
3. How can you save evolving versions of your project without manually renaming the files in Blender?
4. How does the Append function in Blender allow you to use assets from one ".blend" file in another project?

SUMMARY

Organizing objects in Blender using parent-child relationships is a powerful way to manage a collection of objects with a clear hierarchy. By selecting the objects you want to be children and designating the last object as the parent, you can establish a parent-child relationship using the Ctrl+P shortcut or the Object > Parent > Set Parent option.

This hierarchical relationship allows you to control all the child objects collectively through the parent object, making it easier to manage complex scenes, animations, and rigs. Detaching a child object from its parent in Blender is a simple process achieved by selecting the child object and using the Alt+P shortcut or the Object > Parent > Clear option.

Blender offers three options to clear the parent-child relationship: "Clear Parent" removes the relationship completely; "Clear and Keep Transformation (Clear Track)" preserves the child's transformations; and "Clear Parent Inverse clears the parent's transformation from the child while maintaining its current transformations.

Blender provides efficient file-saving and opening methods to manage project files. To save a file, you can use the Shift+Ctrl+S shortcut or File > Save As, while opening a file is done by pressing Ctrl+O or choosing File> Open. Blender's Append function allows you to incorporate assets from one ".blend file into another project by selecting the desired data block and clicking the "Append" button. This functionality streamlines the workflow, allowing users to reuse assets, save time, and avoid starting from scratch when working on complex 3D modeling and animation projects.

PART 2: SCULPTING YOUR VISION IN 3D

People don't use a 3D computer graphics program just to play around with its interface; they use it because they want to create something impressive. The process begins with designing various models, such as characters, settings, props, text, and logos. In this section, we will guide you on how to create meshes, curves, surfaces, and text objects in Blender. These elements serve as the foundation for crafting stunning visuals in computer graphics.

In addition to modeling, lighting and materials play a crucial role in the success or failure of a scene. Therefore, this section also provides insights on effectively setting up lights and utilizing Blender's manufacturing system to ensure that the models you create look their best.

CHAPTER 7: CRAFTING WITH MESHES: FROM SIMPLE TO COMPLEX

Virtually all computer-generated 3D animation, from video games and architectural visualization to television advertisements and feature-length movies, is built on polygon-based meshes. Meshes are normally simpler to manipulate and handle for computers than other types of 3D objects, like NURBS or metaballs. When it comes down to it, the computer hardware actually converts even NURBS and metaballs into a mesh of triangles, a process known as tessellation. Meshes serve as the main building block for the majority of Blender's functionality for several reasons. Whether you're designing a small scene, an animated character, or replicating water pouring into a sink, you'll eventually be dealing with meshes. If you're not cautious, working with meshes can get a bit overwhelming because you must manage each vertex that makes up your model, and the more complex the mesh, the more vertices you have to keep track of.

The majority of the fundamentals for working with meshes in edit mode are covered in Chapter 4. However, this chapter introduces you to several useful Blender features that enable you to deal with complicated models without becoming suffocated by an overwhelming vertex soup. These features will help you work more efficiently and effectively with meshes, making your 3D modeling experience in Blender more enjoyable and productive.

PUSHING VERTICES

A mesh is made up of a collection of vertices and edges. These edges join together to create faces with three or four sides. When you go into Edit mode on a mesh, you can alter its vertices (or edges or faces) using the same standard grab (G), rotate (R), and scale (S) tools, as well as the very helpful extrude (E) tool that operates on all objects. These fundamental actions form the basis of 3D modeling, and some modelers playfully refer to themselves as "vert pushers" because, at times, it may seem like all they do is move tiny points around on a screen until things appear correct. Of course, modeling involves more than just pushing vertices.

There are two primary methodologies when you want to start modeling, and they are:

- **Box Modeling:** Box modeling is a technique where you start with a basic shape like a box or cube and gradually refine it by adding edges and manipulating them. It is similar to sculpting, as you subtract and cut into the shape to create more detail. If you need to add volume, you extrude edges or faces outward, and if you need to reduce volume, you extrude inward or pull edges in. While box modeling is a good starting point, you need to be cautious to avoid ending up with blocky models.
- **Sculpting:** Sculpting is a more organic and free-form approach to modeling. It allows you to directly manipulate the surface of the mesh using brushes, just like sculpting with real clay. This method is ideal for creating organic shapes and intricate details. Sculpting

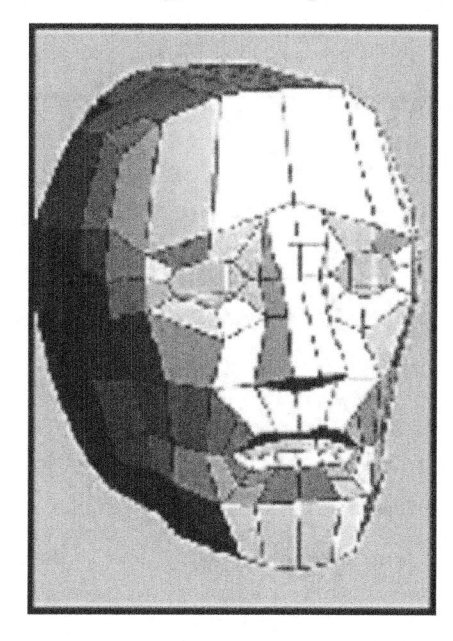

tools in Blender offer a variety of brushes and options for refining the surface of your model.

- **Point-for-point:** Point-for-point t modeling involves placing each vertex of the model deliberately and creating the connecting edges and faces. It is like drawing in three dimensions and appeals to those with a drawing background or a preference for control. This method allows for precise control over the final look and reduces the risk of boxy shapes. However, beginners may tend to add too much detail too quickly, so caution is required.

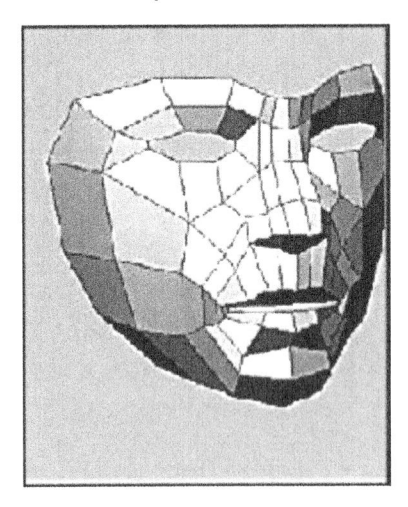

As a modeler, it's common to develop a preference for one method over another based on personal workflow and the specific requirements of a project. However, recognizing the advantages of both boxes modeling and sculpting allows you to leverage the strengths of each technique and even combine them for more efficient and creative modeling. Using the point-to-point technique, which is often associated with box modeling, allows you to quickly establish the basic shape and structure of the model. It provides a solid foundation to work from and gives you a clear outline of the model's form. This approach is well-suited for creating precise and controlled shapes, especially when dealing with man-made objects or architectural elements.

On the other hand, sculpting is ideal for creating organic and natural shapes, where more artistic freedom and creativity are re- quired. Sculpting tools allow you to add intricate details and refine the surface of the model with the ease of sculpting with real clay. This method is excellent for characters, creatures, and any object that demands a more organic and expressive form. By combining both techniques, you can start with the speed and structure of box modeling to establish the overall shape and then switch to sculpting to add finer details, organic features, and expressive elements. This hybrid approach enables you to take advantage of the strengths of each method, giving you more flexibility in your modeling process. Ultimately, the choice between box modeling and sculpting, or a combination of both, depends on the specific needs and goals of your project. Being proficient in both techniques allows you to adapt to various modeling challenges and achieve the best possible results in your 3D creations.

WORKING WITH LOOPS AND RINGS

It does not matter which method you use—box modeling or point-for-point modeling—it is important to also understand the concept of loops and rings to make things much easier for you.

UNDERSTANDING EDGE LOOPS AND FACE LOOPS

An edge loop refers to a sequence of connected edges that form a continuous path, where the initial and final edges are linked to each other. This complete loop is commonly known as a "good edge loop.

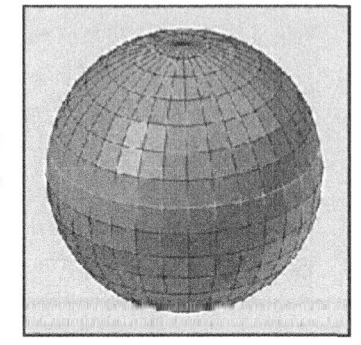

However, it's important to understand the concept of a "badedge loop as well. It's not entirely accurate to label these loops as bad because they may consist of a series of edges that don't connect at the beginning and end of the loop. Instead, edge loops that terminate before reconnecting to their starting point are better described as "terminating edge loops."

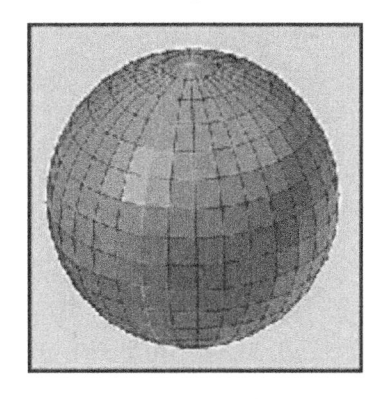

Most of the time, you want to avoid any terminating edge loops in the model. However, you can't always do without them; you might need them to control the flow of edges on the surface of the mesh.

To better understand the distinctions between closed edge loops and terminating edge loops, follow these steps in Blender:

1. Open Blender and create a UV sphere by pressing Shift+A, selecting Mesh, and then UV Sphere. Leave the settings at their default values for rings, segments, and radii.
2. Enter Edit mode by pressing Tab. To select one of the sphere's horizontal edges, hold Alt and right-click on it. This edge loop will encircle the sphere-like latitude lines on a globe, representing a closed edge loop.

1. To deselect everything, press A.
2. Next, hold Alt and right-click on a vertical edge. This selection will include the vertices that connect to the sphere's top and bottom poles, or junctions. This edge loop is an example of a terminating edge loop.

Edge loops are technically defined by four-point poles, which are vertices where four edges intersect. This means that a vertical edge loop won't always complete a full circle. To help visualize this, imagine driving through a metropolis while following an edge loop. At a four-way intersection, you have the option to turn left, right, or go straight. To stay in the loop, you must continue straight ahead. However, if you encounter a fork in the road (a three-point pole) or a five-way (or more) intersection, you can't always to be certain that going straight will keep you in the loop. This means that the loop is going to terminate at the intersection. This is why the horizontal edge loop is made up of four-point poles and connects to itself, while the vertical loop stops at the top and bottom of the sphere with all the edges gathered in one junction.

In addition to edge loops, it is also possible to have face loops. A face loop is composed of the faces located between two parallel edge loops. In the case of a UV sphere, the image below illustrates a face loop selected on a sphere.

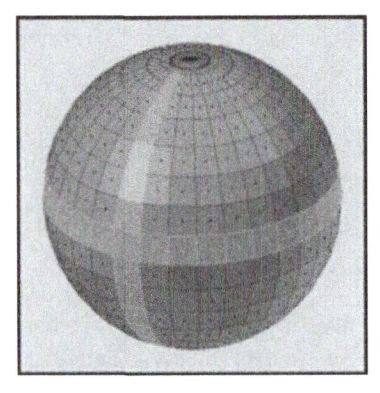

In Blender, you can select face loops using the Face selection mode, similar to how you choose edge loops in the Vertex or Edge selection modes. To select a face loop, enter Edit mode and press Ctrl+Tab to switch to face selection mode. To choose a loop, hold Alt and right-click on a face in the desired direction. For example, to select a horizontal face loop on the UV sphere, Alt+right-click on the left or right side of one of the faces in that loop. Similarly, to select a vertical face loop, Alt+right-click on the top or bottom of a face.

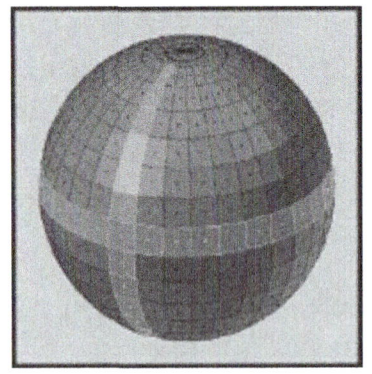

SELECTING EDGE RINGS

Consider the scenario where you only want to select the edges that connect two parallel edge loops, as illustrated in the image below, rather than an entire edge loop or a face loop. In Blender, this selection is referred to as an "edge ring."

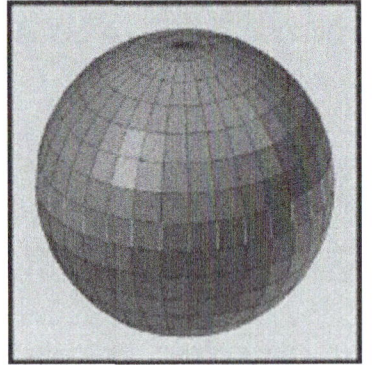

To select an edge ring, enter Edit mode and switch to Edge Select mode by pressing Ctrl+Tab and choosing "Edges."

Then, using the hotkey sequence Ctrl+Alt+right-click, you can select the edge ring. It's important to note that this hotkey sequence only works in Edge Select mode. If you try to use it in Vertex Select or Face Select mode, it will select a face loop instead. By using this technique, you can easily and precisely select the edges that form an edge ring, which can be useful for certain modeling tasks and just me in Blender.

Since you can use the rings and the loops to choose groups of vertices in orderly fashion, you will be saving a lot of time when modeling.

CREATING NEW LOOPS

When you want to add detail to a model, the ability to create additional loops becomes incredibly useful. With the "Loop Cut" feature, you can easily add more detail to your mesh. You can access this feature from the Tool Shelf under "Add" > "Loop Cut and Slide" or by pressingly using the hotkey Ctrl+R. When you activate the loop cut, your cursor will display a pink or purple line, indicating where you can add an edge loop. Left-click to confirm the cut's location, and right-click to cancel the process. Once the loop cut is created, the "Edge Slide" feature is automatically enabled, allowing you to move the loop over the surface of your mesh by moving your mouse. Left-click to set the loop's position. You can perform multiple parallel loop cuts at once using the Loop Cut tool (Ctrl+R) and scrolling your mouse wheel. Alternately, you can change the number of loops in your cut by pressing Page Up and Page Down if your mouse lacks a scroll wheel or if you prefer using your keyboard. Keep in mind that if you add multiple loops at once, Blender skips the Edge Slide capability, as moving multiple parallel edges simultaneously is counterproductive.

In addition to loop cuts, Blender also offers other types of cuts through the Knife tool, accessed by pressing K. While using the knife tool, select the edges or faces you want to cut, then left-click and move the mouse pointer over your model while still holding down.

A line will appear, and when you release K, Blender adds vertices wherever that line intersects the chosen edges.

The Last Operator panel of the Tool Shelf features a drop-down menu titled Type that provides additional options for the cuts:

1. Exact: This creates connected vertices precisely at the points where the knife tool's line intersects the chosen edges.
2. Midpoint: This creates connected vertices at the midpoint of the edges the knife tool intersects.
3. Multicut: Similar to "Midpoints," but it creates edges based on the number of cuts specified, spacing the new vertices equally along the edges the knife tool's line intersects.

It's important to note that the knife tool only operates on the currently selected edges, unlike the loop cut. To make the edges visible while cutting, consider switching to wireframe view or deactivating the option labeled "Limit Selection to Visible." Mastering these cutting techniques in Blender will significantly enhance your modeling capabilities, allowing you to add detail and refine your meshes with precision.

SIMPLIFYING YOUR LIFE AS A MODELER WITH MODIFIERS

When working with complex models that have a large number of vertices, managing and modifying meshes can become challenging. Even with the use of loops and rings, keeping track of vertices and making changes to the model can quickly become a time-consuming and tedious task. Whether you need to add more vertices to achieve smoother surfaces or ensure symmetry in your model, it can become overwhelming. Fortunately, Blen der offers a powerful feature called modifiers" that can help alleviate the monotony. Despite their broad name, modifiers are an incredibly useful tool that can save you time and reduce stress by delegating repetitive tasks to the computer. Modifiers allow you to apply smoothing to vertices, make models symmetric, and perform various other adjustments with ease. One of the significant advantages of modifiers is that they are non-destructive. This means that applying a modifier won't permanently alter the original mesh. You can easily add or remove modifiers, and the changes will only be applied visually without affecting the underlying geometry. This flexibility allows you to experiment freely and go back to the unmodified version at any time.

To access modifiers in Blender, navigate to the Modifiers area of the Properties editor. Click on the "Add Modifier" button to view a list of available modifiers that you can apply to your mesh. Each modifier serves a specific purpose and can enhance your modeling process significantly. By utilizing modifiers in Blender, you can speed up your workflow, maintain flexibility, and focus more on the creative aspects of 3D modeling without getting bogged down by repetitive tasks. The Modifiers section in Blender provides a powerful toolset to enhance and manipulate your models efficiently.

The following are some commonly used modifiers and their functionalities:

1. **Array Modifier:** The Array modifier creates duplicates of your object in a linear or radial arrangement. You can control the count, offset, and rotation of the duplicates. This is

useful for creating repetitive patterns, arrays of objects, or distributing objects along a path.
2. **Bevel Modifier:** The Bevel modifier adds beveled edges to your model, rounding sharp corners and edges. This helps to create smoother and more realistic shapes. You can adjust the bevel width and segments for varying levels of smoothness.
3. **Subdivision Surface Modifier:** The Subdivision Surface Modifier smoothens the mesh by subdividing the faces, resulting in a more detailed and refined surface. This is commonly used to add smoothness and complexity to models, especially when starting with a low-poly base mesh.
4. **Mirror Modifier:** The Mirror Modifier creates a symmetrical version of your model by duplicating and mirroring it across a defined axis. This is particularly useful for modeling symmetrical objects like characters or architectural elements.
5. **Solidify Modifier:** The Solidify modifier adds thickness to a model by extruding its faces. This is useful for giving thickness to thin surfaces, like walls or shells, and for creating 3D-printable objects.
6. **Boolean Modifier:** The Boolean modifier performs Boolean operations like union, difference, or intersection between multiple objects. This allows you to combine or cut out shapes to create complex forms.

Remember that the order in which you stack modifiers is important, as each modifier relies on the output of the preceding one. You can change the order of modifiers by using the up and down arrow buttons. Additionally, you can collapse or extend modifier blocks by clicking the downward triangle next to each modifier's name. To delete a modifier, click the X in the top-right corner of the block.

Utilizing modifiers in Blender offers a non-destructive and flexible approach to modeling, allowing you to experiment and refine your designs without permanently altering the original mesh. By mastering these modifiers, you can enhance your 3D modeling workflow and create more intricate and impressive models more efficiently.

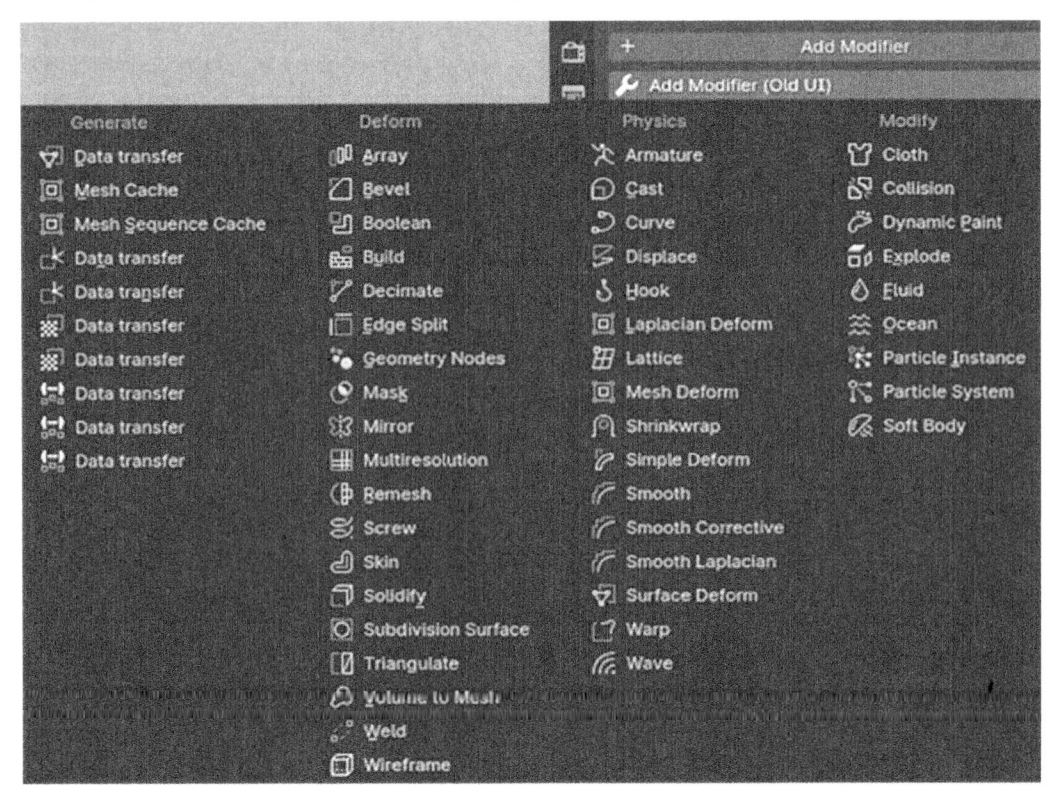

Between the field for the modifier name and the stacking order buttons, you'll find three or four extra buttons. Moving from left to right, the first three buttons control the activation of the modifier for rendering (camera icon), visibility in object mode (eye icon), and visibility in edit mode (editing cube icon).

Disabling a modifier after adding it to the stack, instead of removing and re-adding it, serves several purposes. It allows you to compare the object's appearance with and without the modifier, make edits to the original mesh without the modifier's influence, and optimize computer performance by enabling the modifier only during rendering. The buttons next to each modifier's name facilitate these functionalities.

Certain modifiers, such as Array, feature an extra button at the end of the button block, marked by an inverted triangle icon. Enabling this button applies the modifier to the editing cage during edit mode. The editing cage represents the initial input mesh before any modification is applied. By enabling this button, you can not only see the effects of the modifier in Edit mode but also select and make limited adjustments to the geometry generated by the modifier.

Among all modifiers, the Apply and Copy buttons are the only two that are universally present. Clicking the Apply button results in the immediate application of the modifier's modifications to the original object. To align the original mesh with the modified results, applying the modifier introduces new vertices and edges to the mesh while removing the modifier from the stack.

It's worth noting that the Apply button stands as the sole exception to the nondestructive nature of modifiers, as it deviates from the principle of not altering the original object in any manner. By utilizing Copy but to n, a replicated version of the modifier is generated and inserted into the stack after the original one.

While this function may not be frequently employed, it proves useful when you want to apply a modifier twice, such as doubling up on a bevel operation to achieve a smoother and more rounded edge compared to a single bevel.

DOING HALF THE WORK AND STILL LOOKING GOOD WITH THE MIRROR MODIFIER

When working with the mirror modifier, there are times when your model may not look perfect, especially when trying to create symmetrical objects like faces where one half does not match the other half. However, as a 3D computer artist using Blender, you have a powerful tool at your disposal to avoid the trial-and-error process and let the computer handle the symmetry for you.

In Blender, the Mirror modifier can be found in the Modifiers Properties menu under the Add Modifier section. The image below illustrates the available buttons and options for this particular modification.

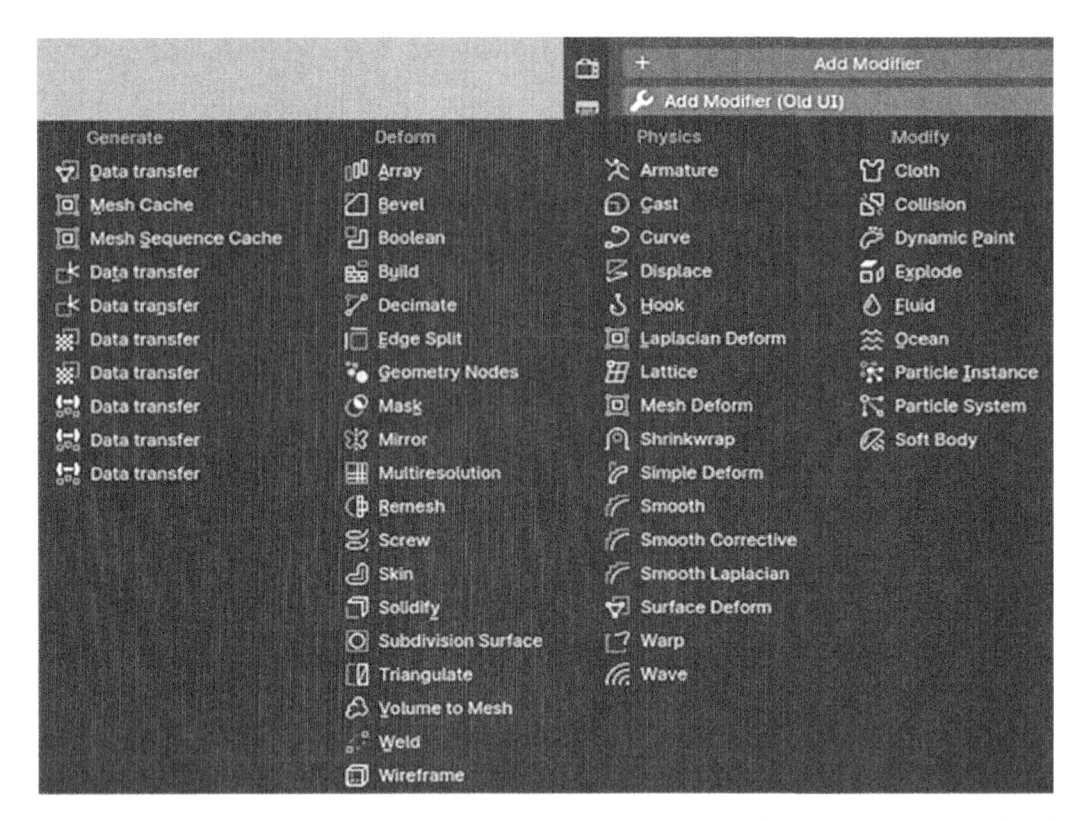

The Mirror modifier in Blender allows you to duplicate an object's mesh data by flipping it along its local X, Y, or Z axes, either individually or in combination. This creates a mirrored copy of the object, making it easy to achieve symmetrical models. What makes the mirror modifier even more impressive is its ability to seamlessly merge the vertices along the central seam of the object, creating the appearance of a single, cohesive piece. The level of proximity required for vertices to be merged along the seam can be adjusted by modifying the "Merge Limit" value.

MERGE LIMIT VALUE.

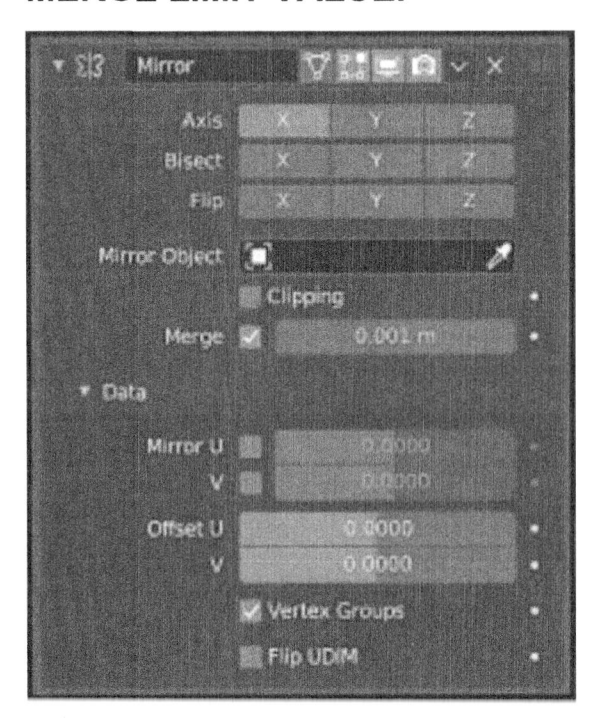

The axis or axes along which your object is mirrored can be determined by selecting the corresponding check boxes for X, Y, and Z. In most cases, the default setup using the local X-axis is sufficient. It is often recommended to enable the Clipping opt ion, which ensures that the merged vertices are constrained to the plane of mirroring once the Merge Limit setting is met. Essentially, when mirroring along the X-axis, all vertices on the YZ plane are required to remain on that plane. This function is great when working on cars or characters, as it prevents you from unintentionally tearing a hole through the middle of your model when you adjust.

its shape with the Proportional Edit Tool (O). Of course, you can temporarily deactivate this checkbox if you need to move a vertex away from the center line. Next, you can use vertex groups to assign vertices within a mesh into arbitrary groups.

No Groups   **Object Mode**   **Edit Mode**

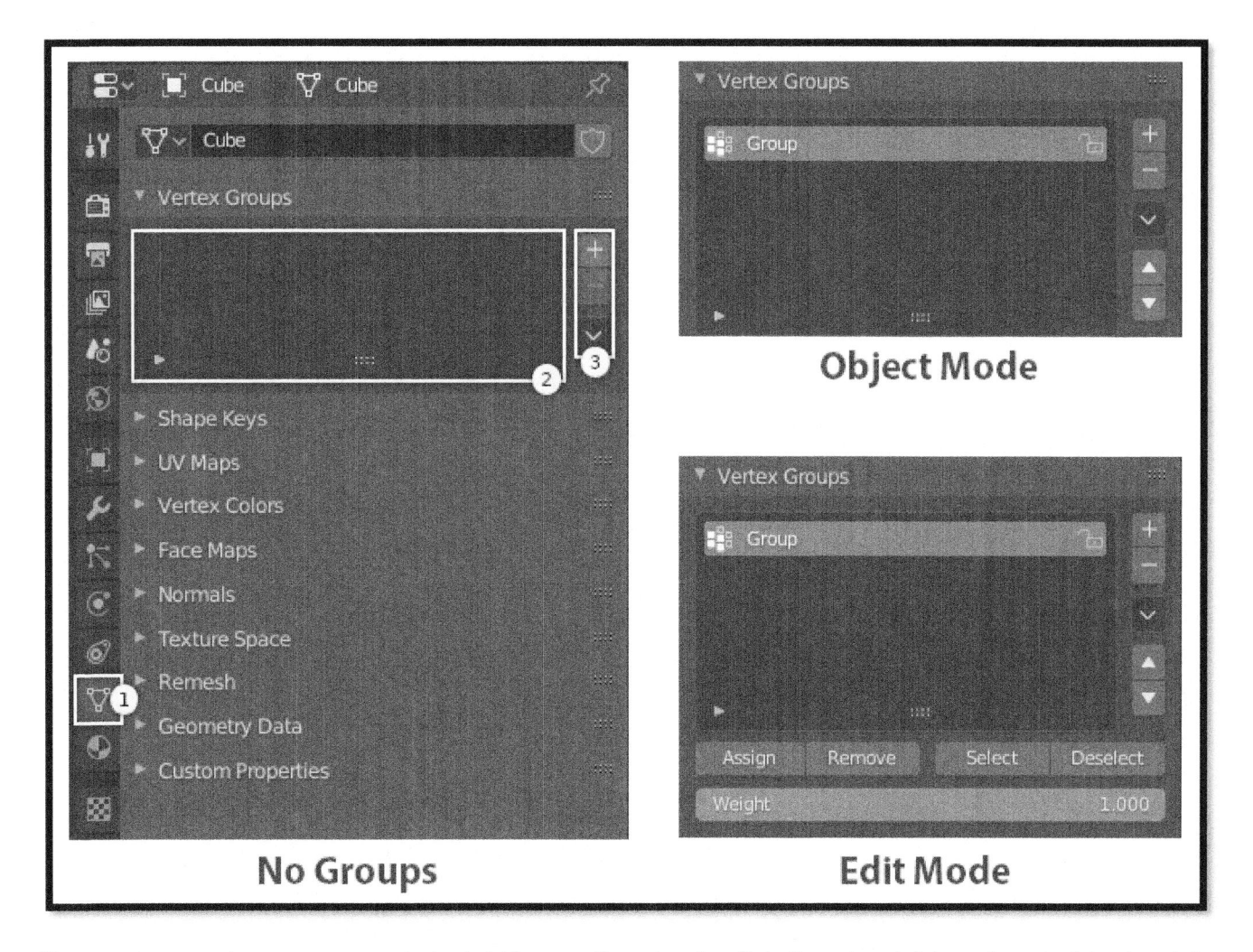

To create a vertex group most straightforwardly, simply click the plus (+) icon located to the right of the vertex groups list in the Object Data Properties panel while in Edit mode. This will create a new vertex group named "Group." Next, select the desired vertex groups in your mesh and click the "Assign" button located below the vertex groups list. Congratulations! You have successfully created a vertex group.

To understand how the Vertex Groups checkbox functions in the Mirror modifier, let's suppose that you have selected specific vertices and assigned them to a group named "Group.R" which represents the right-hand side vertices. You have also created another group named "Group.L" for the corresponding vertices on the left-hand side. However, since you have not yet applied the mirror modifier, you currently have no way to assign vertices to "Group.L." By enabling the Vertex Groups checkbox, an interesting outcome occurs. The newly generated vertices on the left side, which correspond to the "Group.R" vertices, are automatically assigned to "Group.L." Remarkably, this result is achieved even without applying the modifier. This behavior also applies to other modifiers that rely on vertex group names, such as Armature.

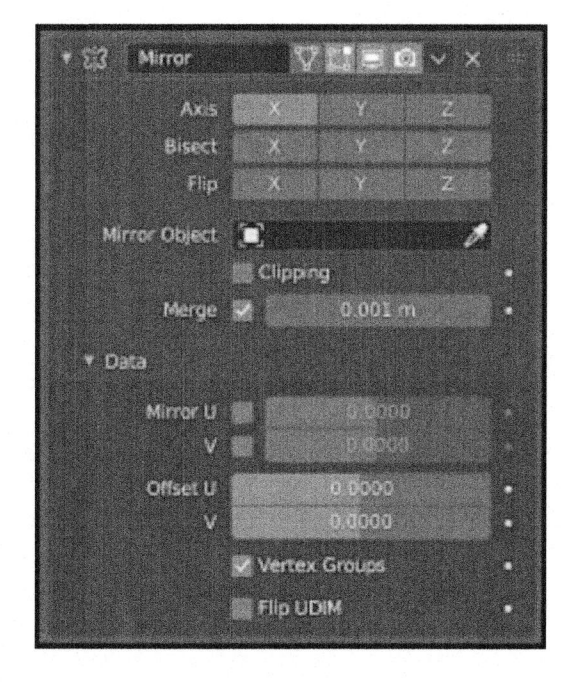

Referencing the image above, the U and V checkboxes under the "Textures" label in the Mirror modifier serve a similar purpose as the Vertex Groups checkbox. However, in this case, they pertain to texture coordinates, also known as UV coordinates. A detailed explanation of UV coordinates can be found in a different chapter of this book, but in essence, they enable the mapping of a two-dimensional image onto a three-dimensional surface.

Enabling these checkboxes in the modifier mirrors the texture coordinates within the UV/Image Editor, potentially reducing your texture unwrapping time by half. To observe the results of these checkboxes, ensure you have a texture loaded and your model unlocked.

wrapped, then access the Properties region in the UV/Image Edit or by left-clicking the "Modified" button (View > Image > Properties or N). It's great to appreciate the power of non-destructive modifiers!

The "Mirror Object" text field at the bottom of the Mirror modifier serves as the final option. By definition, the mirror modifier uses the object's origin as the point of reflection. However, you have the flexibility to choose any other object's origin as the reference point for mirroring. Simply click in the "Mirror Object field and select or input the name of another object present in your scene. This functionality allows you to utilize an empty object (or any other object) as a dynamic origin. It becomes particularly useful when animating a cartoon character splitting in half to bypass an obstacle, for instance, and seamlessly rejoining on the other side.

SMOOTHING THINGS OUT WITH THE SUBDIVISION SURFACE MODIFIER

The subdivision surface modifier is another often-used modifier, particularly for organic models. It is also known as the Subsurf modifier by veteran Blender users. If you have used another 3D modeling program in the past, you might be familiar with the terms sub-ds or sub-divides for subdivision surfaces. If you are unfamiliar with subdivided surfaces, the idea is as follows: Blender subdi-vides the faces on a given mesh into a set number of cuts, or subdivision levels, that you choose. In most cases, you will want to use 1 to 3 subdivision levels. To achieve a seamless transition from one face to the next, Blender moves the boundaries of these subdivided faces closer together. With each subsequent level of subdivision, the result is that a cube with a Subdivision Surface modifier starts to resemble a ball more and more.

It is important to note that subdivision surfaces are treated as modifiers, allowing you to increase the level of detail in your geometry without the need to manually edit each additional vertex. In the previous cube example, even at a subdivision level of 6, you can manipulate the shape by working with just the eight vertices that constitute the original cube when in Edit mode.

Subdivision surfaces are widely used in high-end 3D animations precisely because they enable efficient manipulation of numerous vertices using only a small subset of them. By using a cage, which is a less dense or low-polygon mesh, you can easily control the smooth, organic curves of dense geometry with greater ease.

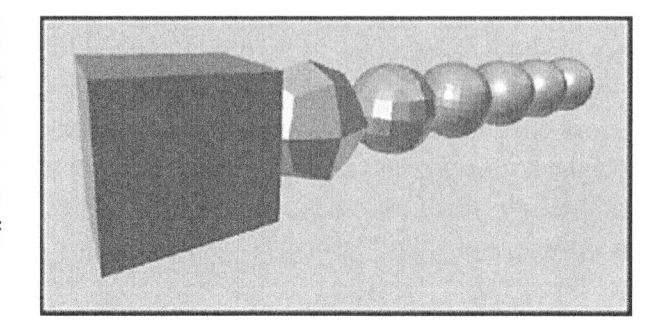

To better understand the potential results of using the Subdivision Surface modifier, let's apply it to Suzanne using the following steps:

1. Start by adding a monkey mesh to the scene by pressing Shift + A and selecting Mesh > Monkey.
2. Next, enable smooth rendering for the monkey's appearance by locating the ToolShelf panel and clicking on the Shading tab. Then, select the smooth option.
3. At this stage, Suzanne will look somewhat smoother than her initial faceted appearance but still retain a blocky look.
4. To achieve a more natural and organic look, add a subdivision surface modifier to the monkey. To do this, navigate to the Modifiers Properties panel and click on the Add Modifier button. Then, select Subdivision Surface (you can also use the shortcut Ctrl + 1).
5. Instantly, you'll notice a significant improvement in Suzanne's appearance. Despite her cartoonish proportions, she will appear much smoother and more refined. Feel free to increase the Levels value in the Subdivision Surface modifier to see how Suzanne becomes even smoother. However, be careful not to set the levels too high (above 3), as this may strain your computer's performance if it is not fast enough.
6. Switch to Edit mode by pressing Tab, and observe that the original mesh acts as the control cage for the subdivided mesh.
7. By using the grab (G), rotate (R), scale (S), and extrude (E) tools in Edit mode, you can directly influence the appearance of the modified mesh within the control cage.

These steps will allow you to experience the transformative effect of the Subdivision Surface modifier on Suzanne's appearance and explore how editing the control cage can further shape the modified mesh.

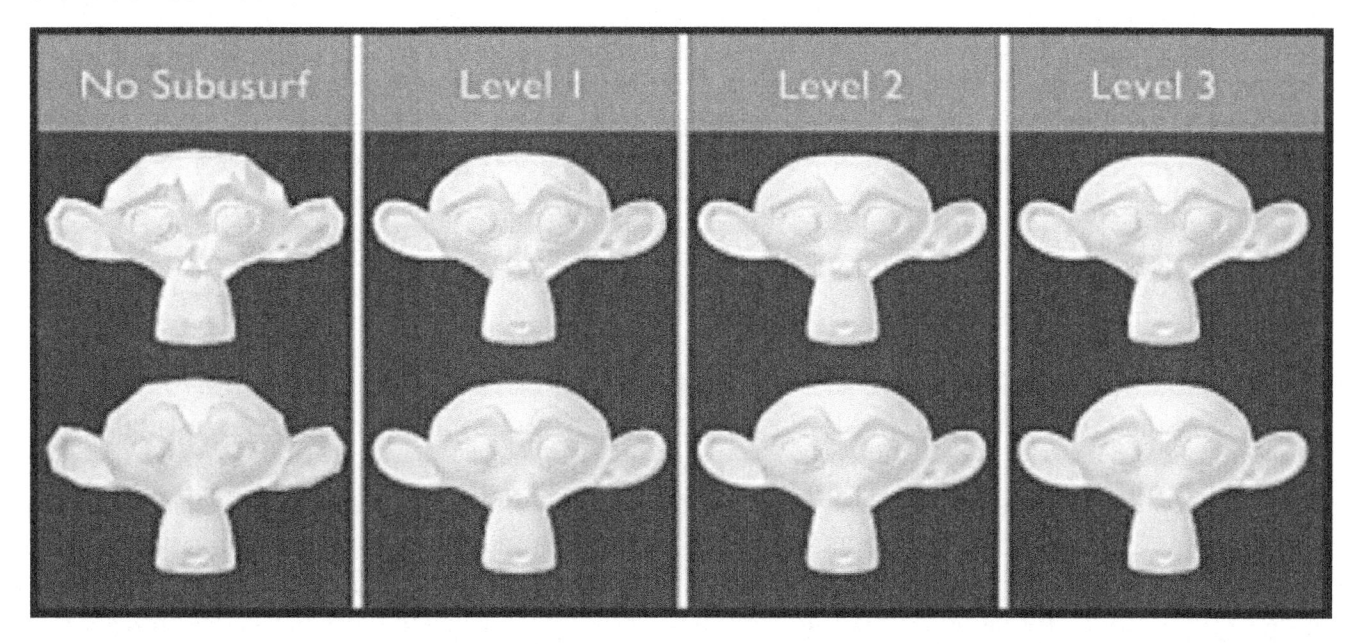

Although the Subdivision Surface modifier is a powerful tool, it offers only a limited number of options within the modifier stack. The Subdivision Surface modifier block can be found in the Modifiers Properties panel, as depicted in the provided image. The first choice you have to make is between the Catmull-Clark subdivision and the Simple subdivision. Catmull-Clark subdivision is the default option, and it effectively subdivides and smoothens your mesh, delivering the expected organic smoothness. On the other hand, simple subdivision behaves more like repeatedly applying the Subdivide operation in Edit mode. It increases the number of vertices in your mesh, but it does not achieve the same level of natural smoothness as the Catmull-Clark approach. Having both options is advantageous since the simple subdivision method may prove useful in certain situations where a straightforward subdivide is preferable.

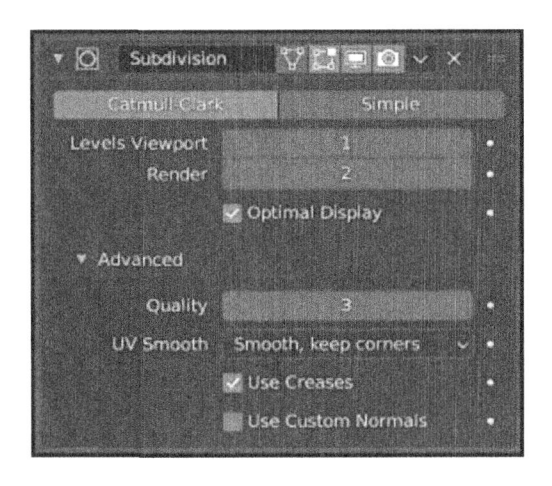

To control the level of subdivision on your model, you can adjust the parameters under "Subdivisions." The first parameter, called "View," determines the number of subdivisions applied to your mesh in the 3D view. It can be set to a whole number between 1 and Typically, people prefer to keep the "View" value at 1 to ensure a responsive and fast 3D view. However, there are instances where you first increase it to 2 or 3 to get a rough idea of the final appearance of the model. After evaluating the results, you can usually reduce the "View" value back to 1 or even 0.

In addition to the "View" parameter, there is another input labeled Render" located under the "Subdivisions" section. This value determines the level of subdivision applied to your model when generating the final version of your scene or animation in Blender. It is independent of the "View" setting and can have the same range of values. Technically, the "Rende r" value is set higher than the "View" value because the goal is to achieve smoother and higher-quality models in the final render. You can adjust the "Render" value within the range available, which is the same as that of the View" value.

In my workflow, which often involves complex projects, we rarely find the need to go beyond a level of 3 for the "Render" value. However, this may vary depending on the specific requirements and complexity of your work. When it comes to texturing, you have the option to enable the "Subdivide UVs" check box. This feature allows you to add additional geometry to your UV map without the need to apply the modifier, similar to how the U and V checkboxes work in the Mirror modifier. By enabling this option, you can save time while preparing your first node for texturing. The "Subdivide UVs" check box is turned on by default because it consistently proves to be a helpful function. Furthermore, in the UV/Image Editor, you can see the results of enabling this feature by turning on the "Modified" check box, just like you would with the U and V options in the Mirror modifier. This allows you to easily observe the outcomes of the "Subdivide UVs" check box.

In my workflow, we typically keep the "Optimal Display" check box selected at all times. This option is particularly useful when viewing the model in wireframe mode because it hides the additional edges generated by the modifier. When working on complex scenes in wireframe mode, hiding these edges can greatly improve clarity and understanding. The effect of enabling the "Optimal Display" option can be seen in the provided image, which demonstrates its impact on a Suzanne model with three levels of subdivision. By concealing the extra edges, the model appears smoother and cleaner in wireframe view, making it easier to work with and analyze.

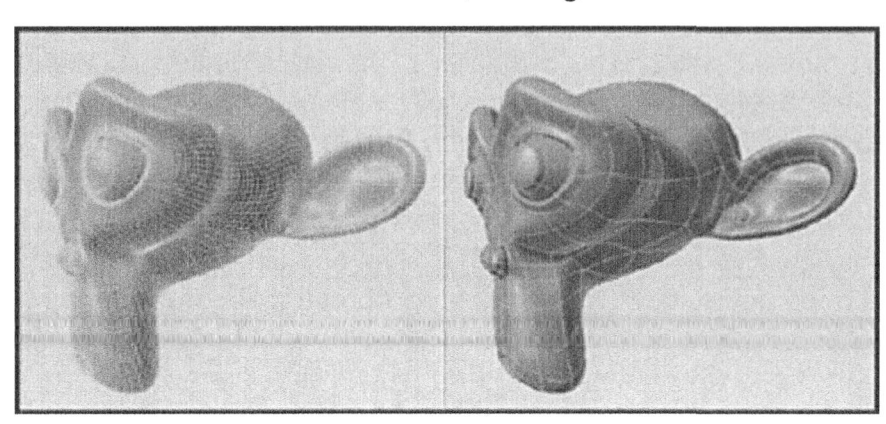

USING THE POWER OF ARRAYS.

The array modifier in Blender is one of the most popular and enjoyable modifiers to use. In its most basic use, this modifier recycles the mesh a predetermined number of times and arranges the copies so that they are uniformly spaced along a line. For example, if you want to arrange rows of seats in a space to resemble a conference hall using a chair model, a great way to achieve this is by combining a few array modifiers. The screenshot we provided shows a scene of a conference hall with rows of seats created with Blender.

Here are the steps on how to create a similar scene:

- Start by creating a chair model.
- Add an array modifier to the chair model.
- In the Array modifier settings, set the count value to 10.
- Set the relative offset to X: 0, Y: 0, and Z: 0.2.
- Add another array modifier to the chair model.
- In the array modifier settings, set the count value to 10.
- Set the relative offset to X: 0, Y: 0, and Z: -0.2.
- Repeat steps 5 and 6 until you have created the desired number of rows of seats.

Once you have created the rows of seats, you can adjust the spacing between them by changing the relative offset value in the array modifier settings.

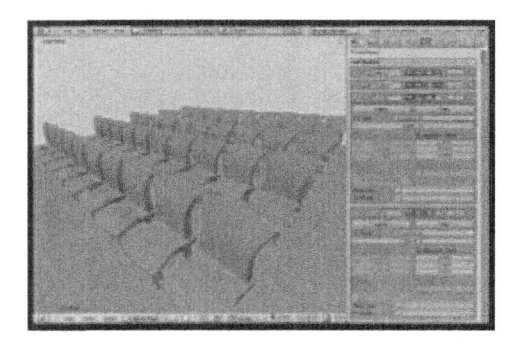

The array modifier in Blender offers a wide range of fantastic features that can be utilized in various creative ways. It allows you to offload time-consuming and repetitive tasks to the computer, which can sometimes make you feel inclined to take a more relaxed approach. For example, you can use the Array modifier to model objects like stairways, chain-link fences, or brick walls with ease.

However, the versatility of the array modifier extends beyond practical applications. It can also be used to create captivating abstract animations, intricate tentacle structures, and even rows of dancing robots. The possibilities are truly limitless when it comes to exploring the creative potential of the array modifier in Blender. The way the Array modifier handles offsets, or the distances between duplicates specified relative to one another, accounts for the majority of its strength.

Three different types of offsets are available with the array modifier:

- **Relative Offset:** This offset is the distance between the copies of the mesh, relative to each other.
- **Object Offset:** This offset is the distance between the copies of the mesh relative to the original object.
- **Constant Offset:** This offset is the distance between the copies of the mesh, relative to the cursor. The object offset and relative offset can be used in conjunction with one another by checking the corresponding boxes. The constant offset can be used alone.

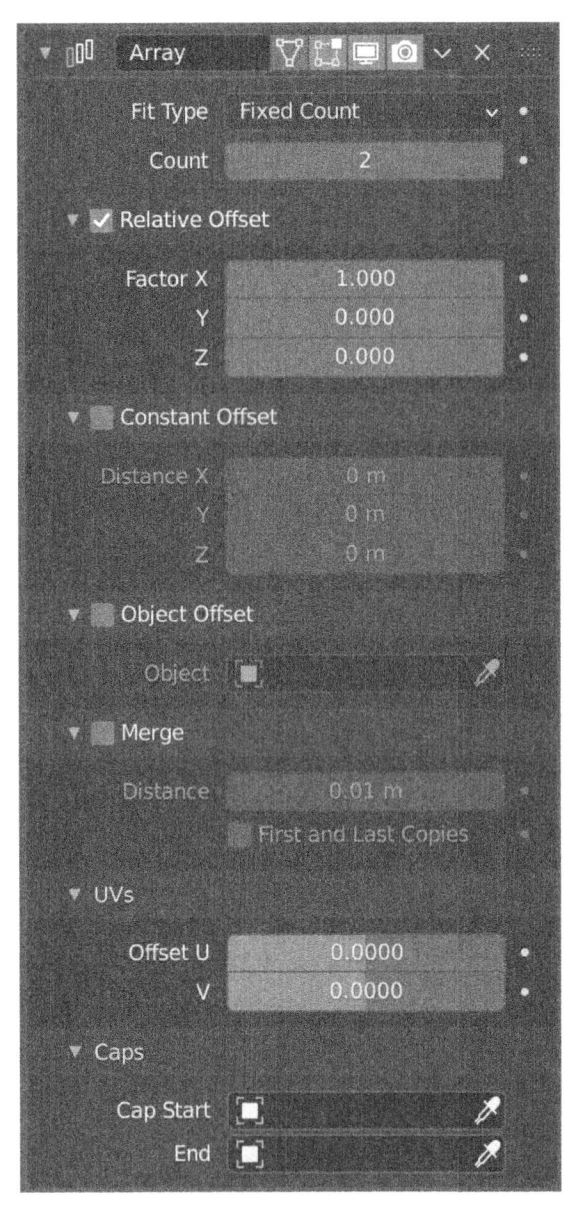

- **The constant offset:** This offset gives each replicated object in the array a fixed distance to travel. For example, setting the X value underneath this button to -5.0 will shift each of the duplicate's five units in the other X direction. The same happens when you specify values for the Y- and Z-axe offsets.
- **The Relative Offset:** Consider this offset to be a multiplication factor based on the object's width, height, and depth. For example, if the Z value is set to 1.0, each duplicated object in the array will be piled on top of the one below it, regardless of how big or small the object is. This type of offset is used by default when you first apply the array modifier.
- **The Object Offset feature** in Blender is incredibly versatile and one of my personal favorites. It allows you to use the position of any object you choose, such as an empty y, as a reference for the offset. This means that the dupli-cates created by the Array modifier will be positioned based on the distance between the offset object and the original mesh.

In simple terms, the Object Offset lets you use another object's position, rotation, and scale to control the placement and appearance of duplicates created by the Array modifier. This allows you to create complex patterns and animations easily.

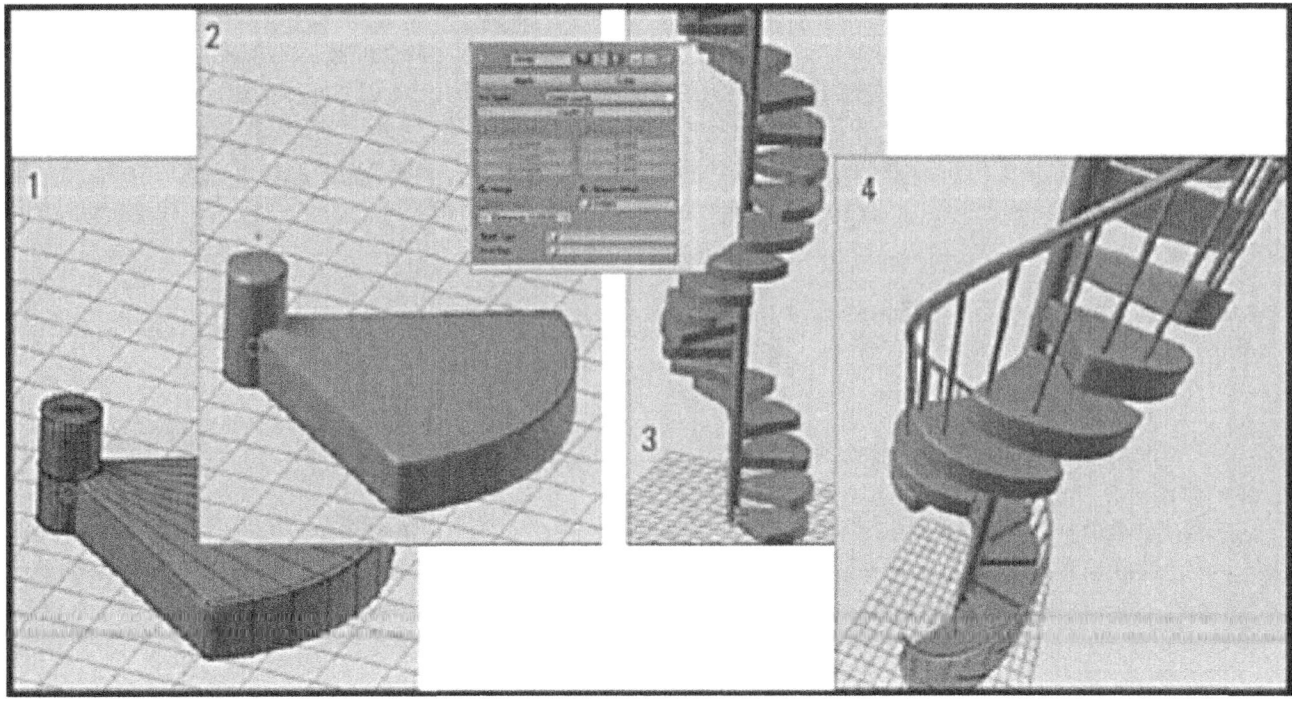

98

- Fixed: With this, you can enter the exact number of duplicates that you like.
- Fit length: This option generates the right number of duplicate objects to fit within the specified distance. This length is not exactly in full units, so keep that in mind. The length you select is multiplied by the original object's scale because it uses the local coordinate system of that item, as seen in the Properties region of the 3DView (N).
- Fit curve: If you select this option, the Object field just below it will allow you to enter the name of a curve object. When you do, Blender figures out how long that curve is and utilizes that length to fill in the gaps with duplicate objects. It's easy to quickly and cheaply make a connected metal chain like the one on the book cover by combining this option with a curve modifier.

REVIEW QUESTIONS

- How do you apply the Subdivision Surface modifier to Suzanne in Blender, and what is the purpose of using it?
- What are the two primary methodologies for starting modeling in Blender, and what are the differences between box modeling and sculpting?
- How can you control the level of subdivision on your model when using the Subdivision Surface modifier, and what are the typical "View" and "Rende r" values used?
- What are the three types of offsets available with the Array modifier in Blender, and how can they be used to create different patterns and arrangements of duplicate objects?

SUMMARY

The chapter discusses the use of the Subdivision Surface modifier in Blen der to achieve smooth and refined 3D models. It explains two primary methodologies for 3D modeling: box modeling and sculpting. The steps to apply the subdivision surface modifier to a model are provided, along with tips on controlling the level of subdivision for optimal results. Additionally, the chapter introduces the array modifier in Blender, which allows for replicating and arranging meshes in various creative ways.

It demonstrates how the array modifier can be used to create rows of seats in a conference hall and discusses the three types of offsets available: relative offset, object offset, and constant offset. The versatility of the Array modifier is emphasized, from practical applications like modeling stairways and fences to creating abstract animations and complex structures. The different options for controlling the number of duplicates, such as fixed count, fit length," and "fit curve," are also briefly explained.

CHAPTER 8: THE ART OF 3D SCULPTING

As computers have become more powerful, computer graphics artists seek greater control over the vertices in their dense, high-poly meshes with millions of vertices. While the Subdivision Surface modifier is useful for adding geometry and achieving organic shapes, it becomes challenging to make specific and detailed modifications. For instance, when sculpting a monster and wanting to create a scar on its face, applying the Subdivision Surface modifier becomes necessary to gain precise control over individual vertices for shaping the scar. By applying the modifier, the additional vertices become a permanent part of the model, allowing direct manipulation.

Despite various selection techniques and tools like the Proportional Edit Tool, handling and manipulating a large number of vertices, such as a million, can still be overwhelming and challenging to keep track of, even if the computer can handle the computational load. Therefore, applying the modification grants artists the necessary control over the vertices, making it easier to sculpt intricate details and achieve the desired results.

Fortunately, Blender supports multi-resolution meshes and sculpt mode, providing artists with sculpting capabilities in the virtual space of 3D. This section will guide users through the process of sculpting in Blender, taking advantage of these features to achieve more refined and detailed results.

ADDING BACKGROUND IMAGES IN THE 3D VIEWPORT

While Blender 3D is primarily focused on 3D modeling, 2D images also play an important role within the software. These images can be used for various purposes, such as serving as backgrounds or providing reference material for 3D scenes.

To add a 2D image as a background in Blender 3D, follow these steps:

1. Use the Shift+A keyboard shortcut to open the add menu within your 3D viewport.
2. Look for the "Im ages and Highlights" section in the Add menu.
3. Within this section, you will find options for adding images. You can choose between adding a reference image or a background image.
4. Select the image file you want to use and choose the "background option.
5. Click the blue "open image" button to import the image into Blender.
6. The imported 2D image will now serve as a background element in your 3D scene, providing additional visual context or reference material for your modeling or animation work.

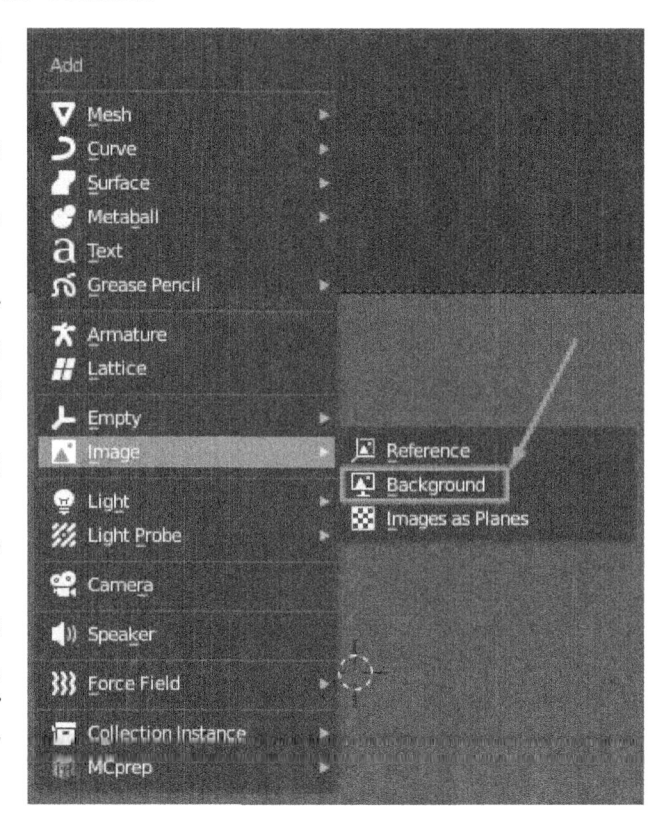

MASTERING THE TYPES OF IMAGE OBJECTS

The following are the types of image objects:

With Blender's mesh editing features, you can make significant alterations to objects composed of vertices, edges, and polygonal faces.

- **Curve/Surface:** In addition to traditional vertex-based editing, Blender offers the option to manipulate mathematically specified objects using control handles or control points. These control points allow for adjustments in length, curvature, and other properties of the object. This feature is particularly useful for creating smooth and rounded shapes or natural-looking settings.
- **Metaball:** Furthermore, Blender introduces the concept of metaballs, which are objects defined by mathematical functions rather than traditional vertices or control points. Metaballs are especially effective for creating organic forms and fluid-like structures. When multiple metaballs are brought together, they seamlessly merge by smoothly rounding the connections, creating the illusion of a unified entity.
- **Text:** This creates a 2D-dimensional representation of text.
- **Volume:** This contains the Open VDB files generated by other software or Blender's fluid simulator.
- **Grease pencil:** You can create this by drawing strokes.
- **Armature:** Armatures are used in 3D modeling to create rigs that enable models to be posed and animated.
- **Lattice:** Lattices are wireframe objects that are not visible in renders. They are commonly used to deform other objects through the lattice modifier.
- **Empty:** Empty objects are null objects that serve as visual transform nodes and do not appear in renders. They are useful for controlling the position and movement of other objects.
- **Image:** Image empties are objects that display images within the 3D viewport. They are used as visual references to assist artists in modeling or animating.
- **Light:** Light emits light and is used to illuminate the scene during rendering.
- **Light Probe:** Light probes are utilized by the Eevee render engine to capture lighting information for indirect lighting effects.
- **Camera:** Cameras represent the virtual viewpoint used to determine what is captured in the render.
- **Speaker:** Speaker empties introduce sound sources into the scene.
- **Force Field:** Force field empties apply external forces to simulations, creating movement. They are represented in the 3D viewport as small control objects.
- **Collection Instance:** Collection instances allow you to select from existing collections. When chosen, an empty object is created with an instance of the selected collection, effectively duplicating its contents.

In summary, Blender provides various methods for editing objects, including traditional mesh editing with vertices, edges, and faces, control point manipulation for mathematically defined shapes, and the use of metaballs for creating liquid-like or organic structures.

CHANGING IMAGE OBJECT PROPERTIES

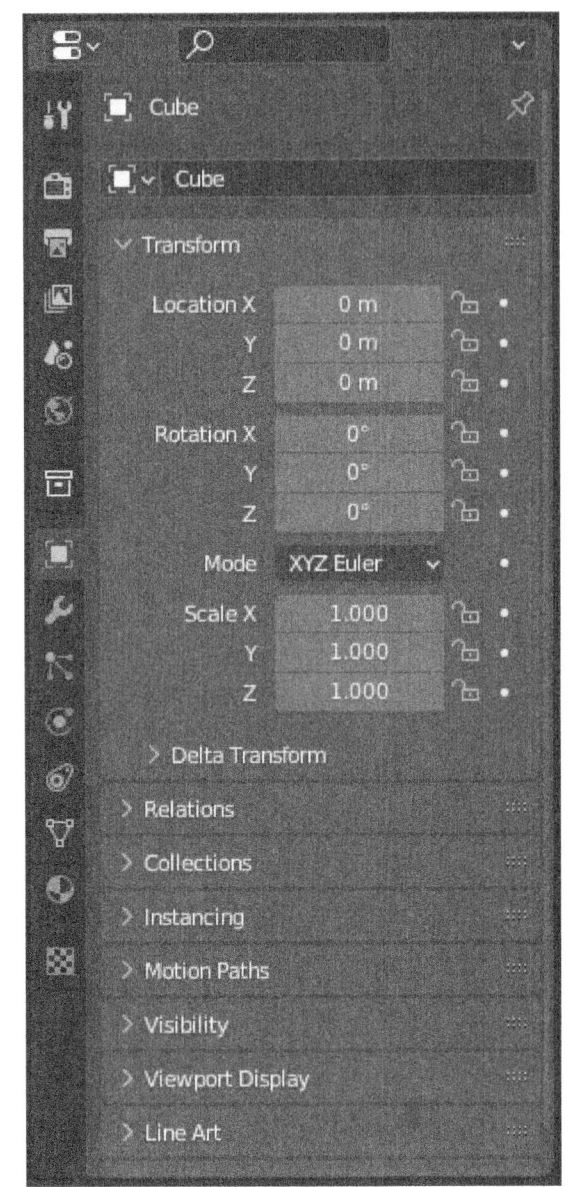

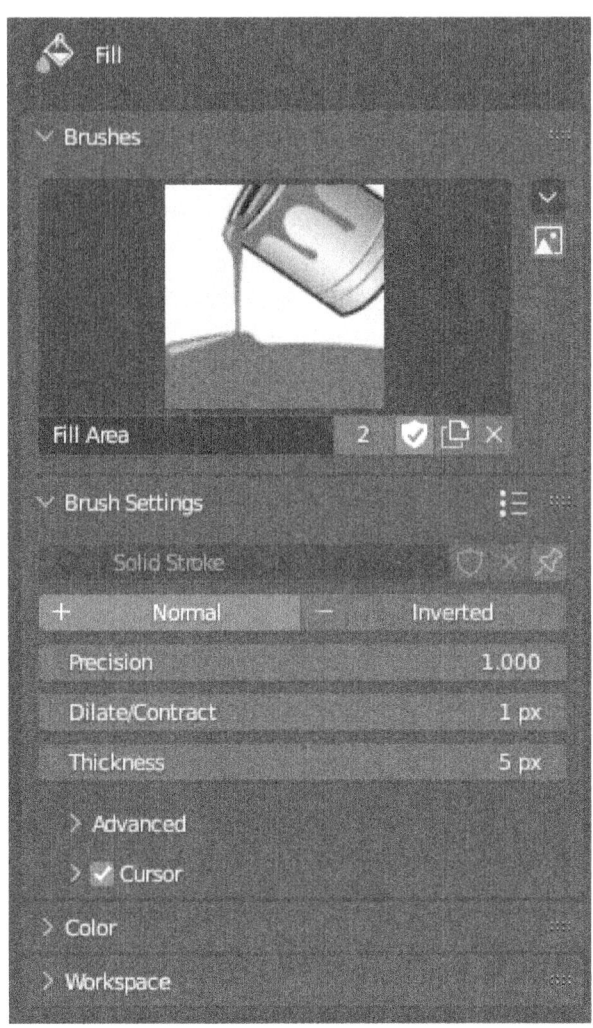

BRUSH TYPES

Creating custom brushes

In Sculpt Mode, you have the option to modify pre-existing brush data blocks or create your own brushes using the controls in the Tool Shelf.

If you choose to create a new brush, follow these steps:

- First, select the Plus (+) button located below the list of brushes in the Brush Panel at the top of the Tool Shelf. This will create a new brush data block.
- To make things more efficient, start with an existing brush as a starting point. Select a brush that has similar properties to the one you want to create.

- After selecting the plus (+)icon, you'll need to give your new brush a name. Type the desired name in the data block field.
- With the new brush data block created and named, you can now proceed with personalizing your brush by adjusting its settings and properties to suit your needs and sculpting style.

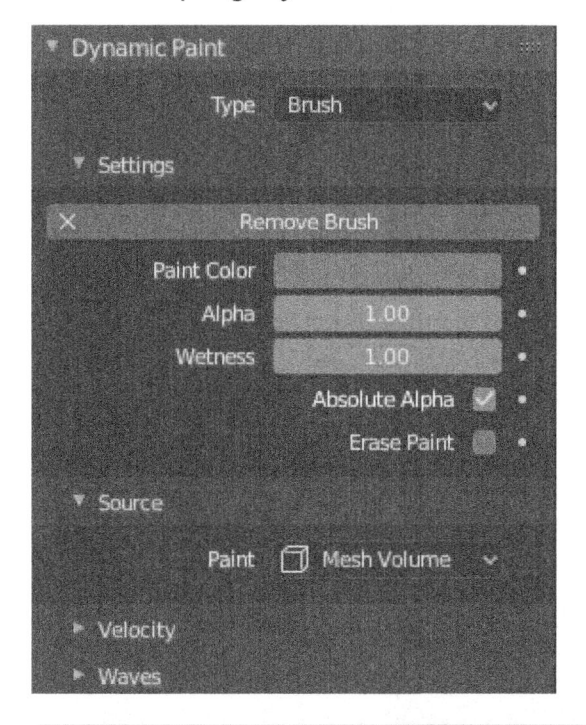

USING BLENDER'S TEXTURE SYSTEM TO TWEAK BRUSHES

You can choose a texture in the Texture tab to affect how your brush behaves. Any texture you have created in the texture properties can be used as a brush while sculpting. Using textured brushes is a great technique to add extra details to your model. To select a texture for your brush, simply left-click the texture square in this panel and choose from the list of thumbnail photos that appear, allowing you to pick an existing texture for your sculpting needs.

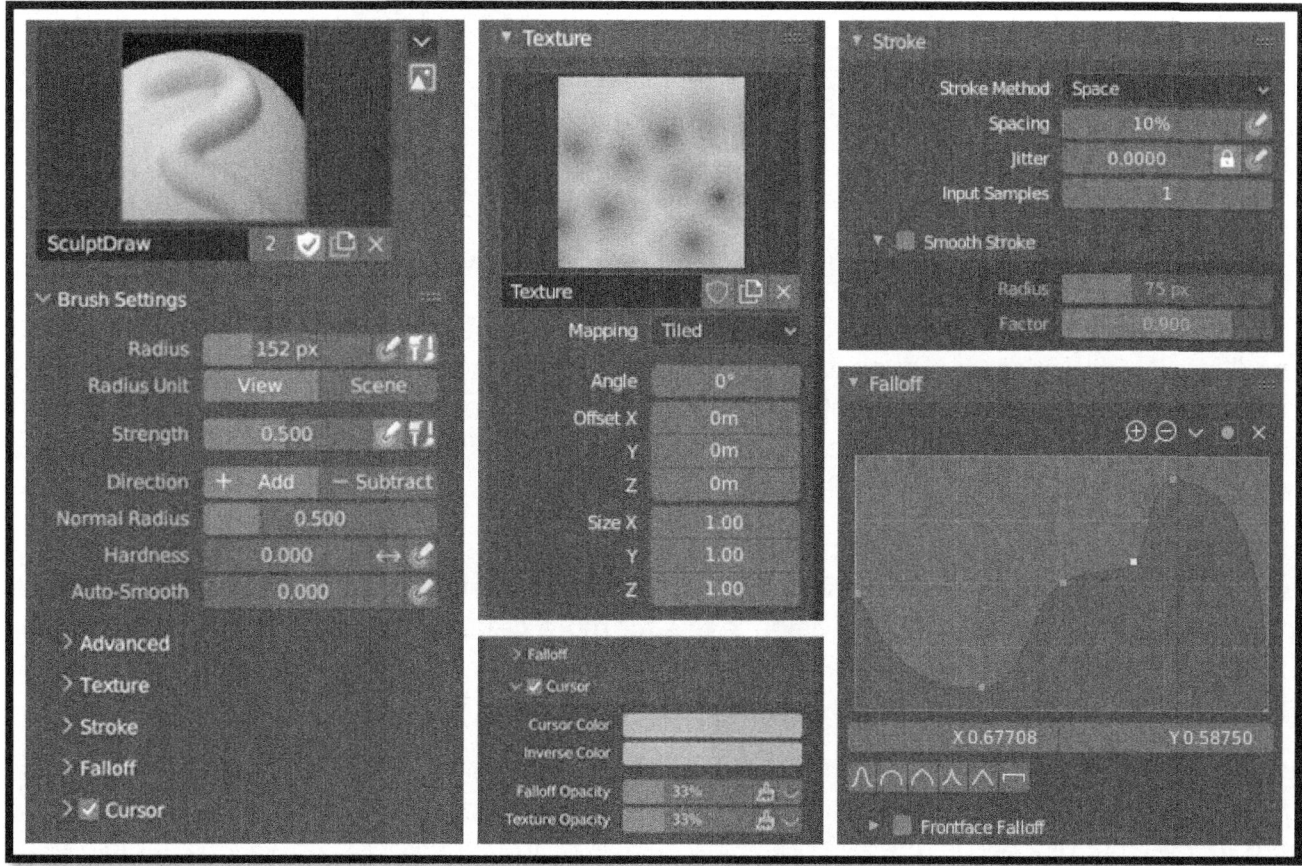

SCULPTING WITH THE MULTI-RESOLUTION MODIFIER

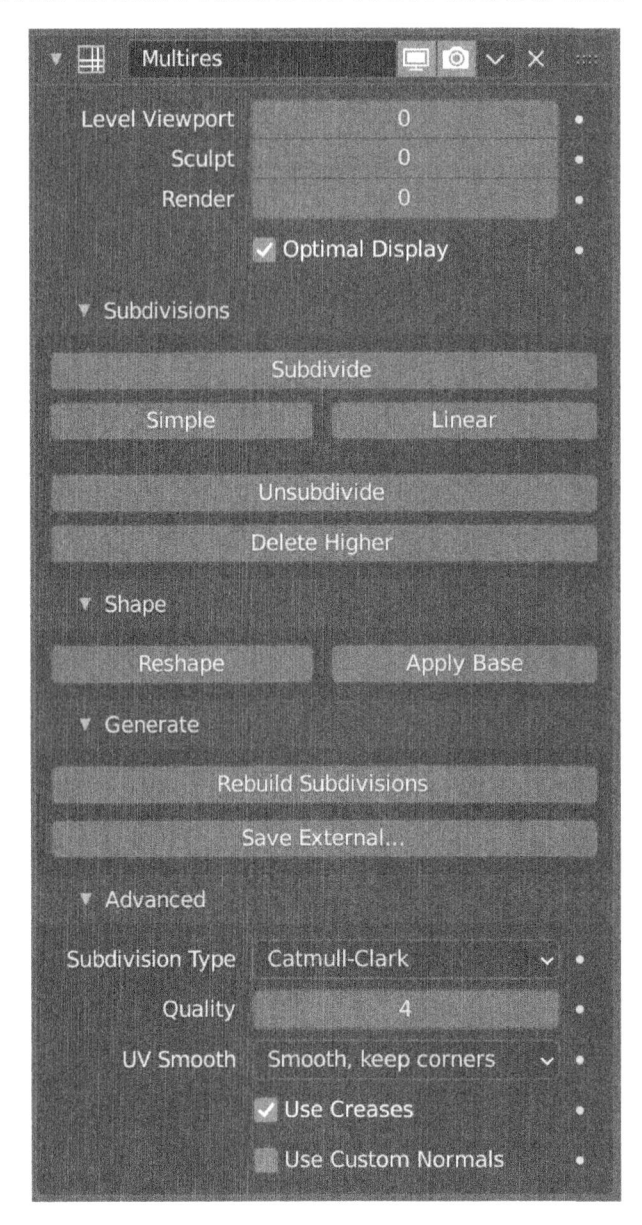

The Multiresolution modifier in Blender has a similar appearance to the Subdivision Surface modifier. By definition, it starts with a mesh having no subdivisions. To increase the level of subdivision, use the Subdivide button. The numbers for Preview, Sculpt, and Render indicate the visible subdivision levels in the 3D viewport during sculpting and rendering. Adjusting these values allows you to control the mesh's level of detail while sculpting and rendering.

Unlike the Subdivision Surface modifier, the Multiresolution modifier isn't limited to six levels of subdivision. You can set any number within your computer's processor and memory capabilities, providing a greater range of subdivision levels for more detailed meshes. You can also choose between the Catmull-Clark Subdivision or Simple Subdivision methods before applying the subdivision.

levels, giving flexibility in selecting the most suitable approach. After adding a level, you have options such as deleting higher sub-division levels and using the Optimal Draw check box to streamline the display in the 3D Viewport. To edit the additional vertices created by the Multiresolution modifier, use Sculpt mode. In Sculpt mode, your mesh behaves like a malleable piece of clay, and You can access a variety of sculpt brushes in the tool shelf (press T) to modify your mesh. A common approach is to start with low subdivision levels to establish the basic shape and then increase levels to add intricate details. This allows you to focus on different levels of detail at different stages of the sculpting process, offering creative freedom and control over your model. While Blender's Sculpt mode works without the Multiresolution Modifier, using the various levels of detail it offers gives you more creative freedom and control in sculpting your model.

REVIEW QUESTIONS

1. How does the Multiresolution modifier in Blender differ from the Subdivision Surface modifier in terms of subdivision levels and flexibility?
2. When creating custom brushes in Sculpt Mode, what steps should you follow to start with a new brush data block and personalize it according to your sculpting needs?
3. How can you use Blender's texture system to tweak brushes and add extra details to your models while sculpting?

SUMMARY

This chapter explores advanced techniques in Blender to cater to the needs of computer graphics artists who seek greater control over their dense, high-poly meshes with millions of vertices. The Subdivision Surface modifier is powerful for achieving organic shapes, but it becomes challenging to make specific and detailed modifications. By applying the Subdivision Surface modifier, Artists gain precise control over individual vertices, allowing direct manipulation for sculpting intricate details. Blender's high-resolution meshes and Sculpt mode provide artists with a powerful sculpting environment in the virtual space of 3D Blender. The chapter guides users through sculpting techniques, utilizing textured brushes, and customizing brushes to achieve refined and detailed results.

In addition, the chapter covers how to add 2D images as backgrounds in Blender, serving as visual references or context for 3D scenes. It also introduces various types of image objects, such as curves, metaballs, texts, armatures, and more, offering a wide range of creative options for artists. The Multiresolution Modifier is explored in detail, providing a greater range of subdivision levels and offering more control in sculpting high-poly meshes. Artists can switch between different levels of detail during sculpting, allowing them to focus on specific aspects and achieve the desired results effectively.

CHAPTER 9: BEYOND MESHES: EXPLORING BLENDER'S PRIMITIVES

While Blender modelers primarily use polygon-based meshes as their primary tool for building objects in 3D space, there are additional types of objects available in Blender. These include curves, surfaces, metal objects, and text objects. These objects often have more specialized functions compared to meshes, but they can be highly beneficial when you require their specific features.

Curves and surfaces are highly versatile and are useful when you need objects to have a smooth and seamless appearance, unlike the faceted look of meshes. They are especially important for achieving mathematical accuracy and precision in models. Metal objects, on the other hand, are particularly effective in creating organic shapes that seamlessly blend, as seen in simple fluids. They can also be used to construct a basic sculpture that can be further refined using the Sculpt mode. Text objects, as their name suggests, allow you to add and edit text within a scene in all three dimensions. For more detailed guidance on handling each of these object types, you can refer to the corresponding chapter. In this chapter, we are going to be talking about the non-mesh primitives.

USING CURVES AND SURFACES

The most significant distinction between surfaces and curves compared to meshes is their reliance on mathematics. Don't worry; there's no need for complex arithmetic here. Simply put, curves and surfaces can be described and understood by computers using mathematical functions, while meshes are defined by the specific positions of each vertex that forms the mesh.

From a computational standpoint, curves and surfaces offer two notable advantages:

Accuracy: Surfaces and curves excel in accuracy, providing a higher level of precision compared to meshes. While meshes can appear impressive, they lack the mathematical definition and ideal shape that curves and surfaces offer, making them more suitable for designers and engineers who require precise representations.

Memory Efficiency: Curves and surfaces are more memory-efficient since they store the mathematical representation of the shape, saving memory compared to storing all the individual points of a mesh. Complex curves and surfaces typically require significantly less hard drive space than their mesh counterparts when representing the same shape.

However, there are some limitations to these benefits. Handling curves and surfaces might be more challenging as you need to use control points, and curves and surfaces don't have radial vertices that can be directly manipulated. Instead, control points are used, either as part of a control cage or floating off the surface, depending on the type of curve. While curves and surfaces can be described as perfect mathematical representations of shapes, the computer introduces imperfections when processing 3D geometry. It converts them into a tessellated form, which can increase processing time, even though it requires less memory for a smooth display. To optimize performance, you can use coarser tessellation with fewer triangles, speeding up the rendering process. However, it's important to note that what you see in software like Blender is an approximate representation of the ideal curve or surface shape.

Both curves and surfaces have their uses in animation, such as defining paths for objects and controlling changes to object properties over time in the graphic editor. Additionally, they are suitable for modeling and have found widespread applications in various industries, including architecture, industrial design, and engineering, due to their precision and efficiency.

UNDERSTANDING THE DIFFERENT TYPES OF CURVES

In Blender, you can add curves by pressing Shift+A and selecting Curve" from the drop-down menu that appears. There are two primary types of curves: Bezier curves and NURBS curves. Bezier curves, which include a particular type called path curves, are commonly used for typography and logos. By default, Bezier curves operate in three dimensions, but you can choose to lock them to a single 2D plane if necessary.

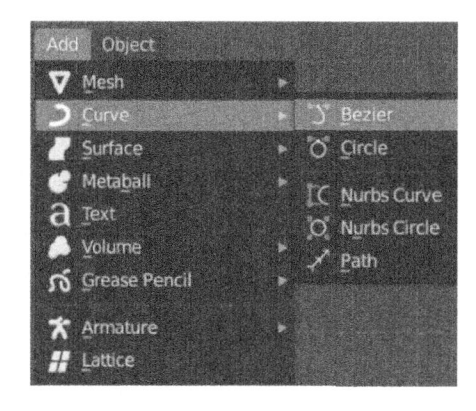

To add curves, follow these steps:

1. In Blender, press Shift+A to open the Add menu.
2. From the menu, select "Curve" to add a curve object to your scene.
3. A drop-down menu will appear, allowing you to choose the desired curve type. Select either the Bezier or NURBS curve.
4. If you choose a Bezier curve, you will notice that it has control points with pairs of handles. These handles allow you to exert more control over the shape of the curve.
5. To access and modify the control points and handles of a Bezier curve, switch to edit mode. You can do this by selecting the curve object and pressing Tab, or by using the mode drop-down menu in the header of the 3D view port.
6. In Edit mode, you can view and adjust the curve's shape by manipulating the control points and handles. Each control point has a pair of handles that you can use to control the curve's shape.

By understanding these steps, you can utilize the Shift+A shortcut in Blender to add curves and choose between Bezier and NURBS curve types. Bezier curves offer greater flexibility for manipulating the shape, especially with the control points and hand. available in Edit mode. NURBS means Non-Uniform Relational B-Spline. Unlike Bezier curves, NURBS curves' control points lack handles. NURBS control points typically don't even touch the actual curve shape by default. As an alternative, the control points are weighted to affect the curve's shape. Higher-weighted control points draw the curve toward them.

WORKING WITH CURVES

Curves have very few dedicated specialty controls. Like with meshes, you can extrude a selected control point in Edit mode by either hitting E or Ctrl+left-clicking where you would like to extrude. Grab (G), rotate (R), and scale (S) also function as intended. Additionally, by selecting the end control points on each curve and hitting Fin Edit mode, you may combine different curves to create a face much like you would when creating a face out of mesh. Pressing F closes the curve, or, in "Blenderese", makes the curve cyclic if the two control points you choose are at the beginning and end of the same curve. Pressing Alt+C while in edit mode will also make any control point on a curve cyclic.

CHANGING 3D CURVES INTO 2D CURVES

By definition, curves are configured to operate in three dimensions. However, you can easily convert a 3D curve into a 2D curve that operates only in a given free-form two-dimensional plane. This restriction will limit the curve's control points to the local XY point.

To change a 3D curve to a 2D curve:

1. Go to Object Data and Properties.
2. Left-click the 2D, but to restrict the curve to operate in two dimensions,.

When working with a 3D curve in Edit mode, you may notice little arrows spread along it. These arrows represent the curve's "normals", which show the curve's direction. To adjust the size of these curve "normals," change the Normal Size setting in the Properties section of the 3D View's Curve Display panel. If you want to hide the curve "normals" entirely, you can simply turn off the Normals checkbox in the Curve Display panel. It's worth noting that curve "normals" are not shown for 2D curves.

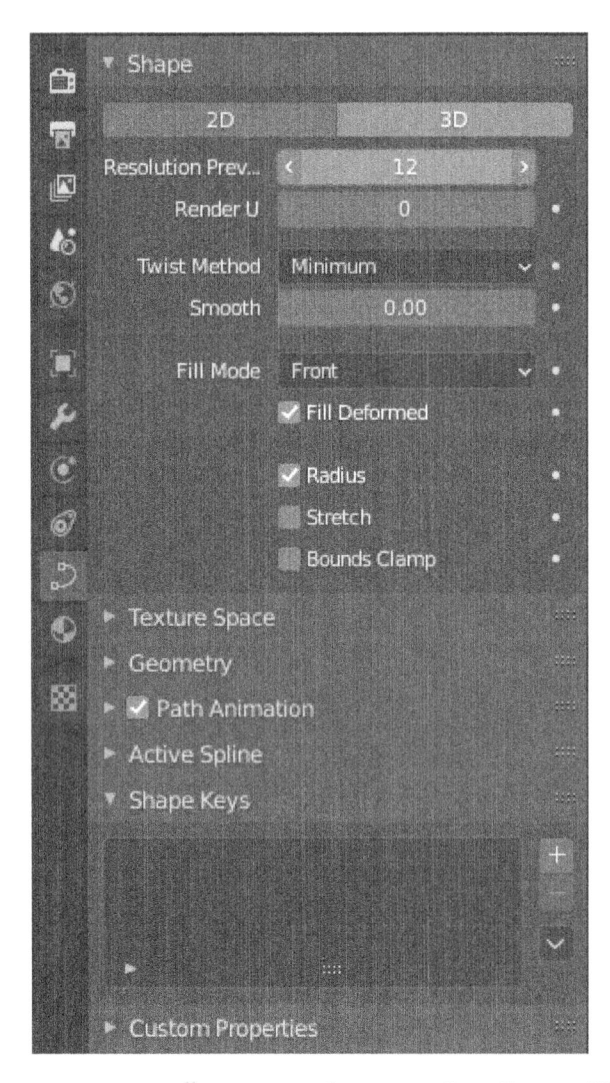

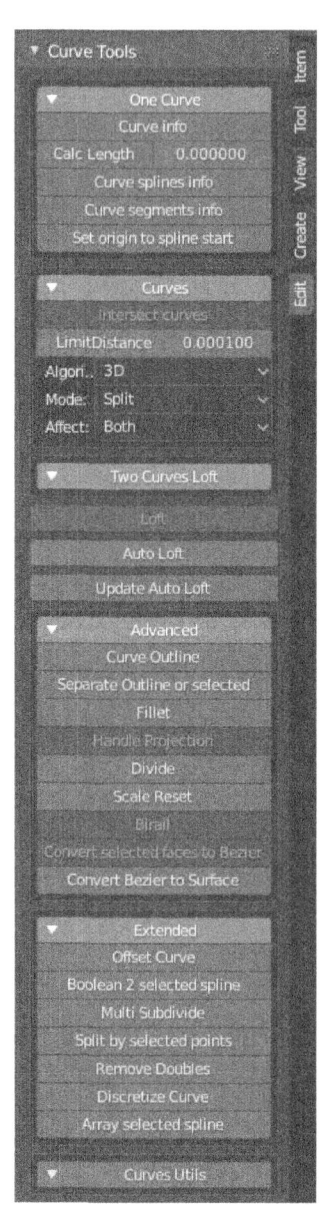

Nevertheless, even cyclic curves have a direction, although in most cases, the direction of a curve doesn't matter much unless you're using the curve as a path. When using a curve as a path, the animated item moves along the curve in the same direction as the curve itself. To change the curve's orientation, you have a few options: you can select Curve > Segments > Switch Orientation from the 3D View's header, click the Curve> Switch Direction button on the Tool Shelf, or simply press W > Switch Direct ion.

All curves, regardless of their type, have significant differences in object data properties. The Shape panel contains some of the most important ones. The functions of the 2D and 3D buttons are already apparent, allowing you to set whether the curve operates in two dimensions or three dimensions. Beneath these buttons, you'll find the Preview U and Render U values, which determine the resolution of the curve. It's important to note that BD is an approximate representation of the true curve, and increasing the resolution here will make the curve more closely resemble its mathematically defined shape.

There are two solution values you may come across:

1. **Preview U:** This is the default resolution and what you see in the 3D view while working on your scene.
2. **Render U:** This is the resolution Blender uses when rendering. By default, the Render U resolution is set to 0, meaning Blender will make use of the value set in Preview U for rendering.

UNDERSTANDING THE STRENGTHS AND LIMITATIONS OF BLENDER'S SURFACES

Blender certainly lags in various aspects when compared to other NURBS-accountable technologies. While you can create bowl or cup shapes using methods like lofting, extruding surface endpoints, or spinning surface curves (known as lathing in other applications), these options are somewhat limited. Blen der lacks certain capabilities, such as using one curve to shorten another's length or projecting the shape of one curve onto the surface of another with NURBS surfaces.

However, there is optimism for the future. Blender has been making progress in incorporating better NURBS tools, although it has been a gradual process. With the upcoming releases, Blender is expected to offer noticeable improvements in this area. Eventually, NURBS may even become compatible with a significant number of mesh modifiers that users commonly rely on. As Blender continues to evolve, it holds the promise of providing enhanced NURBS capabilities and bridging the gap with other NURBS software.

USING METABALL OBJECTS

Meta objects, also known as blobbies, are a fascinating aspect of computer graphics and have been a staple for quite some time. The concept behind meta-objects is simple yet powerful. Imagine two water droplets, and as you push them closer together in a tally, they eventually merge to form a larger droplet.

Meta objects operate similarly, allowing you to control when and to what extent the droplets combine and even giving you the option to separate them again if needed. Moreover, meta objects enable you to perform tasks that are challenging or impossible in reality, such as removing one droplet from another instead of combining them into a single entity. This level of control and flexibility makes them not only useful but also fun to work with.

Meta objects offer unique creative opportunities in 3D modeling and animation, allowing for the creation of dynamic and fluid-like shapes and structures. Their versatility and cool applications make them a valuable tool in the world of computer graphics.

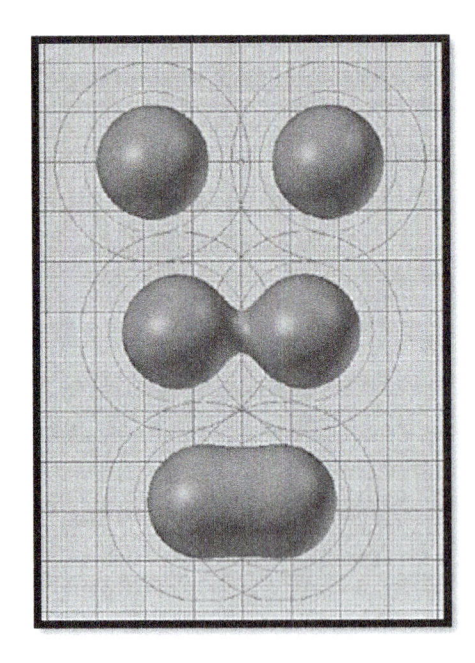

Meta-what?

Similar to curves and NURBS, meta-objects have a mathematical definition that governs every aspect of their existence. Unlike NURBS or meshes, the surface of a meta-object cannot be directly controlled by control points or vertices. Instead, the object's Surface geometry is determined by its underlying structure, such as a point, line, plane, sphere, or cube, and its proximity to other meta-objects.

There are five primary meta-object primitives available in Blender:

1. **Ball:** The surface of a metaball is constructed based on points equally spaced from a single origin. Metaballs can be uniformly scaled and moved, but scaling in only one direction is not possible.
2. **Capsule:** In contrast to a met capsule, which has a single point as its foundation, a meta capsule has two points as its basis. The surface can be scaled both globally, similar to a metaball, and locally along the X-axis.
3. **Plane:** As the name suggests, the fundamental structure of a meta plane is a plane. It can be scaled evenly or along the local X- and Y-axes.
4. **Cube:** A meta cube's foundation is a three-dimensional structure, specifically a cube. This primitive can be independently scaled in the X, Y, or Z axes.
5. **Ellipsoid:** The meta ellipsoid might resemble a metaball at first glance, but it is based on a sphere rather than a single point. If the local X, Y, and Z dimensions are kept constant, it behaves like a metaball. However, you can also scale it along any of the three distinct axes, similar to the meta cube.

A notable feature of meta objects is the ability to switch instantly from one primitive to another when in Edit mode. You can use the Active Element panel in the Object Data Properties of the meta-object to achieve this. The Active Element panel displays the default parameters for each primitive along with the corresponding primitive in the image below. This allows for quick and efficient adjustments to the meta object's structure and shape as needed.

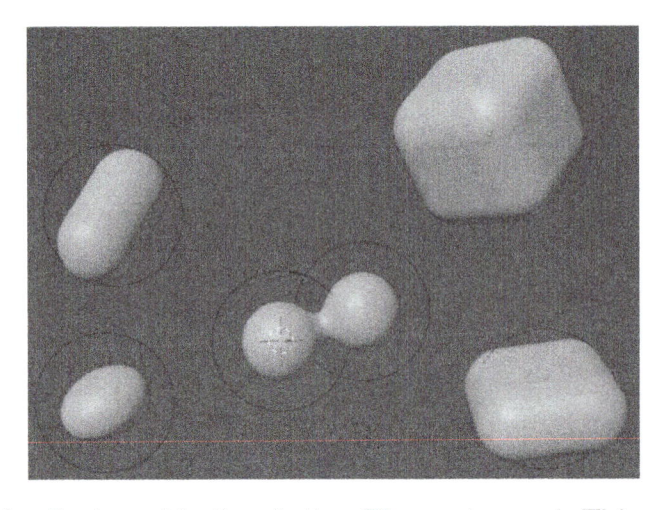

The stiffness value for the selected meta-object is displayed in the Active Element panel. This parameter determines how the meta-object interacts with other meta-objects. A green ring around the meta object's origin in the 3D view serves as a visual indicator of the stiffness value. You can change the stiffness value directly in the panel or graphically by scaling (S) the green ring. To select a specific individual meta-object, right-click on the reddish or pinkish ring outside the green ring. In Edit mode, various values for X, Y, and Z can appear in the Active Element panel, depending on the type of meta-object primitive you're using. You can modify these values both in the panel and in the 3DView using the S-->X, S-->Y, and S-->Z hotkey combinations. At the bottom of the panel, there are buttons to hide the selected meta item or give it a negative effect, which detracts it from the positive, visible meta-objects.

When you merge multiple meta objects into a single Blender object, you can switch back to object mode, and they will be treated as a single object. However, keep in mind that they don't exist in a vacuum, and when two intricate Blender objects composed of metas are combined, they genuinely merge together.

The Metaball panel, located at the top of the Object Data Properties, allows you to control additional features of the meta objects, whether they are in Object mode or Edit mode.

The first two values in the Metaball panel are resolution values:

View: Manages the density of the generated mesh in the 3D view. Higher numbers produce a larger mesh, while lower values produce a smaller mesh.

Render: Functions similarly to the View value but only affect the mesh during render time, as meta-objects can be computationally demanding.

The threshold value is a global control that determines the degree of interdependence between the metas in a single Blender object. An object must have a stiffness value greater than the threshold value to be visible. This number has a range from 0 to 5 and must be larger than the stiffness value.

Below the threshold value, four buttons regulate how meta-objects are updated, as shown in the 3D view:

- **Always:** The default setting, which is the slowest but most accurate. The 3D View updates as quickly as your computer can handle modifications.
- **Half:** Improves the 3D view's responsiveness by lowering the resolution of the meta item as you move or modify it. The meta item displays in full resolution once you're done altering it.
- **Fast:** Close to the fastest setting, Blender hides the meta objects before performing a transform and then re-evaluates the surface afterward. It lacks the visual feedback of Always and Half but performs well.
- **Never:** The quickest update option, where everything is hidden when attempting to change a meta-object, and the 3D view is never updated. This improves performance, especially when using meta-objects linked to a particle system for fluid simulation.

WHAT METABALL OBJECTS ARE USEFUL FOR

When it comes to creating metaobjects, there are two perspectives to consider. On one hand, there is a wide range of potential creations that can be achieved using meta-objects. They serve as valuable tools for quickly generating preliminary models and facilitating basic fluid simulations through particle systems and meta-objects themselves. They still find their place in the realm of prototyping, despite their reduced prevalence with the emergence of more advanced modeling techniques like mult   ires sculpting and subdivision surfaces.

However, there's also a limitation to what can be accomplished with meta-objects. As technology has progressed, their role in rendering and fluid simulation applications has diminished. They may not always provide optimal topology independently and can impose significant computational burdens. Consequently, alternative methods and advancements have surpassed their once-prominent status in certain areas. While meta-objects have somewhat lost their significance in certain uses, that doesn't mean they are entirely abandoned. They are still employed for specific tasks. For example, using metaballs to animate the extraction of life energy from a character with a shimmering halo substance offers quick setup and precise control over the arrangement on the screen. So, meta objects still have their place and can be entertaining to work with. In conclusion, while the prevalence of meta objects may have diminished in some aspects of computer graphics, they still offer unique advantages and can be a valuable addition to an artist's toolkit, especially for specific creative scenarios.

ADDING TEXT

Working with text in Blender has undergone significant advancements over time. Unlike word processing programs such as OpenOffice.org or Microsoft Word, Blender offers unique ways to manipulate text objects. Surprisingly, desktop publishing applications like Adobe InDesign or QuarkXPress share several features with Blender's text objects.

In Blender, text objects are a specific class of curve objects, which means that many of the possibilities available for curves also apply to text. For example, you can use functions like Extrude, Bevel, Bevel Object, and Taper Object to quickly add a third dimension to text objects. This allows you to create fascinating effects with just one text object, as demonstrated in the image below. (Note: Refer to the chapter's earlier section on using curves and surfaces for more details.)

Blender's text capabilities provide artists with the flexibility to transform and manipulate text in creative ways, making it a powerful tool for both 3D modeling and text design. Whether you're looking to add depth and dimension to your text or explore artistic typography, Blender's text features offer a range of possibilities to enhance your projects.

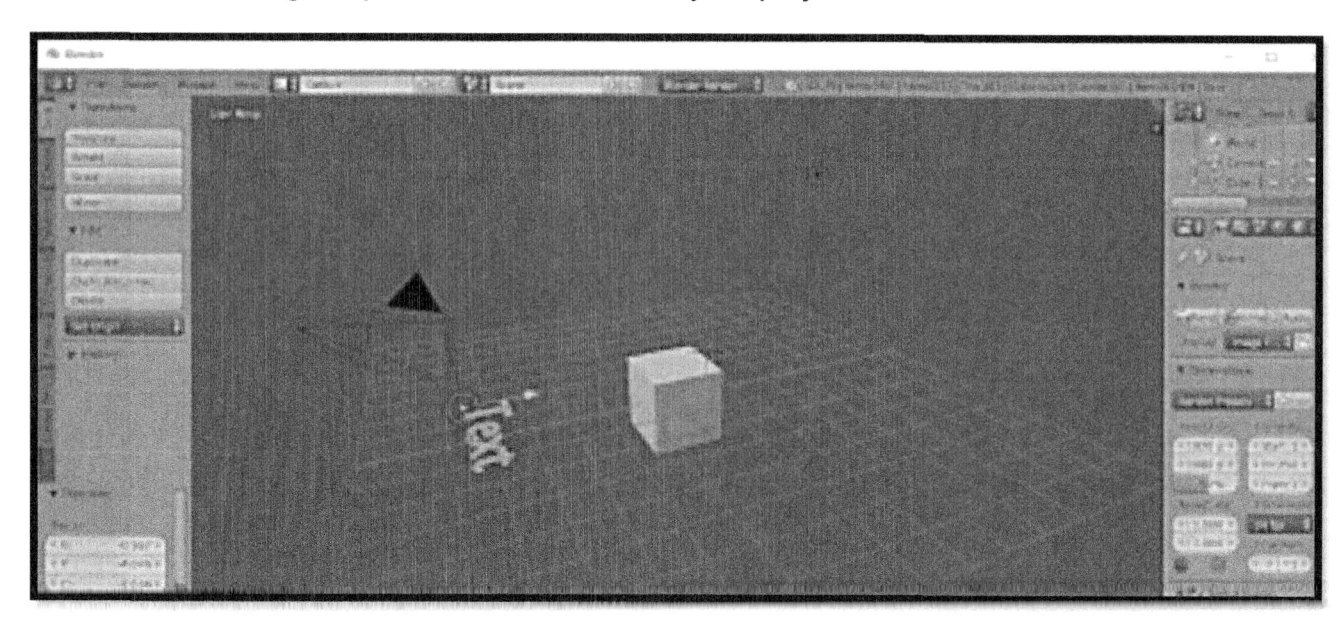

ADDING AND EDITING TEXT

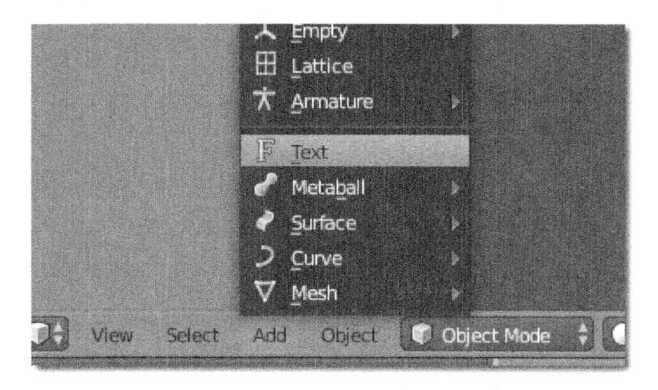

In Blender, adding a text object is similar to adding any other object. By pressing Shift +A and selecting Text from the menu, a text object with the default text "Text" will appear at the location of your 3D cursor. To edit the text, you need to switch to Edit mode. While in edit mode, the controls start to resemble those of a word processor, though there are some differences.

For instance, you cannot highlight text with the mouse cursor, but you can do so by pressing Shift+, depending on the position of the text cursor. Additionally, formatting controls for text objects can be found in the Font panel of the Object Data Properties. In this panel, you can adjust various attributes of the text, such as font style, size, and alignment. The font panel provides options to customize the appearance of the text according to your preferences. Using text objects in Blen der allows you to incorporate textual elements into your 3D scenes, whether it's for titles, labels, or any other text-based designs. With the font panel's features, you can tailor the text's visual presentation to suit your specific project needs.

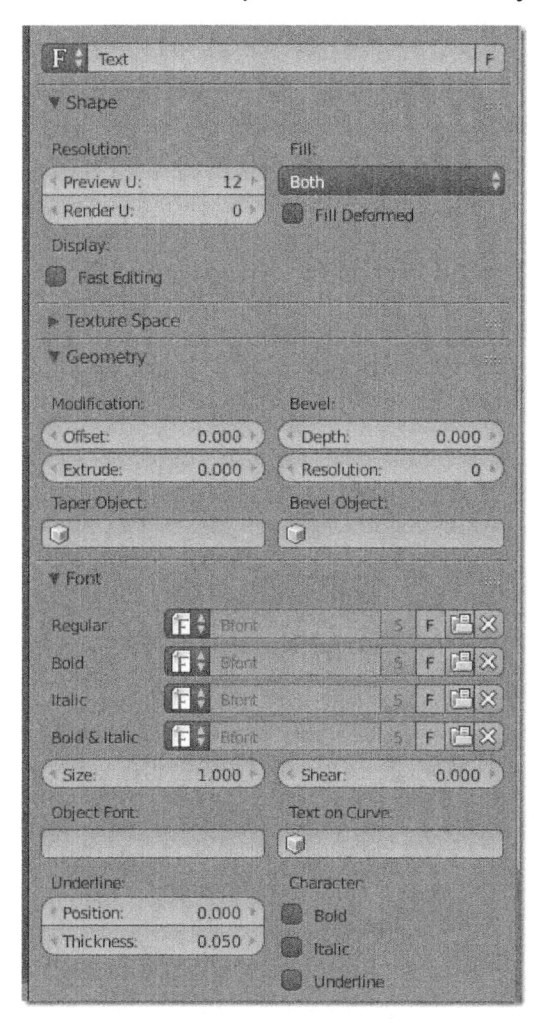

In the paragraph panel of Blender's text editing mode, you'll find a block of alignment buttons that can assist you in aligning your text concerning the text object's origin.

These alignment options include:

- **Left:** Selecting this option will left-justify the text alignment, where the left-hand guide for the text is determined by the origin of the text object.
- **Center:** Choosing the center option will use the origin of the text object as the center point for aligning all the text.
- **Right:** This option will right-align the text, with the right-hand guide for the text being the origin of the text object.
- **Justify:** When you choose Justify, the text is aligned to both the left and right sides, creating a neat and uniform appearance. If a line of text is too short, Blender inserts kerning, or spacers, between the characters to fill the space. It's important to note that using this option requires the use of text boxes.

- **Flush:** The Flush option, with one exception, aligns the text on both sides if the line marks the conclusion of a paragraph, functioning similarly to Justify. Like Justify, this choice also requires the use of text frames to be effective.

These alignment options give you the flexibility to control the layout and presentation of your text in Blender, making it easier to create visually appealing and well-structured text elements for your 3D scenes.

CONTROLLING TEXT APPEARANCE

Blender's approach to managing fonts for text objects is unique and may differ from what you're accustomed to in other tools. Instead of a drop-down menu with a preview of installed fonts, Blender requires you to load font files manually.

Here's how you can do it:

1. In the Font panel of the Object Data Properties, left-click the Load button next to the Regular Font data block.
2. Navigate to the location of your font files in Blender's File Browser. On Windows, it is usually found at C:\windows\fonts, on Linux at \usr/share/fonts, and on Mac OS at /system/Library/fonts.
3. Select the font file you want to use for your text object and load it.

After loading the font, you can select it from the font drop-down list in the Font Panel to use it in your Blender project. Blender also comes with a built-in font that you can use.

It's essential to note that Blender handles bold and italic text differently. You have to load a separate font file for each style, resulting in four font data blocks: Regular, Bold, Italic, and Bold & Italic. By default, the bold and italic versions of the font file loaded in the Regular data block are used for these styles, but you can select different fonts if you wish.

To change the font for your text object in Blender, follow these steps:

1. Access the Font panel in the Object Data Properties of your text object.
2. Left-click on the Load button for the desired font data block (Regular, Bold, Italic, or Bold & Italic).
3. Use the File Browser to select the font file you want to use.
4. Once loaded, the font will be applied to your text object automatically.

If you specifically want to change the font for the Bold data block, follow these additional steps:

1. Enter Edit mode for your text object (press Tab or use the mode selection options).
2. Use Shift+ to highlight the specific text you want to edit.
3. In the Font panel, find the Bold checkbox next to the Character label.
4. Select the Bold checkbox to assign the chosen font to the highlighted characters.

For special characters, like copyright symbols or upside-down question marks in Spanish sentences, you have three options:

1. Check Text > Special Characters to see if the character you need is available.
2. Memorize the hotkey combination for frequently used special characters, as documented in Blender's online resources.
3. Use Text -> Paste File to insert a special character from an external text file into your Blender text object if it's uncommon or not on the menu.

DEFORMING TEXT WITH A CURVE

Having the text flow along the length of a curve is another extremely effective thing you can do with Blender's text objects. By doing so, you can create writing that curves over a doorway, wraps around a bowl, or simply looks weird. The Text on Curve field in the Font Panel is the key to this feature.

Use the steps in the following example to observe how this feature operates:

- (Shift+A -->Text) Add text to an existing image. You are free to fill it with anything you like.
- To control the text's shape, create a curve (Shift+A-->Curve -->Bezier). You are in control of this curve. A NURBS curve can be used in place of the Bezier curve that you are currently utilizing. Additionally, we prefer to have the same origin for my curve as we do for my text object. Although it's only my preference, it works well to keep things simple and manageable.
- In the Text on Curve field, select the text object, then type or click the control curve's name. Blam! Now the text must follow the curve's arc. Any changes you make to the curve in Edit mode will update your text object if you select (right-click) the curve.

CONVERTING TO CURVES AND MESHES

Blender's text objects are indeed powerful, but there are certain situations where using curves and meshes might be more beneficial. For example, Blender allows you to easily convert your text object into a curve or a mesh when needed. You can do this by pressing Alt+C in Object mode and selecting "Curve from Mesh/Text " or "Mesh from Curve/Meta/Sur/Mesh ."

Here are a few reasons why you might consider making this conversion:

1. **Creating Custom Logos or Shapes:** Converting text into curves allows you to modify individual characters and create custom logos or specific shapes with more flexibility.
2. **Font Licensing Restrictions:** If you need to share your ".blend" file but are limited by font licensing, converting the text to curves becomes necessary to legally include it in the ".blend.".
3. **3D Curved Text Effect:** You can achieve the effect of extruded text following a 3D curve by converting the text into a mesh.
4. **Animation Rigging:** Rigging the letters with an armature for animation purposes is possible by converting them into meshes or curves.
5. **Fluid Simulation:** You can use the leaves as obstacles in a fluid simulation by converting them into meshes.
6. **Particle System:** Converting the letters into meshes allows you to generate a particle system based on the letters.

By converting your text object into curves or meshes, you gain more creative control and flexibility to achieve various effects and use them in different aspects of your Blender projects.

SUMMARY

In this chapter, we explored various aspects of working with curves, meta objects, and text in Blender. Cyclic curves, although having a direction, may not matter much unless used as paths. Switching the orientation of curves is possible through different methods, allowing greater control over animated objects moving along the curve. The Shape panel in the Object Data Properties provides essential controls for curves, including preview and render resolution.

We then delved into Blender's text capabilities, which differ from traditional word processing programs. Text objects are a specific class of curve objects, offering unique ways to manipulate text. The Font panel in Object Data Properties provides formatting controls for customizing font style, size, and alignment. Blender's approach to managing fonts involves manually loading font files, and each font style (regular, bold, italic) requires a separate font data block.

Next, we explored the fascinating world of metaobjects, which are blobs that interact and merge based on proximity. Meta objects provide creative opportunities for 3D modeling and animation, offering flexibility and control. We discussed the five primary meta object primitives and how to switch between them in Edit mode. The Metaball panel allows for additional control, such as resolution and interdependence between meta-objects.

Despite the decline in some areas due to advancements in other techniques, meta metal objects still have their place in computer graphics, offering unique advantages for specific tasks.

Lastly, we learn how to deform text along the length of a curve using the "Text on Curve" technique, enabling creative designs like text curving over doorways or wrapping around objects.

Overall, this chapter provided valuable insights into Blender's curve, text, and meta-object functionalities, showcasing their strengths and limitations while highlighting their significance in various 3D modeling and animation scenarios.

REVIEW QUESTIONS

1. What are the main controls provided by the Shape panel in the Object Data Properties for working with curves in Blender?
2. How does Blender's approach to managing fonts differ from traditional word processing programs, and what is the process of loading font files for text objects?
3. What are meta objects in Blender, and how do they interact and merge based on proximity? How can they be used creatively in 3D modeling and animation?
4. Despite advancements in other techniques, why do meta-objects still hold significance in certain areas of computer graphics? What advantages do they offer for specific tasks?
5. How can you deform text along the length of a curve in Blender? What creative possibilities does the "Text on Curve" feature open up for text manipulation and design in 3D scenes?

CHAPTER 10: CUSTOMIZING MATERIALS FOR REALISM

As you work on your models in Blender, you may eventually tire of the default gray plastic substance that all objects have. The world is full of vibrant colors, and you might want to bring some of that vibrancy into your 3D scenes. There's nothing wrong with neutral colors or plastic-like materials but using materials and textures can add a new level of color and realism to your surroundings and models. However, even with the recent updates to Blender's user interface, adding materials and textures to objects can still be a bit perplexing and difficult to grasp.

The purpose of this chapter is to provide you with the essential knowledge to handle Blender's materials with skillful precision. With some practice, you can become exceptionally adept at working with materials. Now, we must clarify that becoming "lethal" with Blender's materials is not to be taken literally. You won't hear about someone being "murdered" by overly intense specular highlights. So, perhaps "fatal" is not the most appropriate term to use here. Instead, think of it as becoming incredibly skilled and proficient in using Blender's materials to enhance your 3D creations.

UNDERSTANDING MATERIALS AND RENDERING ENGINES

By default, when you add a new object in Blender, it is assigned a gray, plastic-like material. If you want to change the appearance of an object, the easiest way is to modify its material characteristics.

You can find the controls for this in the Material section of the Properties editor, which consists of twelve distinct panels.

Context: When you open the Material Properties section in the Properties editor, you'll encounter a context panel. This panel allows you to access a list of material data blocks associated with the selected item and specify some of their essential properties.

Preview: The Preview panel displays images of various pre-made items, such as Suzanne's head, hair strands, a sphere against a sky background, a plane, a sphere, and a cube. These previews serve as visual representations of the content.

Diffuse: The diffuse color of an object represents its dominant hue, which you are going to see on the camera. In this panel, you can adjust this hue and control how it interacts with light.

Specular: One of the intriguing aspects of working with computer graphics is the ability to influence factors that are typically yond our control in the real world. The specular color, or spec, refers to the color of the highlights on your object. In the Specular panel, you can modify the specular color, adjust its intensity, and control how it reflects light.

Shading: Regardless of the settings chosen in the Diffuse and Specular panels, the Shading panel provides a comprehensive range of options to determine how your object reflects light.

Transparency: By checking the box in the header, you can activate this panel, which governs the handling of transparency for your material.

Mirror: If you wish to add reflective properties to your material, you can activate and customize this feature within this panel. In a later section of this chapter, we delve deeper into the concept of reflection and its relationship with transparency.

Subsurface scattering: Have you ever noticed that when you hold your hand in front of a flashlight, the light passes through your palm with a subtle reddish glow? This phenomenon is known as subsurface scattering, or SSS. In computer graphics, we refer to this effect as subsurface scattering, and it occurs when light is scattered beneath the surface of an object, such as your skin. You can control the SSS effect using the options available in this panel.

Strand: Within this panel, you can fine-tune settings specifically designed for using your material with hair particles.

Option: For material controls that don't neatly fit into other panels, you can find corresponding checkboxes in the Options panel. However, it's important to note that most of these checkboxes have a significant impact on both the final appearance of your render and, more crucially, the processing time required.

Shadow: The options available in this panel determine how your material interacts with shadows. You can specify whether the material should accept shadows cast by other objects and how it should handle them, as well as whether the material itself should cast shadows and in what manner.

Custom Properties: You may add custom properties to any part of the Properties editor. They are generally employed by those who Use Blender for more complex tasks that require Python programming. These attributes are added using this panel.

QUICK 'N' DIRTY COLORING

You might be wondering how to genuinely alter a material's color. The quickest and easiest method to do this is to left-click on the color swatch next to the color type (diffuse or specular). When you do this, the color picker for Blender will appear, as shown here.

Blender's built-in color picker is slightly different from those in other graphics programs. To select a color, simply left-click anywhere on the big color wheel. As you click on different areas of the wheel, the color will change accordingly.

To adjust the brightness of the selected color, you can either move the vertical slider located to the right of the color wheel or use your mouse wheel to scroll up and down. This allows you to fine-tune the color appearance to your liking.

Most of the time, you might find yourself leaving the spec color set to white when selecting colors for materials. However, there is one exception.

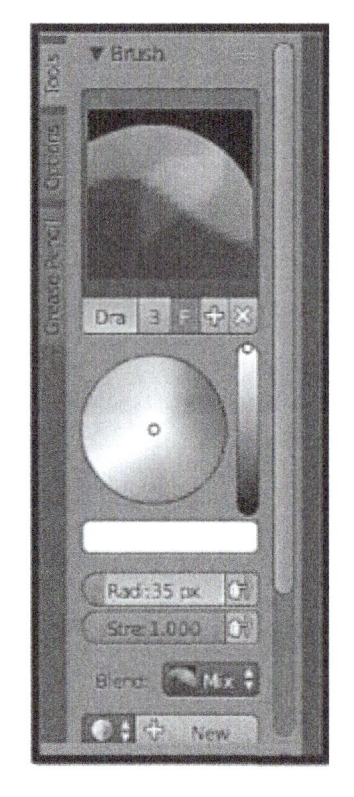

Sometimes, it makes more sense to set the specular color slightly brighter than the diffuse color, especially when aiming for a metallic look in your materials. There isn't a specific formula that dictates when to use the specular color in a certain way versus another. It ultimately depends on your experience and making adjustments based on what appears correct in your final render.

In the context of materials and rendering, specular color refers to the color of the highlights on the surface of an object. For most materials, leaving the specular color set to white works well because it produces natural-looking highlights. However, for materials with metallic properties, such as polished metals, you may want to set the specular color to be slightly brighter than the diffuse color.

When an object has a metallic appearance, the highlights on its surface tend to be more pronounced and brighter compared to non-metallic materials. By adjusting the specular color to be slightly brighter than the diffuse color, you can enhance the metallic look and achieve more convincing and realistic results. There is no strict rule or formula to determine when to use the specular color.

in a certain way; it depends on the specific material you are trying to create and the visual effect you want to achieve. It's essential to rely on your artistic intuition and experience to make such decisions. Experimenting with different values and observing the results in your final render will help you fine-tune the materials to achieve the desired appearance. As you gain more experience, you'll develop a better sense of when to adjust the specular color and other material properties to achieve the best outcome for your 3D scans.

ASSIGNING MULTIPLE MATERIALS TO DIFFERENT PARTS OF A MESH

When you have an object that is initially composed of a single consistent material, it's great if you want to use that material throughout. However, what if you desire to apply multiple other materials to different parts of the object? In such cases, material slots come in handy.

Material slots allow you to define groups of object subcomponents, such as faces in meshes, individual letters in text, or control points in curves and surfaces. These sub-components are then assigned to specific materials, forming what is known as a material slot or material index.

You can create material slots directly from the context panel of Material Properties, but it's important to note that you must be in Edit mode to do so. To understand how this process works, let's imagine you want to model a beach ball and give it the classic pastel-colored panels.

Follow these step:

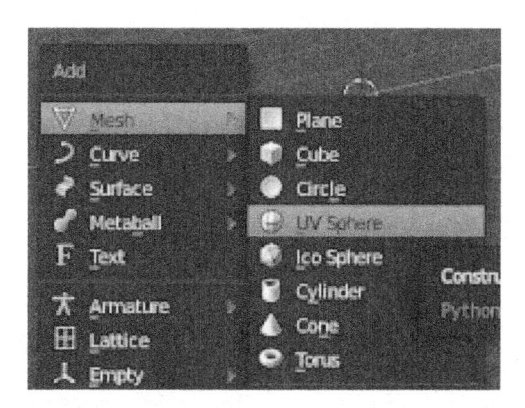

1. Add a UV sphere mesh (Shift +A, Mesh, UV Sphere).
2. Edit the UV sphere using the Last Operator panel in the ToolShelf or the F6 pop-up panel. Set the sphere to have 12 segments, 12 rings, and a radius of 1.00. You can also add a Subdivision Surface modifier (Ctrl+I) and set the fonts to render as smooth in the Shading panel of the Tool Shelf.
3. Tab into Edit mode and switch to Face Select mode (Tab, Ctrl+Tab, Face).
4. Add a new material using the material data block.

5. Click the New button to add a new material or choose an existing material from the data block drop-down menu. This adds your new material to the list in the Material Properties panel.
6. Use the data block text field to name your material. Let's name it "White" for this example.
7. Change the color to white by clicking the color swatch in the diffuse panel. The entire ball will turn white since all faces are currently assigned to this material slot.
8. Use face loop select to select two adjacent vertical face loops (Alt+right-click and Shift+Alt+right-click).
9. Add another new material slot.
10. Click the button with the plus (+) icon in the upper left of the materials list box to create a new material slot named "White.001.".
11. Change the material name to "Blue.".
12. Change the color to blue by clicking the swatch in the diffuse panel and choosing blue using the color picker.
13. Even though the faces are selected, they are still assigned to the white material slot. To assign them to the blue material slot, click the Assign button beneath the material list box.
14. The selected faces will instantly change to the blue color you picked in Step 12.
15. Repeat Steps 6 to 14, working your way around the sphere, creating and assigning colors for the other panels.
16. By following this process, you should end up with four material slots, each representing a different color on the beach ball.

By following these steps, you can create a beach ball with distinct panels of different colors. The material slots feature in Blender allows you to apply multiple materials to different parts of an object, providing you with greater control over the appearance of your 3D models. Material slots are not limited to just meshes; they can also be used with text objects, surfaces, and curves. The process is similar to what we discussed earlier with meshes. However, there is one key difference: when working with curves, surfaces, and text objects, the material slots are assigned to discrete closed entities rather than individual faces. In the case of meshes, you can assign different material slots to specific faces. But with curves, surfaces, and text objects, the material slots are applied to the tire object as a whole. This means that you can assign a material slot to an entire text character or a curve, but you cannot assign a material slot to a single control point or a fragment of a text character. So, while the procedure for using material slots with curves, surfaces and text objects is similar to meshes, but there is a distinction in how the material slots are applied. Understanding this difference is important for efficiently managing materials on various types of objects in Blender.

USING VERTEX COLORS

While material slots allow for the easy assignment of multiple colors and materials to a single mesh, it's important to note that there is a clear distinction between these materials. The hue of one material does not seamlessly transition into another. For example, if you use material slots ineffectively, you won't be able to create a car with a paint job that smoothly transitions from light blue near the ground to a vibrant yellow on the roof and hood. However, vertex colors offer a solution to this limitation. This method is specifically applicable to mesh objects and provides a rapid and efficient way to color a mesh without the harsh edges that material slots can create. Vertex colors function in a rather straightforward manner. You assign a certain color to each vertex in your model. A gradient goes from one vertex to the others if the vertices that make up a face have distinct colors, with the color being most intense at the vertex and becoming more mixed with other colors as it moves away.

It might be quite time-consuming to manually select the color for every vertex in a complex mesh, of course. Vertex Paint mode in Blender helps to solve this issue. By choosing (right-clicking) the mesh object you want to paint in the 3D view, going into Vert ex Paint mode, and then hitting V,. The brush panel is where you'll find a wide range of painting options within the tool shelf. Here, you can select the color you want to use and determine how it will be applied to the chosen object. You have the flexibility to modify the built-in color picker and choose your desired color. To select vertices in the 3D view, simply left-click and drag your cursor over them after selecting your desired color. The color you have specified will be applied to those vertices. If you want to have Blender overlay the wireframe of the object in the 3D view, allowing you to see the exact location of the vertices you are painting on your mesh, you can enable this by left-clicking the "Wire check box under Object Properties in the Display panel.

The tool panel in the tool shelf controls how paint color is applied to vertices in vertex paint mode. The default option for "Mix" merely blends the defined color with the vertex's existing color, based on the Strength slider value. In the 3DView, the current color is added, subtracted, or multiplied with the current vertex color, depending on the choice made in the drop-down selection of the Tool panel. The Blur setting is the only exception, as it tries to mix the colors of the vertices within the specified radius set by the Radius slider. The value of the color you select is used to determine how much of an impact it will have on the colors that are already there by using the Lighten and Darken options. Therefore, painting with Darken enabled won't affect the vertex colors at all if your color settings are set to completely white. However, using that color when Lighten is enabled causes it to show up everywhere you work. If you've used Sculpt mode before, you might be tempted to attempt changing the brush's radius by using the F hotkey. Test it out; it works! The same is true for changing your brush's strength by pressing Shift +F. To build your unique brushes, you may use the brush data blocks similarly to how you do with Sculpt mode. Your mesh may occasionally have certain faces on it that you don't want to get any of the colors you're presently painting during vertex painting. By selecting the Painting Mask button in the 3D View's header with the left mouse button in this instance, you wish to specify face selection masking.

By clicking, you may choose which faces of your mesh to pick after the painting mask is enabled. These faces are the only ones that are impacted by your painting after you do it. This technique is a great approach to isolating a section of your mesh for custom painting without altering the faces around it. If you want the hard-edged color changes that come with material slots, you can get them by using a painting mask.

REVIEW QUESTIONS

1. How can you modify an object's material characteristics in Blender?
2. What is the purpose of this chapter related to blender materials?
3. What is the default material assigned to objects when they are added to Blender?

SUMMARY

The chapter "Changing that Boring Gray Default Material" in Blender focuses on enhancing the visual appeal of 3D models by using materials and textures. While the default gray plastic material may initially suffice, the chapter encourages users to explore vibrant colors and different textures to add realism and creativity to their creations. It introduces material slots as a way to apply multiple materials to different parts of an object, allowing for greater customization. The chapter also explains how to adjust specular colors to achieve metallic looks in materials. Additionally, it delves into the use of vertex colors as an efficient way to create color meshes with smooth transitions between colors. This chapter explores the different panels in the Material Properties section of Blende's user interface. It covers aspects such as diffuse, specular, shading, transparency, mirror, subsurface scattering, strand, options, shadow, and custom properties. Each panel provides various options to control how the material interacts with light and other elements in the scene. The chapter emphasizes that becoming proficient with Blender's materials is about mastering their usage, not about causing harm (as lethal might imply) to the software or the objects.

Overall, the chapter aims to equip Blender users with the knowledge and skills to transform their 3D models into vibrant and realistic creations by effectively utilizing materials and textures while understanding the intricacies of Blender's material system.

CHAPTER 11: TEXTURING TECHNIQUES FOR DETAILED MODELS

If you're aiming for a more precise method to modify the appearance of your object, relying solely on material settings may not suffice, as explained in previous chapters. While Vertex Paint (V) is an option, it may not be ideal if you plan to animate the model, as it can add additional vertices solely for color, leading to performance issues during rigging, animation, and rendering operations.

Moreover, there may be instances where you require material alterations that are independent of the mesh's topology and edge flow. In such situations, employing textures is the recommended approach, which is why this chapter is dedicated to exploring their use. It's important to note that the information covered in Chapter 7 and this chapter complement each other and provide a more comprehensive understanding of how to achieve precise and versatile modifications for your 3D models.

ADDING TEXTURES

In general, a texture is a type of picture that you tile or stretch over the surface of your object to add additional information without increasing its geometry. Textures not only affect the color of your object, but they also provide you with the option to make other changes, including specifying the specularity of some particular model elements.

As an illustration, the skin on a human face tends to be shinier across the nose and forehead and to have less specularity around the eyes. These kinds of phenomena are controllable using texturing. To edit and add textures to a material, go to texture properties:

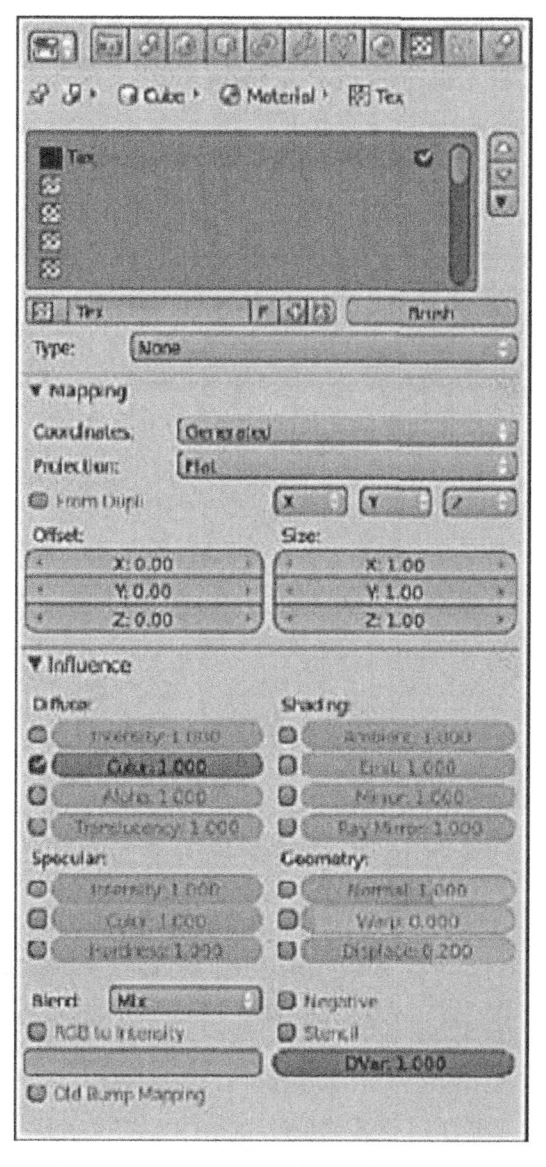

The Texture Properties panel includes a Preview panel that functions similarly to the Material Properties panel. By default, the texture type is set to None, which means the preview panel is disabled. However, you can change this by selecting a different text type from the Type drop-down menu in the Context panel. Just like the list box in Material Properties, the context panel also features a list box at the top. This list box allows you to manage the textures applied to your material, which in turn are applied to your object. However, unlike the list box in Material Properties, you cannot add or remove texture slots randomly. The management of texture slots in the context panel follows a different approach. You have a total of 18 available spaces for texture slots. To edit a specific texture slot, simply left-click on it in the list. The name of the texture is displayed next to its icon for the slots that have a texture loaded. If you want to change the text's name, you can left-click on the texture data-block name field below the list box.

When you select a texture type (other than None) from the Type drop-down menu, a preview panel appears in the Texture Properties. By default, this panel displays the color texture you have selected. However, if you left-click on the Material button below the preview window, the same preview panel you see in Material Properties will be updated accordingly. Without the trouble of switching between material properties and texture properties, you can actively observe how your texture is mapped to an object with this preview type. The preview divides to show the material preview on the left and the texture preview on the right when you left-click both buttons.

The three distinct perspectives of the Preview panel are shown in the image below.

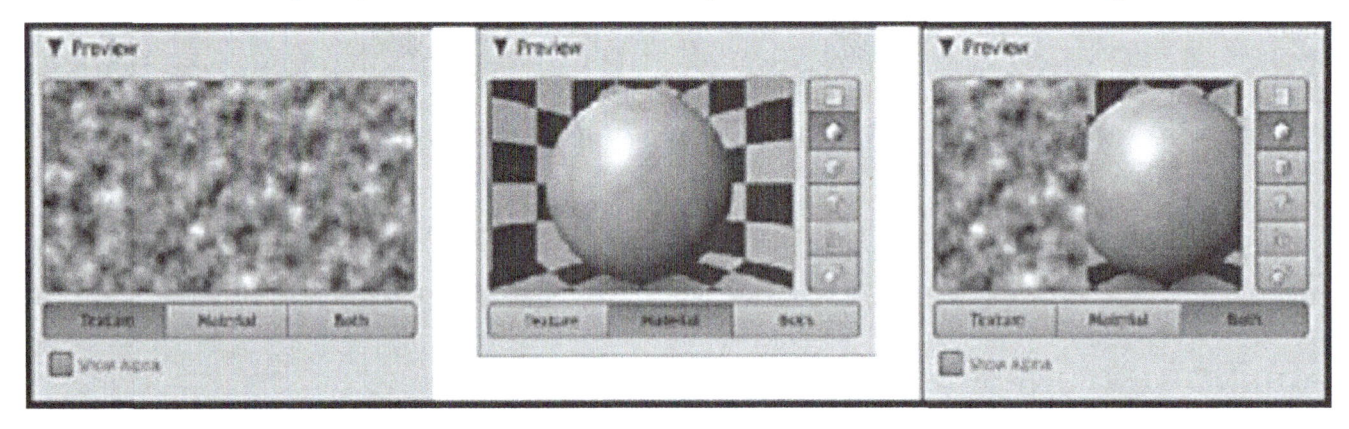

USING PROCEDURAL TEXTURES

In Blender, there are two primary types of textures: image-based textures and procedural textures. Image-based textures involve creating and loading a picture as a texture, while procedural textures are generated within the software using specific pattern algorithms. One advantage of using procedural textures is that you can add complexity to your objects without the need for manual unwrapping, as explained in the "Unwrapping a Mesh" section later in this chapter. The program handles the texture-mapping process for you. However, managing procedural textures may require a bit more skill and effort compared to image-based textures. For example, achieving precise placement of dark circles beneath a character's eyes can be challenging, if not impossible, using pro-cedural textures. Procedural textures are more suitable for creating overall effects than intricate details. They work well for generating textures like the rough surface of an orange rind, providing a solid foundation or base. In Blender's Texture Properties, you can choose from 13 different procedural texture types, in addition to the None texture type, using the Type drop-down box. Apart from procedural textures, another option available is the image texture type. Here are all of the available textures.

UNDERSTANDING TEXTURE MAPPING

Once you have created your texture, whether it's procedural or image-based, the next step is to connect it to your material and, consequently, the surface of your object. This process is referred to as mapping. Mapping involves establishing a connection between a position on the texture and a corresponding location on the object's surface.

You can find mapping controls in the Texture Properties section, specifically within the Mapping and Influence panels, as illustrated here:

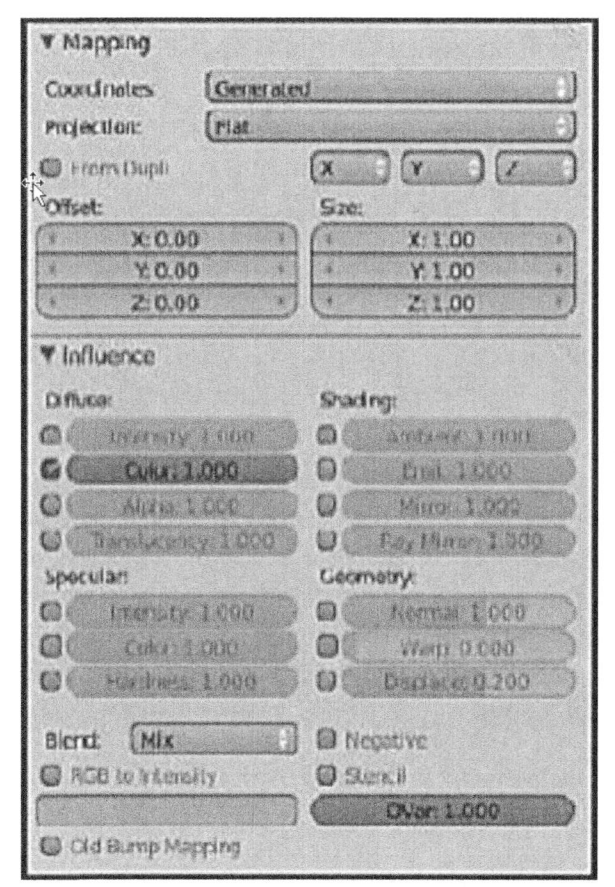

THE MAPPING PANEL

The texture's mapping to the object is controlled by the Mapping panel, which also specifies how the texture's coordinates are projected on it. The Coordinates drop-down menu is the most crucial button.

USING TEXTURE COORDINATES

The several kinds of coordinate mapping are described in the list below:

- **Global:** Selecting this option will define the texture space using the scene's coordinates. As a result, if you have an active object above a texture that has been mapped in this manner, the texture will appear to be stuck in place. Global coordinates have an odd effect, but they can be useful in a few circumstances, like creating fake shadows for a character that is moving.
- **Object:** This option uses another object's location to place a texture on your object. Specify the object by entering its name in the Object field.
- **Generated:** The device generates texture coordinates based on the object's local coordinates, suitable for most situations.
- **UV:** UV coordinates provide precise texture mapping, typically used after unwrapping a mesh.
- **Strand:** Specifically for particle strands, this option maps the texture along the length of the strand.
- **Sticky (camera coordinates):** uses camera location and orientation for mapping.
- **Window:** uses coordinates from the render window (camera coordinates), remaining fixed even during object animation.
- **Normal:** maps the texture according to the surface "normal", useful for angle-dependent effects.
- **Reflection:** maps the texture based on the direction of a reflection vector, suitable for fake reflections.

- **Stress:** Used with dynamic or simulated geometry, stress mapping adjusts transparency based on the difference in texture coordinates.
- **Tangent:** Similar to normal coordinates but uses an optional tangent vector for mapping. Requires enabling the Tangent Shading option.

Texture projection does not affect UV textures, as they explicitly map texture coordinates to the object's surface.

Blender offers four types of texture projection:

1. **Flat:** projects the texture like a slide projector, resulting in distortion on curved or uneven surfaces.
2. **Cube**: Simulates multiple projectors from different angles, mapping the texture onto all sides of a cube. Seams and distortion can still occur on curved surfaces.
3. **Tube**: Allows projection on curved surfaces without distortion, suitable for labeling bottles or applying textures to tubular objects.
4. **Sphere**: Specifically designed for spherical objects, it provides a clean and seamless texture application without noticeable seams. Ideal for spheres and spherical surfaces.

UNWRAPPING A MESH

UV mapping is the most accurate kind of mapping you can employ. You may utilize additional Blender capabilities, like texture paint mode and texture baking, by using UV mapping. UV coordinates are included for free as part of the construction of NURBS surfaces. However, because Blender is primarily a mesh editor, you must put your mesh objects through a process called unwrapping to obtain accurate UV coordinates. Consider a globe and a global map to have a better understanding of this procedure. The latitude and longitude lines on the world map are used to connect points on the globe's three-dimensional surface to the map's two-dimensional surface.

MARKING SEAMS ON A MESH

In Blender, you can unwrap a mesh by selecting all its vertices at once (press 'A' for this), and then, while in Edit mode (press 'Tab' to switch modes), you can either hit 'U or choose 'UV Mapping'-> 'Unwrap' from the ToolShelf. This will display a menu with several choices. Although the menu offers various options, it's generally recommended to select the first one, "Unwrap," unless your mesh is simple or requires a specific approach. Blender's unwrapping tools are powerful, but to make the most of them, you need to define certain seams first. The goal is to convert a 3D surface into a 2D plane, so you must instruct Blender where to make cuts in the mesh. These cuts are called seams."

To create seams for unwrapping in Blender, follow these steps:

1. Enter Edit mode and switch to Edge Select mode.
2. Select the edges that you want to define as seams. You can use edge-loop selection for convenience.
3. Use the Edge Specials menu to mark the selected edges as seams. This can be done by pressing Ctrl+E and selecting "Mark Seam" or by using the UV Mapping section in the Tool Shelf.

4. The marked seams will appear highlighted in orange on your mesh. If you mistakenly mark the wrong edges, you can remove the seam by selecting them and using Ctrl+E or the Tool Shelf to "Clea r Seam."

Once you've marked seams on your mesh, you can proceed with the unwrapping process.

For a clearer view of your work, you can adjust your screen layout by following these steps:

1. Switch the viewport shading of your 3DView to "Textured" by pressing Alt+Z.
2. Create a new area for the UV/Image Editor by using Shift+F10.
3. Set the newly created area to display the UV/Image Editor.
4. If needed, you can easily return to the default UV editing screen in Blender by selecting the screen data block at the top of the Blender window. **The layout should resemble the image below:**

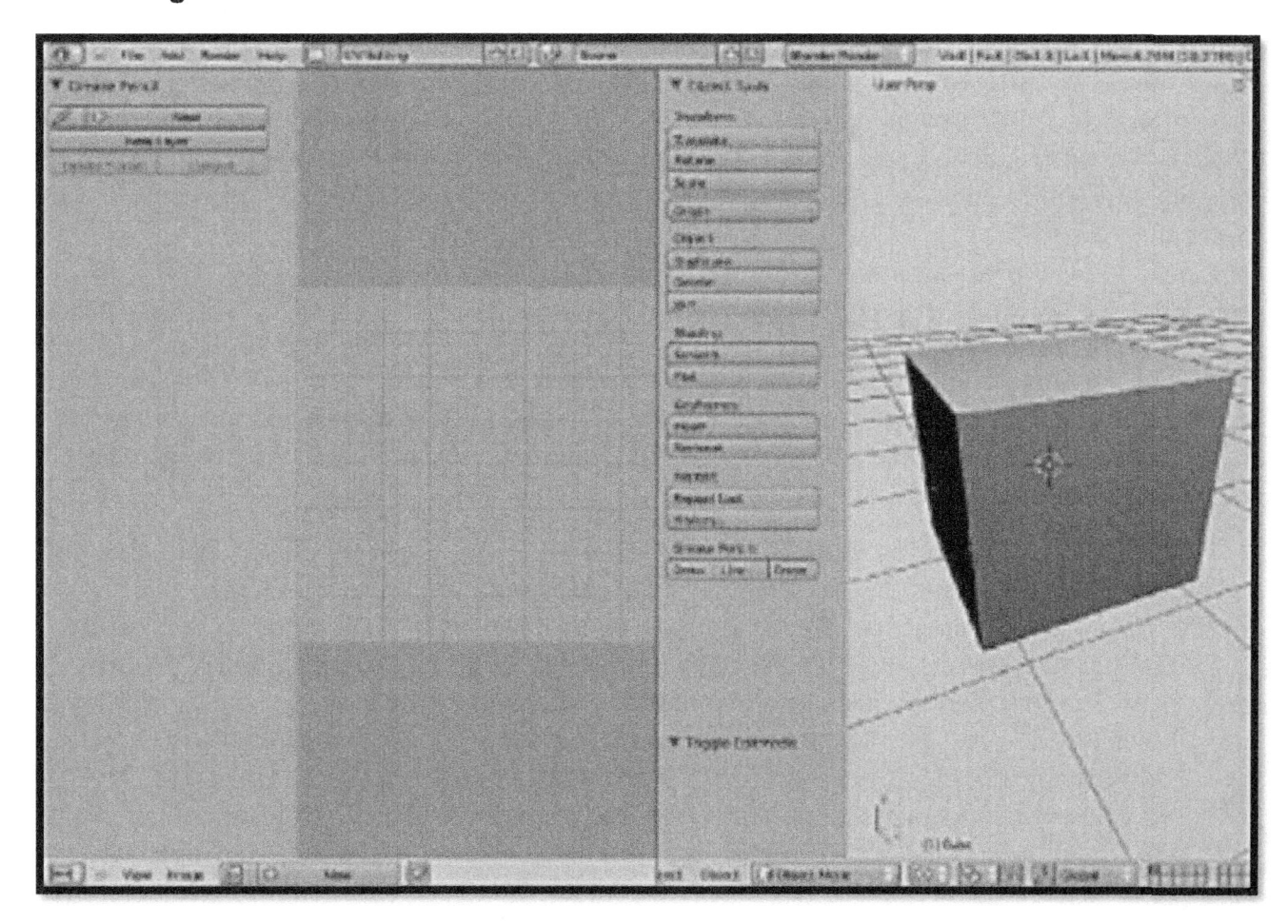

With this layout and your seams properly defined, you can efficiently unwrap your mesh and work on UV mapping. "Happy Blendering!"

ADDING A TEST GRID

To proceed with the unwrapping process in Blender, you'll need an image to map onto your mesh, and using a test grid is a common practice to identify areas of texture stretching.

Follow these steps to add a test grid:

1. Open Blender and go to the UV/Image Editor by selecting it from the Editor Type menu or using the shortcut Shift+F10.
2. In the UV/Image Editor, choose "Image from the header menu, and then click on "New" or use the shortcut Alt+N.
3. This action will bring up a set of options for creating a new image. Give the image a sensible name, such as "Test Grid."
4. Check the "UV Test Grid" box. This will generate a colored checkerboard pattern on the image, which helps in visualizing texture distortion when applied to your 3D mesh.
5. Keep the other settings at their default values for now, such as the image size.
6. The UV/Image Editor will update in real time, displaying the newly created test grid image.

Also, take note that the test grid's height and breadth are equal, making it a square image. It is important to maintain a square aspect ratio because UV texturing is optimized for square images. For optimal efficiency when working with UV textures, it's best to make your texture size a power of two, which means repeatedly multiplying 2 by itself. Commonly used texture sizes are 1,024 square pixels (2" 10) or 2,048 pixels (211) for the next larger size and 512 pixels (29) for the next smaller size. By following these steps and using a square, power-of-two test grid, you can proceed with unwrapping your mesh in Blender and efficiently work on UV texturing. The test grid will help you identify and address any stretching issues, ensuring a better result for your final textured model.

GENERATING AND EDITING UV COORDINATES

Great job! The instructions are clear and well-organized. We made a few minor edits for clarity and formatting. **Here's the revised version:** Now that you have marked seams and added a test grid for reference, it's time to proceed with unwrapping your mesh. **Follow these steps in Edit mode:**

1. Select all vertices by pressing 'A'. Remember that the 'A' key is a toggle, so you may need to press it twice to ensure everything is selected.
2. Unwrap the mesh by pressing 'U' and selecting Unwrap p".
3. Voila! Your mesh is now unwrapped! From this point, you can edit your UV layout to organize the pieces logically and minimize stretching. You can identify stretching by observing the test grid texture. If any squares on the checkerboard appear distorted or significantly non-square, it indicates stretching. Ensure that you are using Textured Viewport Shading (Alt+Z) to see the test grid texture on your mesh. The controls in the UV/Image Editor are similar to those in the 3DView. You can use hot keys such as Grab (G), Rotate (R), and Scale (S) for manipulation. Selection tools like Border Select (B), Circle Select (C), and Edge Loop Select (Alt+Click) work as expected. Additionally, the UV/Image Editor provides a 2D cursor, similar to the 3D cursor in the 3D View, which aids in snapping and serves as a reference for rotation and scaling. When trying to address stretching issues in your UV layout, you may encounter a situation where adjusting certain vertices causes distortion and stretching in another area. To assist with this challenge, Blen d er offers two useful tools: Vertex Pinning (P) and Live Unwrap (UVs > Live Unwrap).These tools work together to improve your workflow.

Here Is an overview of the workflow stages:

1. **Enable Live Unwrap**: activate Live Unwrap by navigating to UVs > Live Unwrap. This feature allows for real-time updates to the UV layout as you manipulate the mesh.
2. **Pinning Vertices**: Identify the vertices that you want to keep in place to avoid unwanted distortion. Select the desired vertices in the UV Editor and use the Vertex Pinning tool (P) to pin them. This ensures that the pinned vertices remain fixed while you make adjustments.
3. **Adjusting Unpinned Vertices**: With Live Unwrap active and some vertices pinned, you can freely manipulate the remaining unpinned vertices in the UV Editor. As you move or scale these vertices, the Live Unwrap feature dynamically updates the UV layout in real time.
4. **Observing the Results**: Continuously monitor the UV light and observe how the changes affect the texture mapping. Check for any new instances of stretching or distortion that may have emerged due to the adjustments. You may need to iterate and fine-tune your modifications to achieve the desired outcome.

By combining the Vertex Pinning tool with Live Unwrap, you can iteratively adjust your UV layout, minimize stretching, and achieve better control over the texture mapping on your mesh. This is an unwrapped and mostly stretch-less Suzanne head.

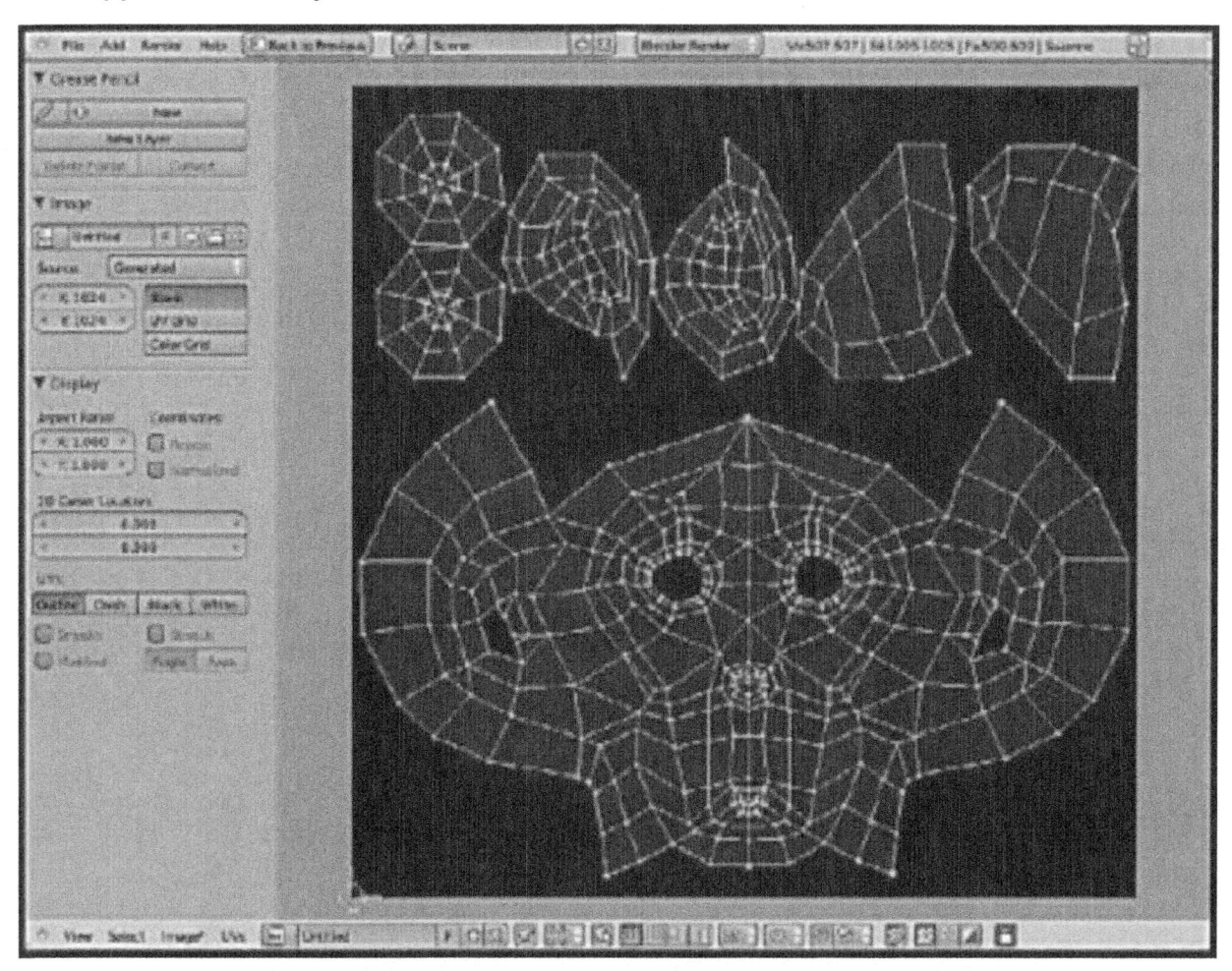

PAINTING TEXTURES DIRECTLY ON A MESH

If you followed the instructions in the earlier chapters of this book, you should already have an unwrapped model with a texture that doesn't stretch. Woohoo! However, let's imagine that, for some illogical reason, you want to use this UV layout to paint a texture for your mesh instead of having a checkerboard as the texture for your object. In Blender, you have the option of painting directly on the mesh or exporting the UV layout to paint in a third-party application like GIMP or Photoshop. We like to combine a few of these techniques. To rough out the color palette and perhaps build some bump and specularity maps, we often paint straight on the mesh in Blender. To begin applying textures to unwrapped geometry, you can utilize Blender's Texture Paint mode. Simply click on the mode button located in the header of the 3D view to switch to texture paint mode. The process is quite similar to Vertex Paint mode, with a few minor differences.

In texture paint mode, you'll find a range of paint options available on the tool shelf. While there are some variations compared to Vertex Paint mode, the overall functionality remains consistent. The ToolShelf provides additional preset brushes and a Jitter slider, offering more flexibility for your painting needs. The Brush data block, however, remains mostly unchanged. Moreover, you have the option to define a texture for your brush in the Texture panel of the Tool Shelf. This allows you to go beyond painting flat colors and incorporate textures into your artwork.

To optimize your texture painting workflow in Blender, it is recommended to set up your screen layout as shown in the image here. This configuration allows you to conveniently work in both the UV/Image Editor and the 3DView simultaneously. Ensure that both the UV/Image Editor and the 3D View are in Texture Paint mode, as this is where you'll perform your texture painting tasks. If you need to make any adjustments to the texture of your brush, you can temporarily move one of the sections to the Properties editor by pressing Shift+F7. From there, you can access the texture properties and modify the desired texture. Now you can unleash your creativity and use Blender's Texture Paint mode to paint directly on your mesh and add intricate details, color variations, and textures to bring your 3D model to life. Happy painting!

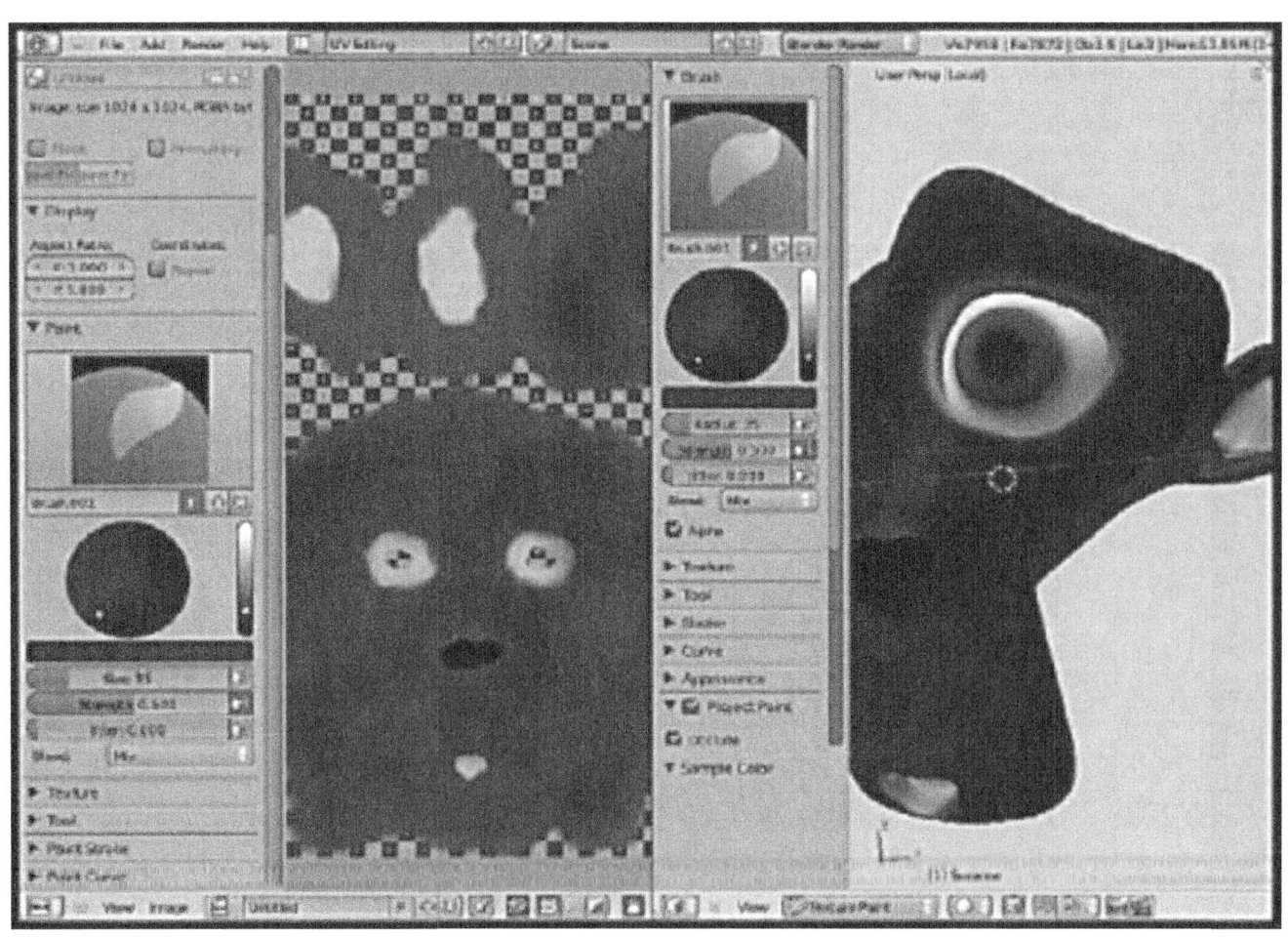

Indeed, while Blender's Texture Paint mode is powerful, certain tasks may be better suited for proper 2D graphics applications like GIMP or Photoshop. If you want to further edit your texture or add more intricate details, it's a good idea to save the painted texture as an external image that you can work on in another software.

To save your painted texture, follow these steps in the UV/Image Editor:

1. Make sure you are in the UV/Image Editor in Blender.
2. Choose "Image" from the header menu.
3. Select "Save As" to save your painted texture as an external image.
4. When the File Browser window appears, choose the format in which you want to store the image on your hard drive. PNG is a popular choice for textures because it offers lossless compression, resulting in minimal file sizes while preserving image quality.
5. Give your image a meaningful name and specify the location on your hard drive where you want to save it.

By saving the painted texture as an external PNG image, you can easily import it into other graphic software, such as GIMP or Photoshop, to perform more advanced editing and fine-tuning. Additionally, exporting your UV layer as a picture can serve as a frame of reference for your painting process, allowing you to understand how the 2D texture will be applied to your 3D model. With this workflow, you can seamlessly integrate Blender with other graphic tools to create stunning and detailed textures for your 3D models. Enjoy the flexibility and creativity that come with combining different software to achieve your artistic vision!

SAVING PAINTED TEXTURES AND EXPORTING UV LAYOUTS

After saving your painted texture as an external image, the next step in Blender is to obtain the UV layer of your object, which is typically required for further editing in your 2D image editor.

To accomplish this, follow these steps:

1. Make sure you are in the UV/Image Editor in Blender.
2. Switch to Edit mode by pressing 'Tab' on your keyboard.
3. From the menu, select UVs -> Image -> Export UV Layout.
4. This action will prompt the appearance of a file browser, enabling you to choose the destination on your hard disk where you want to save your UV layout.
5. The UV export tool provides you with various format options, including the widely-used PNG format as well as SVG (Scalable Vector Graphics) and EPS (Encapsulated Posts) for vector image formats. If your UV layout is in a vector format like SVG or EPS, you can adjust its scale to accommodate any picture size without losing quality.

By exporting your UV layer, you get a visual representation of how your 3D object's surfaces are unwrapped onto a 2D plane. This UV layer can then be imported into your 2D image editor (e.g., GIMP or Photoshop) as a reference, allowing you to paint directly on it or overlay it with your painted texture for precise adjustments and edits. Using the exported UV layer together with the painted texture provides a seamless workflow for achieving detailed and realistic textures for your 3D models. Have fun refining your art and exploring the creative possibilities with this versatile combination of tools!

SUMMARY

This section discusses the importance of using textures to modify the appearance of 3D objects and explains how they complement material settings. Textures provide a way to add additional information to the object's surface without increasing its geometry. Procedural textures and image-based textures are introduced, with an emphasis on the advantages of using procedural textures. The process of UV mapping and unwrapping a mesh is explained, along with tips on avoiding stretching and distortion. The Texture Paint mode in Blender is highlighted as a tool for painting directly on the mesh, and the option to save painted textures as external images is mentioned. Finally, exporting the UV layout for use in 2D image editors is discussed to refine the textures further.

REVISION QUESTIONS

1. What are the advantages of using textures over relying solely on material settings to modify the appearance of 3D objects?
2. How does Blender's Texture Paint mode allow artists to add intricate details and textures directly onto the mesh?
3. Why is it important to mark seams and unwrap a mesh during the UV mapping process, and how does it help in achieving accurate texture mapping?
4. What are the options available for texture projection in Blender, and when would you use each type of projection?

CHAPTER 12: ILLUMINATING YOUR SCENE

This section delves into the various types of lights available in Blender and provides insights into effectively utilizing them in your scenes. Additionally, it explores the process of setting up the environment within your scene using the World Properties settings. These topics play a crucial role in adding the finishing touches to your scenes, resulting in visually stunning and polished outcomes.

LIGHTING A SCENE

The way you light your scene can significantly influence how it is perceived by the viewer. By playing with different lighting techniques, you can create various moods and atmospheres. For instance, using harsh, stark lighting can give your scene a dramatic film noir effect, while low-angle lighting with long shadows can evoke a sense of horror. On the other hand, bright high-angle lighting can make it feel like a beautiful summer day. You can even experiment with unconventional lighting, such as a bluish light with a noise cloud texture, to create an underwater ambiance. In addition to lighting, setting up your environment is equally vital in creating the desired impact. You have the freedom to choose from different settings to achieve various appearances. With the right combination of lighting techniques and other tricks, you can make almost any location come to life in your scenario. The image below illustrates a simple scene with different environmental and lighting setups to showcase the versatility of these techniques.

UNDERSTANDING A BASIC THREE-POINT LIGHTING SETUP

Before delving into the intricacies of lighting a scene in Blender, it's essential to familiarize yourself with some common lighting configurations and terminology. What's interesting is that this knowledge extends beyond the realm of 3D computer graphics and finds utility in professional still photography, video production, and filmmaking. Many photographers and directors prefer to use 3D graphics to previsualize lighting setups before embarking on location for an actual shoot. So, it turns out that you're not just creating visually appealing images on a computer screen—there's more to it than meets the eye!

One of the most widely used lighting configurations is known as "three-point lighting." As the name implies, it involves the use of three separate sets of lights. This setup is commonly employed in interview studios and serves as the foundation for nearly all other lighting arrangements. The figure above provides a top-down perspective, showcasing an example of a typical three-point lighting configuration. By familiarizing yourself with these lighting configurations and techniques, you'll gain a solid foundation for creating captivating visual experiences, whether in the realm of computer graphics, photography, video production, or filmmaking.

KEY LIGHT

To begin creating a three-point lighting setup, the first step is to position your subject in the center of the scene and direct your camera toward it. Once that's done, you can proceed to set up the key light, which serves as the primary source of illumination.

Typically, the key light is the strongest in the scene, responsible for casting primary shadows and creating the brightest highlights. It is advisable to position this light directly in front of your camera, either to the left or right, and slightly higher than your subject. This placement helps avoid the unnerving effect of a flashlight shining from beneath the chin, reminiscent of spooky storytelling around a campfire. Instead, the shadows will naturally fall, enhancing the overall visual appeal and providing a more natural and flattering look for your subject. The key light sets the tone and defines the main features of your subject, making it a crucial element in the three-point lighting setup.

BACK LIGHT

Completing the three-point lighting setup is the inclusion of the backlight or rim light, which serves as the third and final light source. This light is positioned behind your subject, creating a subtle glow that wraps around their silhouette. It is this delicate touch of luminosity that often separates an ordinary lighting arrangement from a truly remarkable one, effectively accentuating your subject and making them visually distinct from the background. The addition of a backlight adds that extra touch of brilliance to ensure your scene truly shines.

Instructions for positioning the backlight in a three-point lighting setup:

1. **Consider different placement options**: There are various opinions on where to position the backlight, so it's worth exploring different approaches to find what works best for your scene.
2. **Option 1**: Opposite the key light. One option is to place the backlight directly opposite the key light. This can be effective in certain cases, but be mindful of the potential competition between the rim effect and the key light's highlights.
3. **Option 2**: Opposite the camera: Another approach is to position the backlight opposite the camera. This can work well, but be cautious if the subject moves, as it may risk causing a glare or distracting the audience.
4. **Option 3**: Opposite the fill light. Some people recommend placing the backlight opposite the fill light. This can create a pleasing rim of light that complements the key light, but be aware that it might appear slightly unnatural.
5. **Experiment and find the best result**: Lighting is subjective, and there's no one-size-fits-all solution. The key is to play around with the placement of your backlight and observe

the outcomes for yourself. Only through experimentation can you determine the optimal position that produces the desired results.

Remember, the most important principle is to ensure that the backlight is directed toward the subject. Beyond that, feel free to explore and discover the lighting arrangement that suits your scene and achieves the desired visual impact. When it comes to the power and throw of the backlight, it's generally recommended to have it less powerful than the key light for a natural appearance.

The throw, on the other hand, can vary since the highlights are on the opposite side of your subject. We prefer a narrow throw, but a wide throw can also be effective, especially for larger scenes. So, that's the basic concept of three-point lighting. It's a versatile approach that works well both in computer graphics and in the real world, serving as a foundation for many other lighting setups. If you want to create a creepy atmosphere, try lowering the angle of your key light. For more dramatic shadows, consider removing or reducing the power of your fill and backlights.

To achieve a mysterious or romantic silence, position your key light behind your subject. And remember, these are just a few examples of what you can explore and experiment with when it comes to lighting techniques. In essence, three-point lighting provides a solid starting point, but there's so much more to discover and learn. So keep exploring, unleash your creativity, and dive deeper into the fascinating world of lighting!

KNOWING WHEN TO USE WHICH TYPE OF LIGHT

When you are comfortable with the fundamentals of three-point lighting, you can utilize Blender to light your scenes. Use **Shift + A --> Lamp** to open the menu shown below to add a new light.

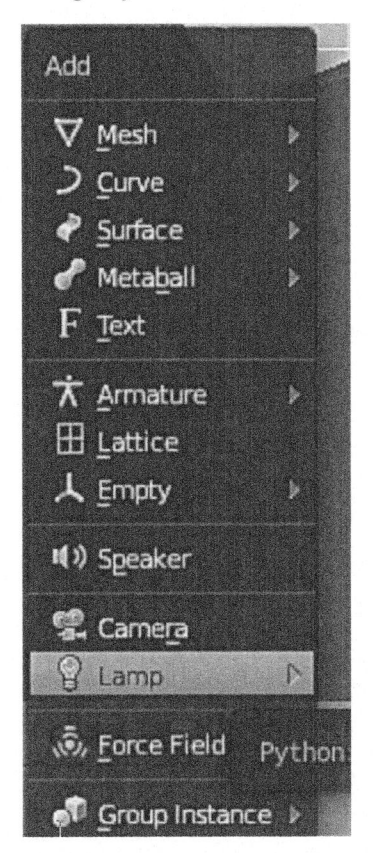

Within the Lamp menu, you have the option to choose from various types of lights, including:

1. **Point**: Sometimes called an omni-light, this type of light originates from a single point in space and illuminates in all directions. By the way, there is only one point lamp in the Blender scene. It serves as a versatile light source, and we find it effective for fill or secondary lighting purposes.
2. **Sun**: The Sun lamp represents a dominant light source that radiates in a specific direction. Its position in your scene is not as crucial as its orientation, as it emits light from a single source. This type of lighting can transform the appearance of the sky, making it a great choice for outdoor scenes that require impactful lighting.
3. **Spot**: The spotlight is widely regarded as the go-to light source in computer-generated imagery for its versatility. It offers extensive have control over shadow characteristics and the area illuminated by the light. Comparable to a flashlight or a theater spotlight, the spotlight provides precise control, making it ideal for serving as a key light in your scenes.

4. **Hemi**: Similar to the Sun lamp, the Hemi lamp can be placed anywhere in your scene without significant impact. The key aspect of the Hemi lamp is its direction. However, compared to the Sun lamp, hemi lighting tends to be softer and less pronounced, as it creates a diffuse illumination resembling a hemisphere of light surrounding the scene. It's important to note that hemi lights in Blender do not cast shadows, making them well-suited for backlighting and filling in shadows. They can also be effective for out-of-door lighting scenarios.
5. **Area**: Area lights are powerful light sources that operate similarly to spotlights. However, they utilize a grid of lights, resulting in softer and more precise shadows. The use of multiple lights in an array contributes to the improved shadow quality produced by area lighting.

Each of these light types has its own unique characteristics and applications. Experimenting with different light setups can dramatically impact the mood and atmosphere of your scenes, allowing you to achieve the desired visual effects and convey the intended emotions to your audience.

LIGHTING FOR SPEEDY RENDERS

In Blender, the lamp offers six additional controls that can be referred to as "cheat buttons" due to their usefulness in achieving unique lighting effects that may be challenging or impossible to replicate in real-world scenarios. These controls play a significant role in enhancing the power of lighting in 3D computer graphics. When utilized effectively, these options can not only improve the rendering speed but also maintain the overall quality of the image. In the lamp Object Data Properties, the image below showcases these controls.

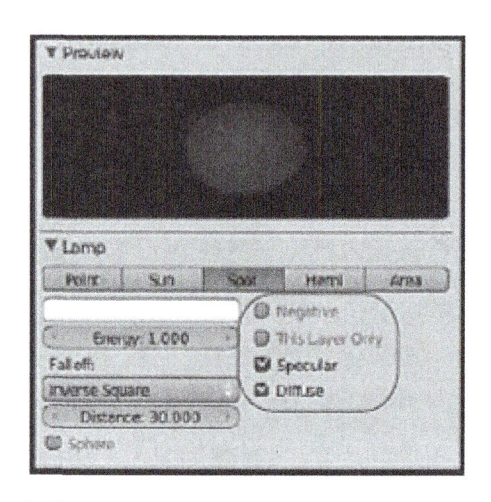

Descriptions of each cheat button in the lamp panel areas follow:

1. **Negative**: This check box allows you to invert the light's output, offering a unique capability in CG lighting. By shining darkness on your scene, you can achieve interesting effects, such as reducing brightness or creating deeper shadows. Adjusting the energy or shadow samples is not necessary when you can simply utilize negative light.
2. **This Layer Only**: Enabling this control ensures that the light illuminates only objects on the same layer. In real-world lighting, Technicians often go through extensive masking or hiding to limit the light's effect to specific parts of the scene. In Blender, you can easily achieve this by enabling the check box and placing your characters on a different layer than the light.
3. **Specular**: In three-point lighting, minimizing the highlights from the fill light is essential to avoid competition with the key light's highlights. In real-world scenarios, technicians often diffuse the fill to achieve this effect. In Blender, you can conveniently disable the lamp's specular highlights by unchecking this box, eliminating any unwanted competition.
4. **Diffuse**: This option provides fine control over highlights without altering the overall scene illumination. By disabling shadow casting and unchecking this box, you can manipulate a movable specular highlight around your subject. Although not frequently used, this feature proves valuable in specific lighting situations.

In the shadow panel, located further down in the Object Data Properties window, you will find the last two cheat buttons, Each is described as follows:

5. **Only This Laye**: This check box specifically affects shadows and operates similarly to its counterpart in the Lamp panel. Enabling this option ensures that shadows are cast only on objects within the same layer as the light source.
6. **Shadow alone**: When this option is selected, shadows are generated without adding additional light to the scene. This can be useful in certain situations where you want to speed up rendering by using other lamps without shadows for primary illumination while relying on buffered spots solely for shadow effects.

These cheat buttons offer a range of creative options, allowing you to achieve specific lighting effects in your 3D scenes and providing more control and versatility in your lighting setups.

WORKING WITH THREE-POINT LIGHTING IN A BLENDER

A recommended lighting rig in Blender often starts with a three-point lighting setup. Here is a typical starting point:

Key: Utilize a buffered spot as the key light. Maintain default settings except for adjusting the spot size to 60 degrees and enabling the Autoclip check boxes for the Clip Start and Clip End values. The key light is the primary light source, and the spotlight provides focused and directional illumination, creating the main highlights and shadows on the subject. Fill: Begin with a Hemi light, setting the energy to 0.5 and disabling the specular option in the lamp panel. The hemi light serves as a secondary light source, filling in the shadows created by the key light. It adds subtle and diffuse lighting to reduce harsh shadows and create a more balanced overall look.

Back: Also use a hemi light, adjusting the energy to a range of 0.75 to 1.0 to achieve a desirable rim light effect. The backlight is positioned behind the subject, emphasizing the edges and creating a subtle glow, separating the subject from the background. Since when the lamp is placed behind the subject, specularity is not as crucial. To ensure it doesn't compete with the key light's specularity, it's recommended to disable the specularity for this light as well. Initially, don't overly concern yourself with the precise location of the backlight, as backlighting in computer graphics often requires tweaking to achieve the desired effect. Getting the location perfect in the initial setup is not critical. This lighting setup is well-suited for studio lighting and works effectively for indoor scenes or when lighting isolated objects. It provides a classic and versatile foundation for various 3D scenes, allowing you to achieve realistic and visually appealing results. As you gain more experience and explore different lighting techniques, you can further refine and customize the setup to suit the specific requirements of your scenes.

SETTING UP THE WORD

When it comes to rendering your scene, lighting is just one piece of the puzzle. Another crucial aspect to consider is the environment in which your scene is set. Factors such as whether it's indoors or outdoors, daytime or nighttime, and the overall ambiance play a significant role in shaping the final look of your image. Additionally, details like the color of the sky, the presence of clouds, and the background scenery all contribute to the overall atmosphere. Thankfully, Blender provides a convenient set of controls for configuring your scene's environment, conveniently located in the World Properties. This allows you to create and adjust the background and surrounding environment, further enhancing the visual impact of your renders.

With Blender's World Properties, you have the flexibility to choose between different environments to set the tone of your scene. You can create a simple "white void" background for a clean and minimalist look or simulate an outdoor setting with a realistic sky and sun. The color and intensity of the ambient light can also be customized to achieve the desired mood and ambiance. Further, Blender allows you to experiment with various environmental effects, such as adding volumetric clouds or fog, to enhance the depth and realism of your scene. These controls offer a powerful toolkit to add depth and complexity to your renders, enabling you to create stunning and immersive visual experiences. In this section, we will explore these controls and learn how to effectively utilize them to craft the perfect environment for your 3D scenes. By mastering the art of lighting and environment configuration, you can elevate the quality and impact of your renders, bringing your artistic vision to life with exceptional realism and atmosphere.

CHANGING THE SKY TO SOMETHING OTHER THAN DULL GRAY

If you've spent some time working with Blender and rendering your scenes, you might have grown tired of the default dull gray background color that the renderer provides. Fortunately, you can change this color to something more appealing. To do so, navigate to the World panel within the World Properties. In this panel, you'll find a color swatch on the left, which determines the horizon color. Simply left-click on the color swatch and utilize the color picker to make adjustments. Next to the horizon color, you'll notice the zenith color.

Interestingly, modifying this color might not seem to have any effect on the background color initially. By Definably, Blender is configured to utilize only the horizon color, resulting in a solid background color. However, you can change this default behavior by left-clicking on the "Blend Sky" checkbox in the World panel. Once selected, the preview will display a linear gradient that smoothly transitions from the horizon color at the bottom to the zenith color at the top.

In situations where you want to focus solely on a model you've created, you can employ this setup with a horizon color of around 50 percent gray and a nearly black zenith color. This choice of colors creates a subtle and visually pleasing background that complements your model and avoids any distractions. By customizing the background colors and experimenting with different gradients, you can add depth and atmosphere to your renders. Whether you're creating a realistic outdoor scene or a stylized environment, the ability to control the horizon and zenith colors in Blender's World Properties allows you to tailor the background to perfectly suit your artistic vision.

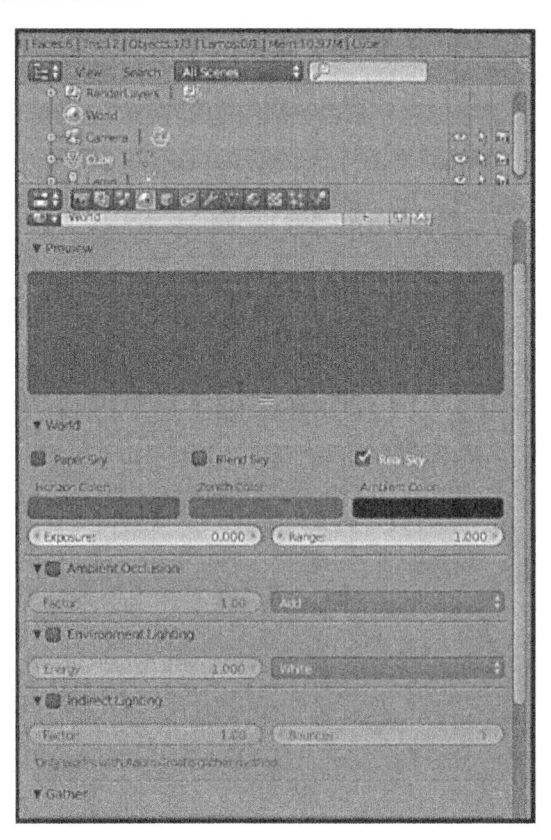

Now, you might be wondering about the purpose of the remaining two check boxes found in the World panel. Allow me to explain their functions to you. The great thing is that you have the flexibility to activate any combination of these checkboxes based on your preferences.

Here's a breakdown of what each option does when enabled:

1. **Paper Sky**: When you enable the Paper Sky setting along with Blend Sky and RealSky, it ensures that the horizon remains at the center of the camera, regardless of its orientation. Additionally, it adjusts the gradient to ensure that both the zenith and horizon colors are fully visible. This option is particularly useful when you want to maintain a consistent horizon appearance regardless of how you position the camera in your scene.
2. **Blend Sky**: Enabling Blend The sky creates a gradient that extends from the horizon to the zenith. If you only enable this option, Without the others, the horizon will always appear at the bottom of the camera view, while the zenith will be positioned at the top. This setting is ideal when you want a straightforward gradient background without any rotation as you move the camera.
3. **Real Sky**: By activating Real Sky, the horizon aligns with the XY ground plane, and the gradient extends along the global Z-axis using the zenith color. One notable advantage is that since the horizon is fixed to the XY ground plane, the gradient rotates along with the camera's movement, resulting in a more realistic background appearance. We find this setting particularly appealing, especially when we're utilizing a texture in the background. It provides a natural and dynamic feel to the scene, especially when there's camera movement involved. With these options at your disposal, you can experiment with different combinations to achieve the desired background effect for your renders. Whether you prefer a fixed horizon, a smooth gradient, or a dynamic real-sky appearance, Blender's World Properties gives you the creative freedom to tailor your scene's environment to perfection.

UNDERSTANDING AMBIENT OCCLUSION

Take a moment to observe the world outside. If it's daytime, you'll notice how everything appears illuminated. Even on a bright sunny day, the darkest shadows aren't entirely black. This intriguing effect is a result of sunlight bouncing off surfaces multiple times, ensuring that nearly all objects receive some level of light exposure. In the realm of computer graphics, this phenomenon is known as global illumination, or GI. Recreating this natural lighting efficiently poses a significant challenge. One of the main reasons for this is the "light only bounces once" rule, which limits the realistic rendering of light interactions.

Another effect of GI is that fine details, creases, fractures, and wrinkles become more noticeable due to all the light that is reflected. This assertion can initially appear paradoxical. After all, it stands to reason that everything should appear even brighter and flatter if the light is reflecting off of everything. But keep in mind that, in addition to reflecting off everything, light also creates tiny shadows from all the strange angles from which it bounces. These minute details are highlighted by those tiny shadows. In outdoor settings, the global illumination (GI) effect becomes particularly noticeable on cloudy days when light is evenly scattered by the clouds. Interestingly, this phenomenon can also be observed in well-lit indoor spaces with multiple light sources, such as office buildings with rows of fluorescent lights along the ceiling. While using a Hemi lamp can partially replicate this effect, falls short of delivering the desirable additional detail that comes with true global illumination because Hemi lamps do not cast shadows.

The unfortunate fact is that Blender's core renderer lacks "true GI functionality. However, ambient occlusion (AO) in Blender does provide a fantastic method for simulating GI. Often referred to as dirty GI or dirt shader, AO identifies the minute details in your object and draws attention to them by darkening or brightening the rest of the model. To enable ambient occlusion (AO) in Blender, navigate to the World Properties window, and click the checkbox next to the Ambient Occlusion panel. Enabling AO unlocks the settings in the Gather panel. In this panel, you are presented with two options for calculating AO: ray tracing and approximation. The image here displays the Gather panel, which showcases the available options for ray-traced AO and approximate AO.

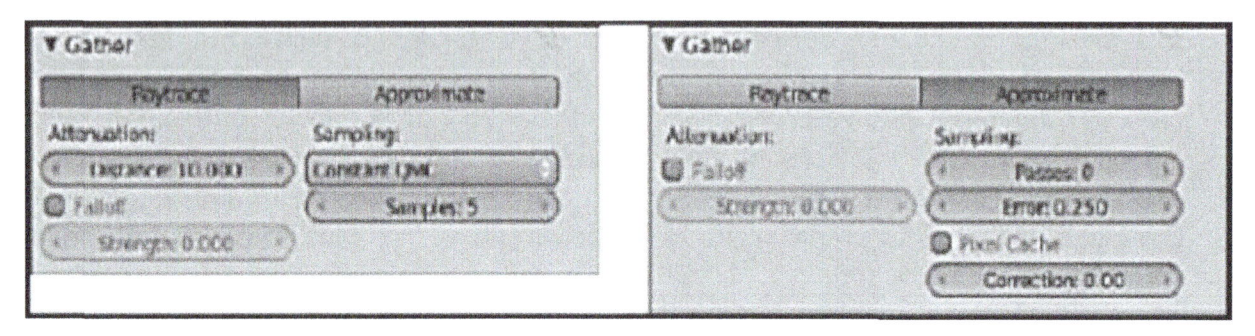

Both the ray-traced and approximate ambient occlusion (AO) methods share several controls in the ambient occlusion and gathering panels.

Let's explore the available options for both types of AO:

1. **Ambient Color**: This color swatch, located in the World panel, determines the source color for the diffuse energy used by AO. Typically, it's recommended to keep the ambient color set to black to avoid washing out the scene's shading. However, when AO is enabled and you adjust the ambient color, the shading becomes more pronounced, resulting in a more realistic and believable image.
2. **Factor**: The Factor r value determines the strength of the overall ambient occlusion (AO) effect. It multiplies the chosen effect from the Add/Multi-Ply menu. Typically, keeping it at 1.0 is recommended, but we encourage you to experiment with different values to see how it impacts your scene.
3. **Add/Multiply**: The Add/Multiply drop-down menu in the Ambient Occlusion panel allows you to control how AO generates shades. Selecting Add brightens the remaining parts of the object, making the details more visible while retaining their original colors. Choosing to multiply darkens the detailed areas, enhancing the object's original shading.
4. **Falloff**: This option, found in the Gather panel, regulates the size of the additional shadows created by AO. Enabling the falloff checkbox enables the use of the strength value field below it. Higher values in the strength field result in subtler shadows.

The additional values provided for ray-traced and approximate gathering serve to fine-tune and optimize their functionality. If you've read about ray-traced lights earlier in this chapter, the settings for ray-traced gathering will appear familiar to you. We suggest using adaptive QMC (Quasi-Mote Carlo) sampling, as it generally produces faster results with good quality. Surprisingly, in many scenarios, ray-traced gathering with adaptive QMC sampling is even faster than using approximate gathering. Other sampling types often yield a more speckled or noisy outcome. When deciding between rays traced and approximate gathering, it's important to consider the trade-offs involved. The ray-traced gathering offers more precise results but can be time-consuming, especially when using a higher Samples value to reduce shading noise in the AO. On the other hand, approximate gathering is faster and avoids the noise issue associated with ray-traced gathering. However, it may require some additional effort to achieve believable shadows, particularly in areas where objects intersect. It's essential to weigh the advantages and disadvantages of your specific projects. The image here showcases the same scene rendered using both gathering methods as well as without any AO applied.

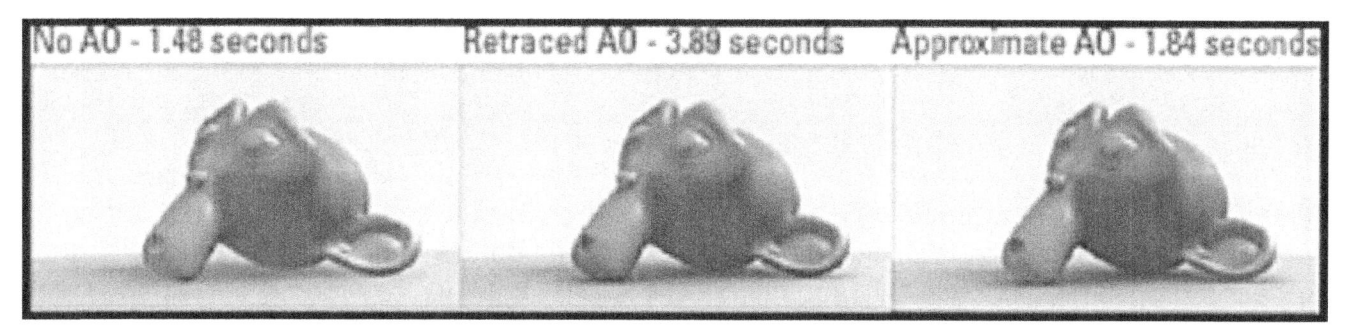

REVIEW QUESTIONS

1. What are the six additional controls, or "cheat buttons," available in the Lamp panel of Blender, and how can they enhance the lighting in 3D computer graphics?
2. What is the recommended starting point for a three-point lighting setup, and how are the key, fill, and backlights placed and configured?
3. How can you change the default background color in Blender to create a more appealing and visually pleasing environment for your renders?
4. What is ambient occlusion (AO) in Blender, and how does it simulate global illumination (GI)? How can you enable and customize AO in your scenes to achieve more realistic and detailed lighting effects?

SUMMARY

In Blender, understanding lighting configurations and techniques is essential for creating captivating visual experiences in 3D computer graphics, photography, video production, and filmmaking. One widely used configuration is "three-point lighting," which involves a key light, a filllight, and a backlight. The key light is the primary light source, positioned in front and slightly above the subject, creating primary shadows and highlights. The filllight serves to soften shadows and create a more balanced look, while the backlight adds a subtle glow to separate the subject from the background. Experimenting with the placement and setting of these lights allows for various lighting effects and moods.

In addition to lighting, configuring the environment in Blender's World Properties plays a crucial role in rendering scenes. Adjusting the horizon and zenith colors, utilizing the "Blend Sky" and

"Real Sky" options, and enabling ambient occlusion (AO) can enhance the visual impact of renders. AO simulates global illumination, highlighting fine details and shadows, making scenes appear more realistic and visually appealing. The choice between ray-traced and approximate AO depends on the project's requirements.

with ray-traced offering precision and approximate results, providing faster results. Balancing these lighting and environment settings enables artists to craft impressive 3D scenes with depth, atmosphere, and realism.

PART 3: BRINGING YOUR CREATIONS TO LIFE

In this section, we are going to be working on animated objects.

CHAPTER 13: BASICS OF ANIMATION IN BLENDER

Creating animations is not an easy task. It involves numerous elements and can require dedicating days, weeks, or even months to animate just a few seconds of content.

Despite the challenges, the process can become deeply rewarding once you complete the animation of a particular object. In this section, we are going to be working on animating objects.

WORKING WITH THE ANIMATION CURVES

With animation curves, known as f-curves, Blender primarily controls and produces animations. An F-curve represents the transition or interpolation between two significant points in an animated sequence.

To better understand interpolation, think back to your elementary school math class when you graphed data or wrote equations for lines or curves on paper. Drawing the line between points involved interpolation, but in Blender, you don't have to do that manually. F-curves handle this for you.

Let's go through an example to illustrate the basic steps of animating in Blender:

1. Start with the default scene in Blender by pressing **Ctrl+N-->Reload Start-Up File**.
2. Select the default cube object and press **Numpad 0** to enter the camera view.
3. Divide the 3D view vertically to switch one of the new regions to the Graph Editor **(Shift+F6)**.

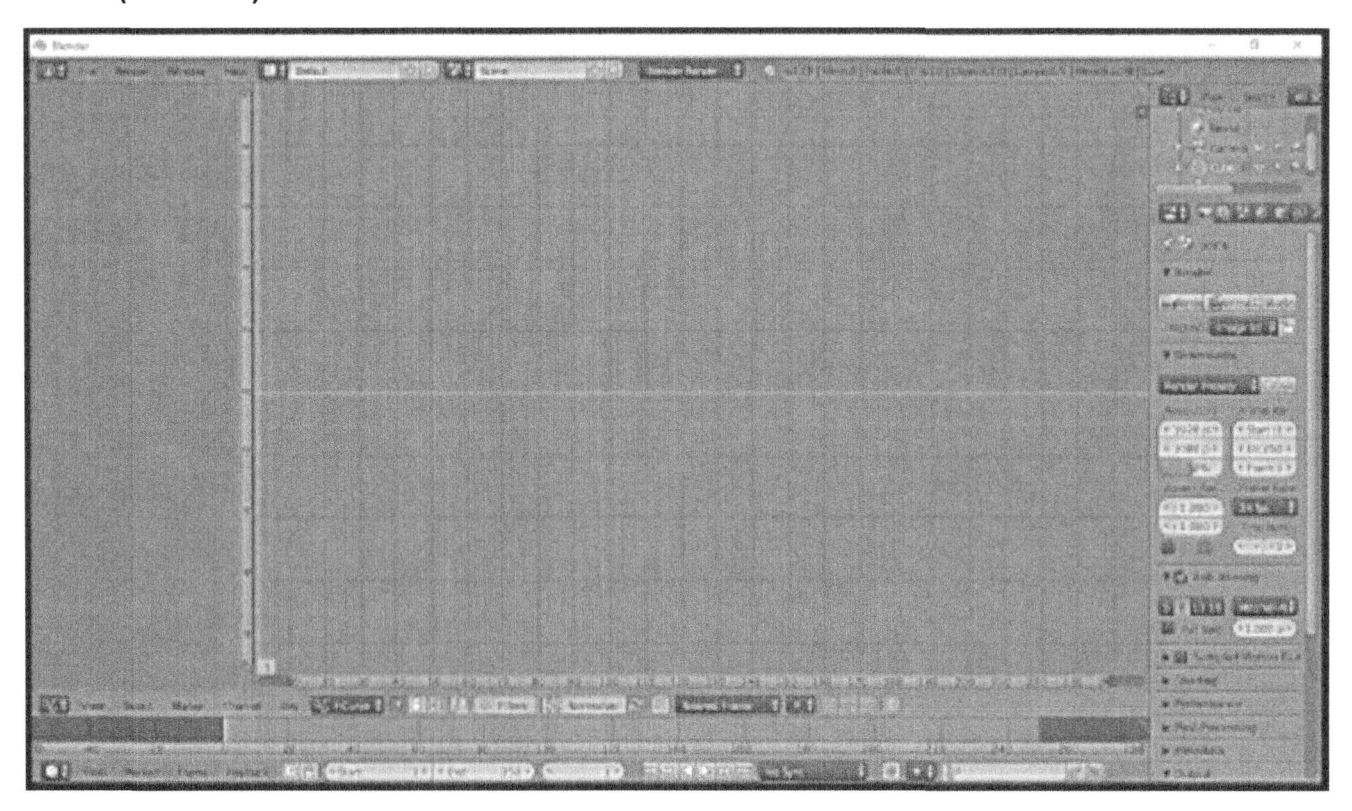

4. Before proceeding, make sure the default cube is selected in the 3DView, then **press I-->Location**.

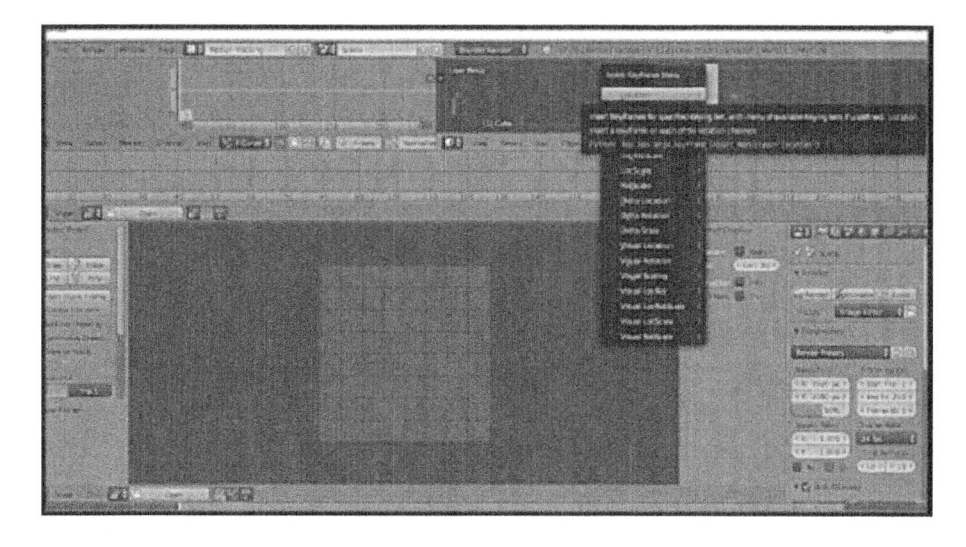

5. This sets the initial location keyframe for the cube. Later in the course, there will be a more detailed explanation of keyframes. You'll notice changes in the left section of the Graph Editor, where a brief tiered list displays elements like Cube, Cube Actio, and Location.
6. On your keyboard, click the up arrow to add ten frames of time to your animation.
7. In the 3D View, grab (G) the cube and move it to another spot in the scene.
8. Once again, **press I-->Location** in the 3D view. The graph editor will display certain colored lines. These colorful lines represent the f-curves, with each f-curve representing a single animated attribute or channel. By left-clicking the triangle on the left side of the block's name to expand the Location block in the Graph Editor, you'll see the three location channels: X Location, Y Location, and Z Location. Move your cursor to the large graph portion of the Graph Editor and press Home to get a clearer view of the actual curves.

Following these steps, your Blender display should resemble the provided image. By utilizing f-curves, you can precisely control the animation of objects in Blender, making it a powerful tool for creating captivating animated sequences.

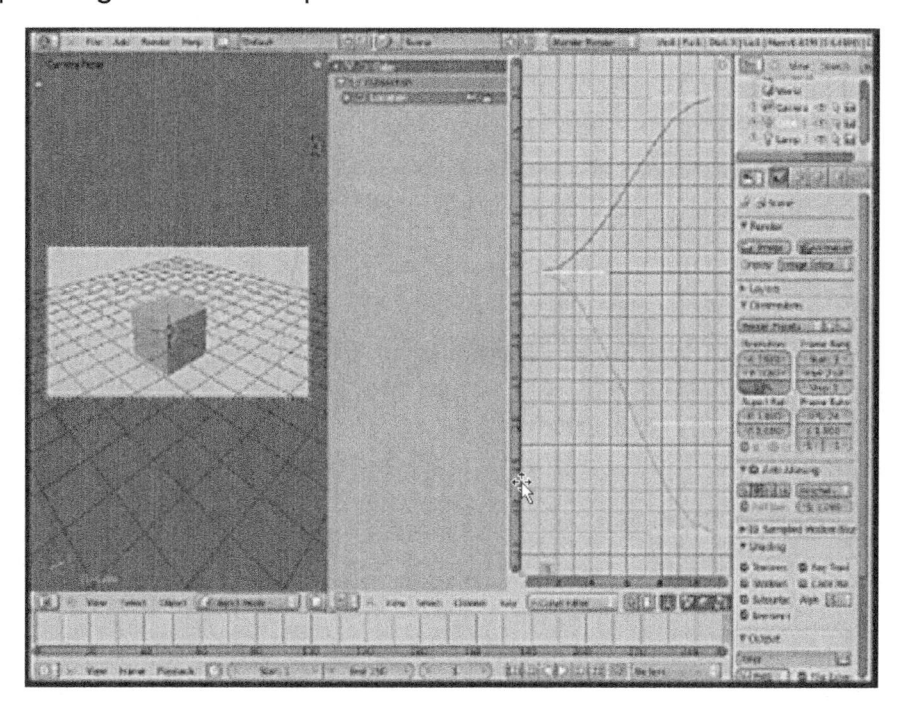

Congratulations! You've just finished making your first Blender animation. What you did was this: A graph makes up the majority of the Graph Editor. On this graph, moving ahead in time is represented by moving from left to right along the X-axis. The value of the channel that is being animated is shown on the graph's vertical axis. Thus, as time progresses, the cube's position changes in the **X, Y, and Z** axes according to the curves you created. By interpolating between the control points, known as keys, that you created, Blender constructs the curves. Playing back the animation will allow you to view the outcome for yourself. **Press Alt+A** while your mouse is still in the Graph Editor. The timeline cursor, which is an agreed-upon vertical line in the graph, pans from left to right. You should see your cube travel from the initial position to the finishing point you specified in the 3D view as the timeline pointer moves. To end the play, press Esc. Scrubbing in the Graph Editor allows for a more controlled viewing of the animation. Scrubbing is accomplished by left-clicking on the graph area of the Graph Editor and dragging the mouse from left to right. You can see the change taking place in the 3D view as the timeline cursor moves in accordance with where your mouse pointer is located.

CUSTOMIZING YOUR SCREEN LAYOUT FOR ANIMATION AND INSERTING KEYS

In Blender, you can create a specific screen layout tailored for animation. To access this layout, you can use the Ctrl+ hotkey or select it from the Screen Layout data block at the top of the Blender window. This animation layout differs slightly from the default layout. The Outliner is larger, and both the Dope sheet and Graph Editor are located on the left side of the screen. Additionally, the outliner overlaps with a second 3D view. However, the timeline from the default layout remains mostly unchanged. You might wonder why this animation layout includes three editors for controlling time in your animation (the Timeline, Graph Editor, and Dope sheet). Each editor offers different types of control over your animation. For example, the timeline provides a central location to manage the playback of the entire animation. The Dope sheet helps you make sense of complex animations with multiple anisotropic properties, while the Graph Editor allows you to focus on individual, detailed animations. You can scrub through the time line and dope sheet by left-clicking and moving your mouse left and right, just like in the Graph Editor.

To complete this animation layout, you can make adjustments in the main 3D view. Change the Rotate manipulator's coordinate space to Normal by pressing **Alt+spacebar->Normal and replacing the Translate manipulator**. This change allows for precise rotation during animation, which can be quicker and easier with the rotate manipulator. Unlike other manipulators, the rotate manipulator doesn't obstruct the view as much. The resulting animation layout will be slightly modified but better suited for efficient and effective animation work.

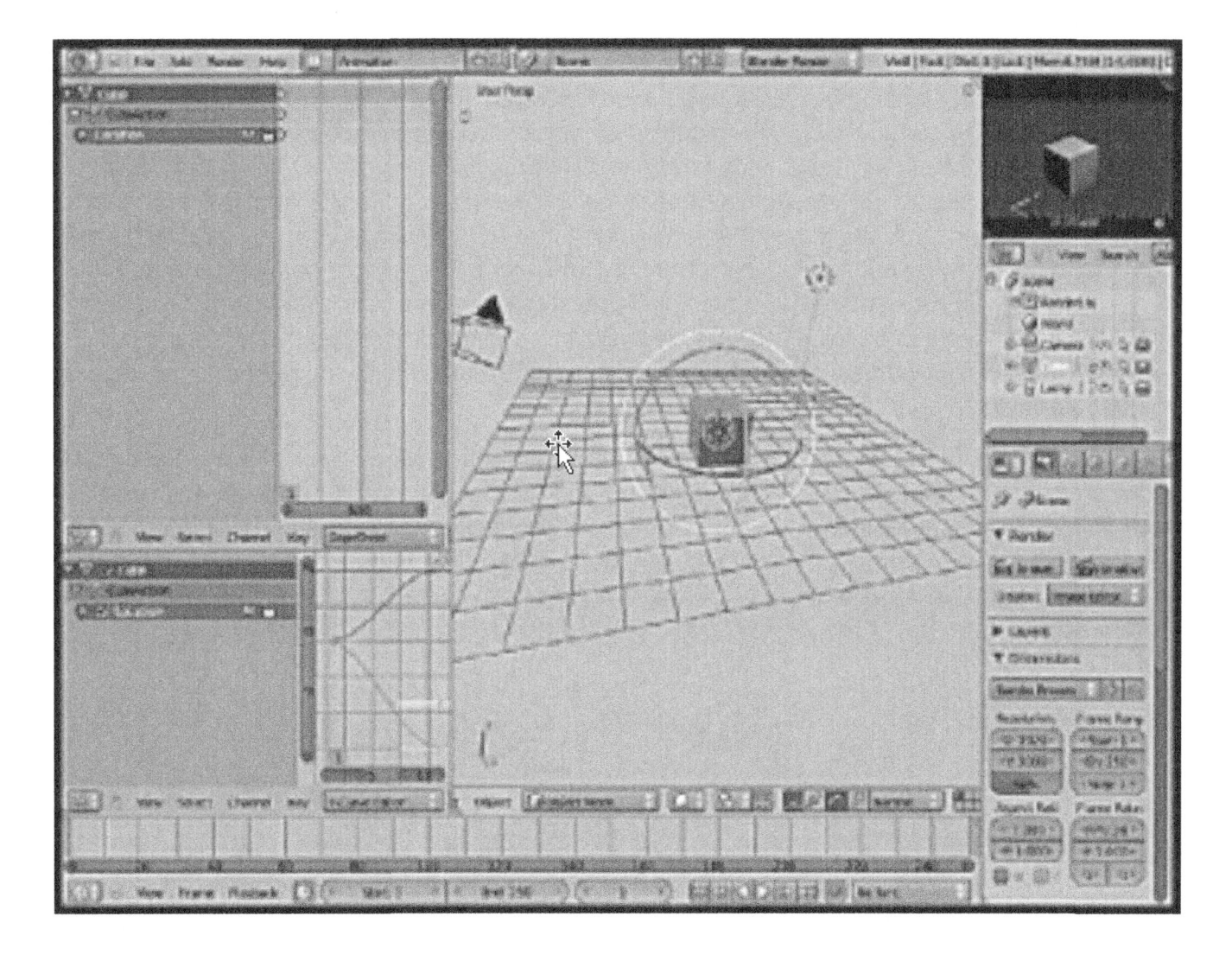

WORKING WITH KEYING SETS

The Graph Editor and the 3DView both have very similar interfaces. The Graph Editor's fundamental controls are described as follows:

- The graph view can be moved around with a middle click and drag.
- You can effectively scale your view of the curve both horizontally and vertically by pressing the keyboard short-cut **Ctrl+middle-click+drag**.
- Zoom in and out with the scroll wheel on your mouse. You can move the graph vertically via **Shift+Scroll**.
- You can move the graph vertically via **Shift+Scroll**
- The graph can be moved horizontally using **Ctrl+Scroll**.
- Individual f-curve control points are selected with a right-click.
- To pick up all or none of the control points, press A.
- To select a border, press B.
- To choose a channel, left-click on it in the Graph Editor's left section.

You can haphazardly add points to a chosen f-curve in the graph by using Ctrl+Left-click.

EDITING MOTION CURVES

The next step after adding keyframes to your scene is to adjust, edit, and modify those keyframes in the Graph Editor, including the interpolation between them. The Graph Editor functions similarly to the 3DView, allowing you to right-click and select specific control points on f-curves or use the Border select key on the key boar d to make multiple selections. The control points in the Graph Editor are not only selectable but can also be edited in the 3D view like a 2D Bezier curve object. The only restriction is that f-curves cannot cross themselves, as it wouldn't make sense for a curve representing motion in time to create a loop. For a more detailed understanding of editing Bezier curves in Blender, Chapter 6 provides extensive information. The V hotkey is used for switching handle types, and selecting and sliding control point handles functions similarly to 2D Bezier curves. However, since f-curves are specifically designed for animation, you have additional controls to modify these curves.

One such control is the interpolation method between control points on a specified curve. By clicking Shift +Tor and selecting Key,>Interpolation Mode In the graph Graph Editor's header, you can modify the interpolation mode used. This allows you to choose from various interpolation options, giving you more control over the animation's motion and timing.

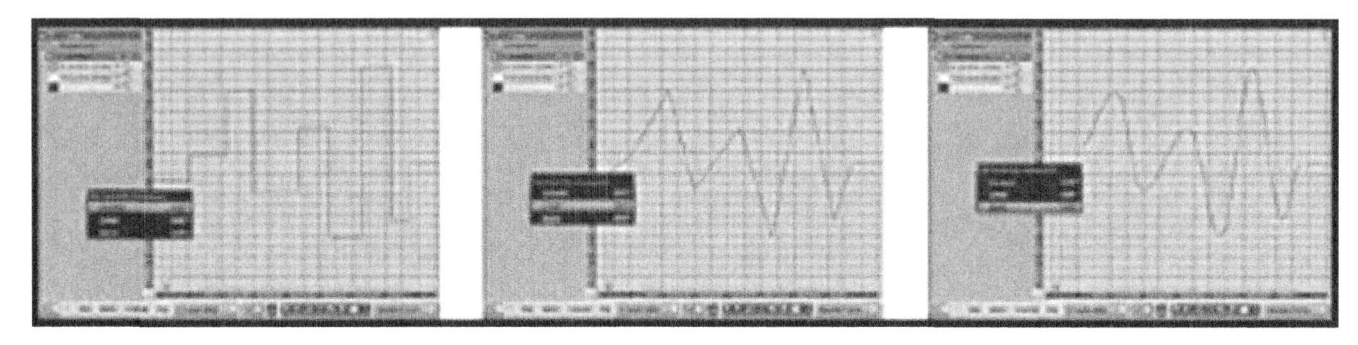

By altering the curve's extrapolation mode, you may also modify what a selected channel does before and following its beginning and last keyframes. By selecting an f-curve channel in the left part of the Graph Editor, hitting Shift+E, or by going to Key-->Extrapolation Mode in the Graph Editor's header, you can alter the extrapolation mode of a curve.

When you do, take note of your two options:

- **Constant Extrapolation**: This is the default setting. The values of the first and last control points are infinitely retained.
- **Linear Extrapolation**: This extrapolation mode takes the directions of the curve as it reaches the first and last control points and extends the curve in those directions, as opposed to retaining the same value indefinitely before and after.

To concentrate on the curves you want to edit, it may be good to conceal unnecessary curves from view if your scene has a lot of animated objects or just one item with a lot of animated characteristics. In the channel region on the left side of the Graph Edi, left-click the check box next to a curve's name to toggle its visibility. Select a channel from the channel region, then either left-click the lock symbol or press Tab to make f-curves visible but not editable. The Graph Editor offers a Properties section similar to the 3D View if you require explicit control over the location of a curve or control point. You raise it in the same manner as well: Either click View > Properties or press N. You can type the precise value here that you want to apply to the handles of the control point you've chosen or to the control point itself.

USING CONSTRAINTS EFFECTIVELY

It is important to understand that being a computer animator is not an easy profession, and cutting corners is rarely an option. However, constraints offer a unique opportunity to achieve complex effects without expending excessive effort. A constraint is a limitation applied to an object to control the behavior of another object. Constraints can save a lot of time and effort in animation, allowing animators to achieve certain effects without tedious manual adjustments. To access constraints in Blender, navigate to the Constraint Properties and click on the Add Constraint button. Alternatively, you can use the keyboard shortcut Shift+Ctrl+C in the 3D View to access the same menu.

In this menu, you will find a variety of constraints that you can apply to objects, each serving a different purpose. Constraints can be used to control object movements, rotations, scales, and much more, making them a powerful tool for creating dynamic and intricate animations. By utilizing constraints effectively, animators can streamline their workflow and focus on achieving their artistic vision without getting bogged down in repetitive tasks. Constraints provide a valuable tool for animators to enhance the quality and efficiency of their animations, making animation a more enjoyable and rewarding process.

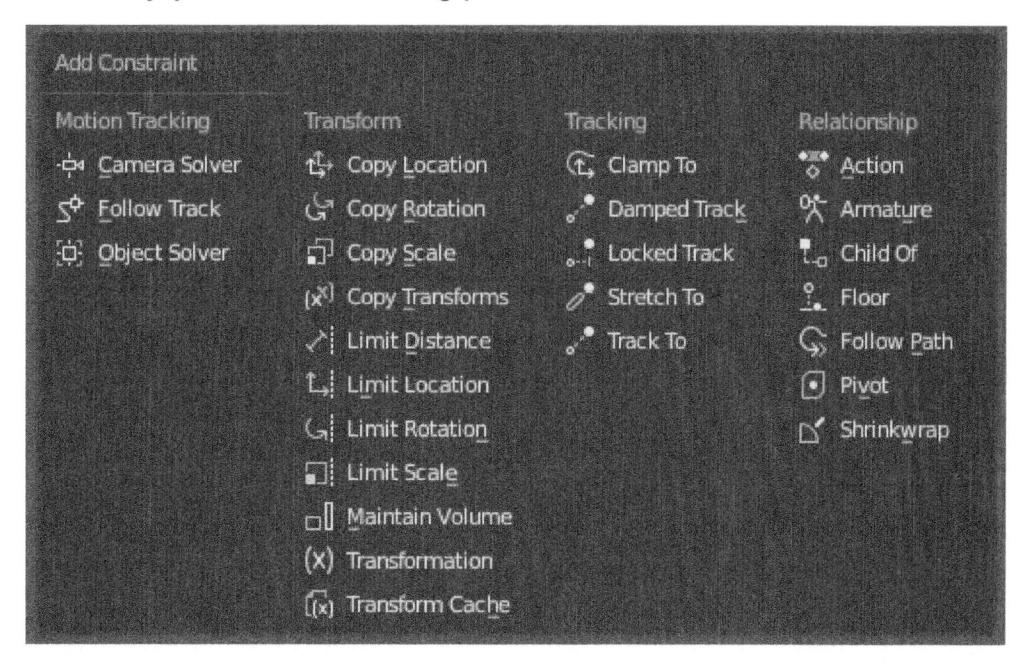

THE ALL-POWERFUL EMPTY

None of the several object types you can use in Blender are as practical or adaptable for animation as the straightforward Empty. An empty is a small collection of axes that represents a position, orientation, and size in three dimensions. After rendering, empty spaces don't even appear. But empties are a fantastic method to take advantage of constraints and choose the best choice for use as control objects. Consider the fact that 3D modelers like to have a turnaround render of the model they develop as a practical illustration of how helpful Empties may be. A turnaround render essentially involves turning the model in front of the camera while it is mounted on a turntable. It's a fantastic method to highlight the model's various sides. Simple models can now be rotated using the global Z-axis by simply selecting the model and doing so. But what if the model has numerous elements or everything is positioned at an odd angle that makes sense only when the Z-axis is rotated? It can take a lot of time and effort to select and rotate all those tiny objects.

You can use the following steps to set up a turnaround.

- **(Shift + A-->Empty)** Add an empty.
- Grab the Em point and place it somewhere in the model's center (G).
- The model should be in the middle of the camera's field of view (right-click, G).
- **(Shift+right-click)** Include the empty in your selection.
- **(Ctrl+P-- >Object)** Make the empty the camera's parent.
- Insert a rotation keyframe **(right-click,I-->Rotation)** after selecting the Empty.
- 50 frames of time in advance.
- Insert a new rotation keyframe **(R-->Z-->90, I-->Rotation)** and rotate the empty in the Z-axis by 90 degrees.
- The rotation of the Empty is obediently matched by the camera.
- By pressing **Shift+F6**, left-clicking, and **Shift+E->Linear Extrapolation**, you can open the Graph Editor and change the extrapolation mode for the Z Rotation channel to linear extrapolation.
- Go to the camera view and play the animation with Numpad 0, Alt+A.

The Empty acts as the camera control in this configuration. Consider a beam that runs from the eye's center to the camera's center, and how that beam is moved by rotating the Empty.

ADJUSTING THE INFLUENCE OF CONSTRAINTS

The influence slider is one of the most helpful options because it for all constraints accessible for all constraints and located at the bottom of each constraint block. The slider operates on a scale from O to 1, with O representing the least influence and 1 representing the most. With this slider, you have the option of letting the characteristics of the target object impact you only partially. But there's more to it. Consider that you're developing an animation in which a figure with telekinetic abilities makes a ball fly into his hand. You can achieve this by animating the effect of a copy location constant on the ball (see the section on "Copying the movement of another object"). The objective is the character's hand, and you begin with no influence. The influence is then increased to 1, and a new keyframe is set when you want the ball to fly to his hand. KERPLOW! telekinetic personality!

USING VERTEX GROUPS IN CONSTRAINTS

After selecting a legitimate mesh object in the Target field, many constraints have a Vertex Group field. You can type or select the name of a vertex group from the parent mesh in the Vertex Group box. By doing so, the restricted object is limited to those certain vertices only. Even the relationship line from the child object changes to point to the group of vertices you've made a part of the group when you assign those vertices to the group and select your new vertex group from the Vertex Group field of your constraint. The image below displays a Suzanne head with a "Child Of" constraint attached to a circular mesh's single-vertex vertex group.

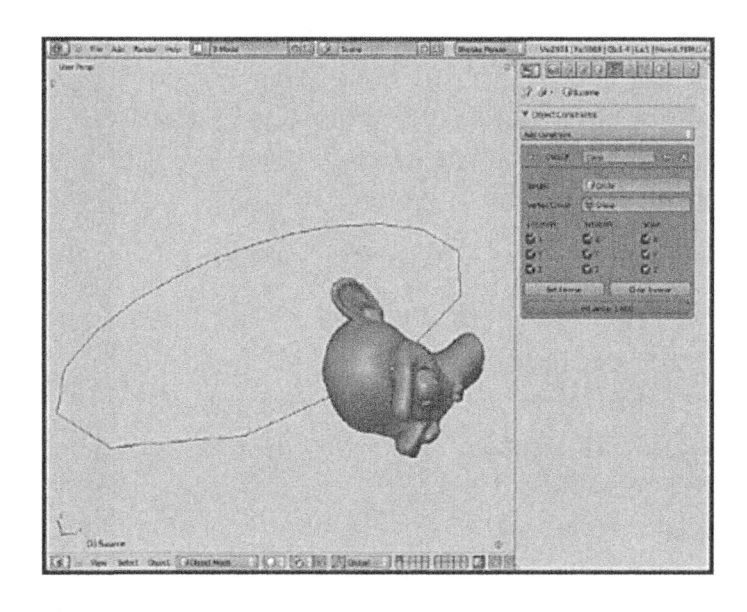

COPYING THE MOVEMENT OF ANOTHER OBJECT

Simple parenting can be beneficial in many situations, but it is frequently not as adaptable as you need it to be. Without also incorporating the location and scale, you cannot manipulate, animate, or use merely the rotation of the parent object.

Additionally, you cannot have a parent object's movement on the global X-axis affect a child object's local X-axis placement. These more precise controls are more frequently required than the relatively haphazard Ctrl+P parenting. To this end, the restrictions Copy Location, Copy Rotation, and Copy Scale provide you precisely with this kind of control. This image depicts how each constraint appears after being applied to the Constraints Properties window.

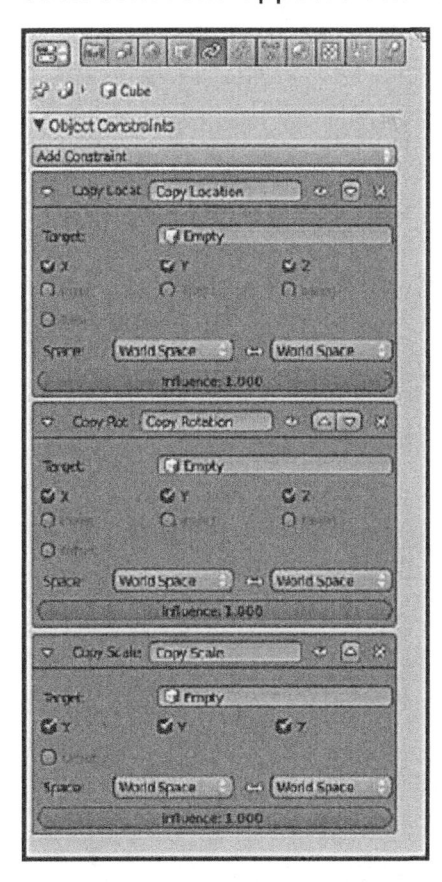

The similarity between the possibilities for these copy restrictions is probably what stands out the most. The item you select in the Target field, however, is the most important setting. Here, you can select the empty object you want to use as your control object or type its name. If you don't, the constraint will not function, and the constraint name field at the top of the constraint block will remain bright red. There are six check boxes underneath the Target field. The checkboxes for X, Y, and Z are already selected, and under them are corresponding checkboxes with the labels Invert for each. The invert check boxes are deactivated by default. Which axis or axes the target item affects is controlled by these checkboxes. The target object has an inverted influence on the constrained object on that axis if both the axis check box and the inverted check box underneath it are activated. Concerning the previous Copy Location example, if you select "Empty" and move it to the X-axis while deselecting the X check box, the cube stays completely static. However, when you move the target empty and enable the X check box and the Invert check box underneath it, the cube will translate in the other X direction.

The offset check box is next, and it's helpful if you've previously changed the location, rotation, or scale of your object before adding the constraint. This feature is disabled by default, causing the confined object to behave precisely like the target object. However, if it is enabled, the object adds the modification of the target object to the values already defined for the constrained object's location, rotation, or scale.

Create a Copy Location constraint using the procedures below for the best visual representation of this:

- Ctrl+N will launch the default scene.
- Grab the standard cube and move it to a different spot (G).
- (Shift+ A-->Empty) Add an empty.
- By pressing Shift+right-click or Shift+Ctrl+C-->Copy Location, you can add the cube to your current selection and apply a Copy Location constraint to it.
- The "Empty" location is where the cube will automatically snap.
- Right-click the Offset Checkbox in the Constraints Properties' Copy Location constraint.
- Back in its original place, the cube moves. The empty grabs (G), and the cube is moved as a result.

PUTTING LIMITS ON AN OBJECT

When animating objects, it's frequently beneficial to limit how far they can be moved, rotated, or scaled. Consider animating a character who is imprisoned behind a glass dome. It's advantageous for animators if Blender makes you keep that character in that area. Sure, you could simply keep an eye on where your character is and visually ensure that he doesn't unintentionally travel farther than is permitted, but why bother if Blender can handle it for you? For the majority of the limiting constraints that Blender provides, the image below displays the constraint options.

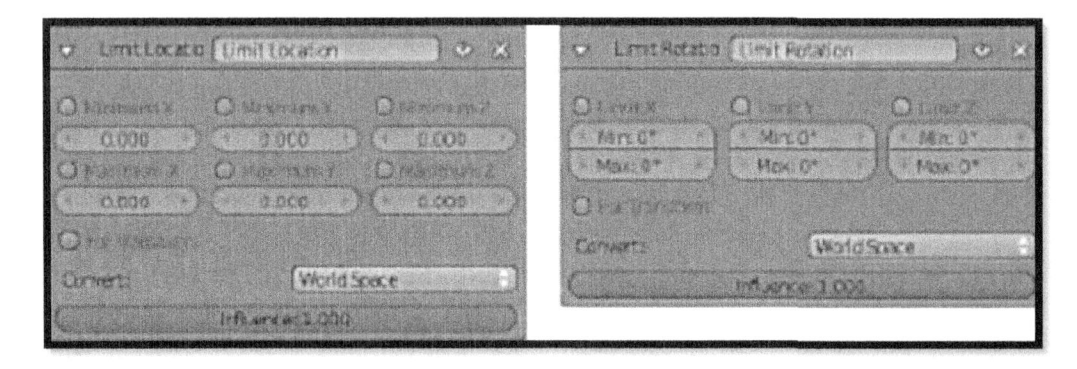

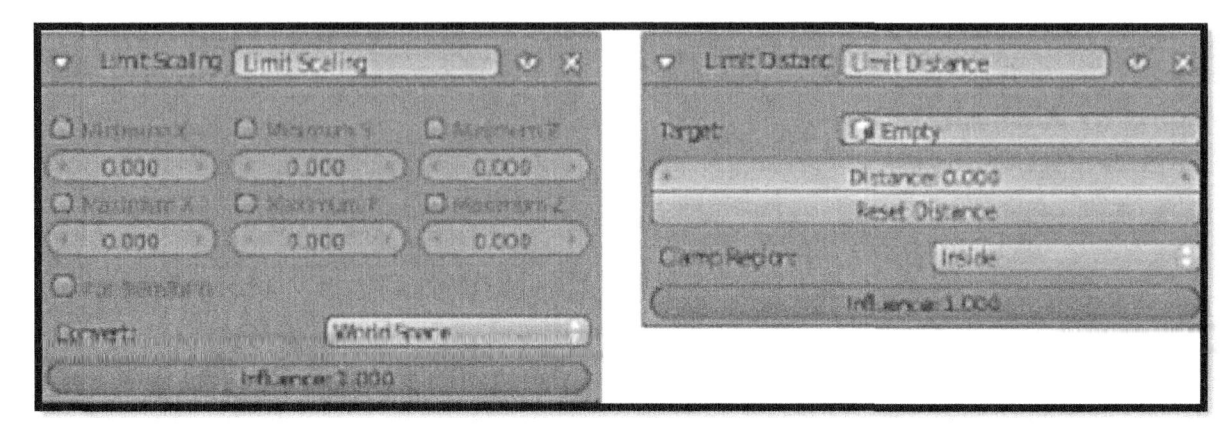

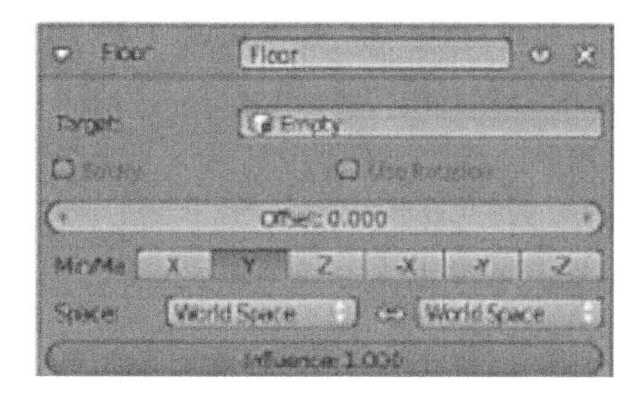

TRACKING THE MOTION OF ANOTHER OBJECT.

Another set of useful restrictions for animation is tracking constraints. Their primary goal is to direct the confined item to point at the target object, either specifically or broadly. Building mechanical devices like pistons or regulating a character's eye movement both benefit from tracking limitations.

SUMMARY

Animation in Blender is a challenging task that requires time and dedication. F-curves control and produce animations, representing the interpolation between significant points in an animation sequence.

To create animations in Blender, start with the default scene, select an object, and set keyframes for its initial and final positions. The Graph Editor displays f-curves representing the animation attributes. You can scroll through the animation to preview the result.

REVIEW QUESTIONS

1. Why is creating animations considered a challenging task? How can it be rewarding in the end?
2. What are f-curves, and how are they used to control animations in Blender?
3. How can you scrub through your animation in the Graph Editor and control the playback of the entire animation in the Timeline?
4. How can constraints in Blender help simplify the animation process? What are some examples of situations where constraints are beneficial?

CHAPTER 14: RIGGING ESSENTIALS - BREATHING LIFE INTO MODELS

Character animation is the process of creating realistic movements for a character. This can be a challenging task, especially when the character is a single seamless mesh. With a single sea1nless mesh, it is difficult to animate detailed movements, such as smiling, wiggling toes, or bending arms. One way to overcome this challenge is to create a rig for the character. A rig is an underlying structure that allows you to control how the mesh moves. Rigs are an essential part of modern computer animation, and they can make the life of an animator much easier.

This chapter will explain the various tools and techniques used to create rigs. You will learn how to create bones, joints, and constraints. You will also learn how to skin the mesh to the rig. By the end of this chapter, you will be able to create rigs for nearly any object in Blender.

WHY USE A RIG?

There are several reasons why you should use a rig for character animation. First, a rig allows you to animate detailed movements. With a rig, you can control the individual bones and joints of the character, which gives you much more control over the movements. Second, a rig makes it easier to animate multiple characters. If you have multiple characters, you can create a rig for each character and then reuse the rig for different animations.

This saves you a lot of time and effort. Third, a rig makes it easier to export your animation to other software. If you want to export your animation to a game engine or video editing software, you can export the rig along with the animation. This makes it easy to import the animation into the other software.

HOW TO CREATE A RIG

The first step in creating a rig is to create the bones. Bones are the underlying structure of the rig. They define the joints of the character and how the character moves. Once you have created the bones, you need to create the joints. Joints are the connections between the bones. They allow the bones to move relative to each other. The next step is to skin the mesh to the rig. Skinning is the process of connecting the mesh to the bones. This allows the mesh to move with the bones.

CREATING SHAPE KEYS

When you animate an object, it needs to be able to deform from its original shape to a new one. If you know what the shape will be, you can model it ahead of time. This is called creating a shape key.

In Blender, you can create a shape key by following these steps:

- Start with the original mesh.
- Edit the vertices of the mesh to create the new shape.
- Save the new shape as a shape key.

For example, let's say you have a cartoon character with bulging eyes. You can create a shape key by editing the vertices of the eyes to make them bulge out. Once you have saved the shape key, you can use it to animate the bulging eyes.

CREATING NEW SHAPES

If you have chosen an object that is compatible with shape keys (such as meshes, curves, surfaces, and lattices), you can begin adding shape keys by accessing the Shape Keys panel located in the Object Data Properties. In this image, you can observe three distinct states of the Shape Keys panel. By default, this panel appears rather empty and unassuming, consisting of a list box and a few buttons positioned to the right of it. However, upon left-clicking the Plus (+) button, a basis shape is appended to the list. The basis shape represents the original form to which other shape keys are associated. Clicking the Plus (+) button for the second time presents additional options enabling you to govern the transition from the basis shape to a newly created shape known as Key 1.

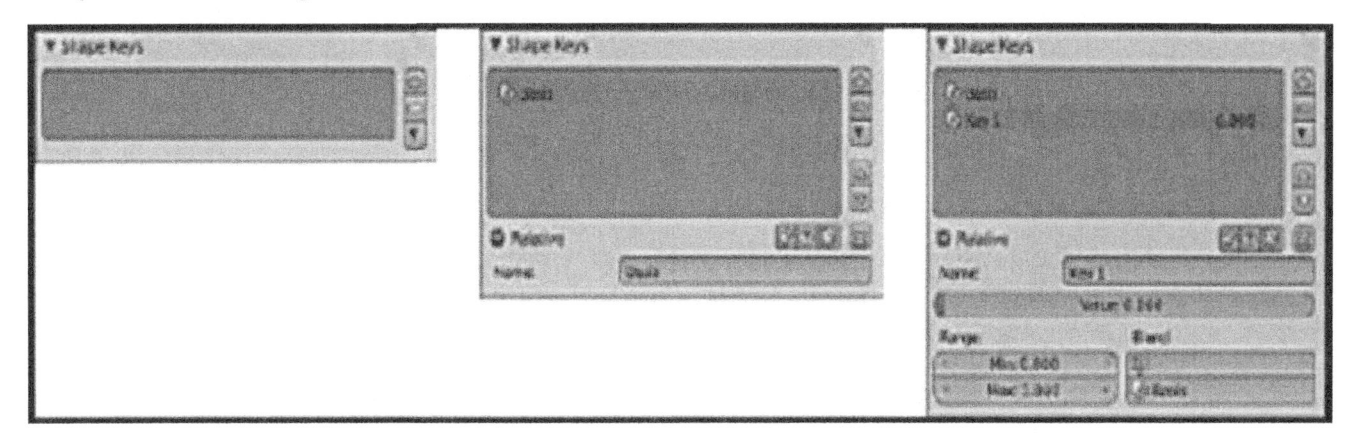

To gain a practical understanding of creating new shapes, it is best to follow a specific exam plan. Let's continue with the bug-eyed monkey concept, using Suzanne as our test subject.

Please follow these steps:

1. Begin with the default scene and remove the cube (press Ctrl+N, right-click the cube, then press X).
2. Add Suzanne to the scene. Apply a Subdivision Surface modifier, set her to appear smooth, and rotate her 90 degrees around the X-axis (press Shift+A, select Mesh, then Monkey; press Ctrl+1; in the Tool Shelf, select Shading, then Smooth; press R, followed by X, and enter 90).
3. Switch to the front view (press Numpad 1).
4. Introduce a shape key by accessing the Shape Keys panel in the Object Data Properties (click on the panel and select the Plus I+] button).
5. The basis shape is now created. All subsequent shapes will be relative to this one.
6. Include a second shape key by selecting the Plus [+] buttons in the Shape Keys (Object Data Properties). If desired, you can rename it.
7. The Shape Keys panel should resemble the last image above. This signifies the creation of Key 1. If desired, you can modify its name by left-clicking on the corresponding field. In my case, we named it "Eye Bulge."
8. Switch to edit mode by pressing Tab. Alter the mesh to give Suzanne bulging eyes. Ensure that the Eye Bulge shape key is active in the Shape Keys pane before making any

adjustments. While modifying the model, avoid adding extra vertices; instead, manipulate the existing vertices to define the desired shape. A convenient way to make Suzanne's eyes bulge is to hover your mouse cursor over each eye, press L to select only the vertices associated with that area, and then, with the Proportional Edit Tool (O) enabled, scale (S) the eyes.
9. Return to object mode by pressing Tab.

The process described above is depicted in the image below. Illustrating the creation of a bug-eyed shape key for Suzanne.

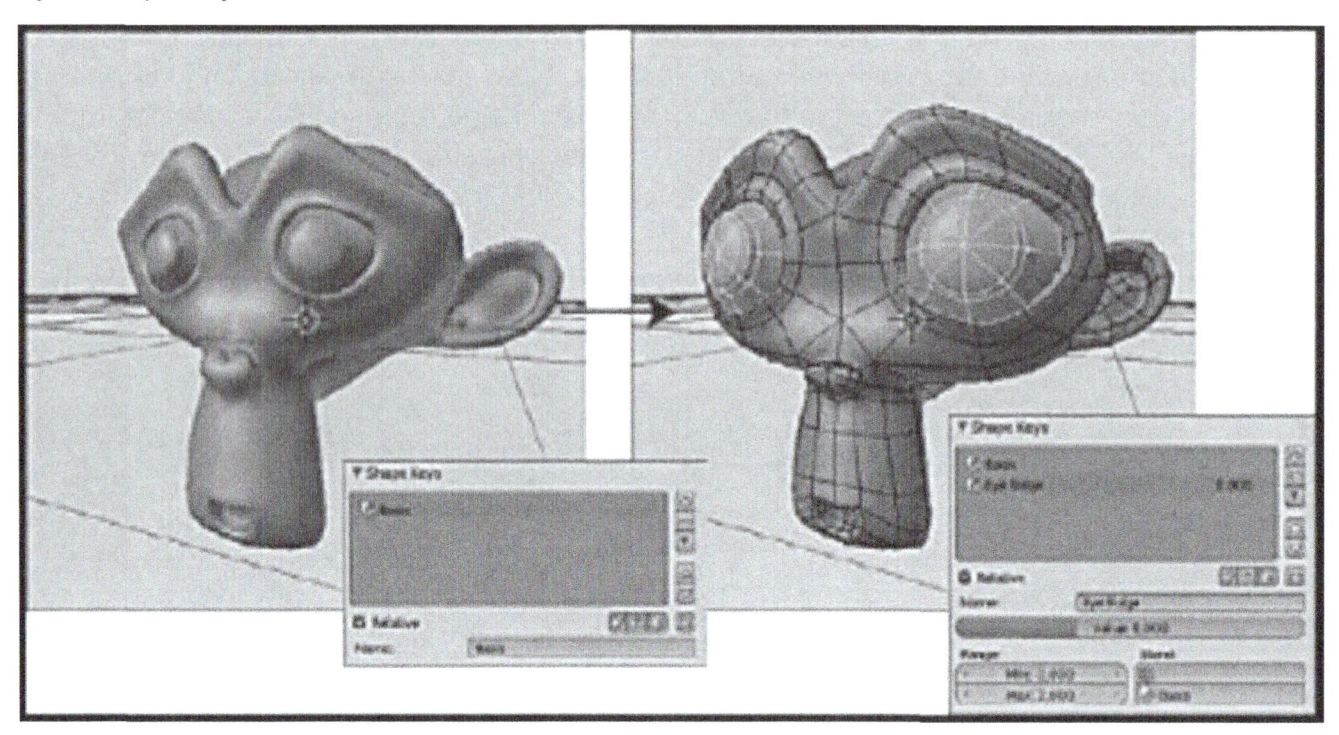

This procedure generates two shape keys: basis and eye bulk. By utilizing the Value slider within the Shape Keys panel, you can seamlessly transition from the Basis shape to the Eye Bulge shape. A value of O signifies that the eye bulge has no effect and only the base shape is visible. On the other hand, a value of 1 indicates that the eye bulge shape is fully active. However, here's where it gets fascinating: Take note of the Range section at the bottom of the panel, featuring the Min and Max values. Currently, the minimum value is set to 0.000, and the maximum value is set to 1.000. Just for fun, modify the Max value to 2.000 and slide the Value slider to the right. As a result, your bulged eyes extend beyond the size initially created by the shape key. Now, adjust the minimum value to -1.000.

and slide the value slider to the left. This causes Suzanne's eyes to pinch inward, reaching a point smaller than the base pose. The image above showcases the outcomes of these alterations. By adjusting the Min and Max Range values, you can achieve even more extreme shapes for your characters without engaging in additional shape key modeling. Isn't that cool?

MIXING SHAPES

Once you've reached this stage, you can proceed to create additional shape keys for the mesh. Suppose you want to include a shape key where Suzanne's mouth becomes larger as if she's screaming due to her enlarged eyes.

To accomplish this, follow these steps:

1. Switch back to the basis key by left-clicking on the basis key in the list box within the Shape Keys panel. It is generally recommended to base most of your shapes on the basis key, unless you have specific requirements. This ensures that you avoid intentionally amplifying or nullifying a shape key. Returning to the base shape sets the foundation for further modifications.
2. Add a new shape key by accessing the Shape Keys panel in Object Data Properties (click on the panel and select the Plus [+] button). You are free to assign any desired name to this key. In my case, we named it "Scream."
3. Enter Edit mode by pressing Tab. Modify the mouth to create an open position using the existing vertices. Be careful not to alter Suzanne's eyes; focus solely on editing the mouth to make it larger.
4. Return to object mode by pressing Tab.

The results of this process are demonstrated in the image below, showcasing the outcome of adding a shape key for Suzanne's screaming mouth. Once you have created the Scream shape key, you can easily combine it with the Eye Bulge shape key to keep Suzanne screaming while her eyes remain normal. The choice is yours, offering the flexibility to mix and match your desired shape keys. Animating the mesh to utilize these shape keys is straightforward. In this updated version of Blender, you can animate nearly everything. Therefore, animating shape keys is as simple as inserting keyframes on the Value slider within the Shape Keys panel. To do this, right-click the Value field and select "Insert Keyframe," or hover your mouse over the field and press "L".

Once keyframes are inserted, split the Graph Editor from the 3D View. Now you can move the timeline cursor forward and witness the joy of Suzanne bulging and screaming. As a bonus, enabling the Show Sliders feature in the Graph Editor (View> Show Sliders) allows you to view the numeric values for your shape keys' influences and even set keyframes for them.

KNOWING WHERE SHAPE KEYS ARE HELPFUL

While it is possible to create an entire animation using shape keys, we don't particularly recommend it. There are other methods available to control meshes, which can provide more natural movement for animating limbs such as arms and legs. However, shape keys are an excellent choice for tasks that cannot be easily achieved through alternative means.

Facial animation, in particular, benefits greatly from shape keys. Capturing the subtle wrinkles, movements, and expressions of the face is challenging without specifically modeling those deformations. Shape keys excel in depicting furrowed brows, squinting eyes, realistic smiles, and phonemes for lip-syncing. Additionally, you can combine shape keys with other controls discussed throughout this chapter to achieve captivating effects such as cartoon stretchiness, muscle bulges, and smooth transitions between different shapes.

ADDING HOOKS

While shape keys are effective for achieving precise, predetermined deformations, they can be limiting when you desire more flexible control over your mesh or when animating objects that move along curved paths. In such situations, an alternative control mechanism called hooks comes into play. Hooks are a unique type of modifier that connects a group of vertices or control points to be manipulated by another object, typically an empty This allows for greater versatility and freedom in shaping and animating your meshes.

CREATING NEW HOOKS

Adding a hook follows a straightforward workflow. Begin by entering Edit mode and selecting one or more vertices or control points. Next, press Ctrl+H and choose "Hook to New Object." This action generates an empty set at the median location of the selected vertices or control points. Simultaneously, a new modifier is added to the Modifiers Properties. Return to object mode by pressing Tab, and you can now manipulate the hook. As you move the hook, all the assigned vertices or control points move accordingly. By adjusting the options available in the Hook modifier, you can precisely control the level of influence exerted by the hook on these vertices or control points. To provide a clearer understanding of the process, let's consider the following example, which illustrates the addition of hooks and the modification of their influence.

To begin, open Blender and load the default scene (Ctrl+N).

- Select the cube and switch to edit mode.
- Ensure that all vertices of the cube are selected. If not, press A until all vertices, which is selected.
- Perform a multi-subdivide operation with four cuts **(W > Subdivide, F6 > Number of Cuts: 4).**
- Choose one of the corner vertices of the cube (right-click).
- Press **Ctrl+Numpad** Plus (+) multiple times to expand the vertex selection.
- Add a new hook by pressing **Ctrl+H** and selecting "Hook to New Empty."
- Return to Object mode by pressing Tab.
- At this stage, the behavior should be as expected. If you select and move the empty, all the hooked vertices will move as if they are parented to it.

Increase the Falloff value in the hook modifier to 1.00 (**Modifiers Properties > Hook-Empty > Falloff: 1.00**).

Now, when you select and transform the empty, you will notice that the vertices follow with a smoother motion, akin to using the Proportional Edit Tool (O) while modeling. For some additional fun, proceed to the next step. Apply a Subdivision Surface modifier to the cube and set it to display the object smoothly **(Ctrl+1, Tool Shelf > Shading > Smooth)**. The transition of the vertices will now be even smoother, as demonstrated in.

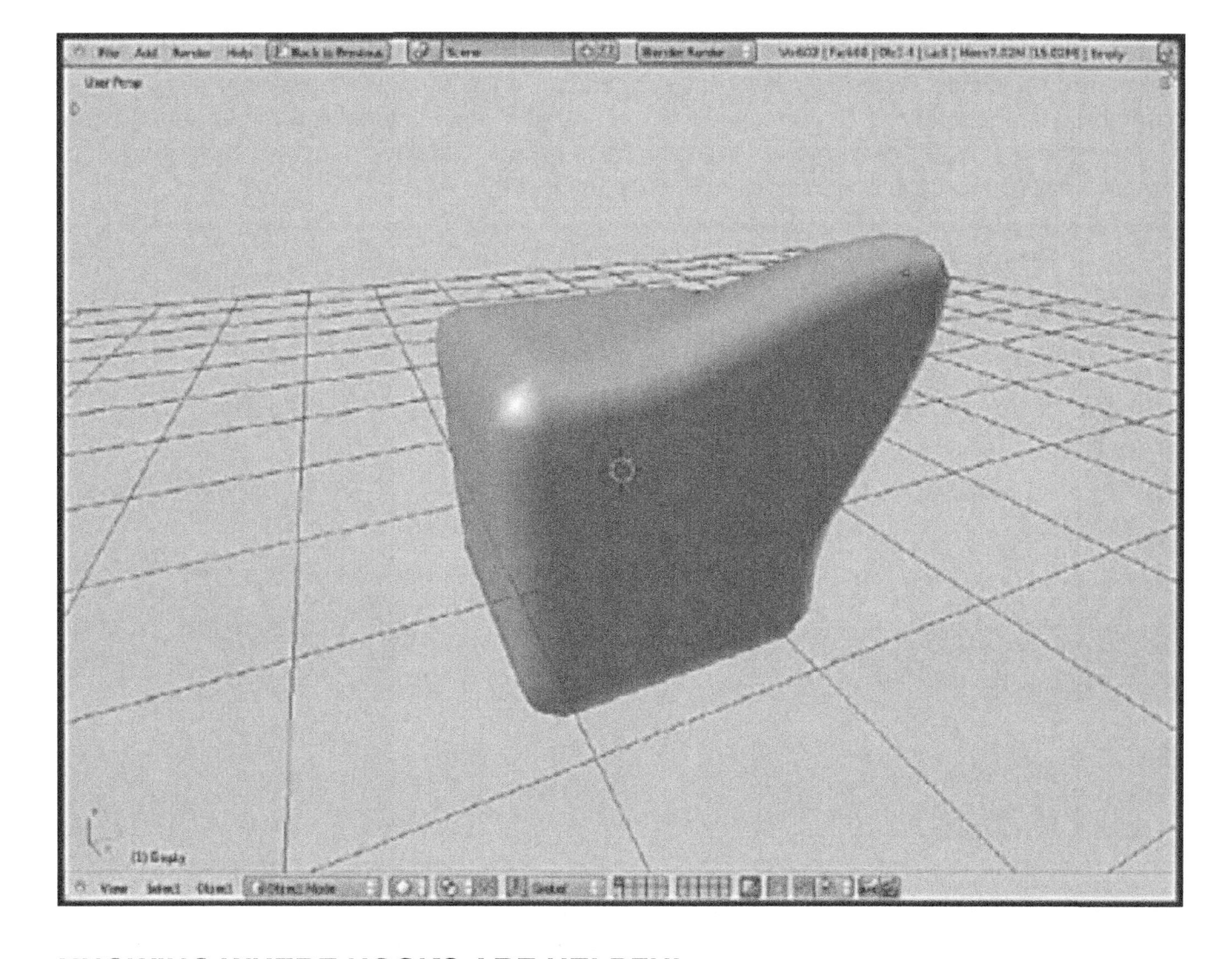

KNOWING WHERE HOOKS ARE HELPFUL

Hooks are particularly effective when it comes to handling significant organic deformations. Similar to shape keys, hooks are useful for producing muscle bulges and exaggerated cartoon-like stretching effects. Interestingly, hooks can also be combined with shape keys, offering additional versatility. While shape keys rely on a fixed basis shape for deformation, introducing a hook can introduce more variation. For instance, in the bug-eyed Suzanne scenario discussed in the "Creating Shape Keys" section, you can apply a hook to one of the eyes to achieve an asymmetric bulging effect. These nuanced details contribute to infusing more character into your 3D creations.

USING ARMATURES: A SKELETON IN THE MESH

Shape keys and hooks serve as effective methods for deforming a mesh, but they lack a well-defined underlying structure. While they excel at creating exaggerated and cartoony deformations, they may produce unnatural-looking motions for more structured deformations, such as bending an arm at the elbow joint. To address this limitation, 3D computer animation took inspiration from stop-motion animation, which often utilizes small sculptures with a metal skeleton known as an armature. The armature provides both structure and the ability to create and hold poses. Similarly, Blender incorporates this concept with its armature system, forming the foundation of most Blender rigs.

To introduce an armature to your scene, navigate to the 3D view and press Shift+A, then select Armature and Single Bone. As depicted here, adding an armature generates a single object resembling an octahedron. In the context of the armature, this octahedron represents a bone. The wider end of the bone is referred to as the head or root, while the narrower end is known as the tail or tip. Typically, a bone pivots around its head.

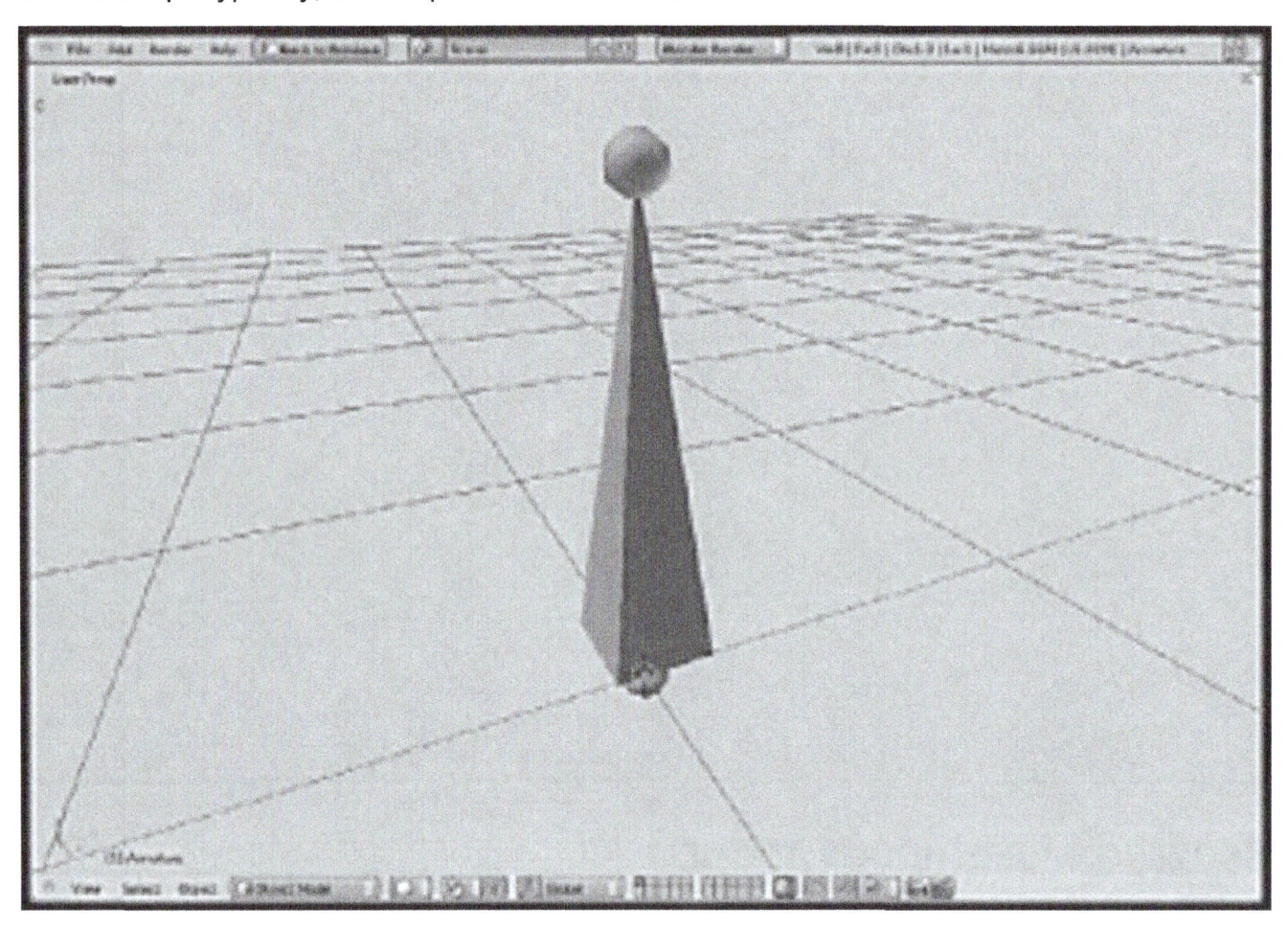

EDITING ARMATURES

You can take a simple single-bone armature and transform it into something more intriguing. Similar to other objects in Blender, you can edit the armature in greater detail by selecting it (right-click) and entering Edit mode. In Edit mode, you can select the sphere at the bone's head, the sphere at the bone's tail, and the bone itself (selecting the bone body simultaneously selects both the head and tail spheres).

There are five methods to add a new bone to your armature:

1. **Extrude**: Select either the head or tail of the bone and press E to extrude a new bone from that point. This is the most common approach for adding bones, and if you extrude from the tail, you instantly establish a parent-child relationship. The new bone comes from the one it was extruded from. These connected bones, tail to head, form a bone chain. The Ctrl+left-click extrude shortcut for meshes and curves also works for bones.
2. **Duplicate**: Choose the body of the desired bone and press Shift+D to duplicate it. This creates a new bone with identical dimensions, parent relationships, and constraints.
3. **Subdivide**: Select the body of the desired bone and press W > Subdivide. This splits the selected bone into two bones while preserving the correct parent-child relationship of the

bone chain. You can also use the Last Operations panel (F6) to perform multiple subdivisions.
4. **Adding**: While still in Edit mode, press Shift +A. A new bone is generated with its head positioned at the 3D cursor's location.
5. **Skeleton sketching**: This advanced feature is highly useful for complex rigging tasks. To explore skeleton sketching, open the Properties region in the 3D View, enable the Skeleton Sketching checkbox, and expand its panel at the bottom of the shelf.

Enabling the Quick Sketching checkbox allows you to draw a red line by left-clicking and dragging the mouse cursor in the 3D View. Each click creates a single, straight line. After drawing, right-clicking generates bones along the drawn line.

Armatures can become complex rapidly, so it's crucial to name your bones as you add them. Let me emphasize this once again: Name your bones as you add them. The most efficient way to name your bones is through the Item panel located in the Properties region of the 3D view (accessible by pressing N).

You can edit the names of your bones in the same manner as you would edit the names for other Blender objects. Simply left-click on the name in the bone field and enter a meaningful name for the bone. Alternatively, you can go to Bone Properties and modify the name using the text field at the top. For instance, if you have a two-bone chain controlling a character's arm, you might name one bone "arm_ upper" and the other "arm_ lower." However, if you find yourself needing to name a large number of bones simultaneously (due to, ahem, forgetting to name them as you added them), the Outliner is the ideal tool for the task.

Expand the armor object to reveal the bone hierarchy within it. With **Ctrl+left-click**, you can rename any bone (or any object) directly within the outliner. This image displays the three different ways you can name your bones.

The image below shows three different methods for naming bones.

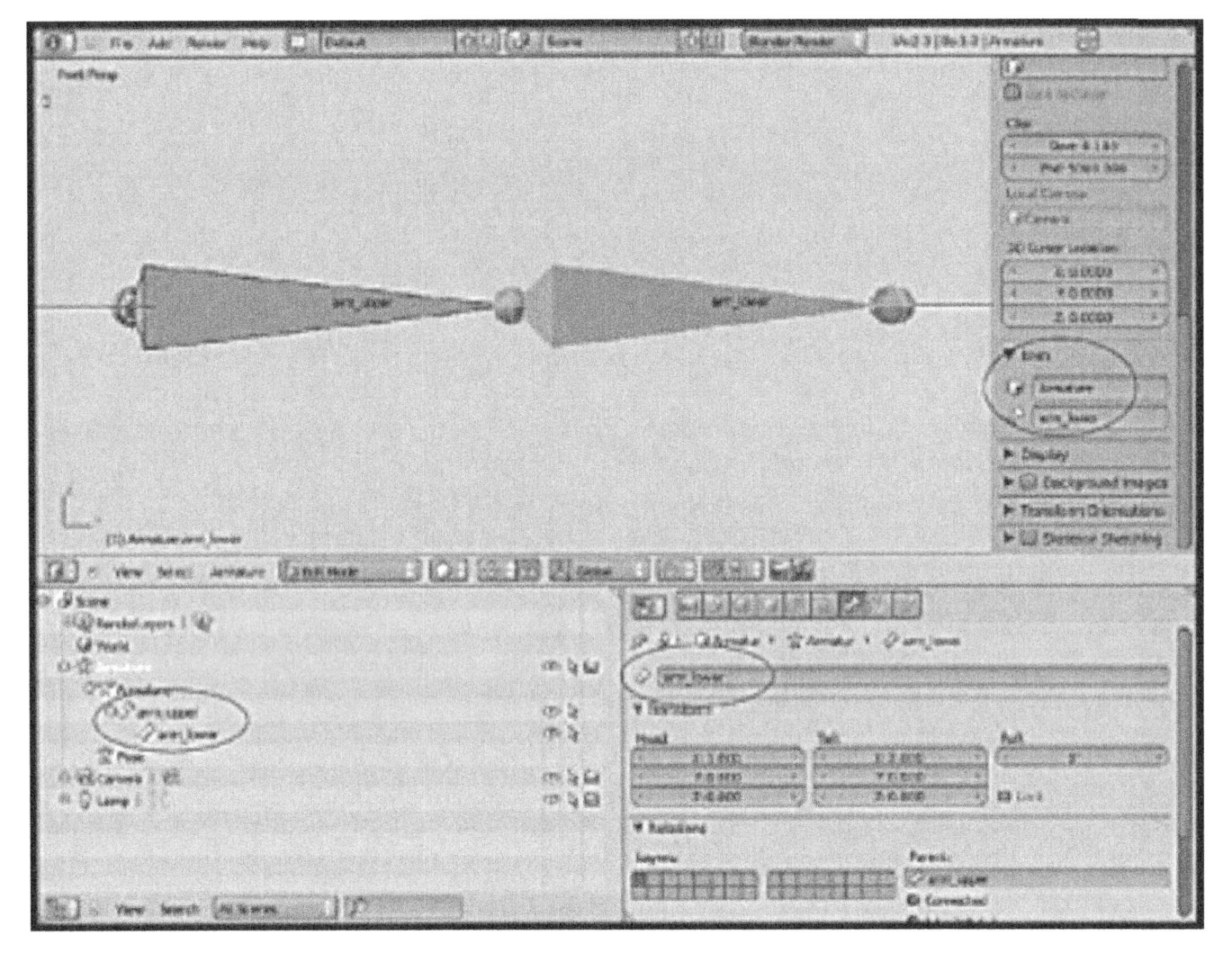

Blender offers a neat approach to handling symmetric rigs, where the left side is identical to the right side. To achieve this, utilize the ".L" and ".R" suffixes in your bone names. For instance, in the previous example of rigging a character with two arms, the bones on the left arm would be named "arm_upper.L" and "arm_lower.L," while the corresponding bones on the right arm would be named "arm_upper.R" and "arm_lower.R." This naming convention provides several advantages, particularly when using the X-Axis Mirror function during rig modeling.

To grasp the concept of symmetric rigs and X-axis mirroring, follow these steps with a new armature created at the origin **(Shift+S> Cursor to Center, Shift+A > Armature > Single Bone)**:

1. Tab into Edit mode for the armature and switch to front view (Numpad 1).
2. Select the tail of the single bone and extrude a bone to the right (E).
3. Name this new bone "Bone.R."
4. Once again, select the tail of the root bone and extrude another bone, but this time to the left (E).
5. Name this new bone "Bone.L."
6. In the Tool Shelf (T), enable the X-Axis Mirror checkbox.
7. Select the tail of Bone.R" and move it (G).
8. Notice how the movement of "Bone.R." is mirrored across the X-axis, affecting the tail of Bone L." accordingly. You can even extrude a new bone (E), and it will be duplicated on

both sides of the axis. This X-axis mirroring greatly accelerates the rigging process. By leveraging X-axis mirroring, the rigging workflow can be significantly expedited.

PUTTING SKIN ON YOUR SKELETON

Armatures and bones are fascinating, but they won't be of much use if they don't deform your mesh. When you create your rig and switch to pose mode using **Ctrl+Tab**, you can manipulate bones by grabbing, rotating, and scaling them. However, the mesh remains unaffected by the bone movements. To establish a connection between the mesh and the armature, you need to bind specific vertices of the mesh to individual bones in the armature. This binding process is commonly known as skinning. Blender offers two main methods of skinning: envelopes and vertex groups.

BUILDING STICKMAN'S CENTERLINE

The T pose is commonly used by modelers as a starting point for character creation and is preferred by riggers. However, some models may choose to model with arms at the sides or in a position between the T pose and the arms-down pose. The choice of pose ultimately depends on personal preference and specific requirements. Now let's proceed with adding an armature to this mesh, starting with the centerline bones, including the body bones, head, and hipbone. **Follow these steps**:

1. Add the armature and begin with the first body bone (Shift +A > Armature > Single Bone).
2. Enable X-ray viewing for the armature in the Object Data Properties to ensure the bones remain visible (Display >X-Ray).
3. Switch to Edit mode (Tab) and move the bone up along the Z-axis until it aligns with Stickman's waistline (G > Z).
4. Select the tail of this bone and move it upward along the Z-axis to the top of the torso (right-click, G > Z).
5. Subdivide this bone into two bones (W > Subdivide).
6. Name the bottom bone "body.1 and the top bone "body.2."
7. Select the joint between the two bones and move it slightly backward along the Y-axis (right-click, G > Y). This adjustment helps align the bones with the natural curvature of the spine.
8. Select the tail of body.2 and extrude it upward along the Z-axis until it reaches the top of Stickman's s head (right-click, E > Z). Name this bone "head."
9. Select the head of "body.1" and extrude it downward along the Z-axis until it reaches the bottom of Stickman's pelvis (right-click, E > Z). Name this bone "hip."
10. By following these steps, you'll establish the initial structure of the armature, including the centerline bones that form the backbone of Stickman.

ADDING STICKMAN'S APPENDAGES

The next step involves creating bones for the arms and legs by initially constructing half of the rig and allowing Blender to automatically mirror the bones for the other side.

Let's proceed as follows:

- Switch to the front view (Numpad 1) and select the head bone. Duplicate it and position the duplicated bone's root at Stickman's left shoulder joint (right-click,Shift+D).
- Note that this newbone becomes an offset child of the "body.2"bone.
- Name this newbone "arm_upper.L."
- Select the tailof"arm_upper.L" and move it to Stickman's elbow position.
- Holding Ctrl while moving ensures the bone remains perfectly horizontal (right-click,G, Ctrl).
- Extrude the tail of arm_upper.L" along the X-axis to extend it to Stickman's hand (right-click,E, X).
- Name this newbone "arm_lower.L."
- From the front view, select the hipbone and duplicate it, placing the head of the newbone at the top of Stickman's left leg (right-click,Shift+D).
- Move the tail of this newbone along the Z-axis to reach Stickman's feet (right-click, G, Z). Subdivide this bone into two bones (right-click,W,Subdivide).
- Name the top bone "leg_upper.L" and the bottom bone "leg_lower.L."

Select the joint between these bones and move it slightly forward along the Y-axis to provide a slight bend at the knee for better deformation (right-click, G, Y).

Parent "leg_upper.L" to the "hip" bone, maintaining offset (right-click "leg_upper.L", shift+right-click "hip", Ctrl+P, Keep Offset).

Your rig should now resemble this.

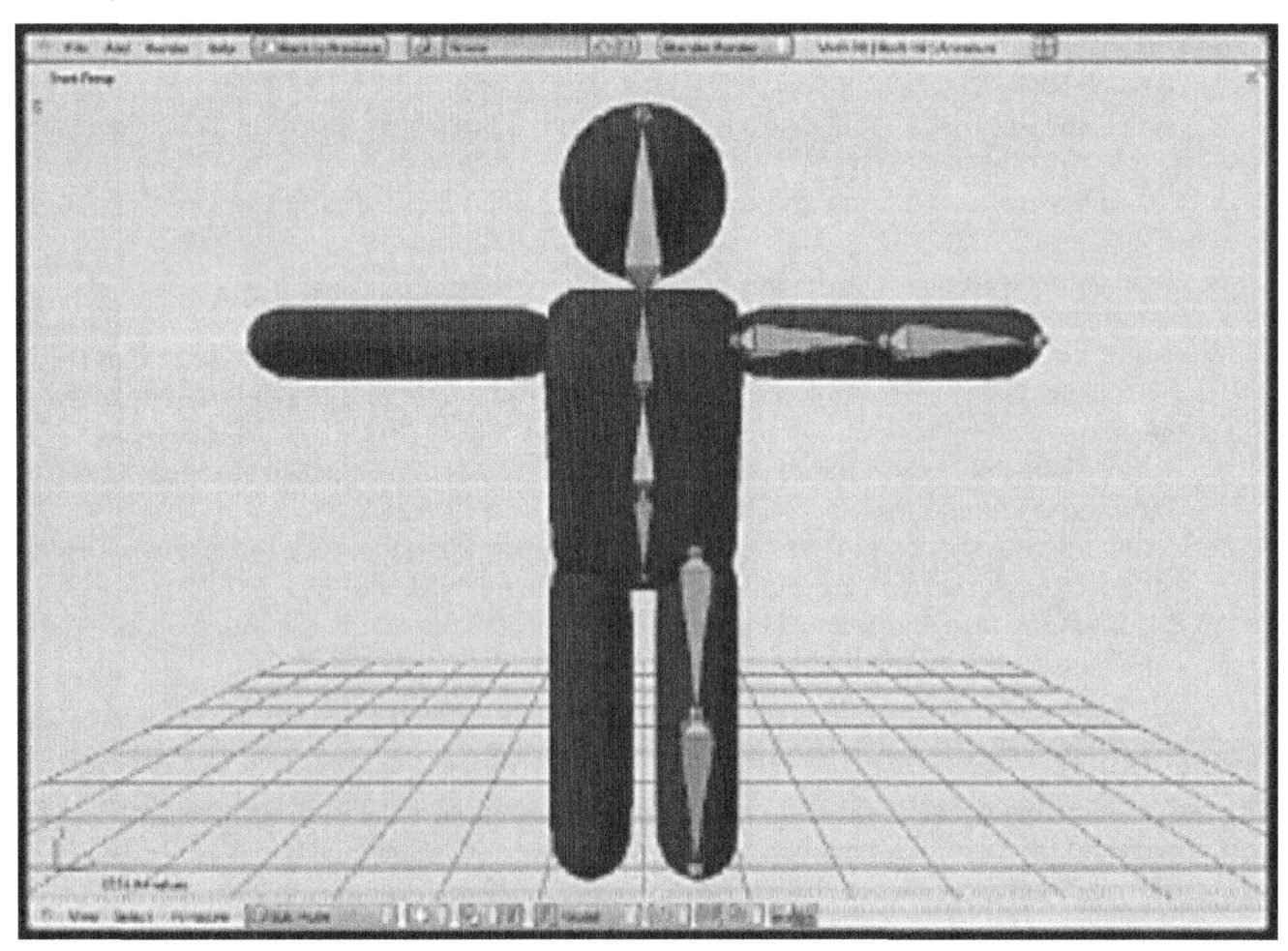

Now comes the exciting part, where Blender automates the process for you. Follow these steps:

1. Select both arm bones and both leg bones using Border Select (B).
2. Duplicate the selected bones and immediately press Esc to cancel the movement (Shift+D, Esc).
3. The duplicated bones will appear in the same location as the original ones.
4. Use the "W" key and select "Flip Nam es" to automatically add the ".R" suffix to indicate that these bones are on the right side.
5. All bones are now correctly named, but half of them are still in the wrong section of the rig.
6. The next step is where the magic happens.
7. Enable X-Axis Mirror in the Tool Shelf (Tool Shelf > Armature Options > X-Axis Mirror).
8. Select all bones (A).
9. Grab the bones briefly and immediately cancel the movement (G, Esc).

- Voila! The bones instantly snap into their correct positions, resulting in a rig resembling this.

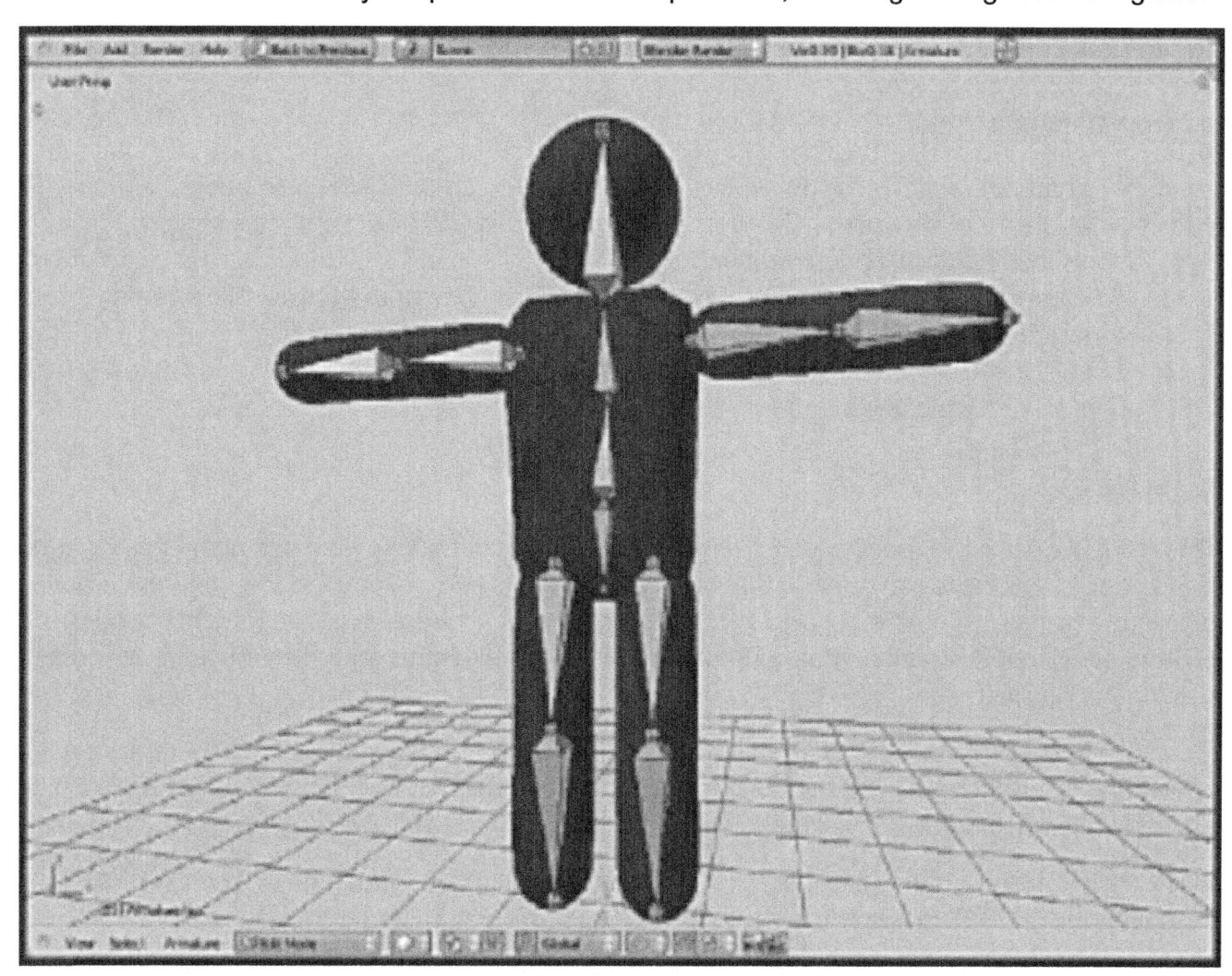

It's worth noting that using Blender's mirror operator (Ctrl+M) to flip the arms and legs to the correct side can sometimes disrupt the roll angles of the bones in the rig. By utilizing the X-Axis Mirror feature, you increase the likelihood of maintaining correct roll angles on both sides of your character's rig.

MAKING THE RIG MORE USER-FRIENDLY.

In summary, there are a few tweaks you can make to improve the usability of your rig:

1. Change the bone display to stick mode in the Display panel of Object Data Properties. This helps reduce clutter and allows you to see more of your mesh while animating.
2. Utilize bone groups to organize your rig. You can create and manage bone groups in the Bone Groups panel of Object Data Properties. Bone groups help with organization and offer the option to define custom bone colors for better visual identification.
3. Use bone layers as an organizational tool to show or hide specific bones in your rig. By moving bones to different layers and hiding those layers, you can streamline your view and focus on the necessary elements. To access hidden bone layers, enable them in the armor panel.

By implementing these adjustments, you can enhance the functionality and cleanliness of your rig, making it easier to animate.

REVIEW QUESTION

1. What are shape keys, and how can they be used to create facial animations in Blender?
2. What are hooks in Blend Blender, and how do they differ from shape keys in terms of mesh manipulation and animation control?
3. How can you add an armature to a mesh in Bender, and what is the purpose of an armature in the rigging process?
4. Explain the process of creating a symmetric rig using X-axis mirroring in Blen der, and what advantages does it offer in character rigging?

SUMMARY

This guide explains the process of creating shape keys, using hooks, and setting up an armature in Blender for character animation. Shape keys allow users to manipulate the mesh by creating different expressions, while hooks enable more flexible control over the mesh or animated objects along curved paths. Armatures, which act as a skeleton, provide structure and pose-holding capabilities.

for character rigs. The tutorial also covers various tips, such as using X-axis mirroring for symmetric rigs, organizing bones with groups and layers, and improving rig usability by changing bone display and colors.

In summary, the tutorial guides users through the process of creating a rigged character in Blender, demonstrating how to use shape keys, hooks, and armatures to achieve different effects and enhance animation capabilities.

CHAPTER 15: ADVANCED ANIMATION - DEFORMING OBJECTS

This chapter delves into the specific techniques and features that make rigged character animation more manageable and understandable. Blen der provides tools such as the Outliner and Graph Editor to assist in handling the intricacies of animating a fully rigged character.

WORKING WITH THE DOPE SHEET

To animate a rigged character in Blen der, you need to make some adjustments to your workspace. Switch to the animation layout and set the 3D view to solid viewport shading. Change the translate manipulator to the rotate manipulator in normal orientation. This allows for easier bone rotation control without the 3D manipulator getting in the way. The dope sheet is an important editor for managing keyframes in your animation. It provides a big-picture view of keyframes for multiple objects and bones. You can Select individual keyframes by right-clicking on them or using column key selection to quickly select all keyframes in a specific frame or column. This is helpful for animating poses and ensuring consistent timing.

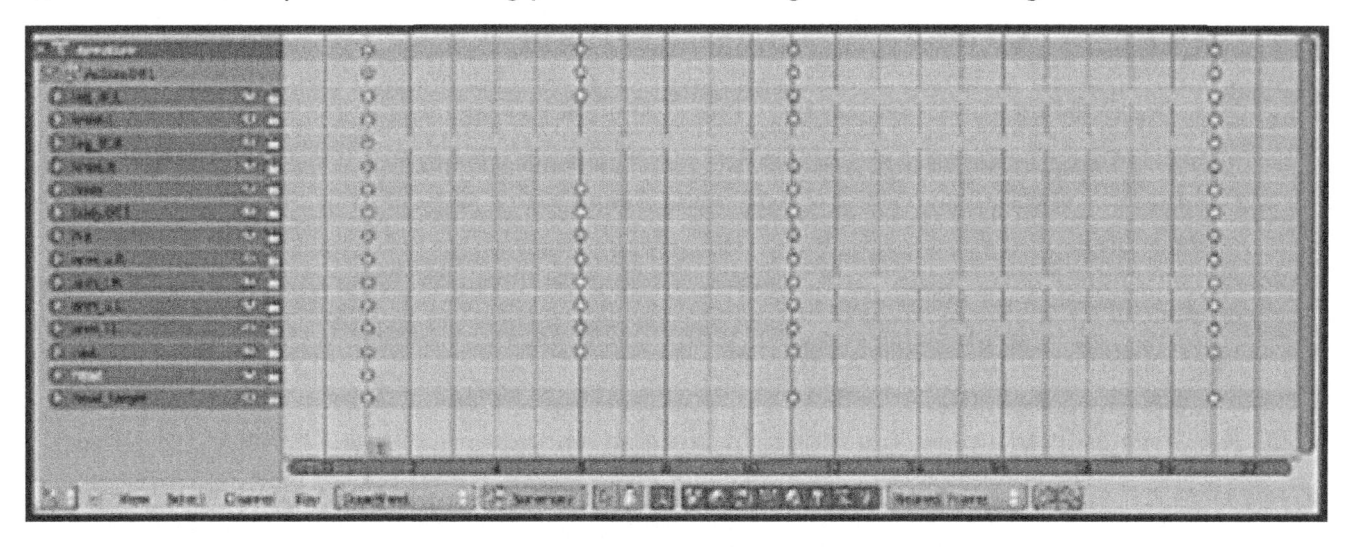

You can manipulate keyframes by grabbing and scaling them. When scaling, be aware that the position of the time cursor affects the relative scale of the keyframes. Pay attention to snapping settings, as Blender's default Nearest Frame snapping helps align keyframes to the closest frame. You can use the Snap Keys feature to quickly fix any keys located between frames. It's generally recommended to use Blender's auto-snap feature, which is enabled by default, for precise keyframe placement. The auto-snap method can be adjusted in the Dope sheet's header, providing options such as snapping to the current frame, nearest frame, nearest second, or nearest marker. By following these tips and utilizing the Dope sheet, you can effectively animate a rigged character in Blender with control and precision.

ANIMATING WITH ARMATURES

Here's a straightforward step-by step instruction for animating with armatures using the Dopesheet in Blender:

1. Plan your animation, considering the motion and timing. Act it out or sketch quick thumbnail drawings to visualize the sequence.

2. Set the timeline to frame I and create the starting pose by manipulating the character's rig. Select all visible bones and insert a LocRot keyframe for everything.
3. Move the timeline cursor to the next major pose and create the character's second pose. If it's a hold or unchanged position, duplicate the keys from the previous pose.
4. Select all visible bones and insert an available keyfram.
5. Repeat steps 3 and 4 for each major pose in your animation.
6. Use the Dopesheet to play back the animation, focusing on timing.
7. Adjust the timing of the poses in the dopesheet to achieve a natural flow.
8. Start adding secondary poses and keyframes for secondary motion between the major poses.
9. Continue refining the timing and details with each pass, tweaking and making changes as needed.

Remember to work in phases, starting with the biggest motion and gradually adding more detail. This approach allows for easier adjustments to timing and avoids the need to shuffle numerous detail keys later on. Take advantage of the flexibility of computer animation to continually improve your work.

PRINCIPLES OF ANIMATION WORTH REMEMBERING

To create captivating animations, consider these tips:

1. **Observe and learn from real-world motion**: Pay attention to how objects move and study their structures. Think about how you can replicate their movements in your animations.
2. **Study early animation principles**: Familiarize yourself with the classic 12 basic principles of animation developed by Disney animators. These principles, such as squash and stretch, anticipation, staging, and follow-through, are still relevant and useful in computer animation.
3. **Choose between pose-to-pose and straight-ahead animation**: These are two primary methods of animating. Pose-to-pose involves creating key poses, while straight-ahead animation is more fluid and realistic. Most animators use a combination of both techniques.
4. **Apply physics principles**: Ensure your animations adhere to the laws of physics. Consider follow-through and overlapping activities to maintain realistic movements.
5. **Use arcs for natural movement**: Most motion occurs in curved arcs, so incorporate arc-like motions when characters change direction or move objects. Straight lines are more suitable for robotic or powerful actions.
6. **Add secondary actions:** Make characters feel more real by incorporating secondary actions like clothing movement, jiggling, and blinking. These details breathe life into your animations.
7. **Master timing**: Timing is crucial for the overall effect of an animation. Control the timing of actions to make them appear believe able, and consider story-based timing to enhance the emotional impact.
8. **Embrace exaggeration**: Animation allows for limitless possibilities, so take advantage of it. Exaggeration can make animations more engaging and fun.
9. **Develop solid drawing skills**: Although not mandatory for computer animators, the ability to draw is beneficial. Drawing enhances your visual perception and understanding of relative proportions, improving your ability to create believable motion.

10. **Strive for appeal:** Create animations that are interesting and captivating. If your animation lacks appeal, it may not resonate with viewers. Aim to make your work enjoyable for both yourself and your audience.

Remember that these principles are not rigid rules. Feel free to break them creatively while still considering their foundational guidance.

MAKING SENSE OF QUATERNIONS (OR WHY THERE ARE FOUR ROTATION CURVES?)

When working with armatures in Blender, you may encounter quaternions, which are used to define rotations in 3D space. They differ from the familiar X, Y, and Z rotations and Euler rotations. Quaternions are employed to avoid gimbal lock issues that can occur with Euler rotations.

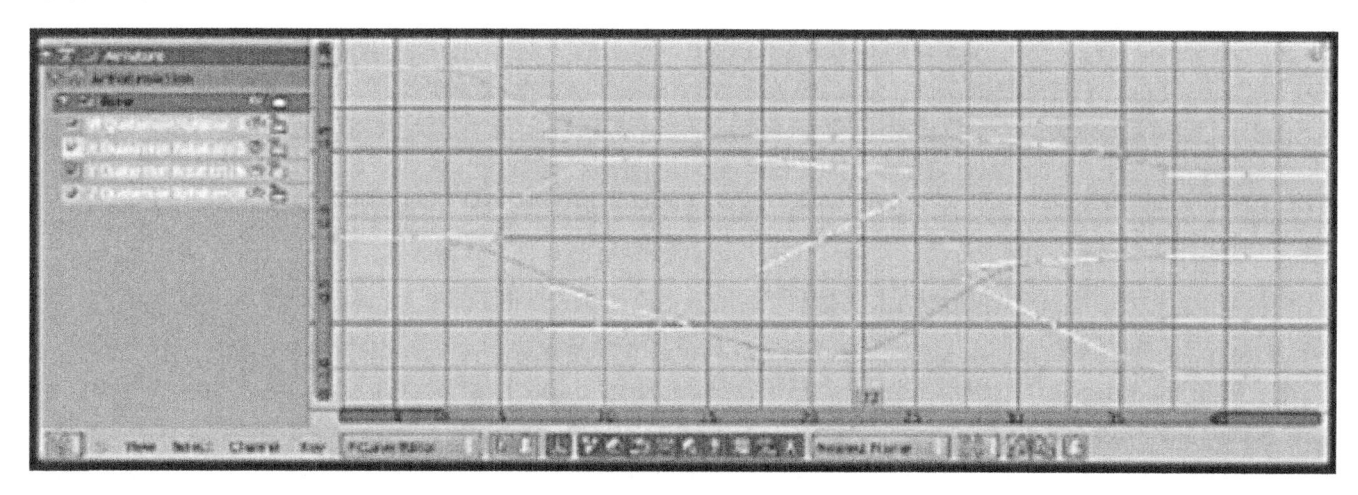

However, quaternions can be challenging to grasp intuitively, especially for non-mathematicians. Instead of trying to understand the mathematical relationship between quaternions and bone rotation, it's often easier to tweak rotations by adding additional keyframes. Blen's a nim at ion systems changed the 2.5 series, including the ability to control the rotation mode of armature bones. To adjust the rotation mode, select a bone and access its bone properties. Look for the Rotation Mode drop-down menu in the Transform panel. The default setting is Quaternion (WXYZ), which is suitable in most cases. But for specific scenarios where gimbal lock is not a concern, such as a bone-defining wheel rotation, you can choose a different rotation mode like XYZ Euler or Axis Angle. By understanding and effectively working with quaternions, you can navigate complex rotations in your armature animations with greater ease.

COPYING MIRRORED POSES

In computer animation, you can let the computer do the tedious work for you.

Blender has three useful buttons in the 3D View's header for copying and pasting poses in an armature:

1. Select all bones.
2. Click the Copy Pose button to save the avatar's pose.
3. Move to a different point in the timeline.
4. Paste the pose back to the character using either the Paste Pose or Mirror Paste options.
   - Paste Pose applies the copied pose exactly as it was.

- Mirror paste creates a mirrored version of the pose, which is useful for creating symmetrical poses.

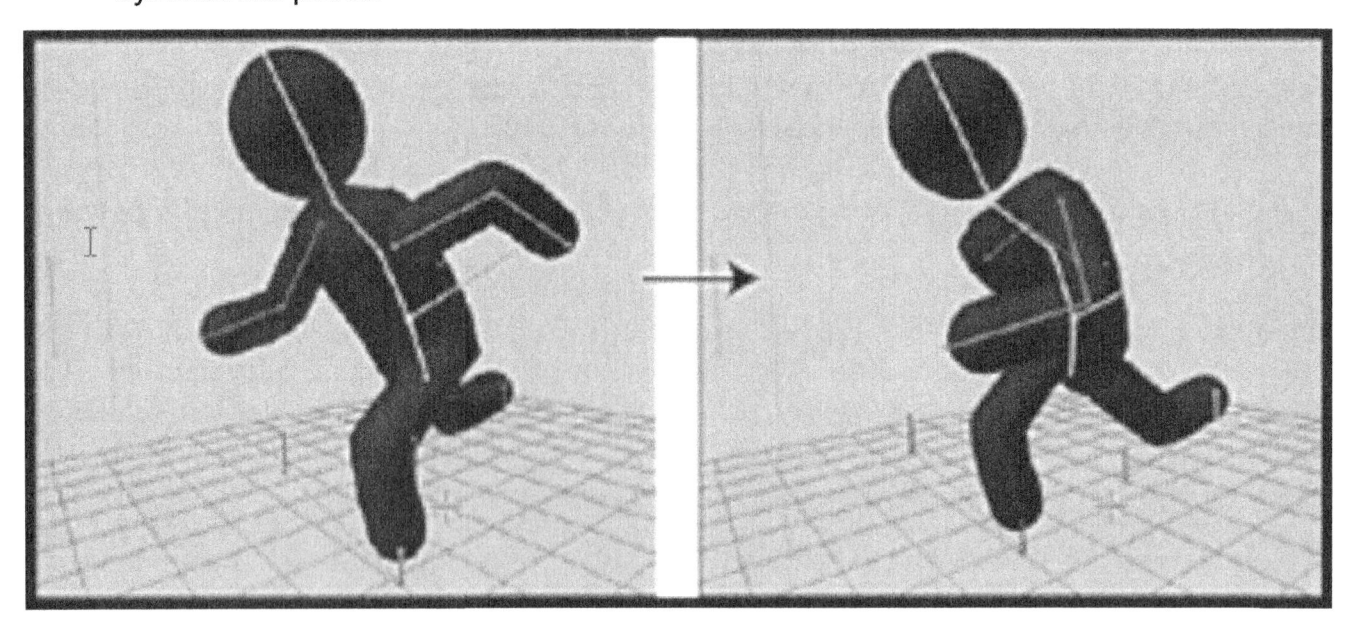

These buttons save time and make it easy to reuse poses in your animation.

DOING NONLINEAR ANIMATION

Nonlinear animation (NLA) is a powerful technique that allows you to create complex animations by combining smaller motion chunks. In Blender, you can create a library of actions, which are collections of off-curves representing different motions or poses. To create a new action, switch to the Action Editor context in the Dopesheet and use the Action datablock to add a new action. Populate your library with various animations such as arm waving, walking cycles, facial expressions, and more. To mix and match these actions, utilize the NLA Editor. Add the NLA Editor to your animation screen layout by expanding its space in the timeline or creating a separate area for it. The NLA Editor allows you to combine and arrange actions, creating more complex sequences. However, it's important to note that while the NLA Editor is a useful tool, it may require further refinement in future Blender releases. Nonetheless, the principles explained here should still be applicable. **To add the NLA Editor to your animation screen layout, follow these steps:**

1. In the animation screen layout, left-click the seam at the top of the timeline and drag it up to create more space for the editor.
2. Since the NLA Editor covers the entire animation, it's practical to prioritize it over the timeline. However, if you still want to use the timeline, you can split it off from another area.
3. Convert the timeline into an NLA editor by changing its type.
4. Your screen layout will now resemble the suggested arrangement.

MIXING ACTIONS TO CREATE A COMPLEX ANIMATION

When you're working with actions in Dopes's Action Editor, you can use the NLA Editor to combine them and create a smooth animation sequence.

Here's how:

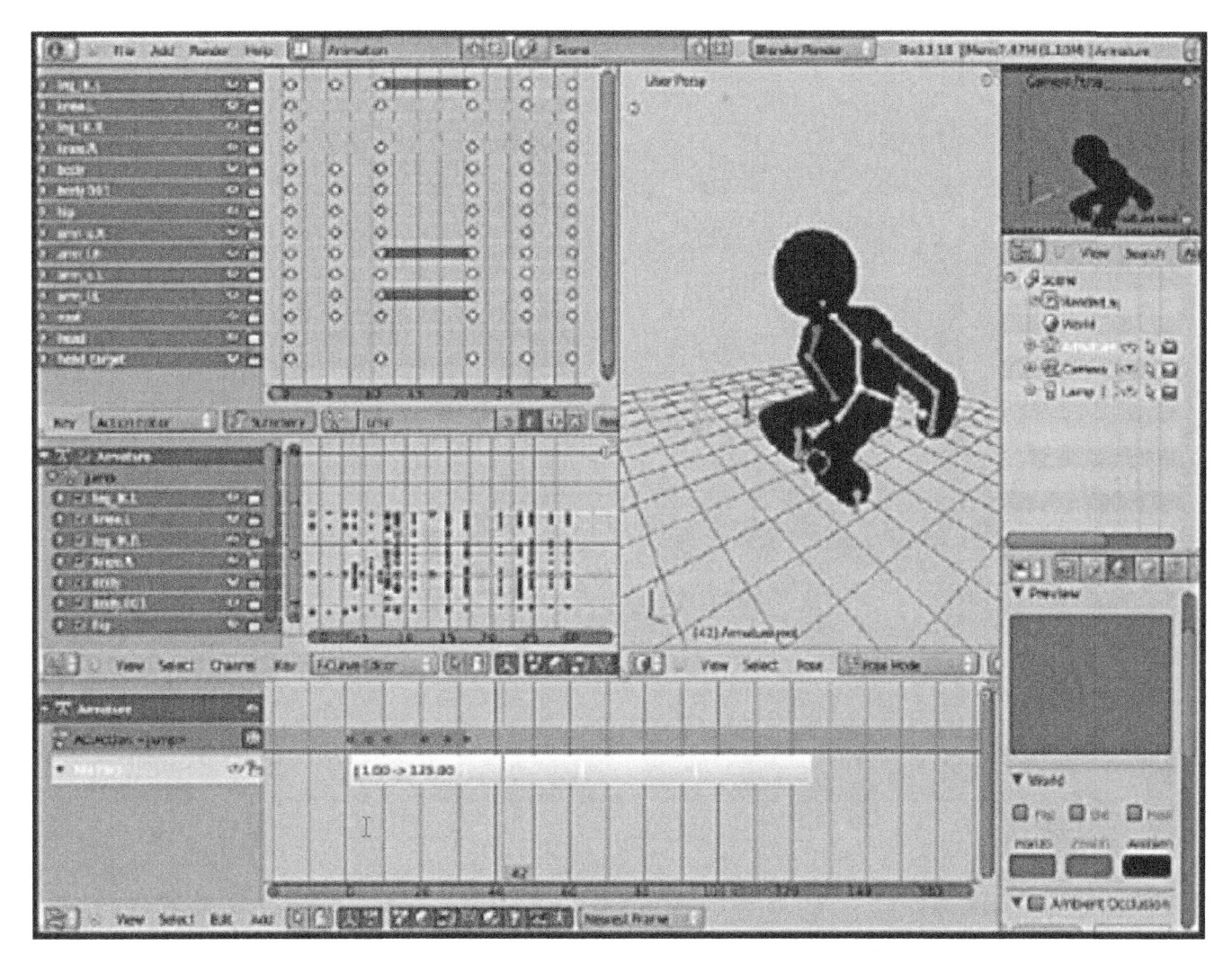

Look for the bright orange bar in the NLA Editor, which represents a track where you can add actions. Activate the track by clicking on the snowflake icon in the channel region on the left of the NLA Editor. This will expand the track and show your current action as a yellow strip. To add a new action, click on the graph area of the NLA Editor and press **Shift +A**. A menu with all your created actions will appear.

Choose the action you want to add, and it will appear in the NLA Editor as a strip. The strip's start position is determined by the time cursor. Repeat the process to add more actions to the NLA Editor. Remember to ensure a smooth transition between strips by adjusting the Blend In and Blend Out values in the Properties region (accessible by pressing N) or letting the strips overlap slightly. By following these steps, you can combine actions and create a cohesive animation in the NLA Editor.

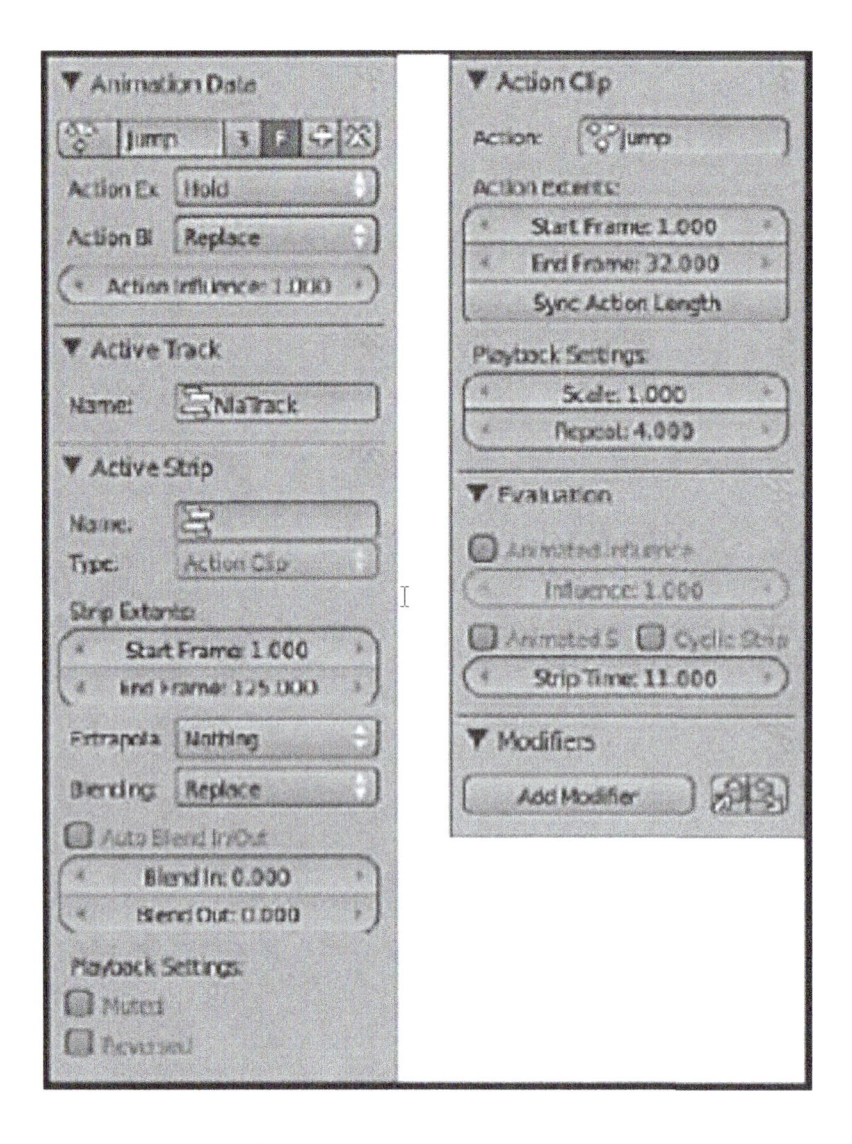

TAKING ADVANTAGE OF LOOPED ANIMATION

In the NLA Editor, you can easily make actions loop and adjust their timing.

This allows you to create cool repeating animations. Here's how you can do it:

1. In the NLA Editor's Properties region, look for the Playback Settings.
2. Find the scale value, which determines the timing of the action. The default is 1.0, but you can change it to make the action faster or slower.
3. Look for the Repeat value below Scale. This value makes the action repeat more or fewer times. You'll see the strip length changes accordingly.
4. To make a smooth loop, it's important to have the first and last poses of the action identical.

Here's how you can do it:

- In the Dopesheet, select the action strip you want to loop.
- Move the time cursor to the first pose of the action.
- In the 3D view, select all bones and click the Copy Pose button.
- Move the time cursor to a point after the last keyframe.
- In the 3D view, click the Paste Pose button.
- Insert a new keyframe. (I-->available)

5. When you go back to the NLA Editor, the action strip will be longer to include the extra frame at the end. It should loop seamlessly when you play it (press Alt+A).

By following these steps, you can create looping animations with different timings in the NLA Editor.

SUMMARY

This chapter covers various aspects of animation in Blender, starting with keyframe indicators, which are essential for creating smooth and dynamic animations. It then delves into animating with armatures, providing a step-by-step guide to creating poses and refining timing using the dope sheet. The chapter also emphasizes the importance of understanding animation principles, including studying real-world motion and applying physics principles to achieve realistic movements. It introduces the concept of quaternions and their use in handling rotations within armatures, offering practical tips on working with them effectively. Additionally, the chapter explores the benefits of nonlinear animation (NLA) and demonstrates how to combine actions in the NLA to create complex and looping animations.

In summary, this chapter equips users with the necessary knowledge and techniques to animate objects and characters effectively in Blender. It emphasizes both technical understanding and creative principles to produce visually appealing and engaging animations.

REVIEW QUESTIONS

1. How can you animate with armatures in Blender using the Dopesheet? Provide a step-by-step guide.
2. What are some principles of animation worth remembering to create captivating animations? How can you apply these principles to enhance your animations in Blender?
3. What are quaternions, and why are they used in armature animations in Blender? How do they differ from Euler rotations, and how can you adjust rotation modes in Blender?
4. In Blender, how can you copy and paste poses, including mirrored poses, to save time and reuse poses in your annotations? Explain the process of using these functions in the 3D View header.

CHAPTER 16: AUTOMATION IN BLENDER: SIMULATIONS AND EFFECTS

Simulations are powerful tools in animation that let the computer calculate realistic motion based on variables like gravity and mass. They are great for complex actions like explosions, fire, cloth, and physics-related movements. Simulations save time by automating the motion instead of manually keyframing every detail. However, some detailed simulations can still take a long time to complete. It's important to learn more about simulations from resources like Blender's official documentation, online tutorials, and books to fully understand their capabilities. This chapter provides an introduction to simulations and opens up possibilities for your animations.

USING PARTICLES IN A BLENDER

Blende's particle system is a powerful tool for creating effects like hair, flocking, and explosions. You can access the controls for the particle system in the Particle Properties panel. When you add a particle system to an object, additional panels appear to help you control the behavior of the particles. This system continues to improve with each new Blender release.

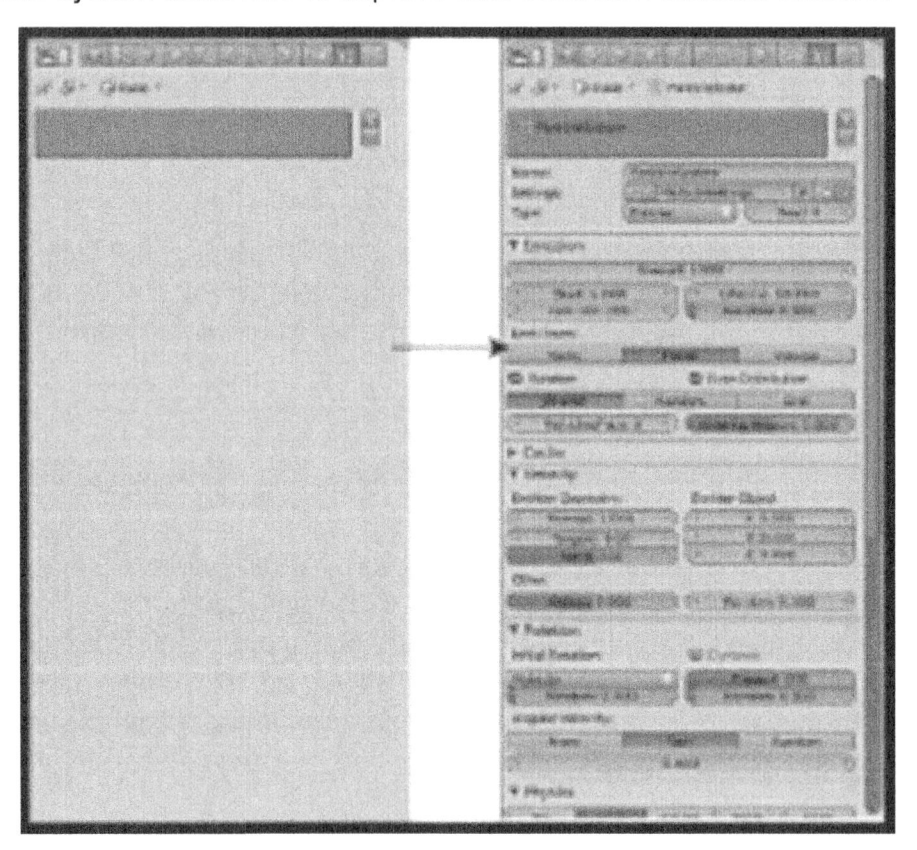

WHAT ARE PARTICLE SYSTEMS USEFUL FOR?

Particle systems in Blender have several useful applications. They are great for creating groups of objects that exhibit similar behavior, making them ideal for simulating physics-based movements like fireworks or a continuous stream of tennis balls hitting a wall. Additionally, particle systems are commonly used for simulating hair and fur by treating the path of individual particles as strands. Blender leverages this technique to generate realistic hair effects. Another exciting use of particle systems is for simulating flocking or crowd behavior. For instance, if you want a swarm of gnats buzzing around a character's head, a particle system can achieve that effect effectively. The image below showcases various configuration panels found in Particle Properties. You'll find the most essential and frequently used panels within this section of the Properties editor. Once you create a particle system, the context panel at the top of Particle Properties provides extensive controls. You can assign a name to your particle system and choose different settings from the Particle Settings data block. It's worth noting that Blender allows objects to have multiple particle systems, and these systems can even share the same settings across objects. Below the Settings data block, you'll find a Type drop-down menu offering two options: emitter and hair. In most cases, the emitter type is used, while hair particle systems are designed specifically for creating manageable hair and fur in Blender.

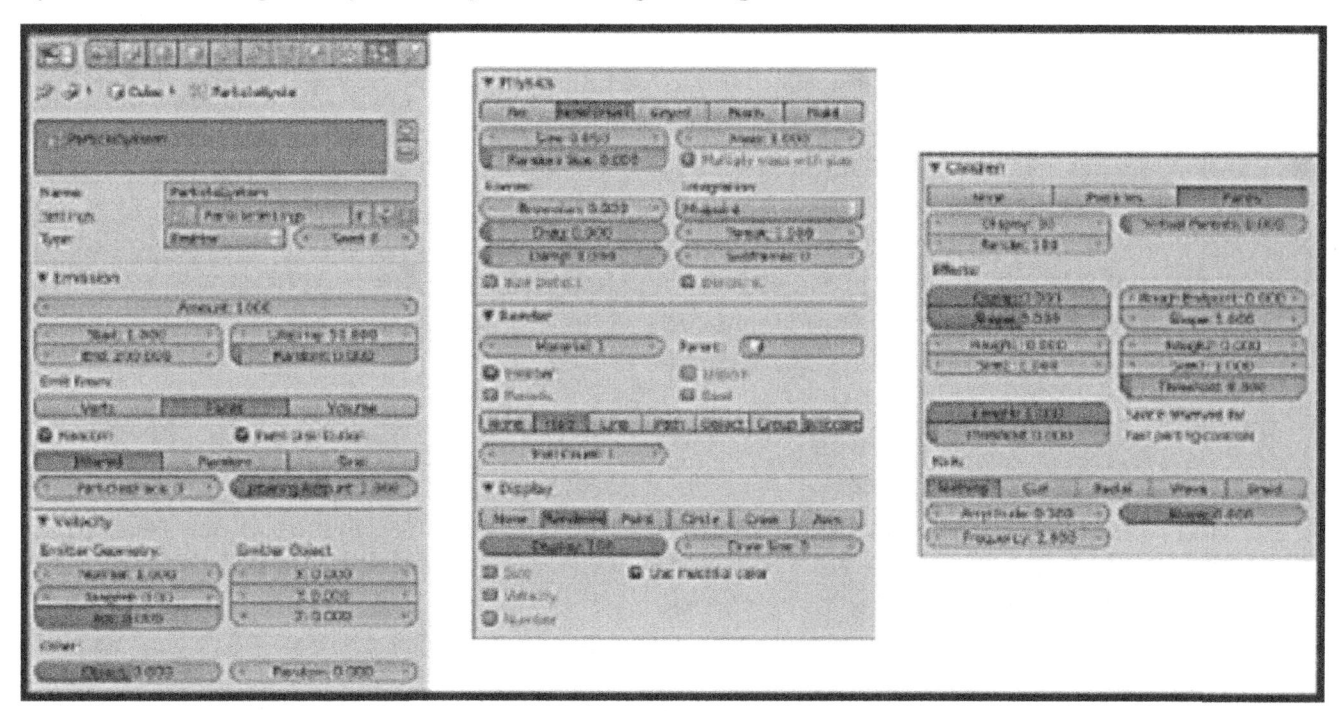

Once you create your first particle system in Blender, you'll find the context panel at the top of the Particle Properties, which provides comprehensive controls. In this panel, you can name your particle system and select different settings from the Particle Settings data block. It's worth noting that objects in Blender can have multiple particle systems, and they can even share the same particle system settings among them. Below the Settings data block, you'll find a Type drop-down menu offering two options: emitter and hair. In most cases, the emitter type is commonly used, while hair particle systems are specifically designed for creating manageable hair and fur effects. If you choose the emitter type, the emission panel becomes crucial for controlling the number of particles and their lifespan in your scene.

Here's a brief explanation of each setting:

- **Amount**: This value represents the total number of particles created by the system. Once the system generates this number of particles, it stops. If you need additional particles, you can increase this value.
- **Start**: This frame indicates when particles start being emitted from the source object. By default, it's set to frame 1, but you can adjust it to delay the particle emission in your animation. Negative values are also possible.
- **End**: This frame marks the point where Blender stops emitting particles from the source object. The default value is set to frame 200. With the default Amount and Start values

(1000 and 1.0, respectively), Blender generates five particles in each new frame of the animation until frame 200 and then stops.
- **Lifetime**: The lifetime value determines how long an individual particle exists in your scene. The default value is 50.0, meaning a particle created in frame 7 disappears at frame 57. If you need particles to exist longer, you can increase this value.
- **Random**: This value specifically affects the lifetime of particles. At the default value of O.O., particles live exactly as long as specified by the lifetime value and die at the end of that time. However, increasing the random value introduces variation, causing particles born on the same frame to disappear at different times, creating a more natural effect.

Particle types, whether emitter or hair, can be associated with five physics simulation models in the Physics panel: None, Newtonian, Keyed, Boids, and Fluid. The default Newtonian setting is the most commonly used, as it simulates real-world physical attributes like gravity, mass, and velocity. However, in certain cases, you may want more control over particles, such as shaping hair on a character. In such situations, keyed physics comes into play, allowing you to control the angle and direction of particle emission using another particle system as the emitter. The Boids option enables flocking or swarming behavior among particles, with dedicated settings to control this behavior. Lastly, the Fluid option provides a physics-based choice similar to Newtonian, but with cohesive and adhesive properties that make particles behave like a fluid system.

To create a basic particle system, follow these steps:

1. Add a mesh object that will serve as your particle emitter. You can do this by pressing Shift + A and selecting "Mesh" followed by "Grid." Remember, any mesh can be used as an emitter, but particles are emitted from the faces of the mesh by default and move away from the face in the direction of its normal.
2. Go to the Particle Properties panel and add a new particle system. Click the plus (+) button next to the particle list box to reveal all the available options for particles. If you play back the animation (Alt+A) at this point, you will see particles dropping from the grid.
3. Decide on the type of physics you want to use to control your particles. Newtonian physics is commonly used for particle systems, but you can also explore the fun and visually appealing Boid behavior for emitter particle systems.
4. Adjust the velocity settings to control the behavior of your particles. You can modify these settings in the Velocity panel under Particle Properties. For Newtonian physics, you can provide an initial velocity to your particles. Start by adjusting the normal velocity, as it produces immediate results. Positive values move particles in the direction of each face's "normals," while negative values move them in the opposite direction. Boid particles don't require an initial velocity, but their settings affect how each particle interacts with neighboring particles.
5. Play back the animation (Alt+A) to observe the movement of the particles. If you followed the tip in step 2, your particle animation may already be playing. If not, press Alt+A to see how your settings influence particle behavior. If the parameters behave unexpectedly, ensure that the time cursor in the timeline is at or before the frame specified as the start value in the emissions panel. You can make live adjustments during playback or press Esc to stop and refine your settings before playing the animation again. We often use a combination of live adjustments and iterative tweaking to refine the behavior of my particle system.

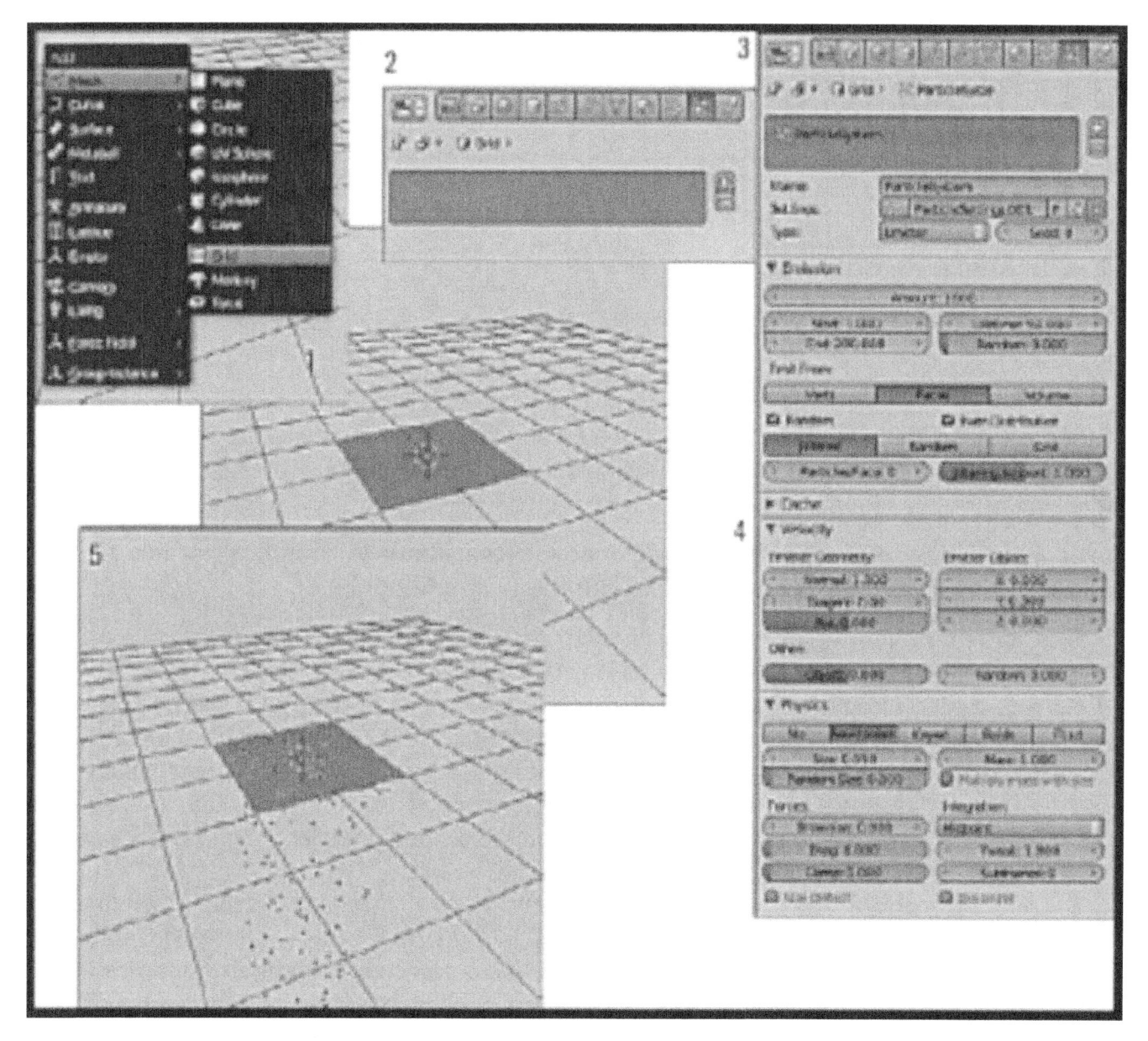

Please note that these steps provide a basic setup for a particle system, and there is much more to explore and learn. We highly recommend taking the time to experiment with different settings and referring to Blender's online documentation for more in-depth information on particles.

USING FORCE FIELDS AND COLLISIONS

After creating a basic particle system, you can have some fun by controlling the behavior of your particles using forces and deflections. Forces are influences that affect the overall behavior of particles, such as wind, vortices, and magnetism. On the other hand, deflectors are objects that particles collide with, impeding their movement. To access the controls for forces and deflectors, go to Physics Properties, which can be found by clicking the last button in the Properties editor's header. The Force Fields panel appears when you click the Force Fields button, allowing you to add force field properties. Similarly, the collision panel appears when you click the collision button, enabling you to define collision settings.

Typically, you use these panels to add force and collision behaviors to objects already present in your scene. You select an object and then add force field and collision properties through the Physics Properties. However, for force fields, there is a faster method. By pressing **Shift+A** and selecting Force Field from Blender's Add menu, you can choose from a variety of forces to add to your scene. Afterward, you can adjust the settings for the selected force from the Force Fields panel in the Physics Properties.

To illustrate how these controls work, follow these steps to create a particle system influenced by a wind force that collides with a wall and bounces off:

1. Create a simple particle system using the steps mentioned in the previous section. Set it up as an emitter particle system with Newtonian physics.
2. Add a wind force field by pressing Shift+A and selecting Force Field, followed by Wind. The wind force field appears as an empty object with circles along its local Z-axis, visually representing the strength and direction of the wind force. Adjust the strength value in the Force Fields panel to see the effect of the wind on the particles. During animation playback (Alt+A), you can rotate the wind object or modify its force field settings in real time to observe how the particles are affected.
3. Add a plane by pressing Shift+A and selecting Mesh, followed by Plane. This plane will serve as your deflector. Move the plane (G) into the path of the particles driven by the wind force. Rotate (R) the plane to ensure that the particles collide with it head-on.
4. Make the plane a collision object by adding a collision panel in the Physics Properties. Congratulations! You've created a deflector. When you play back the animation (Alt+A), the particles should be blown into the plane by the wind force instead of passing through it.

Feel free to experiment with different force fields and deflector settings to create various particle behaviors and interactions.

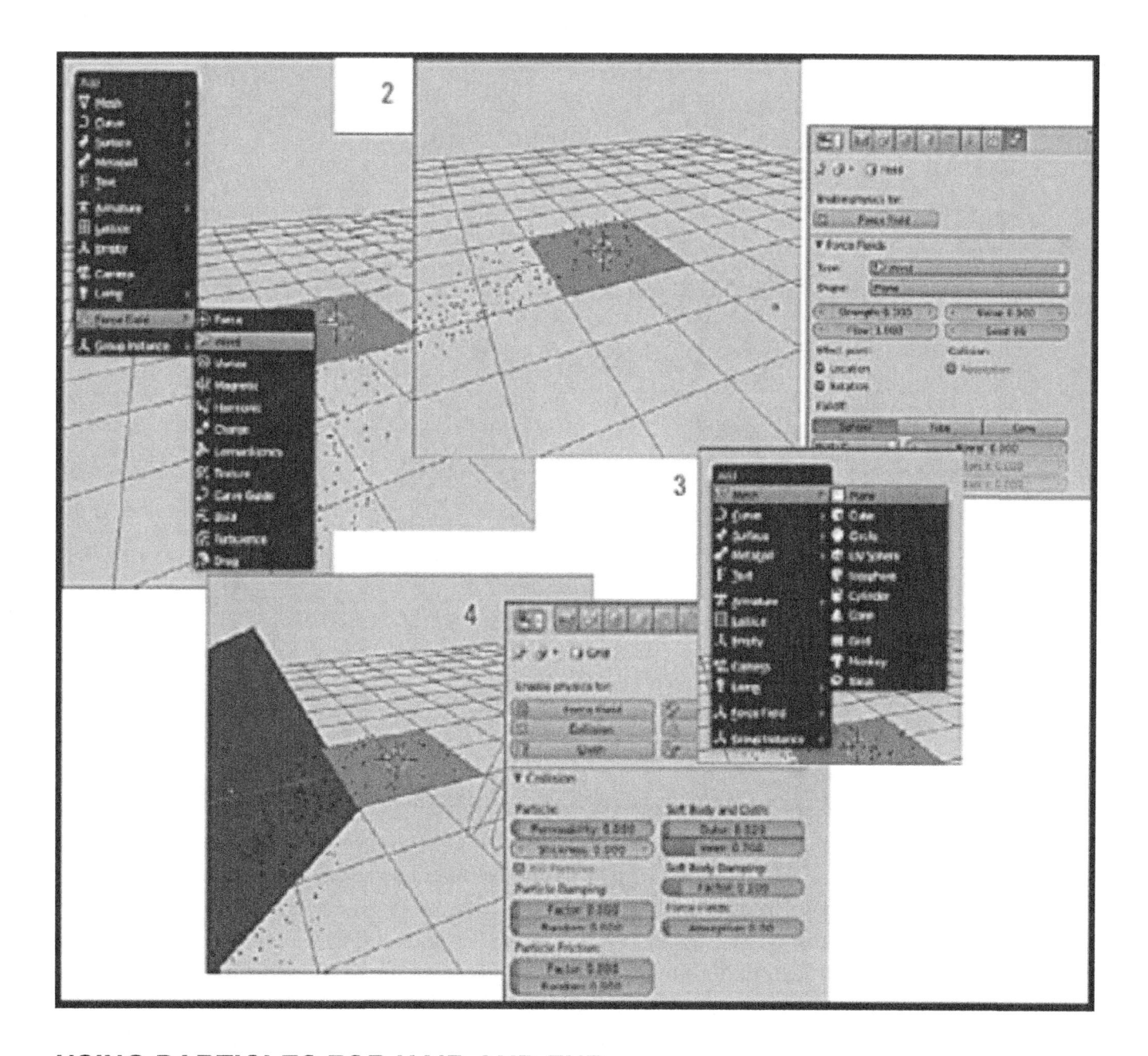

USING PARTICLES FOR HAIR AND FUR

When discussing particles, it's important to mention Blender's hair and fur system. Blender utilizes particles to create realistic hair and fur for your characters. To enable this feature, simply choose the Hair option in the context panel located at the top of the Particle Properties. The setup process is similar to using a regular emitter system with Newtonian physics, but there are two notable differences.

The first difference is that editing hair particles is easier in some ways compared to emitter particles. Blender offers a specialized mode called particle mode, which allows you to customize and style your particle hair. When you enter particle mode, the particle settings are locked, and you can freely tweak and comb the hair to achieve the desired look. Although we cannot provide an accompanying screenshot, you can refer to the image below in the original resource to see an example of an object with particle hair being combed in particle mode.

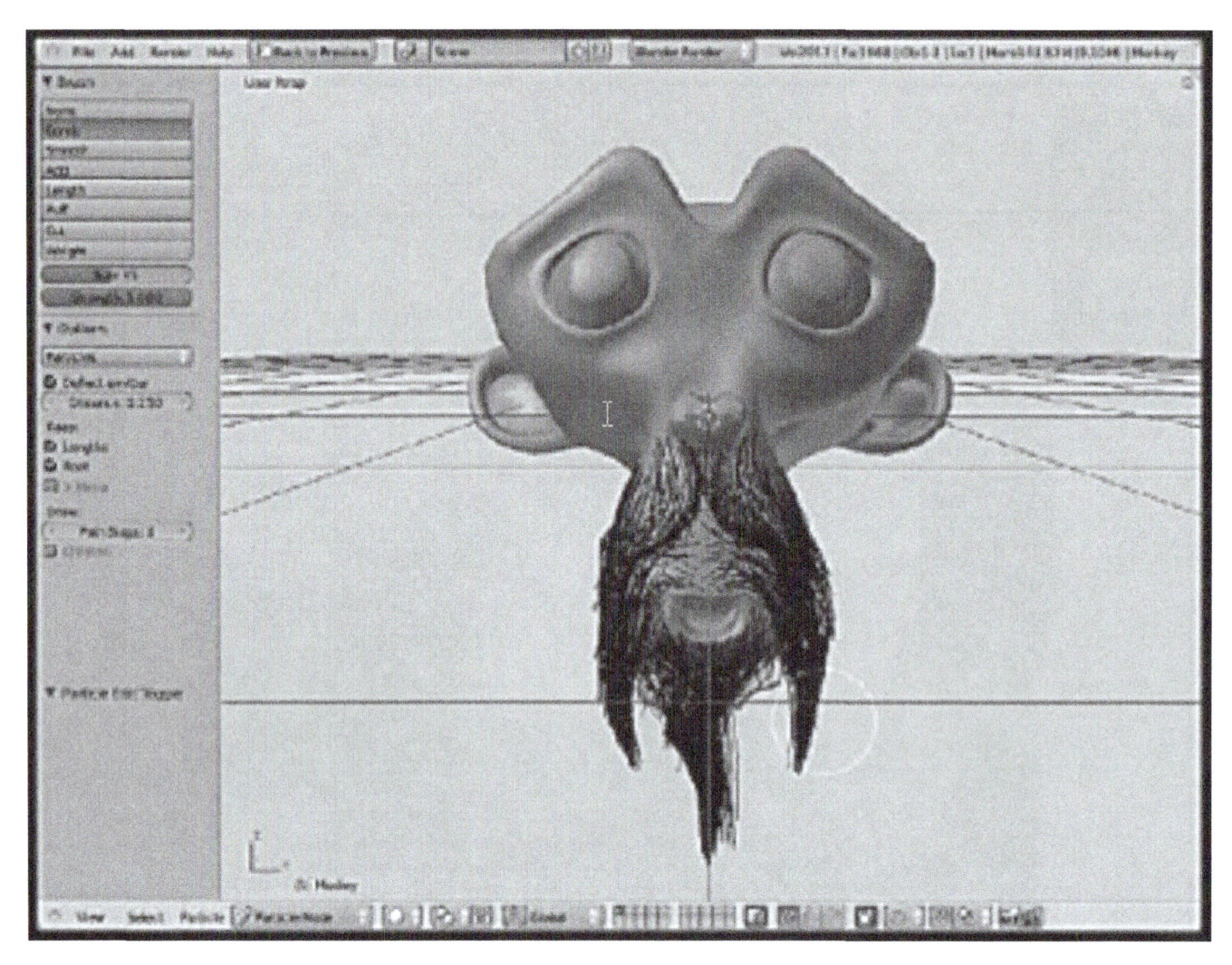

To enter Particle mode, go to the Mode menu in the 3D View's header. Select your emitter object, click the drop-down menu, and choose Particle Mode. In this mode, you have direct control over editing particle hair, including combing, cutting, growing, and smoothing. To access these controls, look to the Tool Shelf (T). Particle Mode provides a circular brush similar to Sculpting and Vertex Paint modes. You can adjust the brush's size and strength using the sliders in the ToolShelf or by pressing Fand Shift+F, respectively. Another aspect that differs in the hair particle setup is the use of child particles. Generating and displaying hair particles can consume a lot of computing power, and during animation, waiting for Blender to draw all the fur in the 3D view may not be desirable. To address this, two solutions work best together. First, reduce the number of visible particles in the 3D view using the Display slider in the Display panel of Particle Properties. This slider changes the percentage of particles displayed in the 3D view, while all particles appear during rendering, giving you the best of both worlds.

However, for characters with abundant hair, simply reducing the displayed particles may not suffice. In such cases, child particles come in handy. In the Children panel of Particle Properties, select the Faces option. Additional particle strands grow from the faces of the emitter, with their locations determined by the surrounding particles. The Children panel has two values: display and render. The display value controls the number of particles seen in the 3D view. For faster animation playback, setting this value to O is often useful. The render value determines the number of child particles each parent particle has at render time. Once your particle system generates hair strands, the next step is to control how Blender renders them.

Here's a quick guide to achieving nice hair:

1. Enable the "Strand render" checkbox in the Render panel of Particle Properties. This instructs Blender's rendering engine to render the particles as strands.
2. Additionally, in the same panel, the emitter checkbox can be enabled to make the emitter visible, which can be helpful when using the character mesh for hair generation.
3. In the material properties, enable transparency and ensure that Z transparency is selected. Set the Alpha value in the Transparency panel to 0. If you're using the Hair Strands preview type in the Preview panel, you may notice minimal visibility due to the O Alpha values. Don't worry; this setting will make sense in the following steps.
4. In the Texture Properties, add a new Blend texture and use the Ramp editor in the Colors panel to control the color and transparency along the length of the hair. The right-hand side of the ramp represents the hair tips and should be completely transparent, while other positions should be opaque.
5. In the Mapping panel, select Strand/Particle from the Coordinates drop-down menu. Enable color and alpha in the influence panel.
6. The Preview panel should display hair strands that utilize the ramp gradient along their length, with semitransparent tips.
7. In the Material Properties, go to the Strand panel and review the settings.

Notable fields include:

- Enable the Tangent Shading checkbox for a shiny hair effect.
- Enable the Blender Units checkbox. By default, Blender measures hair strands in pixels, which works well unless you have a hairy object moving toward or away from the camera. Enabling this checkbox makes the hair size relative to the scene's units (set in Scene Properties) rather than the final render's size.
- Adjust the sizes for the root and tip of the hair strands, considering the Blender Units option. Test renders may be necessary to achieve the desired look.

Other sliders in the Strand panel allow for further customization of the hair strands' shape and shading, which can be fine-tuned through additional test renders.

GIVING OBJECTS SOME JIGGLE AND BOUNCE

Soft body dynamics in Blender allow you to simulate the jiggling and bouncing of objects realistically.

To create a simple soft body simulation using the default cube object, follow these steps:

1. Select the cube and raise it above the 3D grid to give it a height (GZ).
2. Create a ground plane using a plane mesh and scale it up to provide a surface for the cube to collide with (S).
3. Add collision properties to the plane by enabling the collision panel in Physics Properties.
4. Select the cube and add a soft body panel in Physics Properties. This enables soft body physics on the object and adds a soft body modifier.
5. Disable the Soft Body Goal checkbox to ensure the entire cube is affected by the simulation.
6. Play back the animation to observe the cube falling, hitting the ground plane, and jiggling upon landing (Alt+A).

By following these steps, you can achieve realistic soft body dynamics in your animations.

DROPPING OBJECTS IN A SCENE WITH RIGID BODY DYNAMICS

The controls for rigid bodies in Blender are not found in the Physics Properties like in other physical simulations. Instead, you can access rigid body dynamics by utilizing Blender's integrated game engine. **Here's how to create a simple rigid body simulation using the default cube:**

1. Select the cube and raise it in the Z-axis by a few units (GZ). A height of 3 to 5 units is sufficient.
2. Create a mesh plane as the ground (Shift+A, Mesh, Plane) and scale it up to provide a surface for the cube to collide with (S).
3. In the "World Properties," ensure the physics engine is set to bullet and the gravity is set to 9.80. The bullet is the main physics suite within Blender's game engine.
4. Select the cube and open the Physics Properties in the Properties editor.
5. From the Physics Type drop-down menu, choose Rigid Body. This enables the cube to have simulated movement controlled by the rigid body dynamics simulator.
6. Enable the Collision Bounds check box to define boundaries for collision detection. The default box setting is suitable for a cube, but other options are available for more complex meshes.
7. Test the simulation by pressing P to start the game engine. Press Esc to exit the game engine and stop the simulation.
8. To see the simulation within Blender's animation playback (Alt+A), you need to bake the simulation data into Blender's animation system.
9. Enable the Record Animation option in the main header (Game, Record Animation).
10. Start the game engine (P) to run the simulation. Once completed, press Esc to return to the regular interface.
11. The simulation is now baked into f-curves, and you can observe the keyframes in the timeline or graph editor. When playing back the animation (Alt+A), the simulation results should be visible. Note that real-time playback may not be achieved.

To render your baked simulation to a movie file, switch back to Blender's internal renderer using the drop-down menu in the main header. By following these steps, you can create a basic rigid body simulation using Blender's game engine and integrate it into your animations.

SIMULATING CLOTH

Cloth simulation and soft body simulation in Blender are similar but have some key differences. Both can work with open and closed meshes, but soft bodies are better suited for closed meshes, while cloth is more suitable for open ones. The cloth simulator handles self-collisions more effectively, making it ideal for simulating fabric-like behavior.

To create a basic cloth simulation on a default cube, follow these steps:

1. Create a mesh grid and position it above the cube.
2. Scale the grid to be larger than the cube.
3. Apply the Set Smooth option to the vertices of the grid.
4. Add a Subdivision Surfaces modifier to the grid.
5. Enable the cloth simulator in the Physics Properties.
6. Enable self-collision in the Cloth Collision panel.
7. Assign collision properties to the cube in the Physics Properties.

8. Play the animation to see the cloth simulation in action.

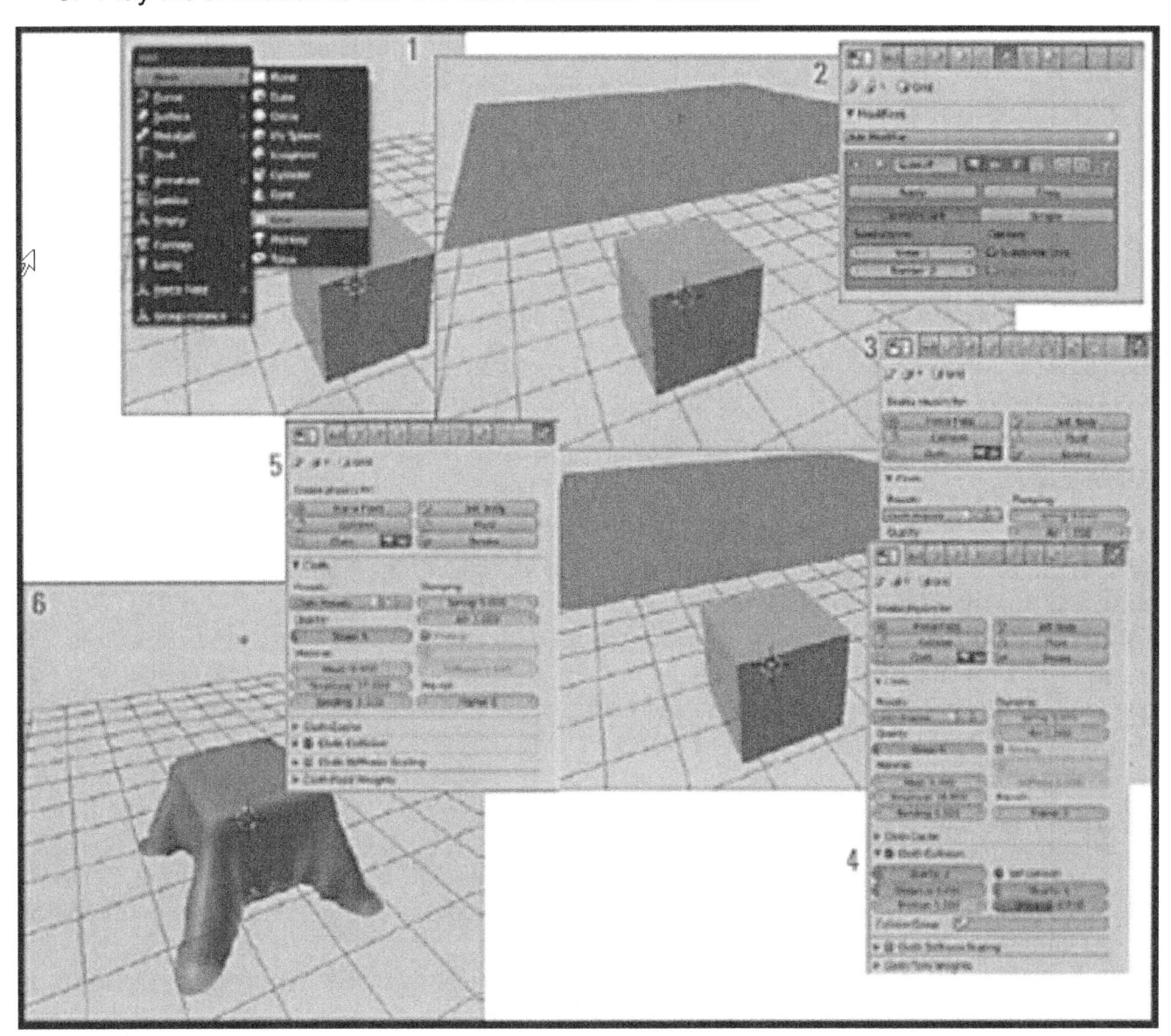

These steps provide a simple setup for a cloth simulation, allowing you to observe the behavior of the cloth draped over the cube.

SPLASHING FLUIDS INTO YOUR SCENE

Blender's integrated fluid simulator is a remarkable feature that adds a lot of value to your projects.

Here's a quick guide to getting started with fluid simulation:

1. Scale up a cube to act as the domain for the simulation.
2. Enable the fluid simulator in Physics Properties and choose Domain.
3. Set the location to save simulation meshes and adjust the resolution settings.
4. Determine the simulation time by setting the start and end values.
5. Create a mesh (such as an icosphere) to be the fluid source.
6. Enable the fluid simulator for the mesh and choose Inflow Type.
7. Optionally, give the inflow object an initial velocity.
8. Select the domain cube and bake the simulation.

9. Monitor the progress of the fluid simulation.
10. Play back the finished simulation and adjust the shading if needed.

By following these steps, you can achieve impressive water-pouring effects in your scenes. You can also add obstacles to control the movement of the fluid as desired.

SUMMARY

In summary, creating manageable hair and fur in Blender involves setting up a hair particle system, using particle mode for customization, and controlling the number of strands with child particles. For realistic hair rendering, you can adjust material settings and use Blend Textures. To add dynamic effects, soft body dynamics, rigid body simulations, and cloth simulations can be applied to create lifelike interactions with the hair or fur. By exploring these techniques and combining them creatively, you can achieve impressive and natural-looking hair and fur effects in your Blender projects.

REVIEW QUESTION

1. How do you create manageable hair and fur in Blender using the hair particle system? Explain the difference between the emitter and hair types and provide steps to set up and customize particle hair using particle mode.
2. What are the different physics simulation models available for particle systems in Blender? How can you use these models to control particle behavior, particularly when creating hair on a character?
3. How can you add force fields and collision properties to particles in Blender to control their movement and interactions with other objects? Explain how to create a simple simulation with wind force affecting particles colliding with a plane deflector.
4. Describe the process of using soft body dynamics in Blender to simulate the jiggling and bouncing of objects. How can you create a rigid body simulation using Blender's integrated game engine, and how can you integrate it into an animation?

CHAPTER 17: EXPORTING AND RENDERING SCENES

Working in Blender is enjoyable, but at some point, you'll likely want to showcase your creations to others. This could involve sharing a still image, a movie, or a 3D model for use in different applications. To achieve this, you have two main options: exporting and rendering. Exporting means saving your scene in a file format that can be opened by other programs. On the other hand, rendering involves creating a final image or movie from your scene within Blender itself.

The type of export or render you choose depends on your specific needs. For instance:

- To share a still image of your scene, you can export it as an image file like PNG or JPEG. To share a movie of your scene, you can render it as a video file like MP4 or AVI.
- To export the geometry and textures of a model for use in a video game, you would use a 3D model file format like OBJOR FBX.
- The exact steps for exporting or rendering will vary based on the specific type and format you need, as well as the version of Blender you're using. However, the underlying principles remain consistent.

EXPORTING TO EXTERNAL FORMATS

Exporting in Blender involves restating the structure of your 3D data so that other programs can understand it. There are two main reasons to export to a different 3D file format. The first is to continue editing in another program, especially if you're working on a project where Blender isn't used.

In such cases, you need to save your work in a format compatible with their tools.

The second reason is video games. Many games have specific formats for loading 3D data, and Blender can export to these formats, allowing you to create custom characters and sets. Blender's exporters are mostly Python scripts. While they generally support the basic specifications of their respective formats, some features may not be fully supported. For instance, exporting equipment or information can be challenging. So, it's important to keep this limitation in mind, as results may vary. To export in Blender, go to File > Export and select the desired format. A file browser will appear, allowing you to choose where to save the new file. The left side of the File Browser includes options specific to the chosen exporter. The illustration below displays the Export menu with a list of available file types.

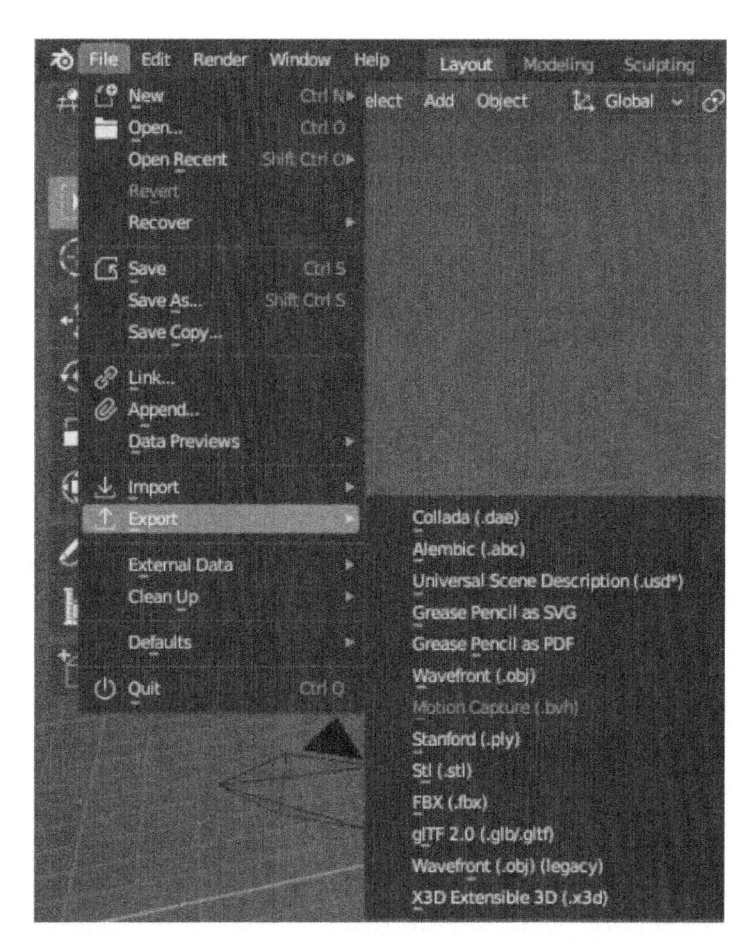

RENDERING A SCENE

Rendering is like capturing a photograph or a movie in the virtual world. It involves taking your 3D data and transforming it into 2D images from the perspective of a camera. These 2D images can be viewed by anyone using image viewers or movie players. Just as you need a camera to take a picture in the physical world, Blender requires a camera in your scene for rendering. Without a camera, Blender doesn't know what to render. So, make sure to include a camera in your scene to enable the rendering process.

CREATING A STILL IMAGE

Rendering still images in Blender is simple and offers three methods. The fastest way is to press **F12** or click the Image button in the Render panel. You can also choose **Render > Image > Render Image** from the top menu. Blender uses the UV/Image Editor to display the rendered output. If it's not open, Blender automatically switches to it while rendering. You can change the display behavior in the Render panel's Display drop-down menu. To save your rendered image, use the UV/Image Editor, press F3, or choose **Image > Save As**. Blender's OPUT panel in Render Properties allows you to choose the file format and control compression. You can save renders as PNG, Targa, TIFF, or Open EXR, and choose between black and white, full color, or color with transparency (alpha channel).

For animations, the process is similar. Set up resolution, filetype, and save location. Ensure the correct start and end frames. Press **Ctrl+F12** or use the Animation button in the Render panel. Rendering an animation can take time, so be patient and enjoy a cup of coffee while Blender works its magic.

CREATING A SEQUENCE OF STILL IMAGES FOR EDITING OR COMPOSTING

Rendering a sequence of still images instead of a single movie file has several advantages. Firstly, it is beneficial for compositing, where multiple images are combined. Still, image sequences allow for alpha channels, which provide transparency for the rendered subject. Since most video formats lack support for alpha channels, rendering still images in formats like PNG, which do support alpha, is necessary for effective composition. Secondly, still image sequences are advantageous for editing purposes. Video codecs often sacrifice image data between frames to reduce file size. This can make editing difficult, particularly when precise cuts are required. By using a sequence of still images, each frame retains all the necessary image data, enabling smooth and accurate editing.

Similarly, rendering still image sequences is practical in various scenarios. When rendering to a movie format, unexpected interruptions such as the need to make changes or system crashes can disrupt the process. Resizing the entire render from the beginning can be time-consuming, especially if each frame takes a significant amount of time to render. With still-image sequences, each frame is saved individually as it is rendered. If the rendering process is interrupted, it can be resumed from the point of interruption by adjusting the Start value in the Dimensions panel of Rendered Properties. To manage the numerous files generated by a still image sequence, it is advisable to create a dedicated folder specifically for the render files. This helps maintain organization, especially when dealing with a large number of individual image files resulting from a long animation sequence.

SUMMARY

In Blender, sharing your creations with others involves exporting or rendering your scenes. Exporting allows you to save your scene as a file that can be opened in other programs, making it useful for collaboration or integration into different workflows. Depending on your specific needs, you can export your scene as an image file (e.g., PNG or JPEG) for still images, a video file (e.g., MP4 or AVI) for animated scenes, or a 3D model file (e.g., OBJ or FBX) for use in video games. Exporting in Blender involves restructuring your 3D data to make it compatible with other programs or game engines. Blender supports various file formats through Python scripts, but some advanced features may not be fully supported. When exporting, you can choose the desired format from the Export menu, and a File Browser will allow you to select the location and save the new file.

Rendering, on the other hand, involves transforming your 3D data into 2D images or movies. Blen de R's rendering process simulates capturing a photograph or a movie from the perspective of a camera in the virtual world. For still images, you can quickly render by pressing Fl 2 or clicking the Render Image button in the Render panel. For animations, you set up the desired start and end frames, choose the file type and save the location, and then render the animation. Rendering a sequence of still images is also beneficial for composition and editing purposes, as it allows for alpha channels and ensures that each frame retains all necessary image data.

This can be particularly useful for smooth and accurate editing, as well as for resuming rendering from an interruption point if needed. It is advisable to create a dedicated folder for managing the numerous files generated by a still image sequence to maintain organization, especially for longer animation sequences.

REVIEW QUESTIONS

1. What are the main differences between exporting and rendering scenes in Blender?
2. How can you export a 3D model from Blender for use in a video game, and what formats are commonly used?
3. What are the advantages of rendering a sequence of still images instead of a single movie file for composition and editing purposes?
4. How do you save a rendered still image in Blender, and what file formats and options are available for saving the image?

CHAPTER 18: EDITING AND ENHANCING VIDEO ANIMATIONS

Welcome to the world of editing and compositing in 3D Blender! In the realm of live-action film and video, post-production often encompasses various aspects of animation. However, in animation, post-production focuses specifically on editing and composing. In this chapter, we'll explore Blender's Video Sequence Editor and Node Compositor, providing you with a concise guide to editing and composing. While these topics are vast and could fill an entire book, this chapter aims to provide you with solid information to get started. You'll learn about Blender's interface for these tools and delve into fundamental concepts like nonlinear editing and node systems.

COMPARING EDITING TO COMPOSTING

Editing involves arranging and adjusting the sequence of rendered footage, whether it's animation, film, or video. Traditionally, editing was done linearly, but with nonlinear editors (NLEs) like Final Cut Pro and Adobe Premiere, you can easily modify shots without disrupting the overall timing. Blender's Video Sequence Editor provides basic NLE functions for editing. Compositing, on the other hand, is the process of combining animations, videos, and still images into a single image or video. It's used for various effects, such as adding credits to the beginning of a movie or making animated characters interact with real-world environments. Blender offers an integrated composer that allows you to create these effects and enhance your scenes with features like blur, glow, and color correction.

WORKING WITH THE VIDEO SEQUENCER

The video editing screen layout in Blender allows you to work with the video sequence editor (VSE). The VSE is where you add and modify sequences called strips in a timeline format. The numbers at the bottom represent time in seconds, while the left side displays labels for tracks or channels. The upper left area is the Graph Editor for adjusting strip properties, and the Preview view shows the footage under the time cursor. The layout includes a timeline for easy scrubbing and playback controls. To optimize the video editing layout, you can make some adjustments. Swapping the Graph Editor with a File Browser displaying thumbnails enables convenient drag-and-drop import of footage directly to the Sequencer. The properties editor can be omitted during editing but added as a narrow strip for the initial setup. The Dimensions panel in Render Properties is essential for setting the project's frame rate (fps) and resolution, ensuring that imported footage matches these settings to avoid stretching or slow motion.

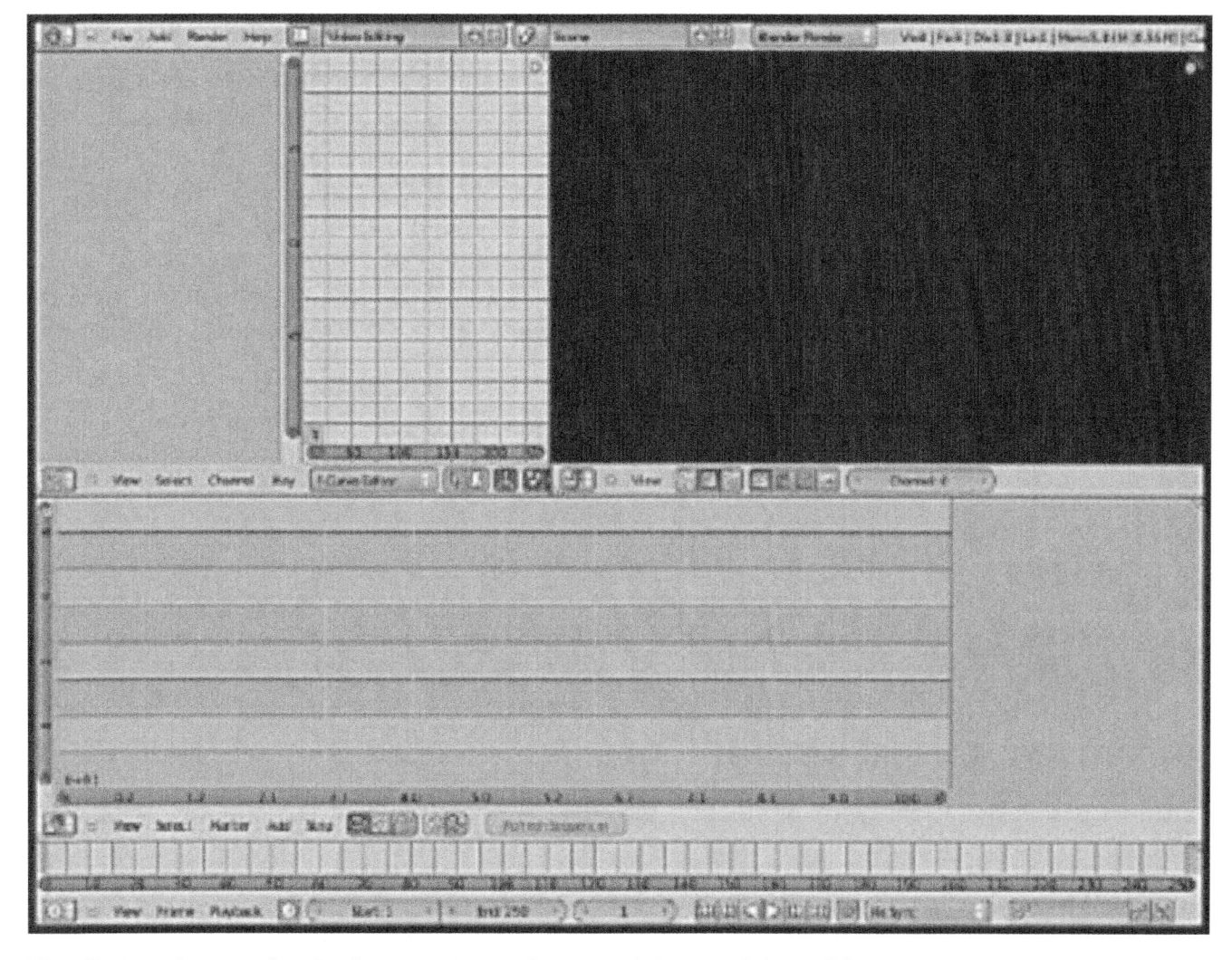

The Properties section in the sequencer is a crucial part of the editing process. Initially, this area appears blank on the right side of the sequencer due to the default layout lacking any loaded strips. However, when you select a strip in the Sequencer, this area is populated with relevant properties, providing you with essential controls for editing operations.

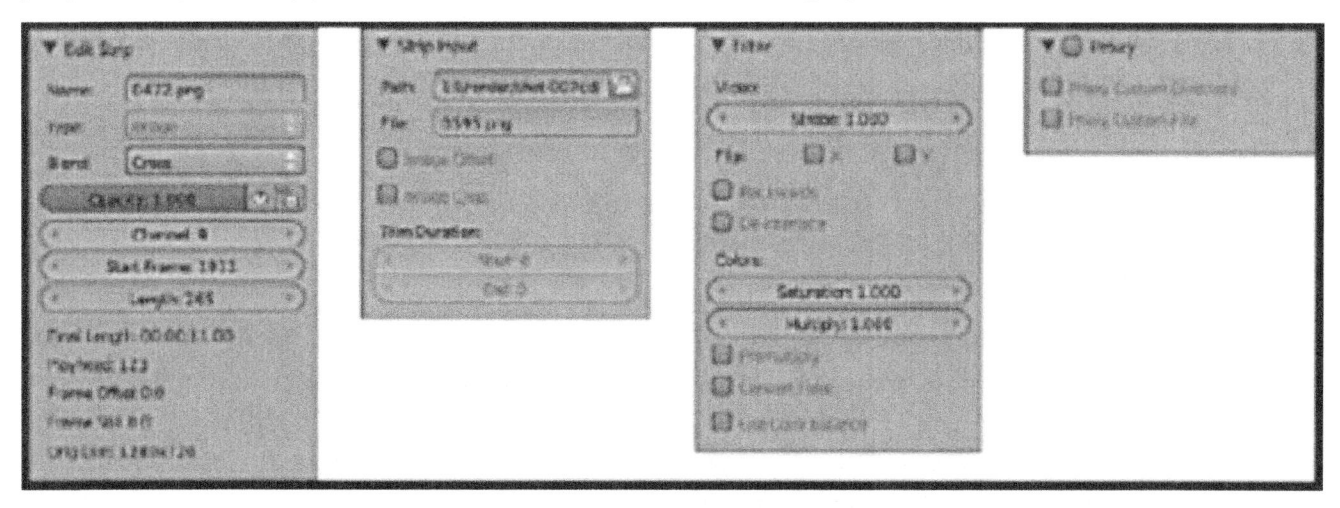

The Properties region in the VSE is where you'll find the most important options for your editing tasks. It consists of five panels: Edit Strip, Strip Input, Effect Strip, Filter, and Proxy. While the Edit Strip, Strip Input, and Filter panels are available for most strip types, the Effect Strip and Proxy panels are specific to certain types of strips.

Here's a brief overview of the commonly used panels:

1. **Edit Strip**: This panel allows you to control the placement and behavior of selected strips. You can name strips, adjust blending with lower channels, mute or lock strips, set the start frame, and change the channel.
2. **Strip Input**: In this panel, you can crop and reposition strips within the frame and control which portion of the strip appears in the sequencer. When working with audio strips, this panel is labeled Sound and offers different controls.
3. **Effect Strip**: This panel appears for effect strips that have editable attributes. It allows you to modify specific effects applied to your strips. Further details on effects can be found in the "Addi ng Effects" section of this chapter.

Additionally, the timeline at the bottom of the screen plays a significant role in controlling your sequence. The Sync drop-down menu in the timeline is particularly relevant for the VSE. It ensures that your audio remains synchronized with your video during editing. Select either AV-sync or Fram-dropping to maintain proper synchronization. We usually opt for Fram e-dropping for better performance. Avoid the frustration of audio and visual misalignment after rendering your edited work. Refer to the image above for the available options in the Sync drop-down menu. With the Properties region and the timeline settings, you can effectively manage your editing tasks in the VSE and maintain proper audio-visual synchronization.

ADDING AND EDITING STRIPS

You can import five main types of strips in the VSE: scenes, movies, still images, audio, and effects.

Each type has specific options in the menu:

1. **Scene**: Selecting this option allows you to choose a scene from your ".blend" file without rendering it separately. It's useful for combining scenes and overlaying graphics on videos.
2. **Movie**: This option lets you select a video file, including both audio and video, using the File Browser.
3. **Image**: By selecting this option, you can choose one or multiple images in various formats. Multiple images are treated as a single sentence in a single strip.
4. **Sound**: Use this option to load an audio file, preferably in WAV format, for high-quality sound.
5. **Effect Strip**: This option provides various effects and transitions for your strips. More details on this can be found in the next section.

When you import a strip, it appears under your mouse cursor in the VSE. Refer to Table 15-1 for helpful mouse actions to enhance your workflow in the VSE. Editing in the sequencer is straightforward. Strips in the higher channels take priority over those below. You can change this behavior in the Edit Strip panel's Blend mode. The Graph Editor is useful for animating values like opacity and volume. **By combining blending modes and the Graph Editor, you can create cool effects like a flickering logo:**

1. Add a logo image to the sequencer.
2. Select the logo strip and set its blend mode to Alpha Over.
3. Insert a keyframe for opacity.
4. Use the Graph Editor to create a random opacity curve.

5. Enjoy your flickering logo effect.
6. Adding effects and transitions

When working in the VSE, Shift+A provides various effect options. Here's a quick rundown:

- **Add/Subtract/Multiply**: Use blends modes instead.
- **Alpha Over/Under/Over Drop**: Use blends modes unless you need specific control.
- **Cross/Gamma Cross**: Crossfade or dissolve between strips.
- **Plugin**: Load VSE plugins (they may have limitations).
- Wipe transition effect with customizable wipe types. Glow: Make bright points in an image glow.
- Transform Basic controls for location, scale, and rotation.
- **Color**: Create color strips, for fades, or background colors.
- **Speed Control**: Adjust the playback speed of individual strips.
- **Multicam Selector**: Switch cameras in a scene with animation.

Keep in mind that the order of selection affects the applied effect.

RENDERING FROM THE VIDEO SEQUENCER

To render your edited sequence from the VSE, follow these steps:

1. Open the render properties.
2. Check the "Sequencer" option in the Post-Processing panel.
3. Enabling this option ensures that the final output includes the strips from the sequencer, not just the 3D camera view.

COMPOSITING IMAGES AND VIDEOS

In the realm of live-action film and video, post-production typically encompasses all aspects related to animation. However, in animation, post-production is more focused on editing and composing. This chapter serves as a brief guide to editing and composing using Blender's Video Sequence Editor and Node Composer. While these topics are extensive and could fill an entire book, this chapter provides sufficient information along with Blender's online documentation (wiki.blender.org) to help you navigate through them. We will explain the interface for these tools, introduce key concepts such as nonlinear editing and node systems, and demonstrate how they can enhance your work, transforming it from "cool" to "mind-blowing."

WORKING WITH NODES

Once you've configured your render layers, it's time to work in the Node Compositor. Blender provides a default screen layout called Compositing, accessible through the Screens data block or by pressing Ctrl+ +- from the Default layout. The Node Editor is the primary tool for compositing, while the other node editors are for more advanced tasks related to materials and textures. To activate the Node Editor, click on the Use Nodes checkbox in the header. This transforms the initially bare Node Editor into a layout resembling the figure below.

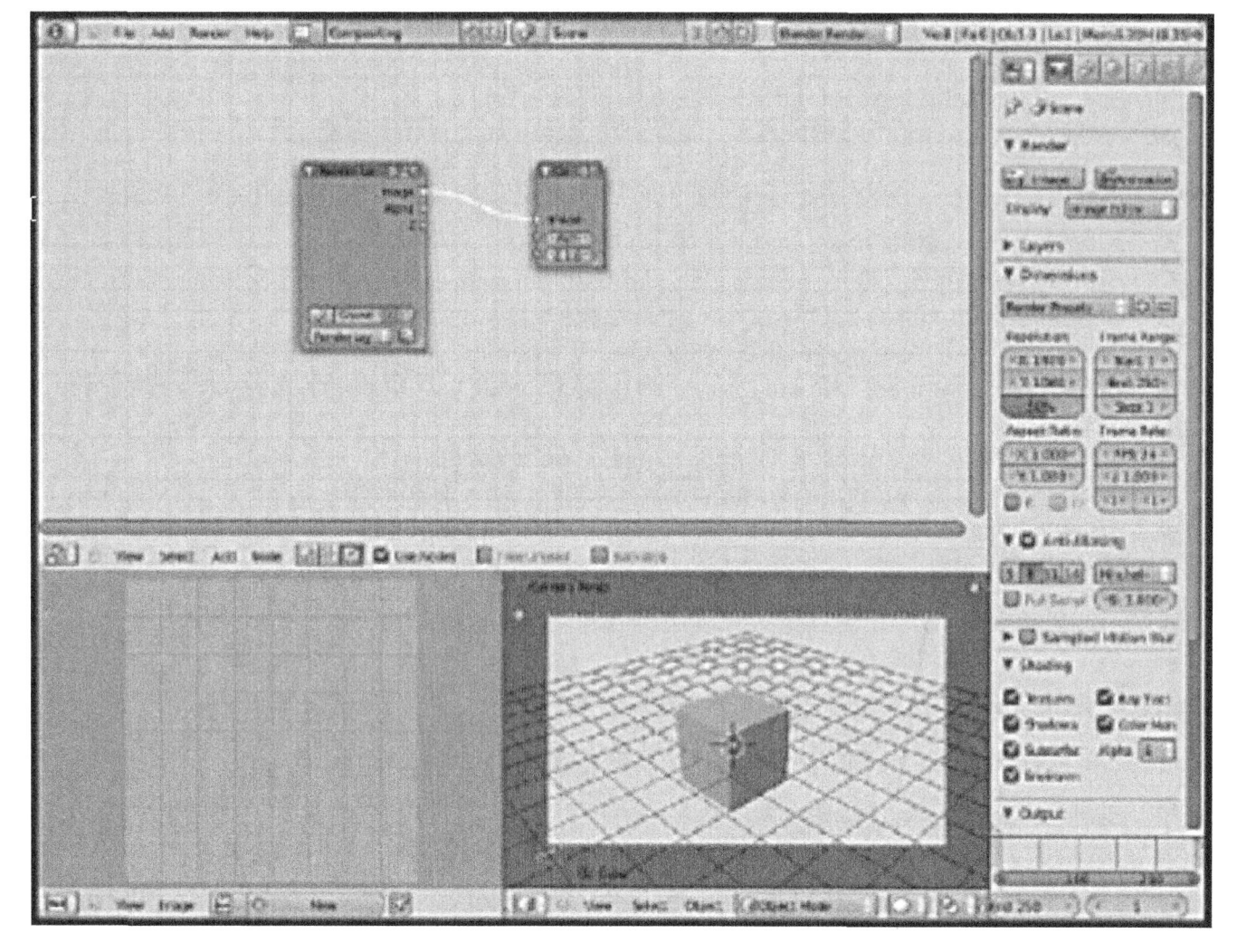

In the Composite Node Editor, you'll find two nodes: an input node and an output node. The Render Layers node, located on the left, serves as an input and has connection points on the right side. It contributes data to the node network. On the right, the composite node is an output node with no connection points on its right edge. It represents the result and acts as the final output when dealing with the node composer in Blender.

CONFIGURING THE BACKDROP

To have a live view of your node network's progress while working in Blender's Node Editor, you can use the Viewer node as an output.

Follow the following steps:

1. In the Node Editor, position the cursor and press Shift+A to add a new node.
2. From the options, select Output>Viewer to create a Viewer node.
3. If the Render Layer input node was already selected, a connection is automatically created between the two nodes. Otherwise, manually connect the render layer's image socket to the viewer's corresponding socket by dragging and dropping.
4. Enable the Backdrop checkbox in the Node Edito's header to display a black box as the composer's background.
5. In the Render Properties' Post Processing panel, ensure that the Compositing checkbox is enabled.
6. Render the scene by clicking the Image button or pressing F2.

7. After the render is complete, return to the Blender interface (press Fl 1), and the black box in the composer will display the rendered results. Anything connected to the Viewer node will be shown in the composer's background.

This setup allows you to work efficiently in the composer, with the live results visible. You can move the Node Editor to the full window size by pressing Shift +spacebar for a better workspace. To adjust the backdrop's visibility, uncheck the Backdrop checkbox or move it around by Alt+middle-clicking and dragging. You can also manipulate the entire node network by middle-clicking, dragging, or zooming in or out using the scroll wheel. Identifying the parts of a node

NAVIGATING THE COMPOSER

Each node in the composer has icons at the top with specific functions (refer to the image below):

1. **Triangle**: expands or collapses the node, hiding its contents.
2. **Plus (+)**: Hides or shows sockets without connections, simplifying the display.
3. **"Equal(Slider)**: toggles the visibility of editable values in the node.
4. **Sphere:** Expands or collapses the view window, available on nodes with an image window.

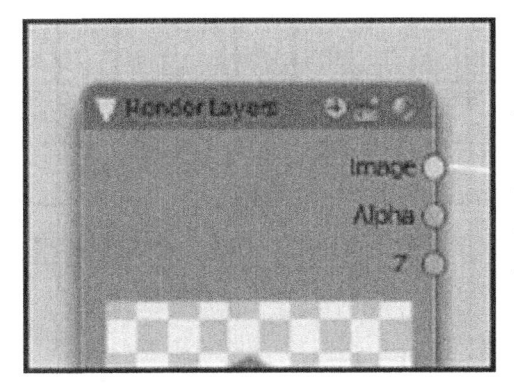

Editing nodes in Blender follow similar user interface behavior as the rest of the program. Nodes can be selected with a right-click, moved using the G key, and multiple nodes can be selected by using the B key for border selection. In the Node Editor, specific hotkeys are commonly used (refer to the table below). When connecting nodes, it is important to consider the colors of the sockets.

Each socket has a distinct color, indicating the type of information it sends or expects:

Hotkey	Menu Access	Description
Shift+A	Add	Open toolbox menu.
G	Node⇨Translate	Grab a node and move it.
B	Select⇨Border Select	Border select.
X	Node⇨Delete	Delete node(s).
Shift+D	Node⇨Duplicate	Duplicate node(s).
Ctrl+G	Node⇨Make Group	Creates a group out of the selected nodes.
Alt+G	Node⇨Ungroup	Ungroups the selected group.
Tab	Node⇨Edit Group	Expands the node group so you can edit individual nodes within it.
H	Node⇨Hide/Unhide	Toggles the selected nodes between expanded and collapsed views.
V	View⇨Backdrop Zoom Out	Zooms out (scales down) the backdrop image.
Alt+V	View⇨Backdrop Zoom In	Zooms in (scales up) the backdrop image.

- **Yellow**: This represents color information for the output image (RGBA scale).
- **Gray**: represents numeric values, often used for masks or transparency (grayscale).
- **Blue**: refers to geometry data such as speed, UV coordinates, and "normals".

Understanding these color-coded sockets helps in effectively connecting nodes and visualizing the data flow within the node network.

GROUPING NODES TOGETHER

Node grouping is a powerful feature in the Node Editor. By border-selecting a section of nodes and pressing Ctrl+G, you can quickly create a group. Grouping nodes offers several benefits. It simplifies the appearance of the node network and provides organizational clarity by assigning specific names to groups. For example, you can have groups for a blurry background or color-corrected characters. Additionally, when you create a group, it automatically appears in the Group menu (Shift +A -> Group). This allows you to easily add the group to other parts of your scene or even different ".blend" files. The ability to apply a pre-defined group's effects to various elements of your work adds versatility and efficiency to your workflow.

DISCOVERING THE NODES AVAILABLE TO YOU

Blender offers a wide range of nodes that can be added to your composer network. Each node has a Fae (factor) value that determines its influence on the image. Values less than 1 reduce the node's impact, while values greater than 1 amplify it.

Input nodes are crucial to the node composer. Here are the key input nodes:

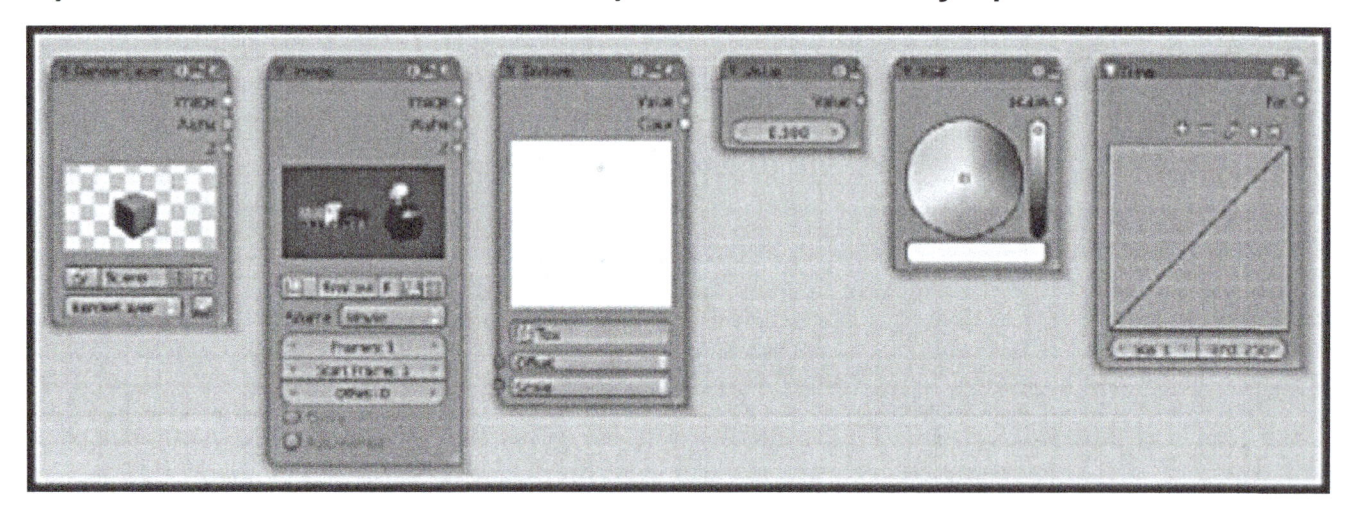

1. **Render Layer**: Sends input from a scene to the composer. You can select render layers from the drop-down menu and use the camera button to render specific layers without re-rendering the entire network.
2. **Image**: This node loads various image data, including still images, image sequences, and movies. You have control over sequence start, duration, and looping.
3. **Texture**: This allows you to incorporate textures created in Blender into the node network. It works well with UV data and enables texture changes without re-rendering.
4. **Value**: Provides scalar (numerical) values as input for other nodes.
5. **RGB**: Feeds solid colors to other nodes, useful for hue adjustments or creating colored backgrounds.

6. **Time**: While less essential with Blender's improved animation capabilities, the Time node remains powerful. It was historically used to animate node attributes independently before integration with the Graph Editor. These input nodes play a vital role in constructing your composer network within Blen de R. Output nodes in Blender are essential for saving and finalizing your render.

Here are the two main output nodes:

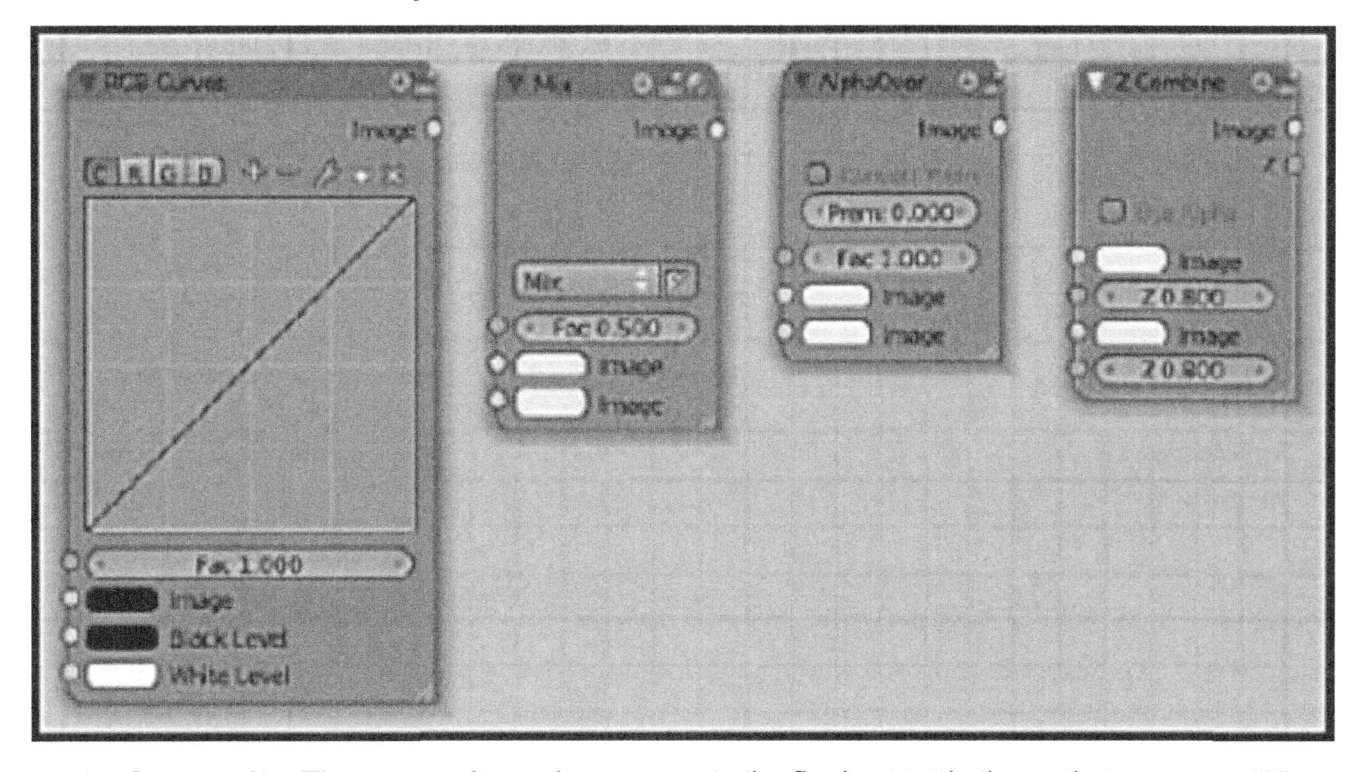

1. **Composite**: The composite node represents the final output in the node composer. When you set up output files for animation or save a render, Blen der uses the information from this node.
2. **Viewer**: The Viewer node serves as a tool for spot-checking specific sections of your node network. It allows you to ensure everything are progressing as desired. The output from Viewer nodes is displayed in the composer's backdrop when enabled. Color nodes significantly impact the appearance and balance of colors in the final output. They directly manipulate how colors are displayed and mixed.

Here are some commonly used color nodes:

- **RGB Curves**: This powerful node uses curves to adjust the combined color or individual red, green, and blue channels of an image. It offers precise control over color adjustments.
- **Mix**: With 16 blending modes, the Mix node combines two input images. It allows you to control the blending effect and is familiar to users of image editing software like GIMP or Photoshop.
- **AlphaOver**: Similar to the Mix node, AlphaOver blends images using their alpha channels. It handles foreground and backgroundimages, and the Convert Premul option helps fix artifacts.
- **Z Combine**: The Z Combine node mixes two sets of image data based on Z-dependent information instead of color or alpha channels. It enables the integration of in-depth information into the composer.

These color nodes play a crucial role in determining the visual outcome of your composition. Vector nodes utilize 3D data to impact the appearance of the final 2D image. They offer advanced capabilities, such as modifying lighting or object movement, without re-rendering. When used in conjunction with render passes and formats like OpenEXR, vector nodes can significantly streamline the workflow.

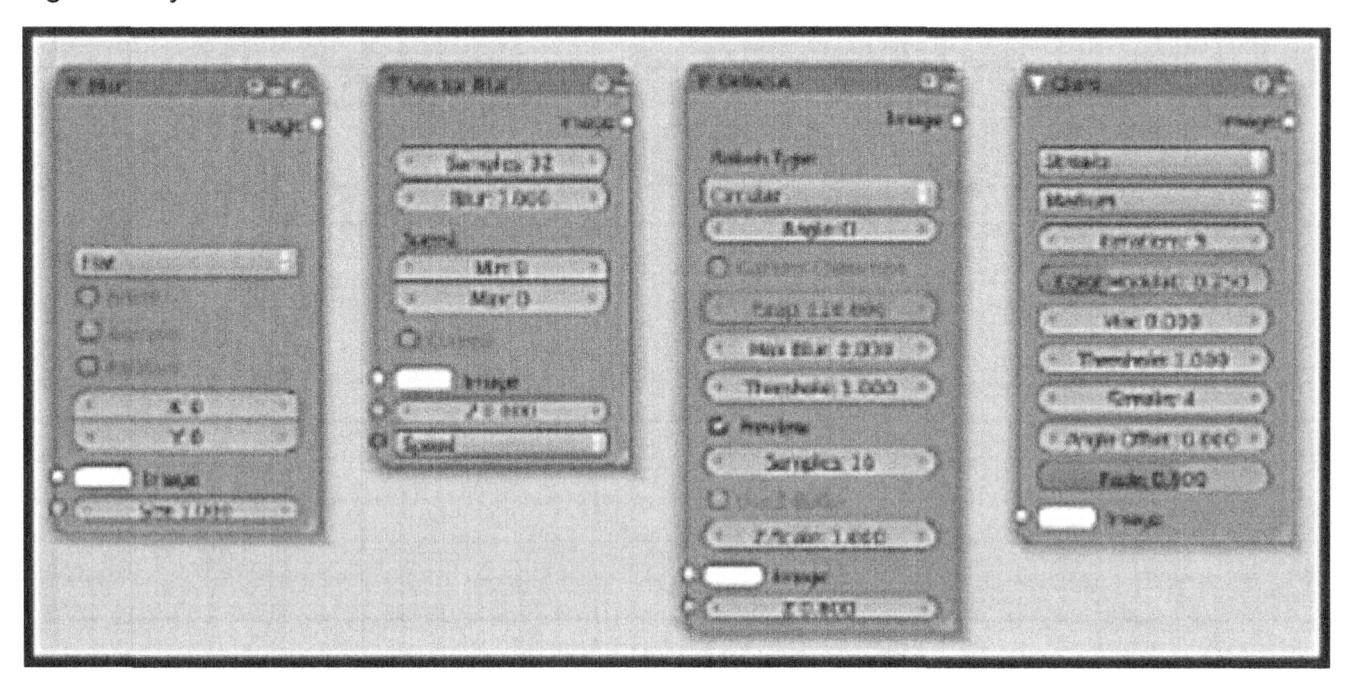

Filter nodes are powerful tools for altering the image's look. They can simulate various effects and transformations.

Here are some commonly used filter nodes:

- **Blur**: applies a uniform blur to the input image. You can choose different blur types and adjust the blur size using the X and Y buttons.
- **Vector Blur**: Generates motion blur based on the speed information from the vector pass. The curved option enhances the natural appearance of motion blur, especially for objects moving in arcs. This node works specifically with 3D data from Blender.
- **Defocus**: Simulates the depth of field effects found in real-world cameras. By adjusting the DOF Dist value, you can set the focal point and create a shallow depth of field effect.
- **Glare**: Add extra impact to the bright areas of the render. Options like fog glow and streaks provide quick enhancements. The threshold value greatly influences the effect's strength, typically set between 0.0 and 1.0. These filter nodes allow for creative image manipulation and can produce impressive visual transformations. Converter nodes serve various utility functions, such as converting data types and manipulating rendered images. Two commonly used nodes are the Color Ramp and ID Mask.
- **Color Ramp**: Visualizes numerical values on a scale, like Z-depth, by mapping them to a color ramp. This allows for better visualization of certain data.
- **ID Mask**: Provides more precise object isolation than layers and renders layers. It allows for targeting specific objects based on their Pass Index value, making them easily distinguishable for further processing.

Matte nodes are designed for using color information to isolate specific parts of an image. Matting, or keying, is commonly used in bluescreen or greenscreen effects where a colored background is replaced with other footage or 3D elements. Distort nodes perform general image manipulation operations such as translation, rotation, scaling, flipping, or cropping.

Noteworthy nodes within this category include:

- **Displace**: Gene rates image distortions like heat waves or refraction effects. Grayscale, color, "normals", or vectors can be used as inputs to achieve different types of distortions.
- **Map UV**: Enables the changing of textures on objects post-render. By utilizing the UV pass and feeding it into this node along with the desired texture, the new texture can be mixed with the image. The ID Mask node can be used for precise texture changes on specific objects.
- **Lens Distortion**: Replicates the effects of different lenses, ranging from wide fisheye to misaligned colors seen in poorly calibrated projectors. It adds unique visual characteristics to the image.

These converter, matte, and distort nodes expand the capabilities of the compositor, allowing for data conversion, precise object isolation, and various image manipulation techniques.

RENDERING FROM THE COMPOSER

To render from the Node Compositor, ensure that the Composing checkbox is enabled in the Post Processing panel of Render Properties. When working on a larger production and wanting to save render passes for further editing without rendering the entire scene, the recommended file format is OpenEXR.

Todo this:

1. Set up your render layers.
2. Go to the output panel.
3. Instead of simply choosing OpenEXR, select MultiLayer. This format saves an OpenEXR file (.exr) containing all the layer and pass information.

By choosing MultiLayer, you can preserve the individual layers and passes within the OpenEXR file, allowing for flexibility and more extensive post-processing capabilities.

REVIEW QUESTIONS

1. What is the main difference between editing and compositing in Blender?
2. How can you optimize the video editing layout in Blender's video sequence editing?
3. What are some commonly used color nodes in the Node Compositor, and what functions do they serve?
4. How can you render from the Node Compositor in Blender, and what file format is recommended for preserving render passes and layer information?

SUMMARY

In summary, the Node Editor in Blender provides a versatile environment for compositing and working with various types of nodes to achieve sophisticated visual effects. Users can connect nodes to create complex node networks that manipulate scene data, textures, and materials. Adding Viewer nodes allows for real-time feedback, and node grouping aids in organizing and reusing specific effects. Blender offers a wide range of nodes, from input and output nodes to color, vector, filter, converter, matte, and distort nodes, each contributing to different aspects of the compositing process. Rendering from the composer can be optimized using the OpenEXR format, particularly the Multi-Laye option, which preserves essential information for advanced post-processing work. By leveraging the capabilities of the Node Editor and exploring the vast array of available nodes, artists can achieve stunning visual results in their Blender projects.

THE PART OF TENS

Ten tips for working more effectively on a blender

These tips we are about to give you are going to make your experience working with a blender more fun. With these habits, you can now work more efficiently and faster.

Use tooltips and integrated search.

Blender is a complex program, but it provides helpful tooltips when you hover over buttons to explain their functions. If the tooltip is not clear, it at least gives you a better idea of what to search for to find help. Additionally, Blender now has a fully integrated search feature that allows you to quickly find specific tools or features within the editor you're working in by using the search hotkey (spacebar).

TAKE ADVANTAGE OF THE QUICK FAVORITES MENU.

Look at models from different perspectives.

When working on 30 modeling and animation projects, it's crucial to regularly orbit around your scene and view it from different angles to ensure accuracy. This is especially important for modeling, as a model may appear perfect from the front but be distorted or misshaped from other perspectives. To facilitate this, you can either split off an additional 30 views or use numeric keypad hotkeys for quick spot-checks from various angles. If you're familiar with 30Studio Max or CAD applications, you may find the Quad View in the 30 window helpful, accessible through the "View" menu by toggling "Quad View" or using the **Ctrl+Alt+Q** hotkey.

Don't forget about addons.

During Blender's 2.5 development, add-ons were introduced to enhance its functionality. Add-ons are trusted Python scripts that expand Blender's capabilities, ranging from small menu additions to large landscape generators. While these scripts come with Blender, many are initially disabled.

To explore available add-ons, navigate to the Add-Ons section in the User Preferences editor (File -> User Preferences or Ctrl+Alt+U). If you come across an add-on that you frequently use, such as the Dynamic Spacebar Menu or a specific importer or exporter, enable the add-on and set it to load by default. Simply click the "Save as Default" button located at the bottom of the User Preferences editor.

Lock a camera on an animated character

When animating a character, creating a new camera and parenting it to the character is useful for animating secondary details while the character is in motion. This technique works well for facial animation on a moving character. **To lock a camera to your animated character, follow these steps:**

1. Add a new camera in front of the character's face (Shift+A -> Camera).
2. Select the camera and add the character's head bone to the selection (Shift+right-click).
3. Parent the camera to the bone by pressing Ctrl+P -> Bone.
4. Now, regardless of the head's movements and rotations, the camera will always focus on the character's face.

To work on the facial animation, simply select the camera (right-click) and switch to its view by pressing Ctrl+Numpad 0.

Name everything

When working in Blender, it's important to give meaningful names to the elements you add to your scene. Opening a ".blend" file after a while and seeing objects labeled as Cube.001, Cube.O1 2, and Sphere.007 or finding a fantastic skin material named Material.O15 can be disorienting.

While ambiguous names might be manageable for small projects, giving materials descriptive names makes them easier to locate later on. In larger projects, proper organization becomes even more crucial. It is wise to not only name everything in your ".blend" file but also establish a well-structured project directory. Typically, we create a separate directory for each project.

Within this directory, we organize subdirectories for models, materials, textures, and finished renders. In the case of animations, the renders directory is further divided into individual shots for better organization.

DO LOW-RESOLUTION TEST RENDERS.

To speed up the process of finalizing a model's look and avoid excessive waiting time, consider the following tips for quicker test renders in Blender:

1. **Disable anti-aliasing**: In the Render Properties, uncheck the anti-aliasing option. This eliminates the time-consuming process of smoothing jagged edges for quick test renders.
2. **Render at reduced size**: Adjust the slider under the X and Y resolution values in the Render Properties to specify a percentage of the final size. This reduces the render time while still providing a sufficient preview.
3. **Disable computationally intensive features**: Turn off features like ambient occlusion (AO), ray tracing, and environmental lighting if they are unnecessary for test renders. Adjust the settings in the Shading section of the Render Properties or the World Properties to disable these options.
4. **Render-specific layers**: If you only need to test a particular model in the scene, disable the layers for other objects. This ensures a speedy and accurate test render by focusing on the required elements.
5. **Use the Border Render feature**: Switch to camera view (Numpad 0) and press Shift+B to draw a box around the specific area you want to preview. This confines the render to the defined region. Remove the border by unchecking the Border option in the Dimensions section of the Render Properties or by drawing a box outside the camera's view area using Shift+B.
6. **Utilize OpenGL previews for animations**: Click the film clapper icon in the 3D View header to render the animation using the OpenGL engine. This provides a quick play blast to observe the action and timing. For a clearer play blast, enable the "Only Render" option

in the Display section of the 3D View's Properties region (View Properties or press N). This hides non-rendered objects, such as rigs, lights, and the grid plane.

By implementing these techniques, you can optimize your workflow by reducing render times during the testing phase in Blender.

HAVE FUN, BUT TAKE BREAKS

Don't hesitate to explore and experiment with Blen der. If you ever wonder about a button's function, simply press it and see what happens. Saving your work before important experiments is wise, but make it a habit to play and try new things. Through this process, you not only learn how to use different parts of Blender but also discover unique and unintended ways to utilize existing features.

Working in 3D is incredibly enjoyable, but it can become addictive. However, excessive computer time can negatively impact your work's quality. Remember to take breaks, rest your eyes, eat, stretch, and even engage in conversations with other people to maintain a healthy balance.

REVIEW QUESTIONS

1. How can you quickly find specific tools or features within Blender's editor using integrated search and tooltips?
2. What are the benefits of regularly viewing 3D models from different angles when working on 3D modeling and animation in Blender?
3. How can you make the most of add-ons in Blender, and how do you enable an add-on to load by default?
4. What steps should you follow to lock a camera to an animated character's face for facial animation in Blender?
5. What are some tips to optimize test renders in Blender to speed up the process and get quicker previews of your models?
6. Why is it important to name everything in your Blender projects and establish a well-structured project directory, especially for larger projects?
7. How can you maintain a healthy balance while working with Blender, and what are the benefits of taking breaks during extended computer sessions?

SUMMARY

This set of tips aims to enhance your experience while working with Blender, making it more enjoyable and productive. To start, utilize tooltips and the integrated search feature to quickly find tools and understand their functions. Additionally, take advantage of the quick favorites menu and employ different views when working on 3D modeling and animation for accuracy. Don't forget to explore and enable add-ons to expand Blender's capabilities. When animating a character, lock a camera to their face for easy facial animation. Always name everything in your scene and organize project directories to avoid confusion. For quicker test renders, apply low resolutions, disable unnecessary features, and use the Border Render feature. Finally, remember to have fun, experiment, and take breaks to maintain a healthy balance and optimize your workflow in Blender.

TEN EXCELLENT COMMUNITY RESOURCES

The Blender community is the true powerhouse of Blender. It is a robust, passionate, and diverse group of individuals engaged in various fields, including animated film production, video game development, scientific visualization, and architectural design.

This community's strength is evident through its organized and motivated nature. Explore the following community resources to witness the breadth and enthusiasm of Blender users:.

Blender.org

Blender.org is the go-to destination for all things Blender. It provides the latest stable version of Blender for download, keeping you up-to-date with new features and developments from the Blender Foundation and Blender Institute. The official Blender User Manual is available online in wiki format, ensuring continuous updates to reflect changes in Blender. Additionally, Blender.org offers a directory of certified Blender trainers for those seeking professional guidance. Explore the Gallery section to appreciate outstanding artwork created by talented artists within the Blender community.

Blender ID

To witness the vibrancy of the Blender community, a single visit to www.blenderartists.org is all you need. This website serves as the primary hub for English-speaking Blender artists. BlenderArtists.org, often referred to as BA.org, hosts forums where artists of all skill levels showcase their work, exchange knowledge on new features, provide helpful tips, participate in contests, and engage in casual conversations.

Notably, the BA.org forums feature an exciting event called the Weekend Challenge. Every Thursday night (GMT), a theme is announced, and participants have until Monday evening to create and render a scene that fits the theme. The community then votes for a winner, who selects the next challenge theme. The Weekend Challenge is not only an enjoyable experience but also an opportunity to test your skills and gauge your abilities. In summary, visiting BA.org offers a glimpse into the dynamic and interactive world of Blender artists, where creativity thrives, knowledge is shared, and engaging activities like the Weekend Challenge await.

Blender Nation

For the latest Blender developments and noteworthy happenings within the Blender community, BlenderNation (www.blender-nation.com) is the go-to news site. It covers events, and book reviews, and offers tutorials. BlenderNation is an excellent resource to discover professional work accomplished with Blender, particularly for busy working professionals who may not actively participate in forums like BA.org. Additionally, BlenderNation provides updates on topics of interest to Blender users, such as new open-source software and events in the broader computer graphics industry.

Blender basics.com

This provides various resources to support your learning journey. On the website, you can access all the sample files. Additionally, they regularly upload video tutorials, supplemental files, and errata updates to enhance your learning experience. The website uses a blog format organized by book chapters, allowing you to easily find information relevant to specific chapters or stay updated with the latest news and information they share.

CGCookies.com

BlenderCookie is a leading resource for Blender education, offering a wide range of high-quality materials. It was among the first websites to provide video tutorials and documentation for Blende's updated interface. Today, BlenderCookie remains dedicated to delivering exceptional examples and tutorials to help individuals enhance their computer graphics (CG) skills using Blender. While most of the content is freely accessible, some tutorials offer the option to purchase supplementary and source files for a nominal fee.

Blend swap

Blendswap is an online repository of diverse 3D models created in Blender. The community contributes to these models, which are conveniently organized by category. Each model is accompanied by a license that explicitly outlines the permissions granted for its usage. Blendswap played a crucial role in the weekend modeling sprints for the recent Blender Institute open movie project, Sintel.

REVIEW QUESTIONS

1. What are the main resources available on Blender.erg, and how do they contribute to the Blender community?
2. How does Blender Artists.org (BA.erg) foster interaction and collaboration among Blender artists, and what is the Weekend Chal-lenge event?
3. What kind of content and updates can be found on BlenderNation, and how does it benefit Blender users and professionals?
4. How does CGCookies.co contribute to Blender education, and what kind of materials and tutorials does it offer to enhance communication skills using Blender?

CONCLUSION

Crafting a conclusion that encapsulates the essence of "Blender 3D Simple & Clear 2024 Guide for New Designers" is akin to capturing the fleeting moment of satisfaction and anticipation that comes at the completion of any great journey. This book has been an odyssey through the realms of Blender, a software that stands as a beacon of creativity and possibility in the digital world. As we bring our exploration to a close, it's essential to reflect on the ground we've covered, the skills we've developed, and the vistas that lie ahead in the ever-evolving landscape of 3D modeling and animation.

Starting with the basics, we embarked on a journey to demystify the complexities of Blender 3D, navigating its interface, understanding its tools, and gradually building our confidence to create within this digital universe. The chapters were carefully designed to ensure a foundational understanding before venturing into more advanced techniques, recognizing that mastery comes from a deep and intuitive knowledge of the basics. As you progressed, each page turned was a step further into the depth and breadth of what Blender offers, from simple models to intricate animations that breathe life into your creations.

Throughout this guide, the emphasis has been on learning by doing—a philosophy that mirrors the ethos of the Blender community. You were encouraged to experiment, to play, and to make mistakes, for it is through these experiences that true learning emerges. The exercises and examples provided were not just tasks to be completed but opportunities to apply your creativity, to see firsthand the impact of light on a scene, the texture on a model, or the fluidity of an animation. This hands-on approach is designed to embed the skills deeply, ensuring they become part of your creative arsenal.

As you ventured into the realms of texturing, lighting, and animation, you were introduced to the principles that underlie these processes.

Understanding these principles is crucial, for they are the foundation upon which Blender operates. They guide how light interacts with surfaces, how materials mimic the real world, and how movement can convey emotion and story. These chapters aimed to not just teach you how to use Blender's tools but to provide a lens through which to view the world, enhancing your observational skills and deepening your appreciation for the intricacies of digital art.

The journey through Blender is also a journey of personal growth and discovery. The challenges encountered along the way are milestones, each one an opportunity to learn more about the software and about yourself as a creator. This book has sought to be a companion in that journey, offering guidance, encouragement, and inspiration. The ultimate goal has been to equip you with the knowledge and skills to bring your visions to life, to transform the intangible into the tangible, and to contribute your voice to the chorus of creators who share their work with the world.

Looking ahead, the path forward is as exciting as it is uncharted. Blender continues to evolve, driven by a community passionate about open-source development and the democratization of digital art tools. The skills you've acquired through this book are just the beginning, a foundation upon which you can build as new features and technologies emerge. The future of Blender and 3D modeling is one of limitless potential, with advances in virtual reality, augmented reality, and artificial intelligence opening new avenues for creativity and expression.

As you move forward, remember that the journey of learning is never truly complete. The landscape of digital art is dynamic, with new techniques, tools, and possibilities emerging continually. Stay curious, stay engaged, and keep exploring. The Blender community is a rich resource of knowledge, inspiration, and support—a community that you are now a part of. Share your work, learn from others, and contribute to the collective growth of this vibrant ecosystem.

"Blender 3D Simple & Clear 2024 Guide for New Designers" has been more than just a guide to a piece of software; it has been an invitation to embark on a journey of creativity and discovery. Blender is not just a tool but a gateway to expressing your imagination, telling your stories, and realizing your visions in the digital realm. The skills you have developed, the knowledge you have acquired, and the creativity you have unleashed are just the beginning. The canvas of the digital world is vast, and your potential to create within it is boundless.

As we part ways on this written journey, the real adventure is just beginning. Armed with Blender, your creativity, and the skills honed through this guide, you are poised to explore new horizons, to create worlds that captivate, inspire, and transform. Remember, the art of 3D modeling and animation is not just about what you create but how you see the world and how you choose to express it. You are an artist, a creator, a storyteller. Embrace that power, and let it guide you to places only you can imagine.

As we reflect further on the essence of "Blender 3D Simple & Clear 2024 Guide for New Designers," it's imperative to understand that the journey with Blender is emblematic of a larger process of learning and growth. The chapters within this guide have not just been about navigating a software; they have been about nurturing a mindset that embraces curiosity, resilience, and creativity. The meticulous progression from simple models to complex animations mirrors the journey of any creative endeavor, where foundational knowledge and skills are the springboards to innovative and sophisticated creations.

One of the key takeaways from this guide is the understanding that mastery of a tool like Blender is not an end goal but a continuous process. The landscape of digital art and technology is perpetually shifting, with new techniques, tools, and approaches emerging. This book has aimed to provide you with a solid foundation, but it is the application of what you've learned in new and unexpected ways that will truly define your journey. The power of

Blender lies not just in its features but in how you leverage them to push the boundaries of your creativity.

The guide has also emphasized the importance of community in the process of learning and growing as a digital artist. The Blender community is a testament to the collaborative spirit that drives innovation and improvement. Engaging with this community, sharing your work, seeking feedback, and learning from the experiences of others are invaluable steps in your ongoing development. This interaction is not just about receiving but also about giving back, contributing to the growth and enrichment of the community that supports Blender's evolution.

Looking to the future, the skills you've developed through this guide open up a world of possibilities. Blender's application extends beyond traditional fields of animation and gaming into areas such as scientific visualization, architectural design, and virtual reality. The convergence of these domains with 3D modeling and animation is creating new opportunities for storytelling, research, and exploration. Your journey with Blender, thus, could take you down paths unimagined, to projects that blend art, science, and technology in innovative ways.

Furthermore, as you continue to explore and create with Blender, remember the importance of developing your own style and voice. The technical skills you've acquired are tools to express your unique perspective and ideas. The most memorable works are those that reflect the individuality of their creator, blending technique with personal vision. This guide has equipped you with the means to create, but it is your experiences, your imagination, and your insights that will imbue your creations with meaning and impact.

The conclusion of this book is not the end of your creative journey but a milestone. It marks a transition from guided learning to self-directed exploration, from following instructions to charting your own course. The path ahead is one of discovery, filled with challenges to overcome and opportunities to seize. Embrace the unknown with the confidence that the skills and knowledge you've gained are the compasses that will guide you.

In closing, "Blender 3D Simple & Clear 2024 Guide for New Designers" has been more than a tutorial; it has been an invitation to embark on a lifelong journey of learning, creating, and sharing. The world of Blender is vast and varied, a universe waiting to be explored and shaped by your vision. As you move forward, keep pushing the boundaries, keep experimenting, and most importantly, keep creating. Your next masterpiece is just a blend file away.

Thank you for choosing this guide as your companion on the journey into the world of Blender 3D. May your creativity flourish, and may your path be filled with innovation, discovery, and success. Here's to the countless creations that await you, and to a future where your digital art makes a lasting impact. Welcome to the next chapter of your creative journey.

Printed in Great Britain
by Amazon